D1209583

Embodied Visions

Embodied Visions

Evolution, Emotion, Culture, and Film

Torben Grodal

OXFORD
UNIVERSITY PRESS
2009

OXFORD
UNIVERSITY PRESS

Oxford University Press, Inc., publishes works that further
Oxford University's objective of excellence
in research, scholarship, and education.

Oxford   New York
Auckland   Cape Town   Dar es Salaam   Hong Kong   Karachi
Kuala Lumpur   Madrid   Melbourne   Mexico City   Nairobi
New Delhi   Shanghai   Taipei   Toronto

With offices in
Argentina   Austria   Brazil   Chile   Czech Republic   France   Greece
Guatemala   Hungary   Italy   Japan   Poland   Portugal   Singapore
South Korea   Switzerland   Thailand   Turkey   Ukraine   Vietnam

Copyright © 2009 by Oxford University Press, Inc.

Published by Oxford University Press, Inc.
198 Madison Avenue, New York, New York 10016

www.oup.com

Oxford is a registered trademark of Oxford University Press.

All rights reserved. No part of this publication may be reproduced,
stored in a retrieval system, or transmitted, in any form or by any means,
electronic, mechanical, photocopying, recording, or otherwise,
without the prior permission of Oxford University Press.

Library of Congress Cataloging-in-Publication Data
Grodal, Torben Kragh.
Embodied visions : evolution, emotion, culture, and film / Torben Grodal.
    p. cm.
Includes bibliographical references and index.
ISBN 978-0-19-537131-4; 978-0-19-537132-1 (pbk.)
1. Motion pictures—Psychological aspects.   I. Title.
PN1995.G6886 2009
791.43019—dc22   2008023667

Printed in the United States of America

Acknowledgments

This book and the ideas in it have been in the making for quite some time and I thank all the people that have contributed with criticism and ideas, not least my students and my friends and colleagues in the Society for the Cognitive Study of the Moving Image (SCSMI). A special thanks to colleagues at the Department of Media, Cognition and Communication at the University of Copenhagen, Andreas Gregersen, Lennard Højbjerg, Mette Kramer, Johannes Riis, Lars-Martin Sørensen, Peter Schepelern, and Casper Tybjerg; and to Murray Smith for reading and commenting on early versions of the book. Thanks to Sally Laird for linguistic revision of the first draft of *Embodied Visions*, to Kenneth de Lorenzi for helping me find films, and to the anonymous referees for their comments on the manuscript.

Some of the material in the book has been published previously in other versions, and I thank the following for kindly providing permission to reuse and reprint this material. A previous version of chapter 3 was published as Torben Grodal, "Love and Desire in the Cinema," *Cinema Journal*, Vol. 43, Issue 2, pp. 22–46. Copyright © 2004 by the University of Texas Press. All rights reserved. A previous version of parts of chapter 6 was published as "Pain, Sadness, Aggression and Joy: An Evolutionary Approach to Film Emotions," *Projections*, Vol. 1, Issue 1 (2007):

pp. 91–107. © Berghahns Books. The introduction to part II contains a graphic representation and text elements that have previously been published as Torben Grodal, "The PECMA Flow: A General Theory of Visual Aesthetics," in *Film Studies: An International Review*, Vol. 8 (Summer 2006): pp. 1–11. An earlier version of chapter 7 was published as "Stories for Eyes, Ears and Muscles," chapter 6 in *The Video Game Theory Reader*, pp. 129–146, © Routledge Inc., a division of Informa pic., 2003. An earlier version of chapter 8 was published by Vistas Verlag in *Festschrift für Peter Wuss*. An earlier version of chapter 9 was published in *Aura*, Vol. 6, Issue 3 (2000). An earlier version of chapter 11 was published as "Subjectivity, Objectivity, and Aesthetic Feelings in Film," in Bondebjerg, ed., *Moving Images, Culture, and the Mind*, 2000, pp. 87–104, by Luton University Press, permission to reuse granted by John Libbey Publishing. A previous version of the appendix was published in *Northern Light*.

Contents

Embodied Visions

1

Introduction

Evolution, Biology, Culture, and Film

Like other fields of research within the humanities and social sciences, film studies are in the midst of a major shift away from the paradigm that has dominated most of the 20th century. That paradigm is based on the assumption that the human mind has no intrinsic nature, no biological architecture, so that humans are entirely socially constructed and infinitely malleable. The extreme version of the social constructivist paradigm claims that humans are controlled exclusively by socially induced systems that are disembodied and abstract, analogous, for example, to linguistic systems or the working of computers. According to this view, biological events in brains play no part in the discussion of culture. Humans are born with what one might call a double blank slate: humans emerged by a kind of virgin birth that erased all traces of our animal past, and the individual is born with no inherent dispositions. For extreme constructivists, minds have only a short history: the product of socialization from birth onward combined with recent cultural history, but not with the long foregoing history of evolution (see Leda Cosmides and John Tooby's critique of the blank slate theory in Barkow et al. 1992). The extreme versions are tacit and implicit and not many will believe them in full. If asked, most humanists or social scientists would admit that at some fundamental level, culture is influenced by biology. However, cultural products are discussed without any reference to research done within a natural science framework.

The new, emerging paradigm may be called *evolutionary bioculturalism*, or simply *bioculturalism*. Many years ago, C. P. Snow described the humanities and sciences as two distinct and conflicting cultures. However, radical advances over the past 40 years in our knowledge of the biological functioning of the human brain have led to a convergence between these two cultures. This new synthesis between matter and spirit, science and the humanities has been described as the "third culture" (Brockman 1995; for an overview of Darwinism in literary studies see Carroll 2008). The present volume is a contribution to this emerging paradigm. It shows how key features of various film genres and narrative forms can be explained within an evolutionary-biological framework. It draws on the flood of ideas and research of relevance for film studies and visual aesthetics that has recently been done within a natural science framework.

Film and Embodiedness

Central to my version of this new synthesis is that the experience of film, litera- ture, music, art, or culture in general consists of processes within living organisms, embodied brains. When we watch a film, our heart rhythms change, we sweat, and our muscles alternately tense and relax throughout. Daniel Stern (2000) has described the transmodal (transsensory) vital feelings that emerge from bodily existence and create the basis for subsequent stages of development and for basic aesthetic experiences. These bodily changes are linked to emotional reactions that also play a central role in memory, cognition, and consciousness (Damasio 1999; Ledoux 1998; Grodal 1997). When we see someone in a film using his hands, the mirror neurons in our foreheads simulate such hand movements (Gallese and Stamenov 2002), and through other mirror neurons the emotions of the facial expressions resonate in us (Schulte-Rüther et al. 2007), just as other people's visual attention resonates in us. And, as Lakoff and Johnson (1999) have pointed out, the workings of our consciousness are built on the functions that serve to control our embodied minds and their movements through space. Evidence for this can be found in the fundamentally metaphorical structure of language and in the canonical structure of narrative. Sublime feelings, or the drive to seek higher goals, represent bodily as well as mental states, and as I show in chapters 6, 9, and 10, films cue such feelings by working on innate dispositions. Likewise, as I show in my account of the PECMA flow (perception, emotion, cognition, and motor action), key aesthetic phenomena in our experience of film can be understood only in relation to the brain's way of processing information from the screen.

Embodied existence and behavior may therefore be described on numerous levels, from high-order functions such as intentionality to low-order biological processes such as sweating or trembling from fear. We may even descend further down the scale to examine the functioning of hormones, neurons, and synapses. In exploring the human mind, it is not possible to draw sharp distinctions between what belongs to the realm of science and what is best described by the tools of the humanities. The natural science research on the human brain and body and its evolutionary history and the humanities represent different approaches to the same object and they benefit from cooperation (Slingerland 2008). Moreover, it is impossible to draw a sharp distinction between the physical brain and the cultural mind since objective physical factors determine certain aspects of the interaction between mind and culture.

Our bodies and brains are shaped by a functional integration and interaction with our niche, our physical and social life world, by a long evolutionary history. A biocultural embodied approach is therefore distinct from, say, Deleuzian ideas of the body, because the embodied mind is described in its concrete ecology and by means of cognitive science. The embodied brain has evolved to solve a series of practical problems that have faced our ancestors. It is therefore not only a body driven by excesses and mysterious Freudian traumas and perversions, as you might think when reading Linda Williams's (2000) descriptions of body genres.

The biocultural approach to culture does not contradict a historicist approach; on the contrary, it offers a radically historical and constructivist view, describing the evolutionary processes and functional concerns that have led to our present human ways of thinking and representing. It also provides tools for describing how and under what conditions culture has supplemented our fixed instincts to strongly increase flexibility, and tools to explain the limits of that flexibility.

The British empiricists believed that we are born with a clean slate and are able to learn only through personal experience. However, already by the 18th century it was obvious to David Hume that it would be impossible, on the basis of pure empiricism alone, to reach an understanding and knowledge of all the myriad facts and relations in the world. Kant provided a preliminary solution by presupposing innate specifications of the mind that would support the processing of sensory data, but had to rely on divine intervention to explain the origin of the design. Charles Darwin solved this explanatory problem by showing that the process of variation and selection through survival over long periods of evolutionary time could account for the design of different species and individuals (Dennett 1995). Thus, animals and humans are born with certain mental specifications and capacities that have been selected by evolution and that have enabled their ancestors to survive. But, as I discuss in more detail later on, dominant tendencies in the 20th century disregarded evolutionary thought and believed in a form of cultural self-creation.

Bodies and brains have evolved through an evolutionary process that has taken millions of years (see, for instance, Björklund and Pellegrini 2002; Mithen 1996; Barrett et al. 2002; Buss 2005). We are able to watch films with brains and bodies that have evolved in a totally different environment. The biology of humans has not changed fundamentally since most of our ancestors left the Pleistocene savannas of East Africa some 50,000–100,000 years ago. For several million years our ancestors lived as hunter-gatherers in small groups on the African savanna, with the men hunting and fighting, and both men and women gathering fruits, roots, and so on. About 50,000 years ago, what is known as the Upper Paleolithic cultural explosion occurred, when language and painting were invented and humans suddenly increased their tool-making skills and began ritually burying their dead (Mithen 1996; Williams 2002). Human culture took off. The next major turning point was the invention of agriculture, which began in the Middle East 13,000 years ago and provided the support for larger and permanent human communities (Diamond 1997). Since then a series of rapid changes have transformed global culture and shifted its basis from agriculture to industry and to the information society. These cultural developments have been carried out by embodied brains of the type that evolved in the original hunter-gatherer tribes of Africa (Barkow et al. 1992; Cosmides and Tooby 1997; Buss 2005), but cultural inventions have also enhanced and modified our innate dispositions and provided new ways of satisfying them (see, for instance, Anderson 1996; Anderson and Anderson 2005, on how films use innate specifications).

The core emotional and cognitive elements that our embodied brains developed in a hunter-gatherer society are perhaps even more obvious if we examine the kinds of visual fictions that viewers prefer, rather than merely observing their social behavior in real life, because many of these fictions reflect core elements in the emotional heritage that enhanced human survival in the past. Films are often made to elicit strong emotional responses and may be based on stories and situations that activate innate emotional dispositions, whether or not these dispositions are appropriate to a modern environment or linked to skills that enhance survival in that environment. Certain central, innate dispositions cue our liking for stories about the attachment between children and parents (see chapter 2) or stories about romantic relations between adults (see chapter 3). Fighting and aggression, as well as bonding with brothers-in-arms, are as prominent as ever in visual fictions and video games (chapters 6 and 7; see also Fox 2005), even though most people nowadays live in societies in which the majority of adults never engage in violent confrontations. Horror stories still often focus on the fear of becoming food for some other, alien creatures (see chapter 5). The central elements in action-adventure films—physical motion, fighting, the quest to find particular objects and mating partners, and so on—represent pivotal ways in which the life of our hunter-gatherer ancestors who roamed the Pleistocene savannas would have been structured. These action-adventure ingredients can be found alike in Homer's *Odyssey* or the stories of *A Thousand and One Nights*, and in numerous modern films and first-person shooter computer games (figure 1.1). Nowadays, however, odysseys are not confined to earth, but can also occur in space, while stones or spears may be replaced by laser guns.

One example of a central cultural activity is the game of hide and seek, whether it takes place as a children's game, as portrayed in Takahata's sad anime film *Grave of the Fireflies*, or is consumed as part of a thriller or a horror story. Steen and Owens (2001) have described how many young mammals, including human children, play games that involve a chase or hide-and-seek, because these games offer good practice in avoiding predators or in hunting prey. Chasing games are one of the most fundamental features of mammalian behavior, while in higher mammals such games have expanded to include other types of playful and hypothetical behavior. The development of social intelligence, the ability to understand other minds, supported the ability to understand the minds of possible

FIGURE 1.1. It is difficult to understand the enormous proliferation of hunter-and-prey scenarios in numerous present-day films except as expressions of innate viewer dispositions for emotional engagements in such scenarios, emotions that were advantageous for our hunter-gatherer ancestors. Here Bruce Willis as John McClane in McTiernan's *Die Hard* advances through a "jungle" in a high-rise building, hunting and being hunted by other humans. *Die Hard* © 20th Century Fox 1988.

prey, and the development of more sophisticated hunting practices was a key element in the formation of modern humans (Mithen 1996; Dunbar 1996). The reason so many film and television viewers choose to watch endless crime, horror, or hide-and-seek action dramas is not only that they have been accustomed to such fictions through long exposure. The reason is also that these dramas appeal to fundamental, innate dispositions in us. Similarly, games of chase can be found among children in all times and places. Films about hiding and seeking fascinate billions of viewers despite the fact that most of them have absolutely no firsthand experience of events resembling the dramatic occurrences in such stories, and despite the fact that watching such films does not enhance the survival fitness of most people in their present-day environments.

At the same time, stories often bear witness to values of a specific culture. The hide-and-seek formula or the adventure travel formula may be used to describe how you hunt down polluters, child molesters, or drug traffickers, but they may also be seen as vehicles for glorifying imperialism. The rise of the detective novel and later the crime film and cop shows is illuminating for the interaction of innate dispositions and cultural constructions. The increasingly complex and populous societies that were the result of urbanization and industrialization in the 19th century created problems of social transparency and moral surveillance. Crime fictions aim at providing orientation and moral surveillance in the new social jungles and also activate a series of innate dispositions like hunting cheaters (criminals), hiding from dangerous others, and interpreting signs and following signs and tracks. They provide gossiplike guesses as to the secret life of others (Dunbar 1996) and exercise social intelligence and understanding of other minds (Baron-Cohen 1995). Thus the development of the crime genres is a product of a double stream of cultural development and innate dispositions.

An evolutionary biocultural approach does not therefore assume that all our actions are determined by innate dispositions; rather, these innate dispositions are flexible frameworks within which we may have freedom to choose. The development of culture has provided new options for satisfying biological dispositions and needs as well as emerging needs. However, Dan Sperber (1996) has convincingly argued that it is not possible to explain how culture is reproduced by referring to cultural exposure alone. We need to explain how certain cultural products are more appealing than others and will therefore be constantly reproduced, "retold." Sperber calls his theory a theory of cultural epidemics: certain cultural items, he argues, spread like epidemics because the biological makeup of our brains makes us particularly susceptible to their appeal, whereas other products will have a very short life because they do not resonate with the people exposed to them. To spread successfully, cultural products must accord with the innate specifications of embodied minds.

Some film genres are understood and appreciated more universally than others. For example, even though some of the values found in action and adventure films may be culture specific, such films relate to very basic, universal ways that humans interact with the world and with other agents, for instance by moving through space to avoid dangers or seeking out goods and mating opportunities. Art films and certain types of comedy, by contrast, often relate to group-specific or culture-specific patterns and values. Resnais's *Last Year in Marienbad* violates basic emotional and cognitive schemas. Understanding the scrambled and diffuse story strains our cognitive capacity. The film has therefore only a limited audience among people interested in experiments with modes of representation, perhaps in combination with a special preference for films that strain our hermeneutic skills.

Evolution and Culture

For decades, the evolutionary approach to culture and history, including the biological underpinnings of culture, has been absent not only within film and media studies but within the humanities in general. There are four main reasons for this. First, the Darwinian evolutionary approach has been conflated with the extreme individualist philosophy of Spencerian social Darwinism; second, any evolutionary or biological explanation was regarded as reactionary, since it supposedly implied that no emancipation or social change was possible; third, because Darwinism had been misused by fascists to defend racism and eugenics; and fourth, because a fraction of humanists were inimical to materialist explanations, either for religious reasons—the most fierce enemies of evolution are fundamentalist creationists—or for more vague dualist ideas of the autonomy of the human spirit vis-à-vis its material support.

Most humanists thought that Spencer's formulation "survival of the fittest" amounted to an espousal of fierce egoistic individualism, and that such individualism lay at the core of Darwin's ideas. However, both Darwinism and neo-Darwinism describe evolution at the level of species, not individuals; it is the survival of the (human) species, not of individuals, that matters (for an overview of the development of evolutionary thought and the differences between Darwinism and Spencerianism, see Laland and Brown 2002). Thus, according to evolutionary theory, altruism and care may be just as fitness-enhancing for the species as a whole as brute competition. The care of offspring is central to the winning mammalian strategy, and the disposition to care is crucial both in children's tales and in love stories. Although many action films and crime stories deal with violent confrontations, the themes of bonding, of solidarity, of helping mates, colleagues, and so on are just as important. The cultural development of morality represents an extension of this disposition to care for others, and the cultural-moral negotiation of values based on different innate dispositions—the process of solving moral dilemmas—is central to most films. Eugenics stems from Spencerian sources, not from Darwinism, and an evolutionary approach emphasizes that all humans have a shared nature; differences in skin colors are late adaptations to different climate zones that do not correspond to psychological differences.

Creationism offers the only alternative to the Darwinian macrohistory of the long process of evolution by natural selection. Likewise, there are only supernatural alternatives to monism, that is, to the theory that intelligent processes are emergent aspects of matter. Dualism—the idea that the mind is based on a nonmaterial spirit that just happens to exist in material brains—is untenable. It is therefore an empirical task to investigate how flexible our brains are in relation to cultural change.

By a long process of evolution in our biology as well as in our culture, our embodied minds have gained flexibility and complexity, reusing basic mechanisms to solve increasingly sophisticated and general problems, for example, by metaphorically projecting different domains on each other (Greimas 1983; Lakoff 1987; Johnson 1987; Lakoff and Johnson 1999; Mithen 1996). This mental complexity is pragmatic in the sense that the embodied brain is like a Swiss Army knife, with numerous different modules and functions (Barkow et al. 1992; Cosmides and Tooby 1997), each of which can be applied singly, or in conjunction with others, in different situations. The modernity thesis initially propounded by Benjamin (1977) claims that modern existence has created entirely new and different psychological mechanisms in modern minds, but such theories vastly underestimate the complexity of perceptual and mental processes, which demand some innate and universal architecture, and the claims they make are contradicted by empirical evidence.

A basic assumption in social constructivism has been that cultural systems exist on the social level and can be explained without reference to their psychological realization in individuals. In *A Cognitive Theory of Cultural Meaning*, Claudia Strauss and Naomi Quinn (1997) show how important theoreticians within anthropology, such as Clifford Geertz, assume that cultural meanings exist in the public space and can be analyzed without describing their psychological realization in individuals. Strauss and Quinn have argued convincingly, however, that it is essential to be able to describe the mental implementations involved, and have come up with certain models for doing so—for instance, cultural learning by means of neural networks. These models provide elements in what Anthony Giddens (1984) called a structuration theory that takes into account the fact that social institutions need to be implemented in human agents.

A central model for culture has been a linguistic one that describes cultures as similar to language systems and discursive systems and has been called the linguistic turn by the philosopher Richard Rorty. The linguistic turn in the 20th century had many sources, such as Saussure, Wittgenstein, structuralism, and poststructuralism. Such linguistic models emphasize cultural differences and de-emphasize how our shared embodied nonlinguistic experiences provide a background for transcultural understanding as well as conflicts between cultures based on interests. Pascal Boyer (2001) has argued that cultural fields such as religion do not constitute a unified system except for a few experts such as theologians who try to make a system out of heterogeneous materials. When anthropologists ask informants about their beliefs, the informants do not simply access ready-made, publicly shared, language-based religious systems. Rather, they try to make some sense out of a rather heterogeneous body of rituals and knowledge by using innate reasoning capabilities as well as cultural knowledge, just as viewers of horror films may make up some ad hoc explanations of what a given film means. Within a given culture, many agents interact on the basis of capacities that are human universals, as well as culture-specific or agent-specific schemes, concepts, and habitus (Bourdieu 1984).

The pertinence of many imaginary constructs and concepts—for example, spirits, fairies, and monsters—is therefore due not only to cultural transfer but also to innate mental dispositions (as I discuss in chapter 5). Rather than assuming that the mind is totally socially constructed and hence completely malleable, a more cautious assumption would be a relative malleability: innate dispositions can be activated by exposure, deactivated by lack of exposure, and modified within certain limits. Thus, although sadism and empathy are both innate dispositions, it has been documented that exposure to violence in film and television may enhance violent behavior (Gunter 1994). The different dispositions may be dormant if there is no eliciting trigger in the environment.

The experience of audiovisual fiction consists in being exposed to acoustic and visual simulations of events in more or less realistic hypothetical worlds. The viewers' experience relies on a great many different practical skills and competencies, many of which are based on innate dispositions that have evolved through millions of years of the animal and human ancestors' interaction with light, space, movement, and so on (see Anderson 1996; Anderson and Anderson 2005). Language and language-like semiotic systems and discourses are important, but they exist on top of numerous embodied mental processes, such as those based on neural networks, that work on quite different principles. Many aspects of perception, cognition, and action occur in sealed modules that work relatively independently of language. This applies, for example, to our sense of balance, to our experience of patterns of motion in action movies, and to our perception of color (Zeki 1993, 1999; Livingstone 2002). Language is not important for those mechanisms that underpin our arousal and hormonal activation in strongly emotion-evoking episodes, in the feelings of intensity that precede meaning and are due to perception alone, or for many unfocused networks of associations (Arnheim 1974; Eisenstein 1949; Grodal 1997). Most viewers will not verbalize such experiences and some experiences elude verbalization.

These perceptions, cognitions, emotions, and muscular movements exist in tandem with certain fundamental features of those parts of the world that have constituted the human niche, the human lifeworld. We are mentally predisposed to be interested in other agents, be they human, animal, or supernatural, and even children growing up in an animal-poor environment are keenly interested in animals or animated fantasy creatures (Hirschfeld and Gelman 1994). Anthropological studies have provided evidence that there exist innate dispositions that support our experience of the world. The anthropologist Donald Brown (1991) has drawn a composite picture of what he calls universal people, based on a list of characteristics shared by people in all known human societies. Furthermore, people all over the world, irrespective of social structure, categorize animals and plants in accordance with similar principles that constitute an intuitive ontology (Atran 1994, 2002; Boyer 1999). As "folk" systems of physics show, the basic principles of physics are comprehended in the same way all over the world, so that, for example, causality can be seen to be an innate mode of inference in humans (Churchland 2002; Carey and Spelke 1994), rather than a product of Western science—contrary to the claims of poststructuralism and critical theory. Notions of magic and the supernatural are side effects of the development of control by reason, including the ability to reason hypothetically and use the imagination in other ways (see chapter 5). The mental mechanisms through which we check that the world is behaving according to laws and expectations, and which are supported by the brain's innate architecture, are triggered when—as is the case with magic and supernatural events—something violates the assumptions developed by everyday experience. Central features of the supernatural, as exemplified in horror films and religious films, are side effects, spandrels, of evolutionary processes.

Because man is a social animal, our perception of the body language of other people and our ability to model the minds of others have been all-important for our survival and social life. Ekman and Friessen (1975) showed how the basic features of facial expressions are innate and universal. Baron-Cohen (2003) and others have described the sophisticated models that we use to model the minds of other people, and films focus on such psychological skills. Neurologists have discovered the so-called mirror neurons that provide automatic brain simulations of the activities of others in the minds of onlookers (Rizzolatti et al. 2002). Thus film viewing may be a biopsychological simulation in a very direct sense, and involve levels far below language and consciousness. The continuous tacit or explicit interpretation of the body language of humans and animals is a key aspect of audiovisual communication (Riis 2003, 2004a, 2004b; Burgoon et al. 1989). The way we move around predisposes us to interact with containers such as caves or houses, and to access points in these containers such as doors and openings, to follow paths and deal with objects blocking movement, to categorize animals and plants, and so on. These basic human–world interactions and categories give rise to the fundamental experiences that, according to Johnson (1987), Lakoff (1987), and Lakoff and Johnson (1999), provide the metaphorical-schematic basis for language and meaning and are concretely enacted and simulated in film.

Contrary to the claims of standard social science theory (described by Tooby and Cosmides in Barkow et al. 1992), the mind is not just a blank slate to be shaped and filled with discourses that determine the experience of the physical and social world. On the contrary, only when the basic experiences of embodied mind–world interaction are in place can language be acquired, as we see when we observe its development in children. In film, language is part of an experiential totality that, for instance, includes vision, action, body language, and affective outbursts. As Damasio (1999) has pointed out, film is a good illustration of how consciousness functions because it induces viewers to simulate our experience of the world. Just as facial expressions, focus, framing, actions, and so on may influence the viewer's experience, so language in film may focus or filter what we hear or see and provide access to other minds. Language in film thus interacts with other layers of experience, just as language in general is one layer in a multi-dimensional mental activity. In chapter 9 I discuss the problem for art films of providing visual representations of abstract categories and symbols. However, certain mental processes may bypass language. Film may therefore in some dimensions provide a better model for a theory of culture and consciousness than language.

Film Studies and Scientific Theories

The developments within a broad range of natural and social science–based studies of humans that I have just described have so far made little impact on film studies. The paradigms that have dominated film studies (and also to a certain extent media studies) since the late 1960s have ignored or been inimical to cooperation with science. In the first 50 years of its existence, film studies, unlike other fields within the humanities, did cooperate with mainstream psychology through the work of, among others, Münsterberg, Eisenstein, Arnheim, and French filmologists. Münsterberg was a professor of psychology and Eisenstein was heavily influenced by Alexander Luria, one of the fathers of modern cognitive-neurological science. Structuralism in the 1960s was inspired by information science. The journal *Communication*, which published the seminal structuralist articles of Greimas, Todorov, Genette, and Metz, was dedicated to reforming scholarship within the humanities in accordance with general scientific principles. Part of the influence exerted by Sigmund Freud pointed to a scientific study of the brain, based on neurological theory, although many other idiosyncratic aspects of Freudian psychoanalysis were deeply problematic.

The structuralist turn in the 1960s was not without problems. Linguistics (and semiotics) became the prime models for cultural studies. At the core of the use of linguistic models was the concept of arbitrary signifiers and abstract systems. Content—semantics—was supposed to be molded by social conventions similar to those involved in the arbitrary systems of signifiers. These theories arose in tandem with first-generation cognitivism, which argued that the disembodied computer could be taken in its entirety as a model for human cognitive processes (in contrast to second-generation cognitivism, which was inspired by neurology and emotion research). Often, indeed, printed texts were taken as a mental model in the semiotic conception of language so that meaning was thought of as abstract, disembodied social systems (see Lakoff and Johnson 1999). No link was made to the way in which physical minds interacted with physical worlds, nor was consideration given to the pragmatic functions of language that might constrain the interpreter's free associations. By contrast, Dan Sperber and Deidre Wilson (1986) argue that language cannot be explained in isolation from nonlinguistic cognitive inference systems. The ability to draw inferences is based, for instance, on perception, so that the understanding of linguistic information bleeds into those general perceptual-cognitive-emotional-motor capacities that we use to understand the world. Clearly, the acquisition of language, perhaps only 50,000 years ago, gave an extraordinary boost to the functioning of these cognitive abilities, as the cultural explosion that began at this time may indicate. However, the development of language probably involved the integration and refinement of existing capacities (see Mithen 1996).

This linguistic influence within a broad range of social and cultural fields entailed isolation of cultural studies from the series of breakthroughs in the understanding of mind-brain that has occurred in the natural sciences, and which has revolutionized our understanding of the human mind. The linguistic turn has been especially problematic for film and media studies because it marginalized previous approaches, such as those of Münsterberg, Eisenstein, Arnheim, and Mitry, which described audiovisual processes as having important perceptual, emotional, and embodied components. The linguistic turn also marginalized the influence of phenomenology, especially that of Merleau-Ponty with his emphasis on the embodiment of experience and his description of agency and intentionality. Christian Metz, for instance, had to give up his phenomenological interests in the hard-core linguistic cultural climate of the 1960s.

In the 1970s, film studies were swept into the maelstrom of critical move-ments. On one hand, the new critical studies within the humanities legitimized themselves as being scientific as exemplified in the Marxism of Althusser and the semiotic-psychoanalytic theories of Jacques Lacan, and the Althusserian-Lacanian film semiotics was later dubbed "grand theory" for that reason. However, the scientific aspects were mainly discursive and the new critical waves ignored or rejected mainstream science, like mainstream psychology, and rejected its meth-ods. The leading film scholar Christian Metz "converted" to Lacanian psycho-analysis. Using a culturalist version of semiotics, Umberto Eco (1970) argued that perception was a totally learned activity (for a critique, see Grodal 1997). The mainstream research was criticized as being positivist and bourgeois, and scholars within the humanities could discuss psychology in ignorance of how it was taught in the psychology departments of their universities. Significantly, film psychoanalysis was focused on Lacan, who was an outsider within the psychoana-lytic community, and not on, for instance, ego psychology. The leading British psychoanalysts in the 1970s were Bowlby and Winnicott, and Bowlby was an important figure in synthesizing evolutionary theory and psychology just as Win-nicott made important contributions to child psychology, but they did not have any impact on film studies.

Grand theory became increasingly influenced by poststructuralist-decon-structivist theories that resonated with avant-garde artists like Laura Mulvey (see Mulvey 1975) who founded their artistic experiments on ideas of transgressing dominant thought forms, like the "logic" of the canonical narrative forms that was seen as an expression of patriarchy. Whereas grand theory was an effort to build up an alternative antipositivistic science based on Marxism, semiotics, and Lacanian-ism, poststructuralists like Derrida denied that it was possible to make consistent theories and totally rejected classical semiotics. Derrida's (and Baudrillard's) mode of reasoning was heavily inspired by biblical exegesis (Grodal 1992), although Der-rida often sampled words from mainstream science. In the 1990s, Derrida (1994) explicitly recast some of his political visions in a religious language.

The rivalry between the humanities and the natural sciences and the effort to claim that reductionist natural science methods were unable to understand the human mind was, as Snow (1993) pointed out in his description of the two cultures, an old one. An important inspirational background for the critical rejection of positivist science in the 1970s was the Frankfurt school, a paradoxical mix of neo-romantic-conservative and radical tendencies. Like previous romantic movements in the 19th century, the Frankfurt school opposed the way in which the scientific spirit of modernity had dissolved the absolute values and enchanted rootedness (see Max Weber, e.g., in Gerth and Mills 1958) of pre-Enlightenment traditional life. The school was influenced by German *Geistesgeschichte* (history of the spirit; Windelband and Dilthey). In contrast to classical Marxist traditions, which emphasized the need to develop the means of production, including science, Adorno and Horchheimer saw a direct line from the Enlightenment and its institutionalization of what they called instrumental reason to the concentration camps and fascism in general (echoed, e.g., in Stam 2000). The only acceptable type of reasoning was the negative idealist critique of the dominant thought forms.

From the late 1980s onward, film studies became increasingly atheoretical (with exceptions like Bordwell 1986, 1989a, 1989b; Smith 1995; Carroll 1996b; Anderson 1996; Tan 1996; Grodal 1997; Plantinga and Smith 1999; Jullier 2002, books that discussed film theory from a cognitive perspective). The dominant trend became a blend of historical studies and cultural studies, focused on interpreting how films were influenced by their social and historical context, and even Bordwell and Carroll (1996) edited a book with the title *Post-Theory*, in which they advocated middle-level research (for a critique, see Grodal 2006).

Historical studies are indeed very valuable, and the historical turn has provided numerous valuable contributions to cultural and film studies. However, the dangers and pitfalls of making historical studies without knowledge of psychological theory may be exemplified with those visuality and modernity studies that are influenced by Walter Benjamin's (1977) essay "The Work of Art in the Age of Mechanical Reproduction" and other works on the history of mentality which presuppose that the human psyche and human vision have changed radically in modernity, implying that the brain and perception can be totally molded by social changes. Thus, for instance, Mary Ann Doane (2002) describes mentalities of modernity and cinematic experiences without considering whether such experiences are psychologically feasible or probable as descriptions of typical viewing experience given present-day psychological knowledge (films are, for instance, easily comprehensible even for people living in premodern cultures; Messaris 1994). Further examples of such modernity studies may be found in Linda Williams's (1994) volume, which, for instance, contains Tom Gunning's (1994) essay on the aesthetics of astonishment, Crary's essay on "modernizing vision," and Friedberg's essay on postmodern vision. None of the authors has any discussions as to whether their claims about the human psyche and ways of seeing are in accordance with what is known about the human brain within modern psychology or neuroscience. Gunning, for instance, claims that early cinema evoked shock, fragmentation and astonishment, and attraction to spectacular events because that somehow corresponded to the modern psyche, which corresponds to the modern, fragmented urban life and its spectacular events, whereas implicitly (and explicitly in Benjamin) coherence and narrative are old-fashioned, premodern.

Bordwell (1998, 139–149; see also Grodal 2003b) has convincingly shown that the characterization of early cinema was problematic, that not all films were fragmented, and further added that it is highly unlikely that those complicated biological mechanisms that support human vision and that have an evolutionary history of millions of years should suddenly change, and change back within a few years when films became less fragmented and more narrative. Entertainment in Roman or modern circuses or stories of miracles and giants with one eye in the middle of the forehead have relied on attractions, just as skilled storytellers have made coherent stories. Ben Singer (2001) follows up on Benjamin and other modernity theoreticians by seeing a link between modern psyches, stress-creating films, and stressful environments, as if stress was a kind of modern pleasure-evoking drug condition, although the physiological arousal system that supports active coping and provides dopaminergic pleasure by moderate activation will cause brain damage in humans and animals by prolonged activation (Ledoux 1998, 239–250).

A more general problem with the modernity thesis is that it relies on too simple ideas of the relation between perceptions and the human mind and thus, paradoxically, is not historical enough. The degree of challenge and shock involved in certain perceptions depends not only on the stimuli in question but also on the cognitive capacities of those exposed to them. Filmmakers, critics, and viewers around 1900 indeed often found that the fin-de-siècle world was full of change, incoherence, and shock, just as people from rural areas might be disoriented in big cities. For those accustomed to traveling by horse, train rides were a novelty. Over time, however, our brains created schemas that made train rides easy to experience. Thus the impact of both cultural and natural stimuli depends not only on the stimuli themselves but on the socialization that takes place at the levels of the individual, the group, and the generation.

The problematic assumptions about the human perceptions and emotions in the modernity theories within cultural studies exemplify why it is important to let historical studies be informed by state-of-the-art psychology. It is easy, although wrong, to argue for historicity on all levels, say, to claim that nonnarrative forms are more modern, narrative forms more premodern. Bioculturalism provides a framework for understanding why narratives are universal, why the skeletons of the Odyssey narrative have appeal even for present-day viewers, but also to explain how cultural interests and biases mold the different versions. Definitions of modernity in terms of "attraction" and in opposition to linear narrative not only are historically mistaken but also seek to present certain universal and transhistorical features of aesthetic expression (such as narrative and lyrical forms) as belonging only to particular historical epochs or certain cultures. The historicity of film is not to be found at the very general level of fundamental forms such as that of narrative. Rather, it is anchored in the specific cultural variations on universal forms, or combinations of forms, along with the new contents with which these forms have been and will be provided.

This book might appear to be lopsided, because it cannot allocate the same space and the same degree of detail in describing historical specificity as to universalism. However, its purpose is not to dispose of historical studies or studies of national cinemas, gender biases, and so on. The purpose is to refine historical studies by using available knowledge from other disciplines to understand what is historically specific and what is based on universal dispositions. The purpose is also to let our short history be seen in the long perspective of the evolution of humans. It is my hope that this book may inspire others to expand the historical dimensions of bioculturalism.

In the book, I show how and why psychological explanations based on evolutionary and biological considerations are highly compatible with historical and moderate culturalist, moderate constructivist, and antireductionist approaches to film studies. Rather than only using language and discourse as a model for understanding audiovisual media, I show how films are simulations of experiences of and for embodied minds in the world and how film involves many different layers and components, each of which has its own historicity and its own speed of change. The basic features of body language, such as the expression of key emotions like hate, fear, love, or disgust, are biologically hardwired and therefore have a high degree of universality and a low rate of change. However, the existence of innate mechanisms does not exclude cultural variation; on the contrary, these innate mechanisms have a certain degree of flexibility, although often by energy-consuming display rules to suppress innate tendencies. The display rules for body language may change more rapidly and create different cultural subgroups, which may in turn lead to interpretative problems for those outside the group. Polite Japanese body language on film and in real life, for example, involves more display rules than Italian body language. The basic features of sexuality are biologically founded, but different cultures or subcultures have different attitudes toward sexuality; often, for instance, there are severely enforced rules as to what parts of the body, and especially the female body, may be visible in public, and many cultures have sanctions against homosexuality. The degree to which displays of violence are accepted varies over time, cultures, and individuals. Films are among the social processes that mold our embodied interactions with the world—embarking not from a blank slate but from our biopsychological dispositions, which provide the framework and parameters for the constant reconstruction of culture.

The Structure of the Book

The book is divided into two parts. The first part focuses on film and culture in the light of evolutionary psychology and comprises chapters 2–6. The second part focuses on how the makeup of the brain explains a series of aspects of film aesthetics.

In chapter 2 I discuss how cultural diversity and cultural development are compatible with the assumption of a biological human nature. I begin by showing that films for children are shaped both by innate emotional needs such as a need for attachment and by cognitive constraints, and also by cultural specificities. I then go on to discuss certain mechanisms that lead to cultural variation and others that promote cultural stability and the existence of universal forms. I give examples of some of these mechanisms through analysis of genre patterns and contrast a functionalist explanation with Altman's postmodern genre theory. Finally, I argue against monolithic theories which claim that given periods or cultures—for instance, "modernity"—can be characterized by certain homogeneous features and argue that cultures such as that of the Enlightenment or modernity are time-spaces in which many different forms exist and interact.

In chapter 3 I compare romantic films with pornographic films and argue that the former focus on the establishment of personalized, exclusive relations— bonds of love—whereas the latter focus on anonymous desire. In addition, the chapter examines the evolutionary roots of love and desire and discusses how films explore the interaction of these emotions with other emotions. Chapter 4 contrasts different approaches to viewers' morality and describes different notions of how the emotions relating to moral conflict are simulated in film. Whereas the psychoanalytic approach assumes that viewers are torn between suppressed perverse emotions and superego morality, postmodernist theorists argue that decentered psyches are a consequence of postmodern life. Cognitive film scholars and scholars inspired by analytical philosophy have argued that we enjoy only the characters in a film who act according to our own moral norms. I discuss to what extent psychoanalytic, cognitive, and evolutionary views of emotions and morality are compatible, using Jonathan Demme's *The Silence of the Lambs* as a test case.

Chapter 5 analyzes the fantastic and supernatural, especially in horror films, and argues that part of the fascination they exert represents an offshoot of archaic mechanisms relating to agency, predation, morality, social exchange, and death, but that other aspects relate to the hypothetical thinking that is such a prominent characteristic of advanced intelligence in humans. I also analyze the way in which superstition is prompted by breaks in causality that are highly salient and activate cause-searching mental activity.

Chapter 6 focuses on the apparent paradox that viewers may be fascinated with stories that have tragic endings, and discusses relations between sad stories and different kinds of social bonding, like offspring bonding, pair-bonding, kin-bonding, and tribal bonding. It argues that sadness is an adaptation to group living and that sad and eventually sublime acceptance and submission are typical of many sad films. Spielberg's *Saving Private Ryan*, Kurosawa's *Ran*, and Yimou Zhang's *Hero* exemplify how sad films articulate tribal attachment and sublime submission in contrast to aggression. I argue that our interest in fiction is not controlled only by a wish for positive emotional experiences, because that would make sad stories unexplained; but that we are for good functional-adaptive reasons fascinated by themes that have a strong existential relevance, whether the topics are sad or happy.

Part II has an introduction that describes a general model of film aesthetics, the PECMA flow model. The model explains how the brain's architecture and the different steps in its processing of audiovisual data support different aesthetic forms, and also how the brain's architecture influences our experience of the reality of film and other types of audiovisual communication.

Chapter 7 discusses the evolutionary and functional roots of narrative, and the way in which different media, from oral and written literature and drama to film and video games, represent experience in different ways. It discusses the way in which narratives are nested hierarchies and looks at questions of story-discourse, linearity, playfulness, and interactivity. Chapter 8 discusses how viewers simulate films and characters and the different theories about how we experience other minds. It discusses several modes of experience, from distanced observation to immersion, and shows how the problem with many rival theories of film viewing is that they rely on erroneous ideas of how we experience everyday life and provide impoverished descriptions of the viewer's experience. These theories rely on third-person emotions such as pity and admiration and exclude central first-person emotions such as love, hate, and fear.

Chapter 9 analyzes some of the concepts used to characterize art films as "high art" and discusses some of the reasons for their limited appeal to a mass audience. The main argument is that the typical difference between an art film and a mainstream film is that the former seeks to portray "permanent" meanings while the latter focuses on "transient" meanings. Our basic experience of the world involves concrete, present, and therefore transient interactions with it. Other experiences, however, draw on two specifically human abilities: our capacity to memorize creates fields of more permanent meanings, while our ability to generate abstract concepts produces experiences that are beyond the transient level of concrete interaction. High art may tone down the middle level of concrete (narrative) interaction between real people and other persons and objects. Art films tend to evoke abstract or subjective permanent meanings, or activate a "lower" level of perceptual meaning, style, in support of the higher, abstract meaning.

Chapter 10 describes the type of phenomena within film aesthetics that are often categorized as subjective. The word *subjective* indicates that the representation is colored by certain inner emotions or shows signs of being filtered and shaped by personal experiences, whereas *objective* representations provide direct access to a given scene, uncolored by embodied mental experiences. The chapter shows how the PECMA flow model can describe how subjective experiences are due to a blocking of vicarious action. The chapter also provides a categorization of subjective features in film.

Chapter 11 analyzes some of the ways in which realism is experienced by viewers. Thus, rather than seeking to define what is real, the chapter describes and characterizes some of the different processes and elements that cause viewers of audiovisual representations to have an experience of realism, based on the premise that realism can be described as an evaluative feeling rooted in perception, cognition, and habituation.

In chapter 12 I make some concluding remarks and sum up some of the major findings of the book. In an appendix, I illustrate the analytical validity of the PECMA flow model in the films of Lars von Trier with emphasis on the means by which Trier cues subjective, lyrical experiences.

Part I

Film, Culture, and Evolution

2

Universalism, Cultural Variation, and Children's Film

In this chapter, I argue that cultural diversity and cultural development are compatible with the assumption of a biological human nature. First, I show that children's films are shaped both by innate emotional needs and cognitive constraints and by specific cultural norms. I thereby refute both the blank slate theory of the human mind—the strong version of culturalism—and the arguments for strong biologism. I then discuss the mechanisms that lead to cultural variation and those that, on the contrary, promote cultural stability and universality. I illustrate the effect of some of these mechanisms on genre patterns and contrast my functionalist explanation with Altman's postmodern genre theory. Finally, I argue against monolithic theories which claim that given periods or cultures—for instance "modernity"—can be characterized by means of homogeneous features, proposing instead that cultures are time-spaces in which many different forms exist and interact, so that heterogeneity is not a property of modernity, but typical of culture in general.

Cultural development since the cultural explosion (Mithen 1996) has been marked by increasing diversity and change in some dimensions as well as stability, in terms of form and function, in particular dimensions of culture. It is not difficult to spot the similarities between Homer's *Odyssey* and Lucas's *Star Wars*, or to find cartoons that use the same type of stick man representations found in drawings that are more than 10,000 years old. But it is equally easy to spot the differences. Although the *Harry Potter* series uses the device of magical empowerment and wizards, just as supernatural tales have always done, these are provided with a relatively modern 20th century setting. An account of culture and film must therefore be able to describe the rich variety of films and cultural products in general, and at the same time explain why certain types and forms recur over time and in different cultures, and thus appear to be human universals.

There are three main ways to explain cultural resemblance: (1) such resemblance is generated by human "nature," human biology, possibly in interaction with the same or similar environments; (2) it is generated by cultural transmission—either through the imposition of a common ideology or freely via influence and tradition; or (3) it is generated by a disembodied human spirit, with or without divine inspiration. Choosing between or combining these various explanations has been complicated by the fact that they have often been used politically. Religions have described the body, "nature," as the source of evil instincts (as well as mortality) and argued that spiritual freedom presupposes freedom from bodily influences, but the idea of human nature has also been used positively to naturalize certain cultural norms. Modern ideas of emancipation embarked from a negation of the religious denial of the body: emancipation meant freedom from culture (including religion) and the happy return to supposedly natural conditions. But in the second half of the 20th century the idea of freedom and emancipation from class, race, gender, and so on was linked to the denial of any connection between culture and biology, biology being seen as a constraint rather than a resource to be developed. Strangely enough, behaviorists such as Pavlov, Watson, and Skinner thought along similar lines: there was no such thing as human nature, and with proper drilling or brainwashing the individual could be molded by society. So the most authoritarian and the most liberal positions shared the same basic notion, that humans are made of an amorphous stuff that is constructed socially; they differed only in their ideas as to who should perform the work of social construction. As a result, explanations inspired by Darwinian ideas of evolution have been under crossfire from both radical and fundamentalist camps. From an evolutionary and historical perspective, such oppositions do not make sense. Culture enhances and refines biological nature and provides new solutions to biological needs. Different cultural products may offer different ways of fulfilling these needs.

Culture and Biology in Children's Films

If humans were born with a blank slate for a mind, we would expect children's stories, especially those designed for small children, to vary immensely. By contrast, if we assume that children have an innate mental architecture and partly innate patterns of development, we would expect their biology to provide a framework for, and impose certain constraints on, the kinds of films that fascinate them. Thus, if children's stories can be shown to have certain universal features, children themselves must have certain innate dispositions and cannot be said to be born with a blank slate. For the blank slate theory of culture to be true, we would have to posit that the biological slate is somehow wiped clean in adolescence or adulthood, ready to be molded by culture. This is not a promising hypothesis, especially since—as we will see in chapters 3 and 5—not only children's stories but films for adults (romances, horror stories, and tales of the supernatural) have a universality that cannot be explained by ideological hegemony alone.

Let us therefore take a look at some of the most popular children's films, such as Wilcox's *Lassie Come Home*, Disney's *Bambi*, Wincer's *Free Willie*, Disney's *The Lion King*, Miyazaki's *Spirited Away*, or Stanton's *Finding Nemo*. Like most children's fiction, these films have certain very prominent emotional concerns that focus on fear and activation of what Boyer and Liénard (2006) called the hazard-precaution system, important for tuning the brain to precaution to danger. Furthermore, the films focus on attachment to some parenting agency, on the creation of reciprocal relations (friendship and so on; Björklund and Pellegrini 2002), and on the urge for exploration and play (Panksepp 1998). These emotions are not merely social constructions but represent vital concerns for any child, and films that are able to offer salient representations of these concerns attract large audiences. As I discuss later, specific cultural values influence the ways in which each particular film is shaped, but the emotional dispositions to which they appeal are innate and represent the biological refinement of features found in other mammals (Bowlby 1982; Fonagy 2001; Stern 2000).

Attachment, or bonding, is linked to the working of two estrogen derivatives: oxytocin, which influences the bonding of mothers and babies, and vasopressin, which influences male parenting behavior and aggression toward other males (Panksepp 1998). Attachment is crucial to the survival of mammals and birds. Children intuitively grasp that this is an innate need and they often find pleasure (or reassurance) in stories that have animal agents and therefore guarantee the quasi-universal existence of parenting behavior (even if, as in the case of fish, parental care is pure invention—take, for example, the way Nemo's father cares for Nemo). In the development of humans, the hormones that support attachment in mammals mutated to promote pair-bonding and romantic love as well (see chapter 3), and many children's stories of attachment have overtones foreshadowing the romantic love that lies beyond the biological development of children. Although children's stories focus on attachment concerns between children and grownups, they may use romantic love to reinforce experiences of bonding. In *Spirited Away* there is a proto-romantic relationship between Chihiro and the boy Haku which fills the gap in support that appears when the parents are temporarily transformed into pigs (figure 2.1). Similarly, Disney's *Snow White and the Seven Dwarfs* focuses on the main character's attachment to the dwarfs, but her attachment to the prince serves as a background and an ending. Attachment emotions are also vitally important to adults, especially in melodramas. Tan and Frijda (1999) have shown how the key scenes in melodramas focus on the reunion of closely related characters that have been separated.

Children know very well that animals do not talk and that the animals in stories have somehow been equipped with human features, but children's tales involving animal agents as protagonists have nevertheless been popular for millennia, just as toy animals are found universally. Thus animals must possess certain features that make them well suited for children's fiction. One explanation is that humans have innate dispositions for detecting and categorizing other creatures, so that animals have a natural salience (Keil 1994; Atran 1994). Moreover, the focus on animals makes it possible to use especially salient agents such as striped fishes, lions, and snakes. Thus, animals are salient agents that children can use to try out various models of agency and test their theories of how other minds work (see chapter 8 and its discussion of theory of mind). But this cannot be the

FIGURE 2.1. Central emotions in films for children are evoked by parental attachment in jeopardy, as in this scene from Hayao Miyazaki's *Spirited Away*, where the 10-year-old Chihiro expresses dejected loneliness because her parents have been transformed into pigs and she is alone in a world of enchanted plenty and lurking dangers. As in other successful films for children, however, she will get helpers and become empowered, and will finally be reunited with her parents. *Spirited Away* © StudioGhibli 2001.

whole explanation; the functional role of animals seems also to be connected to their subordinate position in relation to humans: take, for example, the two cute robots in *Star Wars* who follow their masters with doglike devotion. Donald Winnicott (1971) has discussed the role of transitional objects, such as blankets, teddy bears, dolls, and so on, whose function is to support the child in developing control over his or her attachment to the parenting agencies by actively performing and controlling the care. Humans have generalized their caring relationship to their offspring so that it can also be used in relation to animals, especially small, soft, appealing creatures—even where their diminutive size is an invention, as in the case of toy elephants. The Pokémon company mass produces and mass markets transitional animal-shaped objects that serve to empower children and to articulate their caring capacities. In episode 13 of the sixth season, for instance, the Pokémon animal Pikachu is sick due to a hypercharge of electricity and this activates the parenting behavior of a boy. His transitional object relationship to Pikachu serves as a bridge to a girl-boy relationship.

Both the animal toys that serve as transitional objects and the characters depicted in films or illustrations often exaggerate those aspects of childishness that strongly enforce the strong innate emotional disposition to care for neonates, such as heads that are big in relation to the body (as in the case of Mickey Mouse), large eyes, and motor inadequacy. E.T. is a perfect example of a transitional object that activates feelings of tenderness and care by his helplessness and his exaggerated infantile features. The survival of mammals has for millions of years depended on dispositions to care for helpless offspring. Studies of the development of the design of teddy bears show that in the beginning of the 20th century the head-body proportions were adult, but by a slow process of market feedback, teddy bears in the late 20th century had neonate proportions (Barrett et al. 2002). The preference for childish features need not express only the children's preferences, as teddy bears are mostly bought by adults, just as films for small children mostly involve adults who watch the film together with the children and both children and adults are attuned to the film. That smaller children and grownups share the experience and that children may feel or hear how grownups find helpless characters cute does not mean that children are necessarily indoctrinated into such feelings that are central elements in children's feelings of positive attachment. Like language, fiction consumption relies on innate elements and also needs socialization by exposure to cultural elements that develop such innate capabilities.

When children begin to play and enjoy fiction, they seek to achieve emotional control by assuming a double perspective, that of a child and that of an adult; they play mommy and daddy, manipulate their dolls and teddy bears, and watch stories about transitional objects. The depiction of animal protagonists in films allows them at once to identify with the animals and feel superior to them. This is obvious in scenes of cuteness, such as that of Bambi's first steps or of Bambi on the ice. The fact that we find helplessness in children and animals appealing is a reflection of the strong innate tendency to care for offspring that is vital to all mammals and especially to humans. Children thus experience what it means to care and at the same time develop mental models of parental care that support experiences of security in attachment. Thus films such as *Bambi* or *Finding Nemo* are mental-emotional experiments in dealing with attachment and hazard precaution. Snow White and Chihiro in *Spirited Away* are strongly empowered in their urge to reestablish attachment, Snow White by being a parental agent for the dwarfs, Chihiro by being the heroine who is able to undo her parents' magical transformation into pigs. Woody and Buzz Lightyear in *Toy Story* are afraid because they are trapped in the psychotic boy's house and because they fear that the boy who owns them will move away and leave them behind, but they derive strength from thinking how much this boy will miss them, thus demonstrating their care for him and their expectation of care in return. However, the toys live in constant fear that their owner will acquire a new toy that he will come to love more than he loves them, and that he will therefore abandon his older playmates. *E.T.* and *Free Willy* offer a sophisticated double bind in mastering attachment, because the boys have to overcome their own desire for attachment and adopt the perspective of their loved objects in order to help E.T. and Willy to go home.

The empowerment of the child or childlike agency may be natural, but it is often supernatural, as we see in fairy tales or *Harry Potter*, in anime film (see Sørensen 2008), or in science fiction. The empowerment may be self-developed or derived from one of the magical helpers that abound in fairy tales. The activation of reasonable fear and hazard precaution is central, just as overcoming fear is a key feature of most children's fictions. The stories focus on the terror that dangerous situations evoke, and then describe processes of empowerment and bravery. In contrast to action films for older children and adolescents, where the heroes are absolutely fearless, fear and the overcoming of fear are a recurrent phenomenon in stories for children.

Creating a successful children's movie thus demands certain skills and types of invention that are at once constrained and motivated by the need to produce a narrative concerning emotional events of vital relevance to children: empowerment, the mastery of fear, and the possible temporary loss of attachment to a parenting agency. This is combined with exploratory and playful behavior that has been vital to the successful coping strategies of mammals, especially humans.

Successful stories presuppose using such central emotions and dispositions, but that does not mean that using these emotions is sufficient to make successful films or stories. Numerous stories and films use some of the right ingredients but are not able to mix these ingredients in a way that activates emotions and interest. To make films or to tell stories is an art that demands a series of skills and it is of course very easy to make stories of attachment that lack salience or emotional appeal.

The business of attracting children's attention and allowing them to follow the action involves a further field of options. In the physical portrayal of agency, it seems that salience is important; differences in character and function are often enhanced by using different animals or other highly salient objects. It is easier to distinguish an aggressive character from a friendly one if the aggressor is a wolf or cat and the friendly one is a piglet or a mouse. The ability to display key emotions through the innate features of body language like posture and facial expressions is very important, and exaggerated body language is used to highlight the characters' emotions. The actual physical appearance of the characters varies because a key to success in children's films is salience and emotional relevance, not surface realism. The hero may be a fish like Nemo, a deer like Bambi, a doll like Pinocchio, the toy Woody in *Toy Story*, or a lion pup, whereas the heroes of stories for older children are often more realistic, like Chihiro in *Spirited Away*, and *Free Willie* is a photographed film rather than an animation. However, the hero figures in certain films for adolescents, such as Spider Man (a spider) or Superman (a bird), still have a salience resembling that of many transitional objects.

Built-in cognitive constraints and our need to see emotions develop—from cause, to coping, to final outcome—mean, moreover, that it is important that the story be told in a reasonably linear and canonical fashion. The French structuralists in the 1960s (Greimas 1983; Barthes 1977) drew inspiration from Propp's (1968) analysis of folktales in building their own narrative models. Folktales have circulated widely through oral transmission and therefore have simple, canonical narratives, structurally similar to those found in children's films and stories (see Mandler 1984). In the case of children's stories, the structuralist reduction of the surface story to a deep structure with particular agency and narrative forms appears to correspond with innate dispositions, insofar as children prefer stories that follow such schemas over those that do not.

The Transmission of Mind-Grabbing Functional Bundles

Creating cultural products such as stories is not in principle different from making tools. Certain aspects of a knife, such as its sharpness, are necessary conditions for it to function, whereas length, material, and so on may vary. If a tool that fulfills basic needs is invented in one place, it will soon spread to other places. Jared Diamond (1997) has demonstrated how cultural inventions such as tools, the domestication of animals, agriculture, and so on have continuously spread all over the globe because such inventions have certain objective advantages. Similarly, stories have traveled by word of mouth, spreading along trade routes and through migration, and the same goes for simple functional ways of depicting humans, animals, and other agents. In the period between the cultural explosion some 50,000 years ago and today's globalization, the speed with which culture has been diffused has steadily accelerated, with the Internet as the latest booster of global cultural communication. Cultural artifacts that have achieved wide distribution tend to relate to universal human dispositions and needs such as attachment, the promise of eternal life, and the propensity to believe in ghosts or magical forms of empowerment that supposedly enable us to control the world through our thoughts and wishes without any physical intervention. However, there are often many different ways to satisfy these fundamental needs. Flying carpets, Superman, and the engineering of airplanes all address the same underlying desire on the part of humans to acquire an enhanced, birdlike form of locomotion, while stories of both scientific and magical intervention may all be described in terms of the human desire for control.

Contrary to Jung's theory of archetypes, cultural artifacts are not expressions of innate programs because there is no evidence for innateness of such complex contents. Cultural artifacts like story elements and symbols are, rather, inventions that, like knives and bridges, perform certain functions. If they had not been invented and transmitted culturally, they might not have occurred to the individual mind. Thus Jung's notion of archetypes as innate contents of the mind that will always be consciously or unconsciously present differs from the biocultural approach. The similarity of certain artifacts may, but need not, presuppose the influence of some common cultural tradition; inventions that serve vital needs often arise independently in different places and at different times (Dennett 1995). However, Jung and followers such as Joseph Campbell sampled global cultures to collect universally successful functional bundles (myth elements but also person schemas) that, for instance, could inspire George Lucas to make new variants in *Star Wars*.

Dan Sperber (1996) has pointed out that cultural transmission depends not only on the exposure of individuals to the cultural product in question but on the compatibility between that product and the mental makeup of the individuals who perform the transmission. Sperber's theory of culture has certain similarities to Richard Dawkins's theory of memes. In Dawkins's (1976) *The Selfish Gene* and later publications, he has described what he regards as the cultural equivalent of genes, namely a bundle of information that he dubs a *meme*. The nucleus of the Cinderella story is a meme; the concept of democracy is a meme; the idea of the wheel is a meme. The meme idea has been taken up by, among others, Daniel Dennett (1991) and Susan Blackmore (1999). Memes, like ideas, spread irrespective of whether they are beneficial or detrimental to those humans in whose heads they are replicated, hosted, and transmitted, just as the Internet transmits viruses as well as useful information. The advantage of the term *meme* compared with terms like *idea, concept,* or *schema* is that it emphasizes the anonymous, object-like aspect of mental configurations. However, in contrast to genes, memes do not have a built-in replicator function; they spread due to built-in emotional and cognitive mechanisms in the brain that are attracted by certain phenomena and themes that have been highly relevant for humans (e.g., sex, death, becoming prey) or that posses a high degree of visual or acoustic salience. The problem with existing meme theories such as Blackmore's (1999) is that they do not devote much time to discussing why a given meme is able to "hijack" the brain's attention—how and why, for instance, it relates to innate features of the brain. As Sperber has pointed out in his theory of cultural epidemics, the impact of cultural products depends on whether they serve a function in human brains and are transmitted for that reason. Meme theorists are right in pointing out that ideas and stories—memes—do not necessarily promote the fitness of the individuals who host and transmit them, but even if they work to the detriment of their hosts we still need to explain in functional terms why memes are attractive to their hosts (for an overview of the pros and cons of meme theory, see Aunger 2000).

To avoid the connotations of words like meme, archetype, or myth, I use the term *functional bundle* to describe mental units that are invented, mind-grabbing, attention-grabbing, and widely communicated. For example, the features and functions of children's stories can often be combined in small sets or functional bundles, such as "evil wizard" or "evil witch" (older man or woman able to perform magical and evil acts), or an object of extreme empowerment such as a magic wand or sword. The functional bundle consists of one or several qualities combined with one or several functions: for example, the qualities of being old and ugly with the function of committing evil deeds using supernatural means. The bundle is easy to grasp, and the universal existence of certain bundles, such as the witch-wizard, may suggest that they have not merely traveled but have been independently invented in many different places.

The fact that the functional core of stories can be defined on this relatively abstract level is evinced by the way in which functional bundles may survive even where the stories that encapsulate them have archaic features. An example of such archaism is the use of kings, queens, princes, princesses, and crowns in stories for audiences in societies where these feudal roles belong to a remote past. *Bambi, Star Wars,* and *The Lion King,* for example, are primarily made for the American market, but treat royalty as if it were the supreme and universal social model. The functional core of these roles is "absolute social supremacy based on biological-social inheritance" and the ability to command total attention from other beings. Such roles are easy to learn and remember, just as the function of "castle" is salient as a place of distinction based on physical control by delimitation.

We are able to imagine ourselves as princes or princesses living in castles because our inherited biology supports the desire for social distinction. However, the bundle "prince or princess" is not a product of biology in the sense of being an atavistic biocontrolled remnant of our life on the Pleistocene savanna. Even *The Lion King*, which supposedly takes place in our ancestral home on the savanna, is not based on Jung-like archetypes or symbolic regression, since hunter-gatherer societies had only a relative hierarchy (Maryanski and Turner 1992), not the kind of absolute hierarchy depicted in the film. The Tarzan stories and similar superman stories set in a modern environment relate to an apelike existence in the jungle that has nothing to do with the way of life of Pleistocene bipedal hunter-gatherers in the several million years that followed our ancestors' exodus from jungle to savanna.

Salient functional bundles are comparable to objects such as spears, wheels, bridges, or knives, in the sense that once they are invented they tend to be imitated because they perform easy-to-grasp functions in relation to quasi-universal needs and mental models. Shields, or protective container surfaces, are directly imitated from nature—the shells of turtles—and can easily be transformed, for instance, into magical electromagnetic shields that protect against laser beams or rockets. Peter Jackson's *The Lord of the Rings* trilogy is clearly set in a medieval world, but it is able to fascinate millions today because the imagery it uses (swords and so on) and the concepts and emotions it expresses (allegiance, pledges, etc.) belong to functional bundles that for generations have shown their efficiency as mind-grabbers.

The imitation of existing cultural elements need not be ruled by some uniform ideological agency that forcibly controls the reproduction. Particular functional bundles or mental models may exist side by side with quite other bundles and models. Although Bambi and his family are royal beings, they are also hunted prey who must be careful not to be shot by humans when they venture into the open. *The Lion King* draws on competing political models, depicting on the one hand a quasi-Nazi society that is ridiculed in the film (even though it is not that different from the legitimate model in which the Lion rules by virtue of royal distinction), and, on the other, a hunter-gatherer paradise with a flat hierarchy based on reciprocity. In *Star Wars*, shields and swords exist side by side with advanced technological gadgets. As DiMaggio (1997) observes, following among others Swidler and Lévi-Strauss, culture is a toolkit containing very heterogeneous items. Levi-Strauss (1961, 1964–1971) suggested that what distinguished "primitive thoughts" from those put forward by modern science was that they involved bricolage, the bringing together of what was at hand, contrary to modern thought, which involved unified worldviews based on a complete theoretical and analytical understanding of phenomena. However, cultural phenomena such as film are also bricolage, in the sense that they bring together whatever is at hand and seems to work, even if it is heterogeneous. As Strauss and Quinn (1997) have demonstrated, people can hold contradictory ideas, each of which is activated only in the proper context. However, these ideas are not random but have a local functionality.

Universality and Cultural Specificity

Although biology determines the fundamental framework of children's stories, socialization and cultural norms may explain other important aspects of the specific narrative surface. In *Bambi*, the parenting figure is primarily the mother; the father takes over only after the mother's death, and Dumbo's mother is a lone parent. By contrast, *Finding Nemo* is politically correct: the mother disappears before Nemo is born and the father takes over the responsibility of raising him. The film also excels in transposing an American suburban elementary school environment to the marine environment and includes a funny sequence about sharks that have turned into California-style vegetarians. In *Lassie*, the economic crisis of the 1930s is seen as one of the main causes of the separation between Lassie and her parenting figure, whereas *Free Willie* links the theme of separation to late 20th-century ecological concerns about the violation of Mother Nature and has a more complex double separation theme (the boy from his parents, the whale from his natural environment), while Spielberg's *A.I.* has an even more complex theme of separation linked to questions of authenticity in a futuristic world. *Spirited Away*, on the other hand, criticizes modern consumer society. The film's fairy-tale structure fits Greimas's (1983) analysis of (folk) narrative: it starts from an initial lack and involves helpers, trials, and the breaking of (implicit) interdictions, and these elements are combined with visuals and costumes of Japanese origin that provide the story's universal structure with historical specificity. The Pokémon fictions, meanwhile, are clearly marked by their makers' strong interest in profits from merchandising.

There is thus a hierarchy in the form and contents of films. Certain levels are more fundamental and biologically controlled; others represent cultural variables. A film has a narrative structure, lighting patterns and montage structures, agents with mental characteristics and physical and social qualifications, and so on. Each level may be relatively autonomous vis-à-vis the others, although the various elements may not be totally independent of one another. If I decide to make a film that is told in a canonical fashion, I may decide to tell a story that glorifies white supremacy, but I may equally decide to tell a story about black pride. If I choose to make a canonical film about black pride, I may use a shot-reverse structure, but I may alternatively decide to use long takes and deep focus or narrow-focus swish pans. I can furthermore decide the color scheme, and there will be no clear relationship between my choice in this respect and my decision on whether to use a canonical or uncanonical narrative, or whether to focus on white supremacy or black pride. Not all elements are equally compatible, as I discuss later in this chapter, nor is there a total romantic fusion between form and content that would require a change of form whenever the content is changed. Such a highly specified order encompassing all the elements of a film or any other cultural product is implausible. Even though many of the fundamental aspects of culture work within innate specifications and boundaries, the possibilities for making culturally specific products are unlimited.

The fundamental layers are not to be conceived as language-like systems but rather as a series of mechanisms linked to different functions, situations, and motivations. The human mind is not a general-purpose machine, but a bricolage of different devices, each with its own specific function. The basic emotional mechanisms, such as attachment, desire, romantic love, fear, empathy, and aggression represent universal, biology-based, superior motives for constructing different narratives. We have separate capacities or modules for color vision, for creating narrative structures, for reading body language, for feeling fear or empathy, for making models of other people's minds—the list is endless. Cosmides and Tooby (1997), inspired by William James, have pointed out that humans do not have fewer instincts than animals, but many more, because we are much more complicated beings. It is this multitude of innate instincts and capacities that allows for new combinations and cultural innovation.

The importance of innate specification is most vividly evident in aesthetic devices that are based on cultural violations of features of the natural world. The mimetic impact of photographic images relies on innate human abilities. But even when film violates natural experiences, its effects often depend systematically on the innate specifications of humans. The human eye is preset to perceive the exterior world as ever changing, mostly driven by complex and interacting causal chains. The invention of cinema allowed for an experience that was totally new in the history of humankind: seeing the world freeze. Nothing could be more unnatural or artificial. An extreme culturalist might therefore argue that we need to "learn" freeze frames as a new language. But they would only be partly right, because other innate mechanisms take over in such situations, telling us that if some phenomenon is markedly deviant, it probably arises from some interior, mental cause. Or in other words: innate mechanisms, some of which are sealed off in modules that are cognitively impenetrable (i.e., cannot be influenced by learning) ensure that a freeze frame, unlike a photograph, will be experienced as something subjective. The same goes for effects such as those produced by a fish-eye lens. Because linear perspective is based on innate features of the visual system, a lens with a very short focus will creative subjective effects. Arnheim (1957) illustrated a series of effects that are derived from projecting our basic three-dimensional experience onto a two-dimensional surface. Because the human brain has thousands and thousands of different modules, it is possible to figure out new means of influencing these innate capacities in ways that will be easily grasped by viewers. To say that film relies on innate abilities in humans does not diminish its capacity to find new ways of creating salience, making art.

Mechanisms of Cultural Change and Variety

The exodus from Africa meant that humans spread over the entire planet, and cultural development since then has been characterized by the dynamic interaction of centrifugal and centripetal forces. On the one hand, there has been an ongoing centrifugal differentiation, best illustrated in the variety of the world's languages. On the other hand, there have been centripetal forces: a continuous exchange of artifacts, stories, religions, and so on, especially on the Eurasian continent (Diamond 1997), and the development of social institutions aimed at integration.

The simplest mechanism of variety is what you might call drift. An artist aims to copy an existing artwork or performance, but for some trivial and chance reason the copy is slightly different from the original. The next copy, too, differs slightly from the previous one, and thus over time there will be drift, which may or may not create noise, that is, somehow impede the function of the artwork.

However, changes may also be intentional and arise for functional reasons: for example, if you set out to make a horror film, you may invent changes that make the film a bit more horrifying. This might be called *function optimizing*. David Bordwell (1996b) has provided examples of such function optimizing in relation to the presentation of two people in conversation. At a certain time the shot-reverse-shot formula came to seem the optimal solution, and you might say that the function-optimizing process was then transformed into a (possibly temporary) convention; but as I discuss later, new functional considerations may make other solutions—like using swish pans to conserve spatial continuity or create expressive movement—more desirable. Bordwell (1986) has also pointed out the importance of deadlines in film: setting deadlines is an effective way to generate tense expectations. The development of new, improved techniques for constructing deadlines will give rise to new narrative options. I have argued (in Grodal 1999) that several phenomena that are ordinarily dealt with as being intertextual or as being clichés are end results of function optimization, like a romantic coupling of lightning and storm with dramatic events.

The production of film, like that of other cultural phenomena, demands certain skills that can be invented and learned. Even if it is problematic to see human history as a tale of constant progress, it would be pointless to deny that there is an accumulation of know-how over time—though, equally, know-how can sometimes disappear. A given representation is therefore not necessarily a copy of the way a given artist perceives the world or intends the world to be portrayed, as a romantic poetics would suggest; rather, the artwork is both constrained and supported by the artist's know-how. Thus, the makers of early cinema did not have the same skills to make sophisticated narratives as authors of novels or theater plays, and no need for them because of the interest that the novelty of the medium evoked in viewers. Tom Gunning (e.g., 1994) and other scholars have unconvincingly argued that those features of early cinema that we may regard as primitive first experiments with a medium reveal a sophisticated expression of a modern aesthetics.

It is important to separate the question of art's value for its consumers from the question of progress in solving the technical problems involved in creating art. Primitive art or primitive filmmaking may in some respects be just as valuable as sophisticated art or filmmaking. Drawing three-dimensional pictures requires more skill than drawing two-dimensional ones, but in certain contexts people may prefer two-dimensional images, as we see in the development of art at the beginning of the 20th century; similarly, filmmakers may for various reasons use long shots that diminish depth—for decorative purposes, for instance, or to enhance excitement in a dramatic pursuit. Chihiro's movements in *Spirited Away* are sometimes made more primitive when she is supposed to appear fragile, whereas they are more like a series of jump cuts when dynamic emphasis is needed. In some respects it is easier to use long takes than to construct a heavily edited film made up of material from many cameras. Bazin—contra Eisenstein and others—argued the virtue of long takes, because the phenomenal continuity of time and space were important to him, whereas Eisenstein placed a greater value on expressivity. Cost considerations and the emphasis on spatial expressivity have recently made the swish pan more common, demonstrating that new functional considerations can lead to change and variation. The history of all the arts presents numerous examples of returns to previously abandoned forms and themes. We may call this a change in chosen function.

There are many different reasons behind such changes in chosen function. The changes may be motivated by changes in preference. If, for example, horror film viewers for various social reasons begin to prefer monsters from outer space to monsters from Transylvania, filmmakers will try gradually to optimize their films to suit this new preference. Changes in preference can occur for different reasons; they may, for instance, result from social change: thus many action films made after 1975 have important active roles for women, and Arabs supplanted Russians as the villains in the American action films of the 1990s. Function innovation happens when new ways are invented to satisfy existing preferences; this occurred, for example, with the invention of film and interactive media, or of new genres that satisfied existing emotional preferences. Changes may also be due to influence and interference, as when certain products travel in time or space and therefore create a new context for the products they meet at other locations. Such mutual influences can be seen, for instance, in the interaction between the action films produced respectively in Hollywood and Hong Kong, and in any given case these may or may not be functionally motivated as well.

A special and very important aspect of function change is the *novelty-habituation* cycle. On the one hand, familiarity creates positive feelings, and this fosters the tendency to repetition and the conservation of form and content. Thus, the preference for certain cultural forms such as films need not mean that they profoundly chime with some particular cultural vision; it is simply a consequence of exposure. Thus, two groups of rats were exposed respectively to Mozart and to Schoenberg, and afterward each group was found to prefer the music that had become familiar to them, although the rats overall preferred Mozart (Zajonc 2000). But, as the Russian formalist Sklovskij pointed out (quoting Tolstoy; see Grodal 1997), habituation also diminishes salience over time, so that to reactivate an aesthetic experience and revive salience, you need to create *ostranenie*—estrangement—or variation. The repetition of a stimulus pattern will lead to habituation, lack of arousal, and then lack of conscious attention (Mook 1987, 216–217; Berlyne 1971). This dialectic between repetition and change expresses a very fundamental biological and psychological principle that is easy to understand in relation to food, the metaphorical basis for taste. Familiar food engenders positive feelings associated with safety. At the same time, humans have a tendency to vary their diet, possibly to ensure that they get all the ingredients vital to the body's survival. The modern cycles of change in fashion represent a speeded-up version of the novelty-habituation mechanism, and changes in aesthetic taste need not express deep alterations in function, but rather reflect this fundamental preference for variation (Martindale 1990). Thus the change from three-dimensional to two-dimensional painting around 1900 and the concomitant interest in primitive art did not only, as some have claimed, reflect a crisis of representation (that might have been felt by some intellectual groups), but was also part of a novelty-habituation cycle, and was concomitant with the enormous expansion in realist photographic media. Artists competed with the new photographic media, with each other, and with the paintings from previous periods to create novelty, and some of them might have felt disoriented by the rapid modernization. The transition to two dimensions and abstraction is thus a complex and historically specific event.

Mechanisms of Cultural Universalism and Stability

The mechanisms behind change and differentiation are counterbalanced by mechanisms that promote similar or identical products. These can initially be divided as follows: mechanisms relating to the producing agencies and production; those relating to viewers and other recipients; those relating to permanent, slowly changing, or widely distributed features of the world, and those relating to social institutions.

To the extent that viewers have certain permanent preferences that are due to innate factors, such as innate attractors, the process of function optimizing will tend to create similarities among types of films (and other cultural products). Many artifacts, material as well as cultural, were invented independently in different places and at different times. Similarity need not therefore be the result of influence and imitation, but of the invention of cultural means to perform certain functions. Thus, for example, the similarities between the old Chinese story about Yüeh Hsian, the European fairy tale Cinderella, Disney's movie version, and *Pretty Woman* are partly due to influence, but also to function optimization through a process of bundling, since the core of all four stories is the combination of two goods, becoming rich and acquiring a husband, in which the two benefits reinforce one another. This core motif has therefore been reinvented many times and in many different places, because both the desire for riches and social status and the desire to be married can be found universally.

Function optimizing may in the short term be a mechanism for change, as we can see in the development of the classical Hollywood film. But once certain functions have found optimal solutions within the boundaries of taste and technoeconomic conditions, function optimizing will tend to promote stabilization. Function optimizing can guarantee that there will be a large and enduring audience for a certain kind of narrative, such as many of the tales that have circulated throughout the Eurasian continent and that have been reused at a global level in films.

My description of function optimizing is in some respects a cognitive-evolutionary reformulation of Lévi-Strauss's ideas on myth, as described in *Structural Anthropology* and *Mythologiques I–IV* (1963, 1964–1971). Human beings have certain universal interests and exist in environments that create similarity among stories. However, although storytelling relies on innate mechanisms in the human mind, there is no special machinery in the mind that generates unconscious myth making, as Lévi-Strauss supposed. Rather, these similarities are due to the function optimization of general mental preferences with different *optima*, relating to the different values accorded these various preferences in a given cultural unit (individual, group, class, and so on). *Pretty Woman* fits nicely with the Lévi-Straussian concept of mediation: the mediation of poor and rich, woman and man, heart and brain. Other stories may emphasize different preferences, for example by confirming differences, as in *Bambi* or *The Lion King*, in which innate distinctions prevail.

In the description of the PECMA flow in the introduction to part II, in chapter 3, which concerns love and desire, in chapter 7 on the evolution of narrative forms, and in chapter 5 on the supernatural, I indicate some of the parameters that create similarities based on the mind's innate architecture, whether these serve the purposes of realism, emotion, or fantasy.

Among the mental mechanisms that counterbalance the preference for novelty and change are those linked to familiarity and to urges to perform rituals. Children like to watch the same movie over and over again. Cult movies, too, attract a repeat audience. The repetition of exactly the same narrative creates a sense of both familiarity and empowerment, comparable to that experienced in the repeated recitation of prayers, magic words, curses, and those actions performed by people with obsessive-compulsive disorder (Boyer and Liénard 2006). Films such as *The Lord of the Rings* or *Star Wars* offer their fans experiences of belonging and identity similar to those of tribal or national and religious communities. For such social groups, it is tradition and repetition rather than novelty that provide the fascination because the repetitions serve group integration (see Richerson and Boyd 2001). The urge for novelty and salience varies from individual to individual and over the life cycle; some individuals are powerfully motivated to seek novelty, while others go for familiarity and ritual (see Pervin and John 1999). The preference for novelty or familiarity is also mood dependent; understimulation activates preferences for novelty and excitement, whereas stress and overstimulation promote preferences for unexciting material (see Rubin's [1994] description of how viewers use fiction for arousal management).

It is easier to copy than to invent and change, and producers of artifacts such as films will often copy existing models. Craft traditions may exist over long periods of time and be modified only by the process of drift. The Dracula myths or the traditions of the Western have survived partly by virtue of familiarity and functionality, but also because at a certain point they were simply available, at hand, and easy to copy. Thus within the general framework of functionality there is also the specific historical element of existence and availability. Availability is a more general condition than tradition. Where copying is due to cultural tradition, negative audience reactions will impose sanctions on any deviations from the established norm, thus promoting continuity, whereas copying that arises purely because a given model is available—making production easier—is less bound by rules and may change when other models become available. Hollywood flourished in the physical vicinity of the western landscape and made use of the western lore that happened to be at hand. Ideological elements might or might not then be added. The general features of the Dracula myths were determined and made salient by the mental makeup of humans, but its specifics are due to concrete historical circumstances—including, for instance, 19th-century differences in the levels of industrialization in Eastern Europe and England respectively, combined with the demonization of the less developed area and the personal idiosyncrasies of the author Bram Stoker.

Before structuralism, there was widespread interest in the comparative study of (temporal) cultural transmission, but structuralism tended to favor atemporal studies that were in turn supplanted by the study of specific cultural essences, in the manner of Geertz et al. (see Strauss and Quinn 1997). The study of the dynamic historical interaction between cultures was abandoned. This has had two negative effects: on the one hand, it has promoted the absolutist idea of cultural identities as isolated, opaque worlds (see Kuper 1999), and on the other it has encouraged the notion that the present process of globalization is unique in history. In fact, cultural development throughout the world has been a constant process of differentiation, synthesis, and (re)combination.

The development of the human mind-brain has been characterized by increasing flexibility (Björklund and Pellegrini 2002) as humans spread from their original home to all kinds of habitats, from the desert to the Arctic and even to space. As we have seen, the basic narrative forms focus on those agency functions that guide and control our encounter with different habitats and the problems they throw up. The canonical quest for desired objects may take place in savannas, jungles, or cities or, as in *Star Wars*, involve voyages through space. However, certain universal characteristics of our human habitat provide the backdrop for universally recurrent themes and images in film. The general features of our world, with the earth below, the air above, and the gravitational force that orients the planet, constitute the permanent setting for films, both when the action obeys natural laws and when it violates them—for example, when agents defy gravity and fly in marvelous ways, as in the case of Superman or the Chinese martial arts films. The diurnal cycle of darkness and light is emotionally important (Grodal 2005), and changes in the weather or the season, skies, wind, rain, and sun serve as the focus or backdrop for films, making them universally comprehensible and creating similarities in visual topoi. Yimou Zhang's *House of Flying Daggers* and Kurosawa's *Ran* exemplify the way in which nature, understood in a very general sense, is a recurrent theme in films. Together with sexual reproduction, the biological cycle of growth and decay, in the natural world and in humans, is a universal experience.

Social and cultural institutions may promote cultural recurrence by impeding and blocking certain options—for example, the amount of sexual display allowed in 1930s Hollywood or in modern Bollywood films. Institutions may support certain ideologies and facilitate certain types of cultural communication. Thus, although aggression (alongside altruism and love) is a universal disposition, the specific forms of, say, Hollywood war films are strongly determined by the fact that their production presupposes the cooperation and support of the U.S. military. Many modern institutions try to create social regularity in space and over time and this may be reflected in film.

Film Genres: Function and History

Film genres have been central to the discussion as to whether films are influenced by universal principles or are totally free sociocultural constructions. Structuralist theory in the 1960s and '70s (e.g., Greimas 1983; Todorov 1975; Lévi-Strauss 1963; Chatman 1978) advocated universalist principles and analyzed some fundamental features of narrative texts and it influenced genre theories within film studies (e.g., Cawelti 1976; Schatz 1981). The structuralists lacked, however, an up-to-date psychological background for describing the features and functions of their findings. They used terms like *narrative logic*, *myth*, and so on to vaguely indicate some causal powers in the mind for the regularities found in texts. Such approaches were fiercely attacked in the following decade as expressions of Western logocentrism. Later, from the 1980s onward, the interest in such model building disappeared and the approach to genre studies became increasingly historical.

Rick Altman's article "A Semantic/Syntactic Approach to Film Genre" from 1984 (reprinted in Altman 1999) is a late representative of the structuralist approach, but Altman later (1999) provided a strongly historicist and culturalist-postmodernist theory of genres, arguing against the structuralist universalism that he had previously favored in his description of the semantic and syntactic structures in genres. Altman states, "Only in the multi-era imaginary world of a 'Jurassic Park' do the categories of a previous evolutionary state continue to exist. In the genre world, however, every day is Jurassic Park day. Not only are all genres interfertile, they may at any time be crossed with any genre that ever existed. The evolution of genres is thus far broader in scope than the evolution of species" (Altman 1999, 70). He claims that there are no theoretical, that is, universal, genres, only historical ones. By "historical" he means that these genres arose as a result of local circumstances and exist in an eternal (postmodern) flux.

Part of Altman's criticism of existing genre theories is valid. Contrary to classical genre theories, there are no metaphysically established genres that can be defined by necessary and sufficient criteria. Genres may better be described by means of prototype theory (Lakoff 1987; Grodal 1997). It is certainly true that genres mix, as in horror comedies, for instance. He is right in criticizing notions that genres are unambiguous systems of conventions, whereby producers and consumers of fiction at a certain point arrive at mutually agreed rules as to what constitutes a given genre, what the defining features of an epic or a musical should be, and so on.

However, Altman's description of the historical development of genres is geared toward hiding any trace of continuity of form and function. Although it should be obvious that classical tragedies, comedies, or epics have strong similarities to modern sad melodramas, comedies, or action-adventure films, Altman disregards continuity—everything is aimed at describing discontinuity. He wants to show that different people and institutions have had different genre labels and that genre names vary over time. Thus the terms *musical* and *melodrama* have been used in very different ways in different periods.

The problems with Altman's conception of genre and meaning are especially apparent in his critique of making theoretical genre description based on scholarly analysis. Central to this critique is his objection to Todorov's (1975) analysis of genre in *The Fantastic*. Todorov focuses on ambiguous narratives that contrast elements belonging to the world of reason with elements that seem to point to the existence of supernatural phenomena. Readers of such narratives are thus placed in a position of cognitive dissonance: either they suppress certain information or they accept the existence of the supernatural. Examples of such narratives in literature and film are Henry James's *The Turn of the Screw* and the film version, Clayton's *The Innocents*; Roeg's *Don't Look Now*; and *The X Files*. Altman sees Todorov's definition of genre as theoretical, in the sense that it situates genre outside history. He then objects that Todorov has merely replaced the previous understanding of genre, based on content, with one inspired by formal analysis, and regards this as an old-fashioned approach because it is universalist rather than historical. But he praises Todorov for directing us to the experience of the reader.

Todorov's description of the fantastic is, however, not just a formal portrayal. Todorov deals with stories in which there is a conflict between natural and supernatural phenomena and explanations, and this is not merely a formal problem—it has been a real problem for humankind for thousands of years (see chapter 5). Conflicts between natural and supernatural explanations lie at the core of most religions as well as *The X Files*. Todorov's categorization not only describes existing narratives but can also to some extent predict the course of future narratives (*The X Files* were made much later than Todorov's book). The theme of the conflict between reason and the supernatural has two sides: on the one hand, certain phenomena may cue a reader to the experience of conflict; on the other, the reader or viewer has an innate disposition to experience tension when confronted with conflicting evidence. Pascal Boyer (2001) has discussed why dispositions that make superstition possible are innate and can arise universally.

Todorov does not claim that the reader will experience the fantastic regardless of the content of a given story; on the contrary, he describes a functional relationship between certain types of text and certain types of reader response. Reception studies are right in pointing out that any given film experience depends on the competencies of the viewer. But even though this is true, films are not usually Rorschach tests designed purely to elicit free-floating associations. On the contrary, they are constructed to elicit particular responses, and presuppose certain competencies. Horror films are constructed to arouse fear and they presuppose viewers that are able to feel fear in relation to certain situations. Some viewers may laugh instead, but few if any will be put in a romantic mood by a horror film.

Contrary to what is presupposed by postmodernists, the ordinary viewer's competencies to experience films are to a large extent based on general cognitive and emotional competencies. Producers and consumers of stories about quests and journeys do not need to know anything about the road movie or adventure story genre in order to enjoy or comprehend films in this genre. Understanding representations of journeys and quests is a universal competence derived partly from the common features of human daily life, partly from innate capacities. Bridges may be described as social conventions that regulate how to get across rivers, but such a description would certainly lack important elements, failing to explain, for example, why even wild animals may use bridges because of their obvious functional advantages. One of the oft-cited proofs of how different readers in different cultures understand narratives differently is Liebes and Katz's (1993) classic study of the reception of the TV series *Dallas*. On closer inspection, however, the study shows that the basic understanding of the stories in *Dallas* was very similar in all the different groups; it was only their modal relationships to the serial that differed, so that some took the series more seriously, while others took a more distanced view of it because of their prior knowledge of the genre. Equally, differing values made them judge the characters differently.

Functions and schemas exist on many levels of generality, each allowing for variation and combination. The canonical narrative, including the quest-road movie, is a very general functional schema that can be combined with many other functional devices. A road movie may use the technique of shot reverse, may include freeze frames, and may have several flashbacks, although it is less likely to involve flashbacks than shot-reverse shots. Categorizations at a relatively high level will mostly be defined by very basic human concerns or emotions. Curiosity and moralism are key elements of crime stories; aggression is a key emotion in war and action films, love in romantic stories, fear in horror stories, and so on. Singing and dancing may also be thought of as key human activities, so that one could justify making musicals a separate category, whereas the category flashback films would serve only scholarly purposes, and although some might find it of interest to discuss Cinemascope films, this is not a category that most viewers would accept.

We thus have a hierarchy of functions and schemata, some belonging to the supporting cast, others constituting the stars. There is some logic in this, because a narrative needs to be fueled by certain emotions and contain certain actions, and whether you are ridiculing the pope, Putin, Bin Laden, or George W. Bush, there are certain accepted ways of making fun. Likewise, whether you travel in space or in the Amazon, there are certain actions and emotions—fear, curiosity, and amorous pursuits—that are likely to arise; amorous pursuits, for example, go with almost all the other dishes in the kitchen.

Genre, Function, and Function Compatibility

If we regard a narrative pattern as a specific assembly of functional devices, a given device may be evaluated according to whether it enhances or impedes a certain experiential objective. If you want to make a scary movie, certain devices for rendering it scary are more effective than others. Scenes of dead people suddenly rising up and attacking a living person, or nice girls changing into monsters, are scarier than scenes in which children play with balls.

Some devices are compatible. If you want to construct a passive melodrama (see Grodal 1997), you may open the story by presenting the result, as happens in Wilder's *Double Indemnity*. This is compatible with voice-over narration, because both devices will prevent active expectations. It is also compatible with optical devices that distort prototypical realistic space and realistic objects, because such devices block active coping. Among such compatible features, some will serve to enhance each other. Supernatural agents may go well with the mutilation of humans in horror films and these devices will enhance one another, because it is easier to fight something that obeys Newton and his colleagues than to fight something that obeys supernatural laws. Supernatural agents are also compatible with stereotypical, robotlike behavior. The more compatible and mutually enhancing features you put into a film, the better it will serve its purpose (but, as I will discuss shortly, the more easily identifiable it will be as a formula).

Some compatible features, however, serve to modify each other. Horrific features may be combined with comic ones. For instance, horror stories and comedies both use stereotypical behavior. We can therefore make a comic horror fiction, in which monsters behave in a stereotypical manner. But the comic elements will modify the horrifying impact of the stereotypical monsters. The modification will be compensated for by the humorous payoff, because the latter provides comic relief to the arousal created by the scary elements.

Certain functions are largely incompatible. If you want your story to have a forward drive, you can only have a limited number of flashbacks, for instance, to motivate the behavior of the protagonist. But you cannot have a totally broken narrative and a strong action drive at the same time.

We are now able to explain how it is possible to describe prototypical genre systems and subsystems by means of both historical processes and devices that are rooted in human universals.

Over time, oral storytellers, comedians, writers, and so on will come up with devices that have certain effects. They may, for instance, identify the secrets of running gags, of stereotypical behavior, of strong absurd contrasts. The audience does not need to learn such devices in order to enjoy them, so the problem for comedy makers is not to teach the audience how to enjoy running gags, only to invent effective running gags and get feedback from the audience. There may be certain production traditions, so that a clown, for example, teaches a new clown how to invent jokes and running gags, just as an experienced painter may teach a new painter how to create a painting with perspective. But this does not necessarily presuppose any corresponding tradition among viewers. Viewers notice that a given film is funny or scary or romantic, and they may have some knowledge of the genre involved, but equally they may not. Just as people in remote jungles immediately grasp the experience of three-dimensional photography, so viewers can immediately grasp a running gag.

Over time, traditions of production will develop a standard inventory of comic devices, and this inventory will define a prototypical category. In *Moving Pictures* I listed certain elements of the basic comic inventory and offered a psychological explanation for the way they work (Grodal 1997). Bordwell (1986) has drawn up a similar device inventory for art films, and in chapter 9 I suggest some of the psychological reasons behind these. Certain works will occupy a more central place within the generic category than others; for instance, they may be central prototypes of comedy because they involve a number of comic devices. Audiences do not need to be able to describe the device inventory or the precise narrative structure of a given genre. Genre patterns may raise expectations and certain genre labels may be used in advertising and choosing a given film. However, most viewers have greater experiential than analytical skills and film scholars tend to overestimate viewers' explicit competencies in identifying genre. Altman and others confuse the sophisticated genre skills possessed by professional filmmakers, who actively need to use those skills in practical production procedures, with the passive and more diffuse skills possessed by viewers. Certain types of high art, including various kinds of experimental films, developed precisely because certain professional art makers since the late 19th century have created art for other professionals who enjoy experiments with production-side problems. Such artists may try to instill their products with relevance for a wider audience—for example, by claiming that their experiments are important for political reasons or express existential insights.

As we can see in the examples of horror-comedy and tragicomedy, it is also possible to combine functional devices that belong to different prototypical generic categories. Postmodernists think that this is something new, and often describe it as a transgression of the laws of genre, or an impurity that mocks rigid genre traditions. However, cinema has never had any genre laws or police forces that can bring trespassers to court, although critics and academics may back up their verdicts by claiming that such laws exist. Insofar as many films follow established genre patterns, this is mainly because they have proven their efficacy at the box office (or perhaps among the members of state film funding committees) or at some marketplace where clowns try to make a living. The interaction between producers and viewers may be described as a negotiation, as long as we remember that the negotiated result is not purely arbitrary and conventional. The negotiation consists in the filmmaker's efforts to read what will work in the minds of viewers. Cultural development may alter preferences. Westerns have become less popular as the world of the Western has become part of a remote past. Similarly, many television crime series have replaced the lonely detective with a police team.

But if there are certain devices that are known to have pertinent effects, why don't all filmmakers gravitate toward the kinds of films that maximize those effects? To some extent, this is precisely what they do. There are standard formulas for making love stories, thrillers, horror films, adventure films, and so on. The individual filmmaker tries to vary the concrete realization of these formulas in ways that have been described in structural narratology—for example, by substituting one surface element from a functional paradigm with another surface element. The physiognomies of villains vary a little, and murder weapons vary slightly. Sometimes the adventure takes place in India; at other times it takes place in Brazil.

However, there are problems with repeating an optimal strategy too often, even granted slight modifications in the surface structures. As mentioned above, the novelty-habituation-novelty cycle is a fundamental biological as well as aesthetic principle. Tynianov (1967) pointed out that the development of certain devices is linked to the way in which such devices become automated in the minds of receivers, who will then crave novelty. Psychologists might describe this as desensitization through habituation. A certain style attracts interest by its novelty, then habituation sets in, the style becomes boring, and a new, more interesting style replaces it—not necessarily because the worldview of the viewers has changed, and not necessarily because their psyches have altered in such a way that they have become totally insensitive to the devices that once appealed to them, but for the same reason that people may eat a lot of a certain type of food and then, after a certain time, lose interest in it.

Once a certain period has elapsed, the desensitization will disappear, and a forgotten older style may be revived, as when the Dogma filmmakers reinvented a series of devices that were popular in Italian neorealism and cinema verité, or when the 1980s witnessed the reintroduction of film noir. Most of the features that made film noir attractive in the 1940s were those that also fascinated viewers 40 or 50 years later. In some respects, the new film noir was more effective than the old, because whereas the filmmakers of the 1940s had to experiment with what was then not even thought of as a genre (Naremore 1998), their successors in the 1990s could read scholarly analyses of noir components and had easy access to copies of the old films. So their function optimization was enhanced by previous experiments. It could be argued that the neo noir films are mostly retro films, but in fact the retro element functionally enhances one of the main film noir devices, namely the passive melodramatic blocking of voluntary action. Frederic Jameson (1984) has suggested that retro phenomena express a schizophrenic breakdown of the sense of history, but a functional analysis of aesthetic effects provides a much simpler explanation.

The film landscape is thus a landscape in which optimal strategies linked to core motivations, such as activating a key emotion, will throw up certain prototypes—the mountain peaks, so to speak, since these are the most visible and distinct parts of the generic landscape, while in the flatlands between them we will find the less distinctive combinations. In this analogy, Fleming's *Gone with the Wind*, Wilder's *Some Like It Hot*, and Hitchcock's *Psycho* represent three such mountaintops. Not all viewers want to be on emotional mountaintops all the time; flatland blends may represent quiet entertainment.

Two intersecting causal chains feed into the historical development of film form. One relates to efficiency in the use of significant devices, while the other is controlled by the cycles of novelty and habituation. The cycle of novelty-habituation is even more likely to affect optimal than nonoptimal strategies, because such strategies will be more salient, easier to copy, but also easier to spot as repetitions. Some film noirs have used particular melodramatic effects with such efficiency that they have become highly salient, and the ease with which they can be copied is paid for by the ease with which copies or parodies—such as Carl Reiner's *Dead Men Don't Wear Plaid*—can be recognized. The most distinctive horror film formulas are often parodied, since this may be the only way to prevent a sense of repetition (although repetitions may be attractive for those viewers for whom a ritualistic control of emotions is important). The problems inherent in reusing the most salient formulas mean, paradoxically, that it may be easier to recycle with impunity the more middle-of-the-road clichés, though the price to be paid here is their relative lack of salience.

Different people have different preferences, not only because their exposure to films varies, so that a given film or device may seem more novel to one person than to another, but also because of differences in personality, gender, age, and so on. Young boys enjoy violence more than women and older men. For some people, strong emotional arousal is an asset, while others prefer their films to be gentler and less spiced. For such viewers, strong effects are a negative thing (Rubin 1994). These varying preferences among viewers are most often explained in terms of social categories, whereas less attention has been paid to the—equally important—influence of different character types.

Cultural Time-Spaces, Activity-Spaces, and Cultural Supplementation

The previous paragraphs argued that forms and content elements in stories travel, that some themes and functional bundles live hundreds of years, whereas others are short-lived. This contrasts with the view that any given culture is a set of arbitrary semiotic systems so that any element gets its meaning in relation to the closed semiotic system, and that a given culture or subculture has an essence, for instance "modernity," as discussed in chapter 1 (see also Smelser 1992; Kuper 1999). I will argue that cultures represent specific developments and outgrowths from a universal human nature, and that this is what makes it possible to translate from one culture to another. Furthermore, a culture does not have an essence; rather, it is a time-space characterized by the coexistence and interaction of different elements. Culture often evolves by supplementing existing elements with new elements and that culture is also to be described with what the philosopher Ernst Bloch called noncontemporaneity. Cultural elements travel from place to place, and both history and prehistory have been marked by dynamic changes and supplementations caused by trade, war, emigration, innovation, and so on. The present period of globalization represents a powerful acceleration of trends toward both increasing cultural complexity and the global distribution of form and content.

Burckhard's classic *The Civilization of the Renaissance in Italy* presents a 19th-century version of the idea of a given culture as an essence, while Bloomfield and Lee Whorf's idea that different languages entail totally different worldviews represent classic 20th-century versions of cultural essentialism. The strong version of cultural essentialism argues that it is impossible to translate from one culture to another, because each culture is a unique world that is opaque to everyone but its inhabitants (Kuper 1999). Thus the essence of feudalism was hierarchy; Asian cultures have a different, nonlinear way of thinking, and Asian people have different psyches from Europeans', while ethnic minorities in our communities have their own, distinctive, all-encompassing understanding of the world. Foucault's (1971) *The Order of Things* offers a relatively recent strong version of extreme essentialist culturalism, in which the Enlightenment is seen as having one cultural system, the 19th century quite another. During the Enlightenment, it is argued, everything was logical, coherent, centered, Cartesian, and bourgeois. Others have described the way in which Renaissance bourgeois culture was reflected in the use of perspective in painting, in coherent narratives, and in controlled psyches. Similarly, in the postmodern culture in which we supposedly live now, everything—psyches, genres, sexuality, and so on—is said to be fragmented, heterogeneous, and chaotic. We are allegedly surrounded by signs that the demolition man has been here to do his deconstruction, while we are the *flaneurs du mall* who enjoy the havoc. Versions of such beliefs may be found in Williams (1994), especially in Anne Friedberg's Jameson-inspired description of the postmodern psyche. Thus it is allegedly impossible to study universals that cross the boundaries of individual cultures, or long trends in history that transcend different epochs, because the researcher cannot rise above his or her own culture (see the critique of this position within anthropology in Kuper 1999).

However, there is no reason to believe that such all-pervasive cultural or epochal systems exist. It is easy to find examples that support a given thesis concerning a particular culture or epoch, but it is often equally easy to find counterexamples. The first half of the 20th century might be defined as modern, insofar as it gave rise to abstraction and functionalism, and examples of its modernity can be found in certain paintings from the period, certain buildings, and the so-called absolute films made in Germany in the 1920s. But this thesis can just as easily be disproved by pointing out that most films expressed a perceptual realism, so that the abstract movement in painting was partly a response to the fact that photography had made it more difficult to pursue realism in the other visual arts. Hectic cutting in certain films may exemplify the shock experiences of modern city life, but it is easy to find other films of the period that have long takes. Cutting speed slowed down at the beginning of the 1930s (Salt 2003) due to the introduction of sound, but if you did not know this you might be disposed to argue that the less frantic pace reflected the slowing down of economic and social life during the Depression. Film noir may reflect the traumas of war, but what about the musicals from the same period? Cultural artifacts represent aspects, not essences, of a given culture, and a given film selects one or several aspects of that culture. Musicals from the 1940s articulate upbeat courting and marriage rituals; film noir selects tragic events. It is thus not easy to tell whether a horror film expresses the anxieties of modern man or, on the contrary, was made precisely in order to activate primitive fears that are otherwise dormant in the modern world.

Even in premodern times, life was too complex to be summed up by one or two defining characteristics. An epoch is a time-space in which many different individuals interact within many different spaces, on different occasions, and with different backgrounds, skills, and intentions. A marketplace, a forest, a field, a private home, a wedding, a funeral, a battle, a hunt, and so on constitute different time-spaces that entail different experiences. Each activity-space is relatively autonomous vis-à-vis the others, and is linked to functional clusters and opportunities and affordances that arise from the activity in question. Dance, whether in a musical or in real life, consists of bodily movements, mostly to music; war—in real life and in film—consists of killing other human beings, of displaying anger and aggression, and in some cases expressing solidarity with comrades. Dissanayake (1995, 2000) has pointed out that all cultures tend to enhance particular occasions, spaces, relations, and objects by making them aesthetically special, and promote social cohesion and shared attention. Although funerals, weddings, dance parties, games with small children, or hunts differ from culture to culture, the diverse activities within a given culture tend to differ more from one another than do the various expressions of a given activity in diverse cultures.

Activity-spaces develop and mutate: fights with stone axes are different from confrontations involving armored vehicles; country markets are different from modern shopping malls. The development of a given, relatively autonomous activity thus has a dynamic that need not be in sync, or totally integrated with, the development of other activities. Different activities may be seen as part of the same zeitgeist because they happen to be contemporaneous. Pollock's abstract paintings and *Some Like It Hot* date from the same period. However, the feeling of connection is pragmatic and experiential, arising from the fact that both phenomena—for certain people in the 1950s—were part of the same life world and therefore created explicit or implicit mental links (although other people's experiential life world was constituted differently). However, the two phenomena are products of two different activity-spaces, of different artistic communities that deal with different functionalities and environments, and of the different ways in which their respective activity-spaces have developed historically.

Culture develops through an increasing differentiation and supplementation of activities. Learning a new perspective on the world or a new activity does not necessarily mean abandoning the old ones; on the contrary, people are able to accommodate and access a multitude of views and perspectives, even where these are contradictory. My basic worldview is Ptolemaic: the sun rises over a flat earth each morning and sets each evening. For special purposes such as traveling to distant places or seeing science fiction films, I also use a Copernican worldview that enables me to consider whether I want to fly east or west in order to get to Australia, or to understand why the earth is depicted as a globe in space. People may enter supernatural worlds, read horoscopes, or pray, but this does not prevent them from also entering rational, natural worlds, as discussed in chapter 5. Different films activate different perspectives, but as in the case of the Ptolemaic-Copernican alternatives, these may (or may not) coexist peacefully side by side, and be activated according to context. Thus, new perspectives are often cultural supplements, rather than replacements. In Hitchcock's *Psycho*, we witness how Marion is stressed by driving on a freeway on a rainy night. Although it involves universal coping mechanisms, the experience of driving along a freeway on a rainy night is accessible only to certain people living in a certain period, and to fully appreciate the film viewers may need to have had that experience. But unless the film cuts directly from this stressful drive to a walk by the sea or a peaceful playground or a suburban backyard, there are no active experiential links in consciousness to these other spaces. Although modern life is integrated through economic and other links, it also consists of a series of discrete experiential subspaces that are often connected only in the sense of offering different empirical opportunities for experience. Certain types of crime fiction excel in visiting many different subspaces—suburban houses, nightclubs, offices, and shops—in order to create salience and a feeling of connection that is often purely a product of the fiction itself.

When two contradictory perspectives are suddenly juxtaposed, as in the famous bone-to-spaceship cut in Kubrick's *2001: A Space Odyssey*, both will be activated simultaneously for a brief moment in our consciousness, but on the whole—for reasons to do with relevance and mental capacity—only one such perspective will be activated at a time. Some perspectives are impossible in the sense that it is impossible to construct a full and unified world from them. Neither I nor perhaps the director Gondry is able to create a unified vision of the diegetic world in Gondry's *Eternal Sunshine of the Spotless Mind*, but we may have different mental models to explain sections of the film and certain schemas to explain how they are linked, and we may be intrigued by the salience created by the paradoxes. Likewise, the world in *The Matrix* is "impossible" insofar as the different elements can be comprehended only locally and are linked together only by their coexistence within the same narrative framework.

The mind's pragmatic attitude, which leads us always to attempt to construct a reasonably coherent world out of current stimuli, and the objective limits to our mental capacity, which lead us to limit or exclude alternative visions, have a direct bearing on cultural studies, since researchers and students will often be hijacked by salient examples that are then generalized, as happens with Benjamin's description of the *flaneur* as a symbol of modern city life. But it is easy to come up with several quite different scenes from modern life—a stressed businessman at work, players on a tennis court, or people sleeping, making love, or being stuck on the freeway. Modernity is not an essence; it is a time-space with a multitude of different elements. Although the various mental mechanisms involved may obey laws and serve general functions, the totality of the interaction of billions of people and millions of institutions can only be described historically, because there are no fundamental laws and principles from which we can predict the course of history and culture. Culture develops through innumerable processes and causal chains, the totality of which is unplanned, factual, and pragmatic, and not the outcome of an essence. Despite their critique of grand narratives, adherents of strong culturalism and constructivism often seek to ascribe deep and universal meanings to cultural phenomena, as if they were created top-down by some central culture generator. In fact, cultural phenomena are often synthesized from the bottom up, from various elements, each of which has its own logic, motivation, and history. Cultural elements are not linked with one another by virtue of some overall master plan, but are joined together empirically and historically through the process of cultural evolution.

In this chapter I have argued that films and other cultural products are results of the interaction of a double stream: the innate mental dispositions and the cultural inventiveness to make products that activate those dispositions. Emotions are prominent dispositions, and films invent ways of activating those emotions, and those emotional experiences that are important for children are important selectors of narrative material in films for children. The fine-tuning of such stories may reflect cultural specifics. Prototypical genre categories consist of narratives that aim at optimizing a subset of the human emotions, such as fear, love, lust, or sadness. Storytellers or filmmakers invent agents, props, and actions that are functional bundles, such as wizards and magical wands, that are often universally understandable elicitors of emotions. Functional bundles may travel across cultures, because cultures are not opaque essences, and some experiential fields such as attachment between children and parents have a universal core that supports the spread of mind-grabbing cultural products.

3

Love and Desire
in the Cinema

This chapter compares romantic films with pornographic films. In addition, I examine the evolutionary roots of love and desire. To explain emotions as depicted in films, it is necessary to assume that humans have needs and emotions that are formed in a specific cultural context but that are supported by innate predispositions.

More recent scholarly writings on film have addressed the way in which human culture has developed within a framework nature provided (e.g., Anderson 1996; Grodal 1997; Jullier 2002). In this chapter, I analyze key elements of romantic films and mainstream pornography and show that love stories are concerned with personalized bonding whereas mainstream pornography represents anonymous desire. I examine the way in which romantic films deal with the negotiation of bonds of love. I also offer an evolutionary explanation for the appeal of these film genres, suggesting why women prefer love stories more than men do and men prefer pornography more than women do, although men also like romantic films. My conclusion is that cognitive-evolutionary theory provides a superior explanation for the appeal of romantic movies compared to psychoanalytic theory. But before the analysis of love stories, a brief discussion of the nature of emotions is in order.

Emotions are not primitive drives in constant conflict with culture and the superego. On the contrary, emotions evolved as a way to transcend primitive reflex patterns typical of lower forms of life (Grodal 1997; chapter 1). In mammals, emotions reflect innate motivations that allow flexibility in achieving goals as a result of cognition and learning (Damasio 1994, 1999; Ledoux 1998). Spiders, for example, possess neither emotions nor higher cognition and when threatened are equipped only with the reflex of avoidance (i.e., motivation and execution cannot be separated). In contrast, when humans experience fear, they avoid the dangerous situation in various ways (e.g., by throwing a rock, climbing a tree, or using a laser gun).

Emotions such as love, fear, and empathy are broad, innate motivators for human action. Because these emotions are general predispositions that are developed in order to provide flexibility, they are shaped by culture and individual experiences and abilities.

Emotional centers in the brain are necessary preconditions for storing memories (Damasio 1994), enabling us to remember not only the visual appearance of a snake or the face of a loved one but also to avoid snakes and to express tenderness to our beloved. Thus, our innate emotional nature is not in opposition to our individual or social development but a precondition for variation, adaptation, and learning. In popular language, we reserve the word *emotion* for powerful feelings such as hate or desire. This book, however, employs the broader, psychological definition of the word—that is, emotions motivate tendencies toward action, or as Nico Frijda phrases it, they are action tendencies (Frijda 1986, 69–94; Grodal 1997). Love, empathy, hate, and greed are mental and physiological predispositions that motivate different actions, elicited by different situations. Friendliness, for example, is a set of actions and behaviors, but it is also an emotional disposition that motivates actions, just as depression motivates inaction. Sadness is a reaction to loss, but has also communicative aspects to elicit a reversal of the loss, as when crying solicits help, or sadness is part of a homeostatic regulation of level of arousal.

Seen in this light, the so-called higher emotions of love, friendship, and altruism are neither products of the repression of desire, the body, or castration anxiety nor symptoms of a false consciousness. Instead, these emotions are rooted in innate predispositions. Human consciousness, including the conscious experience of emotions, evolved to enhance the fitness of the species. Although emotional repression certainly exists and most of our brain processes are nonconscious, our conscious experience is often a useful point of departure for understanding emotions in film, just as our conscious experience of emotions guides our actions in everyday life. These claims may seem trivial in the context of folk psychology, but in the context of film theory, they are not. Because of the impact of certain branches of psychoanalysis, some film scholars, following the publication of Laura Mulvey's (1975) article "Visual Pleasure and Narrative Cinema," have tended to regard emotions expressed in ordinary language as distortions stemming from suppression.

Humans share many of their basic emotions and drives with other higher animals. Emotions are functional in relation to the varying tasks that animals and humans must perform to survive (although emotions may be dysfunctional in some situations and for some individuals). Anger and aggression support hunting and fighting, sexual drives support reproduction, and fear supports avoidance of dangerous situations. The film experience simulates situations in which such functional emotions are displayed. Even those emotions and emotional reactions that are typical only of humans (and rudimentarily exist in other primates) are functional: laughter defuses social tension, emotions connected to fairness regulate interpersonal relations, those related to empathy enhance social cooperation, and love supports bonding.

When viewed only from the isolated perspective of a single individual, certain emotions may seem illogical. Yet when viewed from the perspective of humankind as a whole, these emotions are important in facilitating our survival as a species. For example, the care of offspring and altruistic bonds enhance the fitness of the species, although they may not necessarily enhance the individual fitness of an impoverished mother, a hunter who perishes helping his fellow hunter, or a firefighter who offers his life rescuing others. Film plots often revolve around human emotions that enhance the fitness of the species.

A definition of emotions that reduces them to one common origin—for example, desire or sexuality—clouds our understanding of their functions. Not all emotions have their origin in cultural construction; for example, psychoanalyst John Bowlby (1982) has shown that the attachment of children to adults is based on an innate predisposition that cannot be conditioned.

Love and Romantic Stories

Love is one of the dominant themes in fiction and a theme of tales thousands of years old. Love is also a popular theme in film. While there are numerous discussions of desire in mainstream film criticism, love is a relatively rare topic of academic discussion. Some argue that love and desire are the same, that love is merely the cultural expression of desire. I do not agree.

To begin with a definition, (romantic) love is an emotion that motivates an individual to establish and maintain an exclusive and mutual emotional relationship—based on gender—with another person. As long as love is in force, the relationship remains permanent, to death and beyond. But often love decays.

Even if the original impetus for love springs from beauty, health, wealth, friendliness, or intelligence, a central element in the definition of love is that the two people form an absolute and exclusive bond. Love should last even if the original conditions fade away, as in fairy tales, which abound with such stories of love or friendship; for example, the kissing of a frog, which shows an absolute and unconditional commitment despite the appalling exterior, although this absolute commitment is rewarded when the frog is transformed into a handsome prince.

The evolutionary reasons for the emotion of love, and for the behavior it motivates, are rooted in the savannas of East Africa, where some million years ago *Homo sapiens* evolved as our primate ancestors abandoned the rainforests and confronted open terrain. Over the course of millions of years, these primates had developed into large-brained human hunter-gatherers. Our African ancestors survived in the open by developing intelligence (and by walking upright and using their hands). As an effect of this evolutionary process, human infants were born early compared with other animal infants because they had to be born before their heads grew too big for the birth canal. Because of this and because of their slow process of maturation, human infants required more care and resources than their mother alone could provide. The evolutionary solution to this problem was that the human male—motivated by a bond of love—became one of the few male mammals that participate in the rearing of its children (Fisher 1992, 2004; Campbell 2002; Barkow et al. 1992; Buss 1994, 2005). The existence of bonds of love in hunter-gatherer societies is well described in anthropological literature. Thus, in an evolutionary perspective, the love bond was necessary for women as well as for men, or rather, without a love bond, big-headed, intelligent humans would be impossible.

Ten thousand years ago, some hunter-gatherers started farming or became pastoralists (see Diamond 1997), and this meant a fundamental change in social structure, because survival became intimately linked to the possession of land and thus to inheritance of land or other resources such as domesticated animals, buildings, and tools. Many different inheritance systems evolved that hinged on the social regulation of pair-bonding (Barrett et al. 2002), and such practices often conflicted with the formation of a love bond. Many love stories have focused on how economic considerations interfered with love, like Kaige Chen's *Yellow Earth*.

Older love stories like *Tristan and Isolde* attribute powerful and exclusive infatuation to a magic potion that induces an absolute bond. In the romantic film *Sleepless in Seattle*, the main character, Annie Reed (Meg Ryan), provides a partly magical explanation for her total obsession with an individual whom she has never met. Along the same lines, Amélie (Audrey Tautou) is magically destined to find her one and only in Jean-Pierre Jeunet's *Amélie* (*Le fabuleux destin d'Amélie Poulain*).

Modern psychologists are not in complete disagreement with the idea that love is caused by a magic potion. Pleasure related to sexual arousal in general is linked to the release of the neurotransmitter dopamine in the pleasure center, the nucleus accumbens, and adjacent brain structures. Experiments with one of the few monogamous mammals, the prairie vole, have indicated that sexual pleasure becomes individualized so that one person is made special. This is done by means of the estrogen derivative oxytocin and the testosterone derivative vasopressin (Young and Wang 2004) due to the way in which sites for these transmitters are linked to sites for dopamine. By inhibiting their oxytocin-vasopressin systems, scientists have been able to create promiscuous prairie voles. Oxytocin and vaso-pressin seem to be important for creating social bonds (and attitudes). Oxytocin is, for instance, important for establishing a mother-child bond in mammals (see Panksepp 1998). Bartels and Zeki (2004) have made brain scans of people in love and thus established what centers are activated in romantic love and the similari-ties and differences in center activation between women in romantic love and women experiencing motherly love. Therefore, even if there is no magic potion proper, humans may be able to forge extremely strong love bonds if sexual arousal is linked to those oxytocin-vasopressin mechanisms that are able to link erotic arousal to sense impressions of one individual person.

Although there may be reasons we fall in love with a specific person, a central element of "real love" is that the bond is absolute. Frijda refers to the isolation of one emotion from the influence of motives fueled by other emotions as *closure*. He states: "*Emotions tend to be closed to judgments of relativity of impact and to the impact of goals other than their own.* They tend to be absolute with regard to such judgments and to have control over the action system" (Frijda 1988, 354, Frijda's italics). True love, according to both old and new love stories, possesses a very high degree of closure. In romantic love, this emotional closure is often expressed vis-à-vis other concerns—that is, absolute love tries to seal off the emo-tion from other emotions and from considerations that Frijda calls the "care for consequences" (1988, 355; i.e., concern about consequences).

Love as closure has fascinated poets and filmmakers for as long as these arts have existed. Love at first sight is among the most powerful forms of love rep-resented on screen. Charles (Hugh Grant) and Carrie (Andie MacDowell) fall in love at first sight in Newell's *Four Weddings and a Funeral*, an event that is repeated throughout the film. But their loving gazes are not passive media for scopic drives or a patriarchal, sadistic male gaze. Rather, by flirting with their eyes in a universally manifested manner that has been described by anthropologists, Charles and Carrie establish contact and mutually bond. Initially, they look at each other in order to evoke attention and receive information. Carrie's look is emphasized by a human universal that Irenäus Eibl-Eibesfeldt (1989) calls "the eye-brow flash," that is, the lifting of an eyebrow. Their gazes then shift down and away to communicate reticence and modesty. The viewer is not invited to cast an extradiegetic gaze on the actors but to simulate intradiegetic visual attention as a means to communicate a desire for mental and possible physical contact. Thus, the characters' eyes are a means of communication, not of domination (Burgoon et al. 1989; see also Tomasello 1999 for a description of the centrality of shared attention, based on the gaze, for social interaction).

The negotiation of a possible bond of love is between two equals, and their reticence indicates that the bond is not forced but based on mutual consent. Even among animals, negotiation in mating is the rule and rape is the exception. Charles Darwin emphasized the importance of the female's choice of a mate for evolution (with the male peacock's tail as an extreme consequence of such female choices), and after a period of being criticized, the idea gained prominence (see Trivers 1971; Campbell 2002; Geary 2005). Romantic films bear witness to the importance of negotiation in love and bonding. The reticence that both Carrie and Charles express in *Four Weddings and a Funeral* enables the two to save face in the event they fail to establish a bond between themselves. Various modest behaviors serve both his and her ability to control and negotiate their emotional and sexual relations. In many films, the love relationship is slow to develop, as in Ramis's *Groundhog Day*, in which the attunement of the two takes some time. However, a slow buildup serves the same purpose as love at first sight—namely, to guarantee the permanence of the bond (figure 3.1).

Often the bond of love is portrayed as being so powerful that the death of one lover leads to the suicide of the other. In tragic love stories, such as *Romeo and Juliet*, the strength of the bond provides closure that prohibits the lovers from solving conflicts between the love relation and other emotional concerns (such as relations to parents or country). Although love often leads to integration in the prevailing social order, as in *Groundhog Day*, just as often it leads to a conflict with the existing social order, as in Luhrmann's *Romeo + Juliet*, in the different versions of *Double Indemnity*, in Yimou Zhang's *Ju Dou*, and in Bhansali's *Devdas*, because of the economic interests invested in regulating inheritance.

If we follow the logic of Lacanian film criticism, love relationships are based mainly on male patriarchal desires for dominance, which in turn are motivated by the need to repress castration anxiety. Yet in the typical love story, the foundation for bonding is a wish for mutual love. Care is a prominent aspect of establishing that bond, and as the ethologist Eibl-Eibesfeldt (1989) has pointed out, the model for the lovers is often a caring child-parent interaction, so that "baby" may be synonymous with "beloved." This corresponds well with the way in which both relations are oxytocin-based (Panksepp 1998). In *Groundhog Day*, for example, Phil Connors (Bill Murray) has to learn to care for others before he

FIGURE 3.1. To gaze into each other's eyes is typical only of parent-child relations and people in love, and the love bond in evolution is related to offspring bonding. In Harold Ramis's *Groundhog Day*, Andie MacDowell and Bill Murray impersonate the establishment of the romantic love bond, and the mutual and long-drawn-out attunement of Rita and Phil to each other that serves to cement their relationship resembles a parent-child attunement. *Groundhog Day* © Columbia Pictures 1993.

and Rita (Andie MacDowell) may establish a bond of love. In Kasdan's *The Accidental Tourist*, caring for animals and children is a central element in establishing this bond. This is not to say that present or future child rearing is an inextricable element in a love relationship. In Eastwood's *The Bridges of Madison County*, for instance, the dramatic conflict centers on the need to choose between romantic love and the care of children. But to totally ignore that love and sex may be related to procreation and child rearing is problematic.

The Evolutionary Explanation of Love

In this section, I expand on the previous description of the evolutionary origin of love and desire (see also Fisher 1992; Campbell 2002). Lower animals, with the exception of birds, have promiscuous sex lives and provide only rudimentary care for their offspring. The males compete with other males to produce as many offspring as possible and show off for the females with the same purpose.

Most mammals (95–97%, according to Young and Wang 2004) also have rather promiscuous sex lives and fierce competition among males for mating opportunities, but the females are deeply involved in care of their offspring. Few mammal males participate in caring for the young (in contrast to birds), and only among humans (and a few other species like the aforementioned prairie vole) is the female-male-child relationship typically based on the formation of heterosexual couples (although harem building and promiscuity exist); among birds, 90% form heterosexual couples, since keeping eggs warm and feeding offspring is difficult without male-female cooperation.

The reason human males participate in the rearing of offspring and in the formation of couples is, as previously mentioned, the slow maturation of human infants. Thus, through natural selection, the strategy used by birds was reinvented in the formation of heterosexual human couples. Of course, this presupposes the existence of certain strong, innate mechanisms supported by oxytocin and vasopressin that aid in the forging of male-female bonds. These mechanisms enabled personalized and exclusive bonds of love to be formed. Most likely, personalized relations were further developments of attachments that were forged between mammal mothers and their infants. Immediately after birth, a mother receives a kind of imprint distinguishing her offspring from other beings, thus establishing a special relationship between mother and child that motivates the mother to care for the infant.

Thus, we see that sexual desire and love are different innate predispositions that developed in different stages of evolution. The basic elements of desire have a reptilian origin that can be traced back hundreds of millions of years. The predisposition to love developed more recently, perhaps a few million years ago, probably as an offshoot of the fusion and transformation of the predisposition to care for offspring and the predisposition for sexual desire.

As long as humans lived as hunter-gatherers, there were no social reasons to constrain the forging of love bonds. This changed when humans made the transition to agriculture and pastoralism because ownership and inheritance of land and animals provided strong incentives for regulating the formation of heterosexual bonds, marriages, according to economic considerations, so that arranged marriages became much more dominant and a series of different practices were invented like paying bride prices, allowing rich men to keep several wives, and so forth (for an overview of the rationale for a series of different patterns of social control of marriages, see Barrett et al. 2002). Numerous love stories through history tell about the pain inflicted by the clash between economic-social considerations and love. Thus, modern nonarranged love is more in accordance with the lifestyle of our hunter-gatherer ancestors than the way pair-bonding has been regulated in the following 10,000 years of agriculture and pastoralism.

That humans acquired an innate tendency to forge heterosexual bonds does not mean that this predisposition supplanted promiscuous desire. The reptilian and mammalian desire defined on a species level is still in force and in some respects is made stronger because human females have no estrus and can mate all year round. This has served to strengthen the bond of love by giving it a continuous sexual dimension. At the same time, promiscuity is a constant possibility, while for most animals it is an option only during certain periods. However, the evolutionary underpinnings of promiscuity are different for women and men (Buss 1994). Whereas women in the era in which the evolutionary adaptation took place would carry a heavy burden if they were not able to forge a bond that provided additional male resources for bringing up baby and thus tended to look for men with resources, good genes, and a caring nature that indicated willingness to share these resources, men invested less in the total cost of reproduction. They did not invest in nine months of pregnancy and a long period of breastfeeding, so whereas women may produce only a limited amount of children, men might in principle father hundreds of children and let women and eventually some other men carry the cost. Females therefore became choosier than men because of their bigger parental investment (Campbell 2002). Male *Homo sapiens* are clearly less promiscuous than their hominid ancestors, because male promiscuity is linked to intermale competition and eventually linked to harem building, which is again reflected in the relative size of males and females. The difference in size between men and women is much smaller than among their hominid ancestors (Dunbar 1996). However, the stronger male preferences for pornography link back to mental structures that supported a promiscuous male competition for mating rights that is counterbalanced with newer pair-bond mechanisms, reflected in the fact that men also very much like love stories.

Combinations of love and desire are possible. People cheat on their partners; love may fade; and homosexual love and desire are possibilities, as are promiscuity and the formation of harems. That the evolutionary function of sex is procreation and DNA recombination and that the evolutionary reason for the bond of love is to provide resources for the care of infants do not in themselves restrict the manner in which an individual may wish to follow through on his or her innate predisposition to bond. There is no such thing as a natural morality. Even if all people do not experience the kind of dreams and exhibit behaviors similar to those depicted in Kubrick's *Eyes Wide Shut*, structural conflicts occur in both generalized and individualized sexual relations or, to put this another way, in situations involving promiscuous lust and love. It is therefore not the case that only exclusive, heterosexual, individualized bonds are natural. Homosexual love, for example, is based on the same mechanisms as heterosexual love (the question of the possible evolutionary roots of homosexual desire is beyond the scope of this book; see Barrett et al. 2002 and Panksepp 1998 for an introduction to some of the possible explanations). My point is that the bonds of love—homosexual as well as heterosexual—are based on biological mechanisms that developed as part of an evolutionary process. As such, these bonds are not products of specific cultural environments. Likewise, love is not exclusively a derivative of desire, although desire is generally an element of love.

Even if the evolutionary reason for selecting mechanisms that support bonding and exclusive relationships between two people is to enhance child rearing, the functional relationship is still an evolutionary one that need not manifest in a bond of love. A heterosexual bond of love, of some temporal duration, will typically lead to child rearing, just as the wish for children may be associated with love. However, it is not only possible but also common for bonds of love to be forged between people who never have children together. Romeo and Juliet never have children; a homosexual bond like that between Jody (Forest Whitaker) and Dil (Jaye Davidson) in Jordan's *The Crying Game* is not attached to child rearing; and the love between Francesca (Meryl Streep) and Robert (Clint Eastwood) in *The Bridges of Madison County* conflicts with Francesca's concerns about raising her children. Thus, the mechanisms involved with love can be independent of their evolutionary motivation. Equally, other matters such as economic considerations have historically tried to mold pair-bonding, and numerous stories and films tell about the conflict between love and social conventions.

This description of love and desire is in perfect sync with typical gender-based preferences for film genres. While both men and women enjoy romantic love stories as well as pornography, on average women have stronger preferences for the former than men and men have stronger preferences for the latter than women (Kramer 2004). In part, this may be culturally constructed, and more women today view pornography than did so decades ago. Yet cultural construction cannot wholly explain gender-related preferences. The evolutionary explanation suggests that females have a stronger incentive to bond for love than males do and therefore make a greater investment in bonding (Barrett et al. 2002). The interest in forming bonds of love is rational throughout history, as well as today; few women are unaware of the price of being a single mother, and even today women typically have primary responsibility for child rearing. But, as I have argued, women's interest in love stories and in bonding is not inextricably tied to child rearing. The disposition toward bonding has been established through evolution, and the relationship to child rearing is a pragmatic, probable consequence that is not necessarily realized in individual situations. Women and men do not necessarily have to want children to enjoy romantic films.

Women can give birth only to a limited number of children, and the choice of a partner for mating may have fateful consequences; women have therefore developed strong social intelligence. Men are able to produce large numbers of children, and the advantages of providing high-quality care for their offspring may, for a number of reasons, be offset by quantity considerations, although most men throughout history have had children with only one or two women. It is therefore not appropriate to assume ideological indoctrination as the reason that, on average, women prefer romantic stories more than men do, and men prefer pornography more than women do.

Desire and Pornography

Whereas love establishes an exclusive and individual bond between two people, jealousy is the reaction to any sign of deviation from that bond. Numerous cinematic love stories depict this emotion. Exclusive, individualized, and supposedly permanent relationships stand in complete contrast to the relations represented in another important but less respected film genre—the pornographic film or video. In pornography, interpersonal relations are strongly defined as transient, anonymous, and nonpersonal. Everyone wants to have sex with everyone else, and sexual interest in third parties does not evoke jealousy; on the contrary, it enhances erotic desire. Pornographic channels provide a continuous stream of relatively short films so that the viewer may engage in a seamless stream of new erotic encounters. In written pornography, from *The Decameron* to *The Story of O*, a central device is a situation in which it is impossible to identify the partner (who is defined only by his or her genitalia). This is more difficult in visual pornography, yet even here an anonymous body part is all that matters. The seat of identity—the face—is insignificant as a marker of individual identity (or even masked, as in the erotic scenes in *Eyes Wide Shut*). Few people would be able to identify their loved ones by their genitals, but they would instantaneously recognize their face. Important innate brain processes support recognition of the face (Bruce 1988), underscoring the importance of identity in interpersonal relations. In pornography, the role of the face is to express intense pleasure caused by stimulation of erotic areas, underscored by sounds of pleasure, to provide assurance of reciprocity and thereby an unproblematic access to the objects of sexual pleasure. Whereas in love stories protagonists are defined as unique individuals, pornographic protagonists are defined on an anonymous species level, in accordance with the basic reptilian drive system. Erotic signals such as makeup often aim to hide individual irregularities and emphasize gender-typical features and body parts that are considered sensual (Grodal 1997). If in the beginning of a pornographic scene a protagonist is actually provided with an identity, it is only as a spicy teaser, because soon the body will respond automatically to erotic triggers.

In all likelihood, individual identity will disappear with the shedding of clothes. Some pornographic films seek to increase arousal by employing stereotypical social roles—like patient–nurse—as models for anonymous sexual relations and modes of anonymous satisfaction.

A central aspect of pornography is the unlimited and promiscuous access to inspect genitals and other intimate parts of the body. It might seem trivial to point out that visual inspection elicits sexual excitement in the viewer in that such access represents partial acceptance of initiating a sexual relationship and functions as an emotional trigger. Humans and animals shop around and signal their attractiveness through the display of antlers, breasts, hips, penises, peacock tails, and the like. However, all known societies, and even some primate communities, set limitations on the display of genitals, insofar as visual access is an element in the negotiation of intercourse, although different societies have very different boundaries concerning what constitutes private, sexual parts of the body (Eibl-Eibesfeldt 1989, Brown 1991), and all societies have limitations on public copulation.

When our primate ancestors began to live in trees, their olfactory senses declined and their visual capabilities increased. Today, both humans and other primates are very visual animals. However, some film theorists have provided curious explanations of pornography; for example, that visual inspection is an element in the repression of castration anxiety or female otherness or that the highly visual capability in humans is not an innate feature but a recent phenomenon, enhanced by the pervasiveness of visual media (for an overview of the innate architecture of vision, see Zeki 1993).

Linda Williams (2000) has argued that pornography is fundamentally a portrayal of male sadism and perhaps female masochism. This is not the case, however, when it comes to mainstream pornography, in which, generally speaking, all participants express joy and are seduced of their own free will. In mainstream pornography, verbal, facial, and bodily expressions of pleasure and contentment are important elements, and, in contrast to decidedly sadomasochist pornography, in mainstream pornography the body is always willing to be aroused. This is understandable, in that many men fear being spurned or judged sexually inadequate by women; however, despite Lacan, most men are not afraid they will be castrated. An important aspect of pornography consists in arousing men by showing women that enjoy sex; thus lesbian scenes and scenes of women masturbating are part of mainstream pornography to send the message that there are always many horny and willing women around who want to satisfy their sexual needs. Furthermore, due to mirror neurons linked to facial expressions, there is a direct emotional resonance between observing facial expressions of emotional excitement and experiencing that excitement (van der Gaag et al. 2007).

The motivation to form exclusive relations, as opposed to promiscuous ones, should not be confused with the issue of power in relationships. Love may be experienced as an expression of free choice, but it may also be portrayed as a spell; and although promiscuous relations may be established by mutual consent, they may also be defined by power.

My characterization of mainstream pornography is descriptive, not an evaluation of whether it is realistic or beneficial. Viewers (mostly male) seem to enjoy the combination of the visual portrayal of genitals and of promiscuous sex based on mutual pleasure as opposed to force. Yet even if mainstream pornography is diegetically based on mutual consent, some women believe that the portrayal of women who always lust for promiscuous sex appeals more to men than to women and may have oppressive consequences by shaping attitudes toward women in real life. We need to bear in mind that in pornographic films, as in other commercial movies, the performers are paid actors who follow a script. The degree to which, for example, fellatio has become an important part of pornography most likely stems from its cinematic potentials that may also better cue excitement via mirror-neuron-like synesthetic resonance from visual to tactile experiences.

Exclusive love and promiscuous desire need not be in conflict. Many classic Hollywood musicals, as well as Luhrmann's *Moulin Rouge!*, integrate chorus lines in which women and men are anonymous representatives of their gender in plots centering on personalized love. In these films, generalized, promiscuous relations serve as backdrops for individualized, exclusive bonds. Of course, in reality, promiscuous and exclusive relations are often in conflict. Numerous films deal with this conflict, such as *Eyes Wide Shut*, which focuses on Alice Harford (Nicole Kidman) and her husband, Dr. William Harford (Tom Cruise), and their desire to have anonymous sexual relations with other partners. If we follow the line of thought exemplified in Williams's book *Hard Core*, Alice Harford's conflict is between her desire for female pleasure and her patriarchal superego. Williams writes:

> As long as sexual pleasure is viewed as having a proper function and an end—whether that end be reproduction, love, control over another, or even orgasm considered as a climactic goal-driven release—it tends to reside within the relatively parsimonious masculine economy of production. But when sexual pleasure begins to cultivate (already inherent) qualities of perversion; when it dispenses with strictly biological and social functions and becomes an end to itself; when it ceases to rely on release, discharge, or spending for fulfillment; when a desiring subject can take up one object and then another without investing absolute value in that object; and finally when this subject sees its object more as exchange value in an endless play of substitution than

as a value for possession—then we are in the realm of what must now be described as a more feminine economy of consumption. (Williams 1989, 273)

The implication is that emotions linking Alice to her child and to her husband are based on a masculine economy of production and not on valid emotions such as love and parental care. This line of thought assumes the existence of only one or two motivational forces—libido and patriarchal superego—and leads to reductionism.

Actually, the conflict in *Eyes Wide Shut* is not between pleasure and lack of pleasure but between different types of pleasure linked to different emotions. This conflict results in negative responses, such as the shame Alice feels during her sexual dream. The film suggests that Alice's loving relationship with her husband is dominant and her promiscuous feelings are partially repressed. In contrast, in Delbert Mann's *That Touch of Mink*, love is repressed until the promiscuous bachelor (Cary Grant) reluctantly admits to being in love.

Femmes Fatales, Desire, and Lack of Emotional Closure

Analyzing films about love and desire is made more difficult because love often encompasses sexual desire, and powerful emotions are often classified as sexual desire (especially if the protagonist is a woman), even if the emotion in question has nonsexual roots. In several film noirs, for example, femme fatale heroines possess powerful emotions, and although these emotions are linked to greed, the women are often described as erotic. To complicate matters, love stories are often analyzed as if powerful love equates with (promiscuous) sex. Thus, Johnston (1988) argues that *Double Indemnity* is about male castration anxiety and the patriarchal suppression of female desire. This characterization is problematic. Even if sexuality plays an important role in the narrative, this and other noir films center on the dangerous attraction that springs from the conflict that arises when a woman pretends to forge an absolute bond of love and also establishes promiscuous and anonymous relations. The anonymous relations are similar to those depicted in James Bond films, in classical musicals à la Busby Berkeley, or in pornography. Furthermore, they are often based on love or desire being used for nefarious means and thus are a nonclosed form of love or desire.

Vivian (Lauren Bacall) in Hawks's *The Big Sleep* signals that she is seeking a sexual relationship, possibly of a promiscuous nature, yet she is not dangerous; in fact, she later expresses a desire for an exclusive relationship that includes caregiving. And even if the fatal attraction in *Double Indemnity* were based on sexual desire, it would not be dangerous if Walter Neff (Fred MacMurray) were able to transfer his attraction for Phyllis Dietrichson (Barbara Stanwyck) to another woman after he discovers Phyllis's criminal intentions.

Stanwyck possesses a quality of danger as Mrs. Dietrichson similar to that of Jane Greer as Kathie in Tourneur's *Out of the Past* (1947). The dangerous aspect of these two women is in part linked to their desire for promiscuous relations. As a consequence, their desire is nonclosed with respect to its object. However, neither Phyllis nor Kathie is like a heroine of a pornographic film or a James Bond movie in that sexual gratification is not a goal in and of itself; it can easily be combined with other emotions, such as a desire for monetary gain. In a sense, Phyllis and Kathie are prostitutes, using sex for money. But in contrast to real prostitutes, they are dangerous because they lure men into developing strong, exclusive, love-like bonds. The men who fall in love with these women may initially be attracted to them because they emit powerful, generalized sexual signals, and this is due in part to the promiscuity of the setting. However, the men end up desiring exclusive relationships; in other words, they want it both ways. The sexual appetites of the classic femme fatale are not closed—in the sense of Frijda's definition—but are used for private gain. Even modern femmes fatales like Rebecca Carlson (Madonna) in Edel's *Body of Evidence* combine a desire for sex and for money. Thus, these films concern not only desire but also the conflict among emotions, typically sexual desire, greed, and love.

The Role of Choice, Seduction, and Fate in the Portrayal of Love

Establishing a permanent bond of love is a complicated endeavor, often implying mechanisms that in some respects run counter to establishing closure. This bond is often established in the context of explicit or implicit choice, whereby one or both participants compare possible love objects according to a set of preferences. Mechanisms of comparison and choice run counter to forming absolute bonds, and if this process of comparison continues after a bond is established, the relationship is likely to end as soon as one of the participants regrets his or her choice or gets a better offer. In Cukor's *The Philadelphia Story*, Tracy Samantha Lord (Katharine Hepburn) finds herself regretting her choice of a love object and is able to commit herself absolutely only after a renewed round of choosing (involving, strangely enough, symbolic promiscuity).

For narrative purposes, serial love, as in the TV series *Ally McBeal*, is a prime example of a situation in which choices regarding love are made and unmade continuously. While *Four Weddings and a Funeral* emphasizes the fact that Carrie and Charles fall in love at first sight, important parts of the film involve establishing intellectual priorities by investigating alternative options. In *The Accidental Tourist*, Muriel Pritchett (Geena Davis) quickly establishes her priorities, but it takes Macon Leary (William Hurt) the full length of the film to decide to make an absolute commitment to Muriel, mostly because there are class differences between them. He is compelled to evaluate the advantages of her nurturing, intuitive working-class manner in the context of a possible mismatch between her values and his Protestant, work-oriented, middle-class ethic. A central feature in love stories is the emphasis on social-emotional intelligence, whereby both characters and viewers try to find out whether a solid basis exists for permanent love.

Psychological models that focus on choice in love tend to be constructed from the perspective of a single individual, and although individuals often fall in love with another person without love being the immediate response, mutual consent is necessary for a bond of love to be established. Even when the process of falling in love is synchronized, as in love at first sight, the lovers may still need to negotiate their relations.

Words like *flirting, courting,* and *seducing* are traditional terms that express social signals and skills used to persuade another to establish a relationship. These words also express different degrees of control; thus, flirting and courting suggest that the object has some control, whereas seduction implies that a vital interest of the seduced is violated by the technique of persuasion. Tyrannical superego influences do not typically motivate resistance to seduction. Rather, the decision to resist or succumb is more often linked to whether the seducer is an optimal or an acceptable choice of a lover in a given situation.

The process of choosing a love object, as reflected in the postponement of commitment, is supported by involuntary autonomic reactions ranging from feelings of disgust toward the other person to general feelings of tenseness, often expressed in voluntary, goal-oriented behaviors. Our conscious voluntary controls dictate only the so-called striated muscles of the limbs and head, whereas the autonomic nervous system controls the rest of the body (e.g., the heart, vasomotor nerves, and a series of hormones). The autonomic system is divided into two subsystems: the first, the sympathetic nervous system, supports active muscle-driven, mostly aversive acts, including one's delimitation vis-à-vis other people, while the other system, the parasympathetic nervous system, supports relaxation activities such as eating and sex (i.e., incorporative acts). Acceptance appears to be a parasympathetic act (see Grodal 1997; Frijda 1986). The transformation of tenseness and delimitation into acceptance and commitment presupposes the activation of mental and physical mechanisms characterized by relaxation (and involuntary so-called parasympathetic autonomic reactions typical of eating, sexual abandonment, laughter, and sorrow). Viewers and protagonists often experience the relationship as initially characterized by choice and fraught with tension but transformed into one characterized by commitment and relaxation as the two people surrender to destiny.

When Macon finally surrenders to Muriel's wish for a permanent bond, the decision is based on voluntary processes and considerations, but the act of commitment as such is represented as submitting to fate; the deliberating is over and emotional closure can be established. In *The Philadelphia Story*, Tracy's symbolic promiscuous abandonment to Mike Connor (James Stewart) before she finally commits to Dexter Haven (Cary Grant) serves a similar function, in that it creates conditions that promote the establishment of a powerful bond.

One could argue that plot devices such as fate, destiny, and fatalism are used in romantic films merely to provide dramatic emphasis. Yet even when this is the case, the surrender to destiny or fate may still involve emotional elements, such as closure that promotes permanent commitment. A bond of love (or friendship) reduces an individual's free choice in exchange for other gratifications. If, after weighing rational and emotional considerations, a character decides to make a commitment, a feeling of succumbing to fate often accompanies the moment of transformation, as in *The Accidental Tourist*.

In other films, such as Minghella's *The English Patient* and *Double Indemnity*, choices in matters of love are linked negatively to fate because opting for love creates insurmountable conflicts with other values. Just as often, though, a choice is interpreted as destiny, as when—in Hawks's *Bringing Up Baby*—Dr. David Huxley (Cary Grant) finally surrenders to Susan Vance (Katharine Hepburn), submits to his "fate," and commits himself to love even though it negatively affects his work on dinosaurs. In this comic context, destiny is benign and in accordance with the tacit, rational considerations of David's existential options.

Emotions and Culture

The assumption that Phyllis's criminal mind in *Double Indemnity* is an ideological construction is an implicit element of Johnston's (1988) treatment of the femme fatale. According to her theory, women in patriarchal societies are denied the right to sexual pleasure, in that it threatens the sadistic control of women necessary to alleviate male castration anxiety and results in the criminalization of sexually active women. It is true that different cultures have severely restricted female sexuality, often because of economic interests, and horrible practices such as circumcision bear witness to that. It is problematic, however, to overestimate the degree to which publicly professed ideologies or moral norms determine the content of fiction. In most societies, stories of unpunished adultery—of men and women enjoying promiscuous relation—as well as love stories have circulated for thousands of years. Numerous examples can be found in *A Thousand and One Nights* and in *The Decameron*. Many of these stories have circulated in societies as different as those of India, Persia, the Middle East, and Europe. Throughout history, cultures have had double standards whereby men desire women who are sexually active at the same time as they admire women who are virtuous. A banal explanation is that men have different desires as husbands than as lovers. Similarly, women prefer different qualities in lovers than they do in husbands.

The degree to which men and women are allowed to express sexual desire and to experience promiscuous sexual relations is most certainly influenced by social norms and social and economic interests that vary among cultures and over time. Films reflect a wide variety of norms. The degree of sexual freedom accorded Carrie in *Four Weddings and a Funeral* is greater than that given the heroines in stories by Jane Austen. Carrie's freedom is also greater than that accorded Phyllis in *Double Indemnity* but perhaps not much more than what Vivian has in *The Big Sleep*. The perception of Phyllis as somehow limited in her sexual freedom is valid only if one claims that the film postulates a universal link between promiscuity and criminal tendencies and does not view them as individual traits of her character. The portrait is ideological only if all or most promiscuous women on film are portrayed as criminals. Within the explicit context of *Double Indemnity*, Phyllis's problem is not her wish for sexual pleasure. Neither is it a wish for the lethal pleasure described in Oshima's *In the Realm of the Senses* (1976) or the promiscuous rollicking of the characters in the Bond movies. Rather, Phyllis's problem is that she uses her sexuality to achieve nonsexual ends.

The specific norms defining love and promiscuity are negotiated in various manners in different cultures and historical periods. However, in all known cultures, people establish personalized, exclusive love relationships. Stories that describe rampant promiscuity in exotic cultures, such as those told by Margaret Mead, have been exposed as pure inventions (see Freeman 1983).

Establishing exclusive, permanent bonds serves vital psychological functions. For example, a bond of love is often linked to nurturing. The giving and receiving of care are essential to human survival, and their representation activates powerful, positive emotions based on innate tendencies, not desire or repression. In Hawks's *To Have and Have Not*, the fact that Marie "Slim" Browning (Lauren Bacall) is not a virgin does not constitute a problem within the film. However, that both she and Harry "Steve" Morgan (Humphrey Bogart) are altruistic and caring toward one another is a central element of the plot and key to the transformation of a relationship based on sensual attraction into one founded on love. Likewise, in Elaine May's *A New Leaf*, a bachelor (Walter Matthau) initially marries a wealthy, absentminded scientist (Elaine May) with the intention of murdering her for her fortune. Slowly, however, he discovers that she evokes something within him that makes him want to care for her, and these feelings combined with her love for him make him fall in love with her.

It is difficult to imagine a society where everyone wishes to have sex with everyone else, where everyone constantly changes partners without establishing personalized bonds, as in mainstream pornography (although certain hippie communities did attempt to adopt such practices in the 1960s). But according to the underlying theories of certain schools of film criticism, promiscuous desire is the only adequate reflection of human interpersonal relations and love is merely the product of cultural suppression. From this perspective, it is a good idea for Travis Bickle (Robert De Niro) in Scorsese's *Taxi Driver* to invite Betsy (Cybill Shepherd) to a porno movie on their first date. Most viewers, though, do not really share this point of view and consequently are able to understand Betsy's reaction. The abstract descriptions of desire and of the body commonly accepted in film studies, and the lack of definitions of higher emotions like love and of theories that explain the tendency to take care of others, make it difficult to explain why pornography represents such a limited range of human emotions. It also makes it difficult to accept that not only desire but also modesty is an innate human emotion. Modesty is not mainly a symbol of repression but is linked to the desire to control sexual relations.

Sexualizing all interpersonal relations hinders our understanding of the complexity of human needs, as illustrated by the way the term *friendship* has suffered the same fate as *love* in film studies. Thus, the relationship between Roger Murtaugh (Danny Glover) and Martin Riggs (Mel Gibson) in the *Lethal Weapon* series (Richard Donner), and for that matter between all males in action films, is not a friendship but reflects a latent homosexual urge. In the same vein, Johnston (1988) sees the relationship between Walter and his boss in *Double Indemnity* as an erotic one. From her perspective, it is impossible to view friendship as a distinct, nonerotic emotion (that contributed to the survival of our hunter-gatherer ancestors, due to the importance of bonds between hunters and warriors; see also Fox 2005) or as a means by which heroes in modern action films can deal with problems. This argument also excludes the possibility that homosexuals are able to distinguish between love and friendship, or between love and desire. To acknowledge the existence of both homosexual and heterosexual desire does not exclude the existence of emotions that are mainly nonerotic in nature.

Some of the reasons for avoiding discussions of love in film theory appear to be based on considerations informed by simplistic, dualistic concepts, whereby love is inextricably linked to marriage, heterosexuality, children, and traditional gender roles, while desire is linked to emancipation, fluid gender roles, and the body. Modesty and romantic love are further linked to Victorianism, in contrast to desire, which is linked to emancipation (although some feminists oppose por-nography and explicitly or implicitly argue that all pornographic representations degrade women). However, even a modest historical or cross-cultural investiga-tion shows that this interpretation is replete with fallacies.

In some contexts, such as European novels of the 18th and 19th centuries, plots involving romantic love—in contrast to arranged marriages—were a way to express that women wanted free choice in their love interests. A cinematic ex-ample is Kaige Chen's *Yellow Earth*, in which a father's economic considerations are in conflict with his daughter's wishes, fueled by love, for emancipation. In other contexts, the conflict is between love and personal emancipation, as in Benton's *Kramer vs. Kramer*. In still other contexts, anonymous erotic desire is emancipating, as in Buñuel's *Belle de Jour*, or love and desire unite to emancipate, as in Yimou Zhang's *Red Sorghum*.

Mind, Body, and Emotional Conflict in Film Drama

Desire is often considered powerful, whereas so-called higher emotions that are activated by love, friendship, or altruism are considered feeble. According to this logic, a powerful emotion evoked by a film must, by its very nature, have sexual roots. If a protagonist possesses powerful nonsexual emotional motivations, then the character must suffer from false consciousness rooted in repression or serve as a mouthpiece for ideological constructions. However, as Frijda (1986, 1988) points out, emotions are "action tendencies," and to be compelling, to provide momentum (motivational force) and closure, they must be experienced with great intensity. A series of emotions may activate such powerful momentum and closure. As I pointed out in relation to film noir, the desire for monetary gain is often a stronger motivator than sex.

That the strength of emotions equals the degree to which they are basic and primitive has parallels in the theory of human needs and emotions proposed by American psychologist Abraham Maslow (see Ewen 1993). Maslow maintains that there is a general hierarchy of human emotions, leading to his theory of the pyramid of needs. Physiological needs, for food and sleep, for example, are at the bottom of the pyramid. The need for security ranks higher, and the needs for belonging and love rank higher still. Above these is the need for esteem. At the pinnacle of his pyramid, Maslow places the need for self-actualization, including specific metaneeds, such as the love of beauty, justice, and truth. According to Maslow's theory, an individual must satisfy a lower need, a physiological need, for example, before he or she can begin to satisfy needs on the next level of the pyramid.

As long as Maslow's pyramid of needs is regarded merely as a descriptive tool, the model is relatively unproblematic. However, it has less value when it comes to describing a given need's motivational force. In other words, people often have motivational priorities that run counter to lower priorities on the pyramid. For example, mentally ill people, with unmet basic and intermediate needs, often utilize artistic expression to cope with their mental problems, while other individuals will risk their lives to gain social esteem or in the cause of social justice.

The tendency for emotional priorities to conflict with needs on Maslow's pyramid is clearly illustrated in films. In McTiernan's *Die Hard*, John McClane (Bruce Willis) risks his need for safety so that he may protect his wife. In *Kramer vs. Kramer*, Joanna Kramer (Meryl Streep) jeopardizes her need for belonging and love to fulfill her need for self-actualization. Art films, in particular, often deal with higher needs because they portray efforts to create existential consistency in values and emotions (as described in chapter 9).

The film medium can be deceptive, of course, because, as Ed Tan (1996) has pointed out, an emotional experience in the cinema comes at a much lower cost than in real life. We may feel good when John in *Die Hard* risks his life in his prosocial activities, and we may admire heroes willing to take greater risks than the average viewer, or the strength of Romeo and Juliet's love. However, higher needs are not solely the inventions of filmmakers and storytellers and by definition are not weaker than lower ones. In real life, many people commit suicide because of loneliness, sacrificing their physiological needs and physical existence because of frustrated needs for attachment and belonging. In short, distinguishing between higher psychological needs and lower physical ones is misleading because it suggests that higher needs are neither biological nor objective.

Many higher needs developed over several million years, whereas higher culture has existed for only 150,000 years or less and most other aspects of higher culture for only 50,000 years or so (Jones et al. 1992). Thus, higher needs are as objective as lower needs and contribute to the survival and fitness of our species as much as, or more so, than lower needs do. In *Eyes Wide Shut*, Alice experiences a conflicting mix of pleasure and guilt during her promiscuous dream because both modesty and promiscuity are supported by innate predispositions, shaped by culture and socialization. Modesty enhances control of who should father your child; promiscuity is supported by old reptilian mechanisms.

That emotions based on innate tendencies may be in conflict in a given situation points to an important aspect of human emotions that distinguishes them from, say, instincts in reptiles. Although humans have a series of innate emotional predispositions linked to central human concerns, there is no innate system of totally fixed priorities among these emotions. One person risks his own neck to save his buddy; another places high priority on the need for safety. The strength of love versus desire also varies from person to person and from situation to situation. Economic interests may be in conflict with personal preferences. This lack of a fixed hierarchy of emotions and concerns is, in some respects, functional and pragmatic in that it allows individuals to act in accordance with situational contexts and their personal histories. It also provides room for the development of emotions over time.

Because humans experience emotional conflicts, a person may choose one emotion, say love, and reject another, say promiscuous desire, or vice versa. The process of making such a choice involves withdrawing attention from the rejected emotion or impulse, so that it is experienced in an unfocused or perhaps unconscious manner. Even a simple conflict between, for example, being hungry and the desire to work may lead to a temporary repression of an emotional impulse.

Mainstream psychology does not differ from psychoanalysis with regard to whether impulses can be repressed or become unconscious. On the contrary, the fact that no innate fixed hierarchy exists among emotions may lead to repression if no compromise can be found. The basis for our mental and affective architecture is not a few innate predispositions but a series of predispositions, developed in reaction to various practical challenges that arise in the environment. For various reasons, specific cultures may wish to provide fixed hierarchies among emotions and concerns, as manifested in codices of moral norms such as the Ten Commandments. These moral norms function as rules of thumb, heuristics for solving emotional conflicts. However, these norms are not internally consistent. Conflicts among norms will occur in many situations and the norms may not be adhered to by all members of a community.

Film dramas, as well as other dramatic fiction—from *Antigone* to Krysztof Kieslowski's *Decalogue* (1988)—often depict characters experiencing two or more equally powerful but conflicting emotions. In *The English Patient*, for example, the patient has to either betray his country or break his sacred promise to his beloved (to return to save her life); here love and patriotism are in conflict. Curtiz's *Casablanca* deals with a similar issue. In Lars von Trier's *Dancer in the Dark*, the heroine believes that she must choose between telling the truth and subsequently jeopardizing her son's eye operation or being executed and fulfilling her obligations to her son. Numerous films deal with the conflict between the prohibition against killing and the moral obligation to protect family or friends. Nearly all television police officers are torn between their obligations to partners and family and to their job and the pursuit of justice. Moral rules of thumb do not provide clear-cut answers when rules are in conflict; it is left to the pragmatic, ad hoc arguments of the film to depict ways such conflicts can be resolved.

Many filmmakers portray situations in which the salience of a specific situation changes a character's moral priorities, and even the moral-emotional priorities of viewers. As such, film dramas often function as emotional experiments. Viewers enjoy these simulations of real life because they not only evoke different emotions concurrently but also pit the desire for closure against the need to choose between conflicting emotions. In addition, hypothetical simulations provide gratification inasmuch as they represent pleasurable learning processes in which viewers enrich their understanding of the world.

Conclusion

Romantic films and pornography are both based on innate dispositions. The emotions as such are not social or ideological constructions but are based on neural mechanisms that have evolved at different periods of time to solve different problems: procreation in general and providing resources for big-headed babies that are born too early and mature very slowly. However, culture molds the specifics, including how love and desire relate to other deep-seated preferences. Stories are central elements in an ongoing negotiation of how different needs relate to each other.

4

Screaming Lambs and Lusty Wolves

Moral Attitudes and Evolution

This chapter discusses morality from a cognitive and evolutionary point of view. First I contrast different approaches to the question of the relationship between morality and the viewer's simulation of emotions in film. Psychoanalytic research starts from the assumption that viewers are torn between suppressed perverse emotions and superego morality. Cognitive film scholars and scholars inspired by analytical philosophy have argued that the characters we appreciate most are those that act according to our prefixed moral norms. Others argue that today's film viewers have decentered postmodern psyches, not only as a consequence of postmodern life but also as a result of the psychoanalytic critique of the Cartesian subject. I discuss the extent to which the psychoanalytic approach to emotion and morality is compatible with cognitive and evolutionary approaches, and use Jonathan Demme's *The Silence of the Lambs* as a test case for discussion.

Films portray most of the emotions that humans experience, and most of the moral or immoral attitudes and forms of behavior they exhibit. For example, the popular film *The Silence of the Lambs* invites the viewer to witness the actions of a cannibal, Hannibal Lecter, along with those of a psychopath who abuses and kills women in order to skin them and use their skin for making clothes. Slasher films go into even more gruesome detail. Ever since Plato, concerned critics have feared that fictitious portrayals of the more sordid aspects of human life constitute a danger for readers, viewers, or listeners, corrupting them by a process of moral contagion. From the very outset, such concerns were raised by certain critics in relation to the new medium of film (e.g., the Payne Fund studies in the 1920s and '30s). These critics saw the consumption of fiction as a process of social learning (cf. cognitive learning theory and Albert Bandura's [1994] theory of role models). Other critics, however, were less worried. From a traditional Freudian perspective, the psyche is molded in early childhood, and fiction may help to alleviate the pressure from suppressed drives and provide catharsis, cleansing the psyche of the negative effects of such drives. The use of psychoanalysis in film studies deviates from the classical Freudian perspective insofar as many perversions are described as arising from a repressive regime (e.g., Mulvey 1975). Noël Carroll (1998) has argued that viewers have fixed moral and emotional positions that cannot be influenced by fictitious representations; films at most offer them a deeper insight into the moral and psychological attitudes they have already adopted. Carroll's position differs alike from mainstream cognitivism, from Bandura's cognitive learning theory, from mainstream social psychology, and from neurologically based emotion theory (Damasio 1994, 1999; Ledoux 1998). Murray Smith's (1999) approach bears some resemblance to Carroll's; he argues, for example, that the reason viewers like Hannibal Lecter is that Lecter has certain positive moral traits, but at the same time he suggests that human beings have an innate disposition to be intrigued by immoral and perverse activities.

Let us project these various views onto *The Silence of the Lambs*. The concerned critic would worry that certain viewers might learn how to be cannibals or psychopaths from watching the film, or come to share some of the characters' emotions. The classical Freudian view would be that the film alleviates the pressure from sadistic drives. A Lacanian feminist might take the view that the film expresses a patriarchal-oedipal fear of the feminine; Carroll would probably claim that it could be used to deepen the viewer's preestablished understanding of deviant characters and moral norms. Murray Smith (1999, 227) has suggested that, despite Hannibal's cannibalism, viewers like him for his positive features. But he has also (in a private communication) argued that our interest in Hannibal reflects "our innate fascination with the bizarre, strange, horrific, immoral, etc." The choice between these different explanations has implications for our self-understanding and our understanding of human nature and culture. It also impacts on the self-understanding and social status of the film analyst, because film analysis is often based on introspective reports, and what critic would admit to sordid gratifications unless such gratifications were perversities shared by all humankind?

Moral Norms, Natural Dispositions, and Decentered Minds

The normative values that we attach to emotions and behaviors arise from a cultural context that did not exist when the oldest layers of the emotional dispositions inherited from our animal ancestors were molded by the evolutionary process. Hannibal Lecter and those viewers who enjoy his aggression may be judged as sadists, but it makes little sense to see predators such as cats as sadists when they toy with their prey. At some remote point in our own prehistory, the distinction between moral norms and instincts ceases to be meaningful.

Morality has developed in two phases. The first is based on evolutionary adaptations that became imprinted in the DNA and reflects what was fitness enhancing in a Pleistocene hunter-gatherer environment. The radical expansion of the frontal lobe in humans compared with other mammals has further enabled cognitive processing and modification of emotional impulses and therefore also moral considerations evaluating different emotional impulses and different possible actions. As Frijda (1988) has pointed out, some emotional tendencies strive for closure, for giving action priority to a given emotional impulse, whereas other emotion-supported mechanisms express care for consequences, and such a care might be pragmatic, as well as a consequence of moral reasoning of the types discussed by Kohlberg (1984) (see also Krebs 2005). The second and shorter phase is based on culture and social institutions that have sought to constrain and mold our innate instincts and emotional drives to modify those instincts by enhancing moral considerations and to establish common moral norms to forward social interests of groups, subgroups, or individuals.

The evolution of the biological components consists of a heterogeneous body of adaptations. A cluster of adaptations relate to bonding and altruism. The basic altruism is the biological urge for mammal mothers to care for their offspring. As I discussed in chapter 3, evolutionary pressures extended the bond to possibly include the father (see Fisher 1992, 2004) to secure additional male resources for raising infants. On the other hand, a constant source of violence, male jealousy, developed because it enhances the chance that these resources will actually benefit the male's genetic offspring: taking care of someone else's offspring (and therefore genes) does not make evolutionary sense (Buss 1994; Barkow et al. 1992), although violent jealousy is clearly dysfunctional in a modern society. Evolutionary psychologists have further argued that there are advantages of group altruism (see Sober and Wilson 1998; Cosmides and Tooby in Barkow et al. 1992) and this made it necessary for humans also to develop powerful innate mechanisms for cheater detection to counter those that want a free ride on group altruism. Christopher Boehm (in Katz 2000) has argued that ideas of fairness related to minimizing bullying behavior of stronger individuals have biological underpinnings. Our empathy with other humans developed as a tool to enhance the survival of the hominid group, and Dolf Zillmann (2000) and Tan and Frijda (1999) have shown how issues of fairness and justice, or the sight of justice in jeopardy, strongly activate the emotions of film viewers.

The innate dispositions do not add up to an essence: empathy is often linked to a "tribal" sense of community that excludes nonmembers (Richerson and Boyd 2001), as is amply demonstrated in the vast number of films in which groups confront outsiders, like the white settlers confronting the Indians in Westerns. Our aggression developed because it enhanced our fitness as hunters and our survival vis-à-vis other hominid groups. Thus our dispositions consist of a huge variety of action tendencies, backed up by various motivating emotions. Some of these dispositions are part of our stop-go or approach-avoidance mechanisms, as in the case of love and empathy versus hate and sadism. As we saw in the previous chapter, other emotions, such as love and desire, may sometimes exist in symbiosis and at other times conflict with one another. Powerful innate dispositions remain within us, even though they may no longer serve to enhance our chances of survival or no longer be considered laudable in terms of our present cultural development. Thus a certain conflict between our basic emotional dispositions and our shifting moral norms would seem to be inevitable. We may not believe that we have innate drives toward violence or even cannibalism that need to be constantly alleviated either in real life or by symbolic means. Freud's idea of drives as a constant river that will create pressure if stopped by a dam, that is, by moral inhibitions, is not quite correct. Dispositions need not be activated or activated in full. But from an evolutionary point of view it seems probable that we have dispositions for violence and sadism as well as for empathy, love, and care, because of the clear survival value of such dispositions for our ancestors—although it should be understood that the different dispositions function in relation to different contexts. Films may lure spectators into taking pleasure in aggression and even sadism, even though present-day morality condemns such activities as detrimental to society, and they lack the survival value they once had under the prehistoric conditions in which they developed. However, even present-day societies rely to some extent on violence.

In certain respects, the postmodern critique of the view that humans are Cartesian subjects with a self-conscious center accords with evolutionary psychology. Although an individual's socialization is one factor that may influence his or her innate dispositions, such dispositions are also situation and context bound. The brutal warrior of the battlefield turns into the tender lover at home, and yet another context may lead him to kill in jealousy or to mistreat his wife. Carol Clover (1992) has observed that the audience of slasher films may start out cheering the psychopath when he assaults his victims at the beginning of the film. Later on, the same audience gives full support to "the final girl" and empathizes with her suffering and bravery during her showdown with the psychopath. The audience's reactions are thus prompted by the immediate film context, rather than by a fixed set of moral attitudes, in accordance with psychological research that shows that moral attitudes are context dependent (Krebs and Denton 2005). However, contrary to the view implicit in postmodern theories, such shifts between different emotions and actions are controlled by functional patterns that have evolved in relation to vital human concerns and are elicited mainly in situations that cue functional responses. Although, for instance, the kind of cruelty exemplified in splatter films is dysfunctional in a modern context, such films create contexts in which cruel motives and forms of behavior are made salient and may even appear functional and justified to the viewers in the context provided by the film.

Culture, socialization, and individual development may for various reasons create tendencies toward enforcing more stable (transsituational) moral attitudes. Population pressure led to the invention of agriculture roughly 13,000 years ago, and humans came increasingly to live in much larger groups than their hunter-gatherer ancestors. This in turn made it necessary to develop new, culture-based systems for regulating social life: David Sloan Wilson (2002) has argued, for instance, that religious systems were invented to enhance fitness at the group level by providing the rituals and metaphysical underpinnings for the moral norms and moral surveillance (see also Boyer 2001) that promoted the group's well-being and survival. Richerson and Boyd (2005) have discussed how group living increasingly relied on cultural enforcement of norms. Today, films play an important role in the cultural negotiation of different needs and in regulating personal interaction. Films offer a plethora of different scripts for calibrating our emotions and our moral norms, and while some of these scripts advocate unified moral systems, others allow for our being both Dr. Jekyll and Mr. Hyde.

Moral Conflict or Perversion

Moral norms are cultural institutions that were developed to restrain situation-induced behavior and the free expression of innate dispositions by individuals in order to promote the kind of behavior deemed by society, or by special groups within it, to benefit the community as a whole. Although moral capacities such as our sense of fairness, decency, and so on are based on innate dispositions, the precise definitions of what is just, fair, decent, and so on are determined by culture. Moral judgments are therefore essentially normative, not descriptive. Moral norms may be modified over time as a result of changes in the social structure. Thus some of the behavior that was considered perverse in the Victorian age is today regarded only as a harmless deviation from the norm. To some extent, psychosemiotics has served to maintain the Victorian and Bible Belt attitude toward sexuality. Thus, some of the terms that Freud used to describe people in desperate need of treatment have been employed by psychosemioticians to describe the experiences of normal viewers. Looking at nudity or indeed watching film scenes of any kind is denigrated as a form of scopophilia or voyeurism. Passive behavior is linked to masochism; aggression is taken to indicate anal sadism; the term *fetishism* is used extremely loosely, and so on. In order to describe the audience's emotional involvement in film, it is therefore important to distinguish between:

1. Activities that, according to our present-day norms, can be described as pathological deviations (e.g., cannibalism, necrophilia, exhibitionism in relation to children, other forms of sexual abuse of children, and voyeurism in a strictly clinical sense). With the exception of cannibalism, none of these pathologies has ever been an accepted mainstream practice in any known society.
2. Activities that are not pathological, but which to varying degrees conflict with moral norms or legislation. This gray zone includes the brutal use of force, humiliation of the weak, lying, stealing, cheating on your partner, and so on.
3. Activities that are socially accepted or positively evaluated.

My main focus is on the "gray zone" in category 2: on behavior that expresses a tug-of-war between innate dispositions and moral or legal norms and thereby activates moral dilemmas in the minds of the audience and a conflict between different dispositions. Such conflicts are represented in mainstream films and give rise to public discussion. By contrast, category 1 activities of the kind displayed in snuff movies or pedophilia films belong to the domain of the police and psychiatrists. A mainstream film such as *The Silence of the Lambs* would appear to contradict this: the hero, a cannibal, advocates category 1 dispositions, and the film also portrays a psychopath who abuses and kills women. But I think that the typical viewer's interest in this kind of film reflects only what Murray Smith (1999, 234) has called our "limitless natural curiosity in and fascination with the bizarre and the horrific." The film engages us because, as Smith has argued, we have a natural interest in deviant phenomena that arises from a key fitness-enhancing feature of human beings: the curiosity that enables us to monitor our environment for both beneficial and dangerous phenomena. However, Hannibal's cannibalism is not the reason he has proved so popular with audiences and entered the select group of modern mythical characters that includes Dracula, Sherlock Holmes, and James Bond. Nor, on the other hand, do audiences like him just because he is sometimes nice to Agent Starling. Yet the fascination he evokes does have something to do with Starling, for she too has somehow entered the mythological universe: she and Hannibal are a pair. Only *The Silence of the Lambs* enjoys this mythical quality to the full; the sequel, Ridley Scott's *Hannibal*, is much more ordinary, and in Michael Mann's *Manhunter*, Hannibal is not the main focus of the film at all.

Freud, Cognitive-Neurological Psychology, and the Theory of Attitudes

My analysis of the possible reasons for audience fascination with *The Silence of the Lambs* bears certain resemblances to Freudian analysis. The focus of Freud's psychology was on moral conflicts and their relation to the human drive system, and on the suppressions that can make us partially or wholly unconscious of our motives. Although modern cognitive psychology, by contrast, emphasizes the role of consciousness and totally rejects the theories of Jacques Lacan, it recognizes elements of Freudian theory. Before embarking on a close analysis of the film and the fascination it exerts, I will therefore comment on the similarities and differences between a cognitive-neurological and a Freudian understanding of the mind.

Like that of modern cognitive-neurological psychology (CNP), Freud's point of departure was late 19th-century neurology and Darwinism. Both CNP and Freud see the mind as a dynamic system with a series of functions that are sometimes in conflict and can sometimes be reconciled. There is no Cartesian center, no homunculus within the system that has absolute authority. Like CNP, Freud claimed that large parts of the mind were temporarily or permanently out of reach of conscious processes. However, Freud maintained a dualist understanding of the mind in which physical and psychological processes are seen as working in parallel, whereas the prevailing view in modern CNP is monist: mind is seen as a special emergent aspect of matter. Freud furthermore believed that sexual drives were at the root of most mental activities, and he saw the mind as being relatively unspecified at birth but as acquiring its "software" in early childhood by means of a rather limited range of experiences associated with the child-parent relationship (the Oedipus complex, the primal scene, etc.). This is the most problematic aspect of Freud's work, and in this respect it differs sharply from the view advocated by CNP, which on the one hand emphasizes the fact that human beings have a number of innate dispositions, and on the other sees personal development as arising from an interaction between these various innate dispositions and numerous environmental factors. Anxiety, for instance, cannot be explained solely in terms of sexual repression, but may also be a consequence of exposure to dangerous and traumatic events (Ledoux 1998).

Some of the speculations on evolution that Freud developed in his old age, such as his theory of the death instinct, are also problematic. Freud arrived at his death drive hypothesis by observing the effects of shell shock suffered by soldiers in the First World War. Subsequently, however, these effects were found to be a consequence of neuronal deterioration in the part of the brain called the hippocampus (Ledoux 1998, 256–258). More important, neurological research has shown that the experience of anxiety cannot solely or mainly be attributed to sexual repression. The neural systems that elicit fear are different from those involved in sexual arousal, and although certain people may develop anxiety out of fear of the consequences of their sexual urges, the prime function of fear and aggression is—logically enough—to protect animals and humans against danger. Anxiety is often caused by overload damage to the fear centers in the brain, as happens to patients with post-traumatic stress disorder. Thus the tendency within film and literary studies to describe all bodily phenomena in sexual terms is extremely misleading.

However, this should not blind us to the fact that other parts of Freud's account of mental processes have been confirmed by strict neurological research. Some of his central insights relate to the ways in which the mind seeks to control or reconcile conflicting thoughts and impulses. The neurologist Ramachandran has summed up some of the central mental mechanisms that Freud was the first to describe: denial, repression, reaction formation, rationalization, confabulation, and projection (Ramachandran et al. 1999, 153–154). Experiments with split-brain patients initiated by Gazzaniga in collaboration with Joseph LeDoux (1998, 32) have demonstrated radical examples of confabulation, that is, the invention of stories to account for actual behavior. I have argued (Grodal 1997) that aspects of Freud's theory of humor still provide the best explanation of several features of comic texts.

A sharp rebuttal of Freud's conception of mental life and that of CPN has been put forward by Noël Carroll (1998, 319–342), who has proposed a theory of the emotions in art that he calls clarificationism. His aim is to demonstrate that viewers or readers cannot be influenced by or learn from fiction; all fiction can do is to reactivate or clarify experiences and insights acquired elsewhere. The problem with this position is not only that it seems to run counter to learning theory (Bandura 1994), but also that it presupposes a Cartesian subject who is always aware and in control of his or her own experiences and has rather clear-cut moral ideas. Carroll's criticism of the abuse of psychoanalysis in film studies is important and well argued, but his clarificationism appears to revert to Cartesian positions that have been criticized by, among others, Damasio (1994).

The question of whether normal viewers might come to empathize with or even simulate morally problematic emotions and actions is a special case within a more general problem of social psychology, namely the relation between emotions, attitudes, and actions. A series of experiments have shown that context is just as important as attitude. A famous experiment conducted by Darley and Batson (1973) consisted of asking seminary students to go to another building; some of them were told that they would have to speak there about the Good Samaritan, others that they would have to give a talk on seminary jobs; and while some were told to hurry, others were told that they had plenty of time. On the way to the other building, the experimenter had placed an actor simulating a person in dire need. Many of the seminary students hurried straight past him. Their behavior did not depend on their professed attitudes, or on whether they were supposed to talk about the Good Samaritan or about jobs. The most important variable was whether they had been told to hurry or to take it easy. Their eagerness to be good students overruled their moral attitudes in another field. In Milgram's famous experiments, participants agreed to expose other people to high-voltage electric shocks because the experimenter asked them to do so. One set of attitudes linked to empathy may be offset by another set of attitudes, such as the desire to be a good seminary student or a good participant in an experiment. Carroll, however, presupposes fixed attitudes that are independent of context.

We may believe that it is wrong to kill our fellow humans. Film viewers may stick to that attitude when seeing certain films—for instance, films that show the pain of the death penalty like Robbins's *Dead Man Walking* or Darabont's *The Green Mile*. But the same viewers may see *The Silence of the Lambs* and actively want Lecter to kill and eat. Viewers may become powerfully emotionally involved in films dealing with a main character who is treated unjustly. But they may also enjoy stories about crooks. The audience may object to injustice when the film cues them to identify or empathize with the victim, because they experience the injustice in this case as a major loss of control, but the same audience may enjoy witnessing cheating when it is portrayed from the point of view of the crook. Thus the experience of watching a film does not necessarily clarify the viewer's moral norms; different films make different attitudes salient, and in the course of their lifetimes viewers see thousands of films advocating strongly divergent moral norms. It would be difficult to test how this influences the strength of the viewer's various attitudes and his or her behavior over time. The negotiation of values and the individual viewer's efforts to construct consistent moral systems take place to some extent at the conscious level, but may also be unconsciously influenced by exposure to different real-life and fictional value systems.

Personalized Morality and Law-Based Global Morality

The moral norms presented in films very often appeal to emotions and forms of behavior, such as hate, revenge, and sadism, that conflict with the moral norms of modern societies. In films, the New Testament's prescription to turn the other cheek to an aggressor is often supplanted by an Old Testament morality that demands at the very least an eye for an eye, and often a tenfold payback for any offence received. Hannibal Lecter is, admittedly, teased and humiliated by the warden. But he is also a murderer and a cannibal, and although we may find him more intriguing as a person than the warden, our moral standards would not normally lead us to approve his stated intention of eating the warden. In practice, however, many viewers regard this planned revenge as quite satisfying and justifiable. My students argued that the warden deserved such a fate because he was a bad guy, and their argument certainly accords with the film's emotional cues. The police officers that keep an eye on Lecter's cage may not be the nicest people in the world, but by normal standards they do not deserve to be killed and mutilated. However, because the officers oppose Lecter's desire for freedom, viewers accept his response, finding his actions quite funny and understandable (figure 4.1). Hannibal harasses the mother of one of his abduction victims by exposing her to a perverse sexual fantasy. He first asks her whether her nipples became hard when her little girl sucked them. He then states that a man's leg may still itch when it is amputated, and proceeds to ask her where she would itch when her little girl was slaughtered. The question is based on a cluster of metaphors that are not completely unambiguous, but surely imply that the mother might get an erotic kick out of her daughter's murder. Besides creating an erotic atmosphere, the only "justification" for the abuse of the mother—a senator—is that she collaborates with the warden.

Viewers are therefore invited to rationalize and have empathy with the story and its characters from a more basic, tribal moral system in which the world is divided into "us" and "them." If some of them offend some of us, we are entitled to use any means to humiliate and eventually kill them. But among ourselves it is important mutually to protect one another, show solidarity, and so on. Hannibal helps Agent Starling, so he is good, even though he is a cannibal. The warden, the senator, and the policemen oppose Starling and Hannibal and are thus considered bad. Such a morality cannot be deemed perverse, since it probably represents a default mode going back to the time of our hunter-gatherer ancestors, when members of each small group may have felt tribal solidarity with one another but lived in potentially mortal conflict with other groups. The them-versus-us mentality also corresponds to the typical moral attitudes of children. It is not an

FIGURE 4.1. The moral attitude of viewers may be influenced by the cinematic guidance of a given film and viewers may even to some degree empathize with monsters by following their perspectives. Here, Anthony Hopkins plays Hannibal the Cannibal in Jonathan Demme's *The Silence of the Lambs*. His brutal acts are partly legitimized as being a kind of self-defense, as here, where he is killing two policemen in order to escape from the cage in which he is imprisoned. *The Silence of the Lambs* © Orion Pictures Corporation 1991.

irrational morality; the principles are easy to learn and may be consistent. But it is limited in scope, and historical developments have replaced it to a certain degree with a more global morality based on laws, principles, and social institutions. Other films propagate these more global moral norms.

A classic and in some aspects problematic cognitive theory of morality was made by Lawrence Kohlberg (see Krebs and Denton 2005). Influenced by Piaget's theories of development, Kohlberg proposed that humans developed their moral sense in steps toward higher and more universal norms. The first four stages are as follows:

1. Morality is defined in terms of avoiding punishment, respecting the power of authorities, obedience for its own sake, and avoiding damage to persons and property. This is typical of small children, and also typical of authoritarian relations.

2. Morality is defined in terms of a negotiation, through making deals and engaging in equal exchange. Older children and groups will experiment with this kind of nonhierarchical morality, based on personalized exchange.

3. Morality is defined in terms of upholding mutual relationships, fulfilling role expectations, preserving one's reputation, and giving care. Trust, loyalty, respect, and gratitude are important moral values. Such moral systems depend on a certain degree of social transparency, because more complex social-moral systems may be victimized by cheats.

4. Morality is defined in terms of maintaining a social system from which one benefits by obeying the rules and laws, and contributing to society.

I will add that category 4 moral systems reflect the needs of large societies, in which both the control of violations and cheating and the learning of norms and laws are institutionalized. Thus the development from stage 3 to stage 4 represents not only the typical pattern of individual development but also the historic development of social moral systems, from those adapted to the hunter-gatherer group to those which cater to more complex modern societies in which cooperation in large groups is important. Such societies therefore develop moral norms and legal institutions that facilitate downscaling of selfishness and emphasis on common norms.

However, Kohlberg's description has been criticized for being too idealistic and general, because it does not reflect actual moral behavior. The moral values of the higher stages are often incompletely internalized and not fully backed up by innate dispositions, and people often dispense with adherence to these norms, in real life as well as when they are film viewers. Jonathan Haidt (2001) argued (contra Kohlberg's rationalism) that moral evaluations are often emotional, quick, and intuitive and eventual rational justifications are produced post hoc, as when people rationalize why they like Hannibal Lecter. Moral intuitions are often based on innate features but fine-tuned by culture and context. If therefore a film produces a scene in which the hero needs to use torture to extract some vital information, viewers may feel that the torture is just, although in other settings they would find torture immoral. Krebs and Denton (2005) have therefore argued that people's emotions influence their moral judgment and reasoning.

Different moral systems offer a variety of options for any given film. Filmmakers may choose to make one of the four moral stages salient in a particular film, or mix the different stages. The typical police film focuses on stage 4 morality, that inscribed in national or universal laws, but often in combination with a stage 3 morality in which role expectations are important, like being a good cop. In contrast, Coppola's *The Godfather* from the outset maintains a stage 3 morality in which notions of right and wrong are linked to role expectations and reputation within a subgroup but in conflict with society as a whole. War and action films may in principle adhere to a stage 4 morality—for instance, by presenting the hero's goals as patriotic—but in fact promote personalized moral norms of stages 2 or 3, showing, for instance, forms of bonding based on individual exchanges of support or emphasizing the need to achieve a reputation for bravery, and may also violate the rights of out-groups if they are in conflict with in-group interests. Some gangster films present a stage 1 morality, in which the hero struggles to fulfill his personal goals and optimize his preferences within an established power hierarchy. By contrast, many art films (as I discuss in detail in chapter 9) focus on establishing a coherent value system of their own, although certain "transgressive" art films experiment with amoral value systems. Different viewers may have different moral stages as their basic model, but may also enjoy other stages; for example, "going up" and enjoying a lofty, altruistic morality, or "going down" to a more primitive morality, based on individualized bonds, exchange, and revenge, or a group morality based on notions of us versus them.

The implicit conflict between a more limited morality (based on personal allegiances) and more sophisticated moral attitudes based on general norms and laws may be softened in various ways by the use of genre. Genre systems often serve as a way of allowing deviating moral systems and forms of gratification to exist in a socially acceptable form in certain circumscribed environments. In this respect, film genres resemble other types of social conventions: compared with a normal party or normal office life, for instance, a ball may allow a greater display of bare flesh, a greater intimacy between the sexes, and even the exchange of caresses. Soccer, American football, or boxing involve levels of physical aggression that in other circumstances would be highly illegal. In chapter 8 of Grodal (1997) I discuss how humor often serves as a switch that allows the audience to deviate from emotional-moral norms—for instance, by laughing at other people's sufferings. James Bond films involve a level of promiscuity and violence that would be unacceptable in other circumstances. Certain genres, such as slasher movies, are acceptable only to a minority of viewers. Sexual display, violence, or the replacement of empathy with laughter have the same emotional roots whether they are articulated in an unmarked realistic situation or defined by a specific code, such as that of the ballroom, the playing field, or a particular film genre. The same emotional circuits are activated whether a given event takes place in a game, a film, or in real life. But genre marking serves a double function: it both allows the participants or viewers to enjoy the deviating morality and serves (in principle) as a warning not to transfer these deviant moral norms, emotions, and forms of behavior to locations outside those covered by the code. Such markings do not, however, prevent certain individuals from learning, over time, to adopt these deviant norms.

The Silence of the Lambs uses different genre markers to sugarcoat the moral behavior presented in the film. The first such marker suggests that the film has deep allegorical meanings. The allegorical hints are contained in the title of the film and in the story of Agent Starling's attitude to the slaughtering of lambs. It implies that there is some deep relationship between pain and sexuality: Starling's virginal qualities are suggested in her efforts to show empathy and to save the lambs, or victims. The allegorical and opaque form in which the lamb theme is presented veils it from closer scrutiny and suggests that the message of the film cannot be judged by normal moral standards. The second genre marker encourages us to perceive the film as a special kind of horror-slasher thriller. Hannibal is linked both to the figure of the mad, perverse scientist and to Dracula-type monsters that drink blood. Such figures are marked as belonging to varying degrees to a realm of fantasy governed by other laws, including other moral norms. The scene in which Hannibal is put into an excessively monstrous iron helmet that prevents him from biting and eating other people signals that we have moved beyond realism (but also shows that he is abused by the warden, cueing us to take pity on him).

Starling and the Gallant Beast

The key to the success of *The Silence of the Lambs* lies in the pairing of Starling and Hannibal and in the way they interact with each other. The novelist and the scriptwriter who created them appear to have been influenced by Freudian theory, insofar as their relationship is seen as incestuous, Starling's involvement with Lecter replicating her strong ties to her father. From a cognitive perspective, however, it is important to explain how their relationship can activate emotions in the viewer that do not presuppose childhood traumas. The film first presents Agent Starling (Jodie Foster) as a kind of modern nun. She is working hard to control her body by strenuous exercise on an FBI training ground. To make sure the viewer doesn't miss the point, the camera focuses on a sign that reads: "hurt, agony, pain, love—it." Starling's control of her hard, muscular body is thus overtly labeled as sadomasochistic. But she is then confronted with pictures of girls who have completely lost control of their bodies by falling victim to a serial killer. This prefigures her confrontation with aggressive male sexuality.

She is assigned to contact Hannibal Lecter, a cannibal and brilliant psychologist, in order to get his help in understanding the mental profile of the serial killer. This leads to a prolonged encounter with aggressive male sexuality. First Lecter's warden makes a pass at her, and then an inmate screams at her that he can smell her cunt, and finally Lecter forces her to repeat this exclamation and demonstratively sniffs at her to inhale her bodily odors. He then proceeds to harass her sexually, indulging in fantasies about her provincial background and the way her virgin body must have been attacked by sleazy boys in cars. This is followed by an attempt to psychoanalyze her by prying into her most intimate experiences. Agent Starling has been warned that it is dangerous to let Hannibal "get inside" her head, but Hannibal slowly but firmly opens her up, forcing her to sell access to her intimate self in exchange for information about the serial killer. Finally, having coerced her intellectually into admitting him as a partici-pant in her private life, he provides her with a certain amount of information. This pattern is repeated in all their encounters. He starts by painting a highly pornographic picture of Starling in relation to men (for instance, asking her if she fled the farm where she worked because the farmer forced her to engage in fellatio). Then he gets her to reveal various intimate, nonsexual experiences, and finally provides her with information relevant to her pursuit of the serial killer. This information mainly concerns sexual deviations or involves descriptions of how men look at her body.

Objectively speaking, then, their meetings are a series of sexual harassments in which the "virgin" is assaulted by the "beast" and forced from the active posi-tion that she holds in her other relationships into a (controlled) passive position in relation to Hannibal (see Thompson 1999, 103–130). Her relationship to him might even be described as a sort of initiation. But most viewers will probably not remember and interpret their encounters in that light, even though the film and its sequel overtly speak of Hannibal's love for Starling. There are several reasons for this. The first is that throughout their encounters Hannibal is con-fined to a prison cell so that he cannot physically approach her, so his innuendos cannot be followed up in practice. The second reason has to do with Hannibal's Freudian implication that Starling's sexuality has been blocked by some child-hood trauma and that Hannibal may somehow cure her of this. The third reason is a consequence of the second: the film suggests—as mentioned above—a deep allegorical meaning that the intellectual wizard Hannibal may be able to unravel, and his innuendo is therefore excused by his superhuman insight, which places him beyond good and evil. The fourth reason is that Starling is partially able to control him because she appeals to his protective instinct; he even hypnotizes a fellow prisoner who has offended her into committing suicide. And finally, Hannibal pays for her acceptance of his sexual harassment with information that actually helps her in her task. The narrative development therefore supports the view that Hannibal is a helper in a fight against an evil torturer and murderer. Thus, the viewer is sexually engaged but cued to rationalize this arousal in a non-sexual framework of intellectual detection and crime prevention, backed up by

Starling's brave rescue of the serial killer's last victim. Moreover, the serial killer, as a victim of his own confused sexuality, provides a contrast to Hannibal, who seems to know everything about the subject.

The film creates a story in which the viewer can both have his cake and eat it. Hannibal Lecter and Starling work together to punish a heinous criminal and there is pleasure in this moral endeavor to punish these cruelties and in observing Lecter's care for Starling and her project and seeing how he helps Starling in her pursuit of the serial killer. Viewers can empathize with the selfish brutality that he shows and even be fascinated with his wish to eat his enemies and other expressions of power. At the same time, viewers can empathize with Hannibal's sexual aggression toward an object that is sexually attacked, yet at the same time protected. Viewers can identify with the control and care expressed in Agent Starling's behavior, and they may even enjoy Starling's meek appeal to Hannibal and the way in which she gives in and accepts a passive position in pursuit of her professional duty. Moreover, viewers can enjoy this arousal at one remove, protected at once by Hannibal's distancing monstrosity and by the courteous and highly civilized aspects of his character. Women may fully give in to Dracula in Coppola's *Bram Stoker's Dracula* due to the supernaturalism, but certainly not to Hannibal. This causes a lot of clumsy episodes in the sequel, for a relationship between a virgin-knight and an aggressive-caring monster in a cage and chains is one thing, but it is quite another to try to further their relationship without these blocking remedies. After all, Hannibal is a cannibal and the film does not cater to cannibalistic emotions, only for moral slumming.

The Male Gaze and Female Mating Strategies

Laura Mulvey (1975) has claimed that most Hollywood films are vehicles for the male gaze. Although this characterization is beside the point in most films, it certainly rings true in relation to *The Silence of the Lambs*. Apart from her boss, all the men in the film direct their gaze at Agent Starling's body, and this intrusion reaches its peak when the serial killer, Buffalo Bill, stares at her seemingly defenseless body through his night binoculars. Roger Ebert (1991) observes, "The movie has an undercurrent of unwelcome male attention toward her character; rarely in a movie have I been made more aware of the subtle sexual pressures men put upon women with their eyes." However, Mulvey's Lacan-inspired explanation, that the purpose of the male gaze is to veil a male castration anxiety, is unfounded (see Grodal 1997). Males throughout the animal kingdom look at females to gauge their suitability as mating partners and, where appropriate, to gain the female's attention and arouse her interest.

The film's achievement, however, lies not merely in secretly or overtly cueing aggressive sexuality, but in demonstrating the problems this causes for women. The narrative is ambiguous. On the one hand it shows how Starling conquers and punishes men who back their male gaze with violence. On the other hand it shows her mentally giving in to Hannibal's gaze and his verbal attacks. For evolutionary reasons, female mating strategies are different from those of the male. Men do not invest as many resources in child rearing as women, and tend to follow a more promiscuous and philandering strategy (see chapter 3). Women have traditionally wanted to attract the best possible mate (and the best possible provider of additional resources for the child; see Kramer 2004, 2008). By their beauty, clothes, skills, and so on, they passively or actively emit information about their attractiveness. At the same time, they reject most offers in order to maximize their preferences. Contra various chauvinist mythologies, there are good evolutionary reasons for women to have a strong innate opposition to coercion, because this would lead to a catastrophic and traumatic lack of control. In evolutionary terms, millions of years without contraception underpin women's emotional hostility to coercive sex. Preference for strong men who can provide resources and protection has often been in conflict with women's essential need to retain control over their own bodies. Fictional works and courtrooms are full of examples of what can go wrong—intentionally or unintentionally—in the negotiation of these two different mating interests and strategies. The fine-grained female balance between passively or actively emitting signs of sexual attractiveness and the actual regulation of that contact by go-stop-play is a continuous source of male misunderstanding and aggression. On the one hand, Starling provides a role model for female control, but on the other her passive acceptance of Hannibal's aggressive sexual innuendo is certainly intended to give pleasure to male viewers.

Clarifications, Rationalizations, or Emotional Roller-coaster Rides

It is unlikely that films such as *The Silence of the Lambs* offer viewers any moral clarification, though nor can we assume that normal viewers risk moral contagion by watching it. What is clear, however, is that the film portrays a complex web of emotions and offers viewers rich possibilities to rationalize their ways of finding gratification, even if some of these conflict with some of their moral attitudes. There are two ways of explaining films: one is to take what is shown as a kind of mimetic truth, so that reality itself is ultimately responsible for what is portrayed; the other consists in seeing the film as a crafted and communicated product aimed at cueing certain emotions and cognitions. Clearly, the filmmakers' purpose in *The Silence of the Lambs* is not only to offer a realistic account of certain sordid aspects of the world but also to give viewers a trip on an emotional roller-coaster. Its moral patterns consist partly therefore in rationalizations. Most violent films provide reasons for why their heroes have to kill dozens of crooks; many films describe rescue operations in which dozens of people are killed before a few hostages are saved. A mimetic description of *The Silence of the Lambs* would emphasize that the blend of sexual aggression, intellect, perversion, and care that we see in Hannibal can be found in real people too, and that serial killers such as Buffalo Bill exist in real life, as do upright modern police officers such as Starling. The communicative approach, by contrast, would suggest that the positive aspects of Hannibal's character also serve to allow viewers to rationalize their film experience and make the emotions involved more acceptable.

The Silence of the Lambs goes to extremes in its efforts to allow viewers to accept double standards. Many films, by contrast, stick to their explicit standards. As mentioned above, they may focus on different levels of morality and have different degrees of moral complexity: both *Bambi* and Ephron's *Sleepless in Seattle*, for example, are morally uncomplicated. Films may also be simple in the sense that each individual scene is morally unambiguous, although the film as a whole may be more complex, with different moral norms governing different scenes: the characters in one scene, for instance, may demonstrate a lofty morality, while group violence, revenge, and torture reign in other scenes. Wallace's *We Were Soldiers* or Kotcheff's *First Blood* series offer examples of such mixtures.

The cognitive, neurological, and evolutionary approach to film differs strongly from the Freudian in many respects, but it also has affinities with Freudian criticism—for example, in recognizing the importance of the conflict between innate drives and moral norms, and the importance of nonconscious or vaguely conscious motivations. However, the approach assigns a much lesser role than the Freudian to sexual double standards in a landscape where many other dispositions, such as the disposition to violence toward outsiders, to fight for resources, and so on, play equally important roles in creating moral heterogeneity. Emotions and moral norms are not unambiguous, and conflicts often arise between different aspects of norms and different emotions. Moral norms consist of several layers, and violent mainstream films often portray moral norms that are closer to those of our ancestors' personalized world than modern norms based on laws and complex social integration. Viewer behavior is, as pointed out by Krebs and Denton (2005), strongly influenced by context. Although viewers may seek to establish a certain consistency in their attitudes, values, and behavior, and even at times succeed in doing so, such consistency is fragile and may be influenced by film contexts in ways of which they are not fully aware.

5

Undead Ghosts and Living Prey

Fantasy and Horror

This chapter discusses the evolutionary roots of films with a supernatural con- tent, inspired by cognitive-evolutionary studies in fantastic phenomena (e.g., Boyer 2001; Atran 2002; Barrett 2004; Norenzayan et al. 2006). It discusses the reasons for the salience of counterintuitive phenomena and shows how themes related to agency, predation, death, morality, and social exchange are prominent in fantastic films and horror films.

Works portraying fantastic, supernatural, and religious phenomena constitute an important area of fiction. Indeed, certain genres are defined by these subjects. Such genres include fantasy films (often made for children), science fiction, and hor- ror. However, many art films deal with supernatural phenomena as well. From an Enlightenment perspective, one might assume that the scientific worldview would slowly but steadily replace a worldview based on or involving magic and the super- natural. Max Weber called this tendency disenchantment. But disenchantment is clearly not the whole truth. On the contrary, the number of fantasy films is by no means decreasing. In fact, genres such as science fiction or horror, which involve the significant use of "nonstandard physics" or fantastic and supernatural scenes, are more widespread today than they were in the 1930s. Art films, too, continue to deal with supernatural phenomena: take, for instance, Tarkovsky's films, Trier's *Breaking the Waves* and *The Kingdom*, or Wenders's *Wings of Desire* (see chapter 9).

The mental capacities that enabled us to envisage supernatural and fantastic experiences evolved because they enhanced our chances of survival, because imagination, the ability to visualize alternative future scenarios, is vital to the intelligent and flexible management of behavior (Björklund and Pellegrini 2002; Boyer 2007; Pellegrini et al. 2007). Such imaginative ability is also a by-product of our search for causality because insights in causes and effects enhance survival, so the mind is on a constant lookout for causal explanations. However, the world is full of complex chains of events, and without the aid of science that may disprove causal links (say, relations between black cats and misfortune, star constellations, day of birth, and fortune), minds and cultures will accumulate valid causal links side by side with invalid links. The principle "x followed y; therefore y caused x" is often helpful, but the world is also full of random contiguities. If an accident happens just after a black cat has passed, we may without justification infer that the cat was the cause of the accident. The interest in radical deviations from or negations of laws and common sense is in a paradoxical way a function of our innate rationality. Changes, deviations, and novelty attract our interest. As soon as events are slotted into familiar and well-explained patterns, they lose their salience, unless they prompt us to further action. Few phenomena are as deviant and therefore as attention-grabbing as supernatural figures or events, and these will therefore activate strong interest even when they are merely portrayed in words or pictures. Moreover, we have an innate tendency to draw causal inferences that may sometimes lead us astray. Films not only use but may also abuse our natural tendency to infer too many causal relations (Grodal 1997) because films are free to activate hermeneutic mechanisms by creating mind-boggling coincidences.

To mold the intentions and functions of animal and human agencies is extremely important in a natural world, and thus brains tend to overgeneralize and invent supernatural agencies as causal reasons for natural or social events. Our ability to create fantastic worlds, moreover, has evolved in tandem with the development of language and other forms of communication: the more advanced our media of representation, the more liberated they are from those aspects of reality that constrain our unmediated perceptions.

Realism and Fantasy in Films

In order broadly to define what we mean by the fantastic and supernatural, we might start pragmatically by defining their opposite, that is, by investigating what we mean by "the real." We have a basic everyday sense of the world, a sense that is upheld both by our innate dispositions and by our acquired knowledge of the normal appearance of agents and objects and the natural and psychological laws that govern their behavior (see Hirschfeld and Gelman 1994). Our various innate senses and cognitive abilities, in combination with our life experience, provide the foundation for our experience of reality, although some aspects of reality are more dependent on cultural knowledge than others. Certain visual norms, for instance, provide the intersubjective basis for our recognition of such objects as faces, houses, and trees. These norms consist of numerous different elements: the color of tomatoes, the number of eyes in a human face, or the average proportions of the human body. They may also consist of more general laws of causality, derived from the knowledge that thoughts cannot directly create or kill living beings; that dead people cannot regain life; that animals cannot speak, and so on.

All humans possess the imaginative ability to alter mental representations based on these realistic norms, and such alterations may be more or less extensive and fundamental. A minimalist alteration would consist in changing a single perceptual feature—for instance, by imagining or painting blue tomatoes or sculpting a very tall thin man à la Giacometti. One can depart more radically from reality by altering more features—for instance, by changing the color of all natural objects (see Ryan's [1991] description of levels of fundamentality in deviations from realism). Another type of fantasy alteration consists in creating metaphorical links between objects and phenomena at the level of individual features. In Disney's *Fantasia*, the imaginary world is filled with links between objects that have certain formal similarities, such as mushrooms and Chinese hats. Fantasy films like *Fantasia* also delight in the metamorphosis of form—for example, speeding up the slow processes of animal or plant growth and transferring them to other features of the world. These accelerated transformations make the world less stable: objects may suddenly morph into something quite different. Fantasy films may also create synesthetic associations between sight and sound: for example, deep tones may be linked with the motion of large animals such as rhinos, high tones with small animals (for the natural background to certain types of synesthesia, see Grodal 2005; Baron-Cohen and Harrison 1997). Changes that occur mainly at the level of individual features will often be regarded as expressions of fantasy, but not as fully fantastic.

However, it is also possible to create a completely fantastic world, in which fundamental features and laws are altered so that, for example, thoughts impact directly on the physical world (as in fairy tales or in Cronenberg's *Scanners*), the distinction between life and death is annihilated, or body and soul exist independently of one another. Invisible beings or beings that are defined only in relation to one sense or a few senses (such as ghosts, which can be seen but not felt) also represent a fundamental change in the basic laws of nature. The way in which we categorize phenomena in the animal, plant, and mineral kingdoms and in the realm of abstract concepts is governed by innate mental dispositions (Hirschfeld and Gelman 1994). Violations of such categories—for example, when plants walk and talk, as some of the trees do in *The Lord of the Rings*, or when robots and cyborgs transgress the boundaries between the animal and mineral kingdoms—play a key role in the realm of the fantastic. Another common device is to alter standard human features, deforming them in various ways or mixing human and animal features.

Film is not only well suited to presenting a realistic portrayal of the world; it also offers unique scope for fantastic representation, as Méliès demonstrated in the early days of cinema. Through the devices of montage, double exposure, matte photography, and so on, it is possible to give an audience an apparently realistic, photographic experience of the fantastic: disembodied spirits, metamorphoses, flying humans, and suchlike. Recently, digital image manipulation has increased still further our ability to render the fantastic visible. Fantastic phenomena become credible through visualization, because seeing is believing. Even if our ability to judge reality leads us to conclude that such pictures are unreal, they remain real to our senses and emotions. This is especially true of narratives and moving images. Merely looking at a drawing or a photograph of a monster does not necessarily require the kinds of comprehensive cognitive activities that imply the existence of the monster, whereas in order to be able to follow a fantastic narrative, and especially a film narrative, the audience needs not only to be perceptually involved but also to engage in a massive cognitive reconstruction of the fantastic world and its laws. In order to simulate a film narrative, the viewer must lend some of his or her feelings to the protagonists and speculate about their destiny. Thus the viewer must either avoid seeing fantasy films altogether or temporarily attribute the status of reality to the supernatural phenomena presented in such films. A viewer who has followed the sufferings of Bess in Trier's *Breaking the Waves* will ardently wish for her to be saved. So when the viewer witnesses with his or her own eyes the bells in heaven that promise salvation, disbelief will be in conflict with the perceptions, cognitions, and emotions that the film has activated.

The Emergence of Reason and Superstition

Most of our mental equipment as humans developed long before we acquired the ability to draw pictures or create verbal descriptions—perhaps as recently as 50,000 years ago. At this point, a cultural explosion took place that was also manifest in the sudden appearance of burial ceremonies. Interestingly, our relationship to death and to the burial of dead people is central to much fantastic fiction.

Until this cultural explosion, animals and people lived in a world in which their senses and consciousness were exposed mainly to the real and concrete, with the exception of marginal phenomena such as mirror images, dreams, and delusions. Of course, the faculty of memory and the ability to imagine simple hypothetical scenarios had developed steadily over millions of years and meant that the brain had a certain degree of independence in relation to directly perceived reality. Even the earliest humans, who had no language skills—let alone films— must have been able to imagine simple series of actions such as going down to the river or finding possible prey, and such abilities to imagine counterfactual scenarios are probably, as argued in Boyer (2007), expansions of a series of different mental capacities. But it was only with the acquisition of the capacity for language, painting, and drawing that it became easy for human beings to imagine and represent not only reality but also hypotheses, fantasies, and lies. The first cave paintings are rather realistic representations of animals and people, but later on stories, paintings, and drawings began to portray imaginary creatures, angels, and devils as well. This new capacity for advanced hypothetical representation led to the development of culture and science as well as to the invention of imaginary monsters.

Our brains have not entirely adjusted themselves to the new situation in which what we see and hear is not necessarily real. The lower levels of the brain continue to react relatively independently, regardless of the judgments reached by higher levels of the brain about the reality status of a given phenomenon. The low-level "zombie modules" still adhere to the principle that seeing is believing, or rather, complicated aspects of reality are dealt with only by the superior levels of the brain. Gilbert et al. (1990) have argued, based on experiments, that the default mode of processing information is to believe it as soon as one has comprehended it, and that to disbelieve incoming information demands additional mental work that may not be done or may be forgotten, and this fits well into an evolutionary framework in which belief is the basic mode, disbelief an additional process. This is indeed an interesting result that contradicts dominant theories of fiction. It is often said that our understanding of fiction involves the suspension of disbelief, but it might be more apposite to say that understanding fiction involves the ability to suspend belief caused by seeing, hearing, and imagining. The lack of this ability to control and suspend belief leads to superstition. Carroll's (1990) theory of art horror makes assumptions compatible with Gilbert et al.: thoughts have causal powers, for instance, in relation to emotions irrespective of reality status.

Fantasy representations often therefore have a sensual and emotional impact comparable to the impact of real phenomena. The invention of film has strengthened the human ability to simulate real and invented phenomena. We see and hear terrible monsters—they impact directly on our senses. The digital revolution, moreover, has vastly reduced the price of producing visual fantasy. Earlier fantasy films often required expensive sets, props, and costumes and elaborate postproduction work, but it is now relatively cheap to produce hundreds of flying saucers or monsters. Similarly, it used to be highly complicated to show, for example, a human being changing into a monster, but modern morphing techniques such as those inaugurated with *Terminator 2: Judgment Day* have made metamorphosis cheap.

The fact that our lower mental capacities do not really distinguish between sensory impressions originating in complex, factual reality and those produced by human artifacts was demonstrated by Spielberg in his Pinocchio-inspired film *A.I.: Artificial Intelligence*. The main character, David, is a cyborg constructed to love the human that functions as his mother. At one point in the film, when David is in an extremely dangerous situation, he is comforted by a mild cyborg woman who resembles his mother. Her face and voice are expressive and she emanates a strong emotional power, despite the fact that on several occasions we see her in profile and thus notice that her face is only an ultrathin masklike surface, connected by a thin steel construction to a mechanical robot body. The knowledge we thus gain about her reality status has no influence on our experience of the powerfully humane signals that emanate from her face, seen *en face*. Our emotions are triggered by low-level perceptual mechanisms in the temporal lobe that have direct access to our stored memories and emotions (Zeki 1993; Ramachandran et al. 1999; van der Gaag et al. 2007). The function of these low-level modules is "cognitively impenetrable" (Pylyshyn 1991). Our cognitive knowledge cannot fully influence the effects of these low-level modules, which are "sealed." On numerous occasions in the film Spielberg emphasizes the way in which emotions are triggered by artifacts. Later on, David meets the blue fairy, a lifelike figure that also makes a strong emotional impact on David and on the viewer. We are influenced by the cinematic representation of singular components of human facial expressions even if we know that they are just visual devices.

From experiments with babies, we know that humans have innate knowledge about the basic physical laws that govern our experience (see, e.g., Churchland 2002; Carey and Spelke 1994). Even small babies show signs of being intrigued by any violation of these fundamental laws. At a very early age, they acquire assumptions about, for example, object constancy (objects do not change when they are partly hidden), causality, gravity, and so on. These basic physical laws are not something that we learn from science; rather, we have innate dispositions that allow us to deduce them from basic experiences—dispositions that evolved because they enhance our fitness. It is a widespread misconception that so-called primitive people cannot distinguish between natural and supernatural phenomena. The French anthropologist Pascal Boyer (2001) has demonstrated the contrary with numerous examples. The supernatural is interesting precisely because it violates universal common sense. The Christian miracles or the story of the virgin birth attracted attention precisely because of their strong, salient deviation from everyday experience.

Although singular counterintuitive phenomena are mind-grabbing, it is easier to remember more complex events and agents that behave in accordance with naturalist specifications rather than with counterintuitive and supernatural specifications, because the memory process is supported by a series of standard schemas and standard assumptions. Boyer (2001) and Barrett (2004) have shown that religious and supernatural stories are often minimally counterintuitive, meaning that most of a given supernatural being's capabilities are intuitive, in accord with innate ontology, although a few features are counterintuitive. Jesus may walk on water and be resurrected, but eat, sleep, and walk just like other people; the stepmother in *Snow White* has a few counterintuitive features, but a lot of her features are intuitive. Boyer argues that such a setup, which uses a few counterintuitive features combined with many intuitive features, facilitates reasoning about, say, supernatural agents because we may use most of our standard inference systems. A story with too many counterintuitive features would be difficult to comprehend and remember. Norenzayan et al. (2006) have discussed how the most successful fairy tales are those that contain only two or three counterintuitive elements. *Little Red Riding Hood* has a speaking wolf and the deviant story element of grandmother coming out in one piece and alive from the wolf's stomach; however, we can imagine most of the other story elements by using standard inference systems. We understand how the little girl walks through the wood and how the hunter may cut open the stomach of the wolf by using a knife. Thus, although fantastic, counterintuitive features are mind-grabbers, they may also provide cognitive burdens, and therefore successful fairy tales find an optimum between salience and mental costs by using a few counterintuitive features together with the mostly intuitive features. Films may have more counterintuitive features because there is an external storage medium that may partly diminish the memory burden, but still viewers need to be able to process the film cognitively.

Science and Black and White Magic as Means of Control

The rationality of animals and humans developed as a mean of controlling the environment. Our ability to predict causal chains increases our chances of survival.

Imaginary alternatives to our normal, rational methods of control may offer other benefits, such as the pleasures readers and viewers derive from witnessing omnipotence in the *Harry Potter* series. Stories for children and adolescents, in particular, often indulge in depicting the joys of magical environmental control. In the world of fairy tales, the heroes are supplied with magical props and skills that enable them to move directly from wish to wish fulfillment without any physical mediation.

The pleasure we derive from imagining the ability to control the world by thoughts and wishes alone might lead one to conclude that wish fulfillment is the key element in fantasy. But quite often the breakdown of normal causality in fantasy involves a radical loss of control. The Dracula films offer a typical example. Dracula is not subject to the laws that govern normal folk, so ordinary people become defenseless when he attacks. It is only through the introduction of magical remedies and rituals (McCauley and Lawson 2002)—the use of crosses, garlic, silver bullets, and so on—that ordinary humans are able to regain their ability to control events. The battle between black and white magic features in numerous tales of the supernatural. White magic may enable the hero to work wonders, but witches such as Snow White's wicked stepmother are also endowed with supernatural capacities to do evil. Snow White is visible to her evil stepmother even when she goes into hiding with the seven dwarfs. Science fiction worlds like that of *The Matrix* portray both good and evil techno-magic. Thus, even if part of the motivation for the supernatural is empowerment, another part is derived from fear—for instance, by activating dispositions developed to spot invisible predators, as I will discuss later. Furthermore, Boyer and Liénard (2006) have discussed how a small set of central worries in relation to hazards that in the era of evolutionary adaptation have been fitness enhancing, like fear of contamination and fear of other people, is often central in obsessions.

The fantastic world is rarely one in which all causality is absent; rather, it is a more unstable world in which normal causality can break down and new, magical laws emerge. The world portrayed in the *Lord of the Rings* trilogy lacks the stability of the normal world because mental categories such as good and evil have become physical forces on a par with magnetism and gravity, projecting their influence through time and space and purifying or contaminating the souls of those affected. Popular religions such as Christianity or Islam involve the same sort of ambiguity. On the one hand the supernatural powers of God or the devil present additional dangers, in the form of devilish temptations and the possibility of eternal damnation, but on the other hand they offer additional ways to control the world—for instance, through faith, prayers, good deeds, grace, and promises of eternal life. Karl Marx proclaimed that religion was the opium of the people, but it is not as simple as that. The fantastic makes life more complicated, more colorful, and more uncertain, because it increases both poison and antidote. We can see a parallel here to the way in which science both identifies new dangers and invents new means to cope with them.

The Fantastic as Double Bind

A special variation of the fantastic focuses on the conflict between natural and supernatural causality, in which the conflicting evidence evokes a strong cognitive dissonance that can be resolved only by the decision to reject or believe in supernatural phenomena. We see this conflict in Henry James's story *The Turn of the Screw*. Similarly, Roeg's film *Don't Look Now* elicits powerful cognitive dissonance because it at once proves and disproves that the protagonist's dead daughter is alive. The TV series *The X Files* depicts a similar conflict between belief and disbelief in supernatural causation, with the two main characters, Mulder and Scully, representing the two conflicting views. Indeed, literary scholar Tzvetan Todorov (1975) has argued that the term *fantastic* should be applied only to those stories that provoke this kind of conflict in the addressee by presenting fictional features that alternately confirm and disconfirm the existence of the supernatural (see chapter 2). The fantastic represents the borderline between the marvelous and the uncanny. However, I find such a restricted definition of the term *fantastic* problematic. We label both the marvelous and the uncanny fantastic, because whether you feel happy at the appearance of good fairies or frightened by Dracula, the fascination of such representations is due in both cases to the way in which they deviate from standard physics and biology.

Fictions about the conflict between belief and superstition may nevertheless play a special role in present-day culture, because the development of science has deepened the gulf between natural and supernatural explanations. Over the past 250 years, the cognitive dissonance elicited by such ambivalent fictions has therefore evoked particularly strong emotions, since the "natural" salience of the supernatural has been amplified by the way in which scientific development has strengthened the rejection of the supernatural. Even though prescientific societies also drew a clear distinction between natural and supernatural causality, the two systems were not necessarily seen as mutually exclusive; rather, the supernatural was regarded as a supplement to the natural. Modern science, however, has increased the fear evoked by the loss of control associated with any supernatural violation of natural laws. Some films, such as Spielberg's *Close Encounters of the Third Kind*, portray a New Age religiosity in which the intervention of the supernatural elicits a form of sublime abandonment, but in many films the breakdown of natural laws evokes the fear of losing control. Mulder believes in all kinds of aliens in *X Files*, but their doings are mostly unpleasant.

In fantasy films or stories, emotional and moral qualities are often able to exert a direct influence on the world, so that virtue and vice, for instance, become quasi-physical forces or agencies. That the mind thus plays a central and supernatural role may be the key to the paradox that many art films—films addressed by intellectuals to other intellectuals—have a strong element of the supernatural. Bergman, Tarkovsky, Wenders, Kieslowski, Lynch, and Trier, among others, all make use of supernatural elements in their films. In Trier's *The Kingdom*, the supernatural is mainly seen as the good alternative to the evil rationalistic world of medical science. Intellectuals may derive a double pleasure from the violation of natural laws. Their work may attune them to be extra sensitive to the salience of any deviation from normal logical procedures; moreover, these mind-oriented humanists may envy the prestige that science has won by its success in controlling the physical world, and experience a certain pleasure in seeing science outwitted.

Scientists as well as occultists may be intrigued by inexplicable phenomena. In confronting scientists with supernatural phenomena, as he does in *Stalker* or *Solaris*, Tarkovsky may partly be drawing attention to the limitations of natural science. But perhaps he is also motivated by the thought that any violation of the known laws of science will make a greater impact on scientists, and that the resulting cognitive dissonance will evoke a more powerful emotional conflict in them than in other people.

Art films are often constructed in such a way as to activate the viewer's curiosity about what Roland Barthes (1974) has called the hermeneutic code. Art films arouse this curiosity on the perceptual-stylistic level, activating the brain to find more signs of hidden meanings than can actually be identified, and tend to articulate lofty, abstract, and allegorical meanings. The concrete actions and goals that characterize mainstream films are absent or toned down (see chapter 9). Supernatural phenomena and themes involving cognitive dissonance serve extremely well to heighten our perception of veiled meanings in films like *Stalker*, Kieslowski's *The Double Life of Veronique*, or Lynch's *Lost Highway*. The supernatural often blocks human action, thereby giving rise to lyrical, saturated emotions (Grodal 1997). To the extent that the supernatural is experienced as benevolent, these lyrical feelings may even become sublime (as at the end of Trier's *Breaking the Waves*, or in Spielberg's *Close Encounters of the Third Kind*).

Magical Agency: Hunter and Prey

In *Religion Explained*, Pascal Boyer (2001) has pointed out that fantastic and religious representations deal primarily with a limited set of phenomena relating to five areas: agency, predation, death, morality, and social exchange.

Central to the supernatural and counterintuitive are the importance of agency. Intentional beings possessed of magical skills—heroes that can fly, invisible ghosts, cosmic beings with supernatural intelligence or physical abilities—play a central role in almost all fantastic stories. Such agencies are also, of course, integral to most religions: angels, gods, and devils are close relatives of magical heroes and monsters. Before the age of machines, practically all actions were carried out by living beings, so that any powerful effects would be ascribed to some living agency, natural or supernatural. We still have difficulty in understanding stochastic processes or in conceiving of the world as an impersonal and purposeless process. On the whole, films capture our attention only if they include at least one agency that has intentions and emotions. Understanding the world in terms of (supernatural) agency is therefore naturally appealing.

Whereas the real world consists mainly of minerals, plants, or empty space, with some living beings scattered around, in the fantastic world the density of living beings is much higher. Even space is densely populated with a variety of beings, and ultrafast vehicles reduce the vastness of the universe. The animation of the world enhances feelings of good and evil. In Disney's *Snow White and the Seven Dwarfs*, animated trees stretch out their branches to grasp Snow White, and there are evil eyes everywhere that may belong to evil creatures. But when dawn comes, Snow White finds herself surrounded by the benevolent eyes of animals who want to follow her. Films such as the *Lord of the Rings* trilogy portray a world rich in a variety of good and evil beings, including animated plants.

Pascal Boyer thinks that an important reason for our continuing to imagine supernatural agencies is that our ancestors were both hunters and prey. On the one hand they were weak creatures, constantly on the lookout for dangerous predators; on the other they were predators themselves, always watching out for potential prey. Our mental equipment is therefore preset for constant agency detection, whether of predators or prey, and this results in a tendency to overdetect. Justin Barrett (2004) has given a name to this mental disposition: HADD, which stands for hyperactive agency detection devices. The disposition to be constantly on the alert for possible dangerous agencies needs to be relatively immune to experiences that disprove the grounds for watchfulness. If our ancestors had ceased to look out for danger in the forest after discovering on 999 occasions that the sound that had alerted them was just a branch waving in the wind or a twig snapping underfoot, they might have been eaten on the 1000th occasion. No matter how much evidence we assemble to disprove the existence of the supernatural, any sign of some new, inexplicable phenomenon will continue to possess a salience for us. The image of lurking aliens that want to prey on humans remains highly salient; and millions of people in the United States claim to have seen or even been abducted or abused by aliens. Even though such ideas may have been induced by watching films, they continue to have a powerful hold on our imagination due to innate dispositions to hyperdetect agencies for hazard precaution reasons.

In most countries today, there is a fair chance of being killed by or in a car—in the United States alone, 30,000–40,000 people die annually in car accidents—and hundreds of thousands die from smoking cigarettes or from other types of substance abuse. Very few, on the other hand, die from attacks by animals. Yet few people are scared of cars or cigarettes, whereas many fear wild animals, even when they are locked up in cages. The idea of roaming wolves still activates the imagination of Danish children, even though wolves have been extinct in Denmark for hundred of years. People fear intentional killers, but not their fellow drivers who may kill them by accident. In horror and science fiction films, *Homo sapiens* is still the prey, deliberately hunted by beings that use tentacles to ensnare them or that prey on humans from within, as in Ridley Scott's *Alien*, or suck their blood, as in the Dracula films or Wachowski's *The Matrix*. Random dangers do not catch the imagination, and threats to the earth such as the gigantic meteor in Bay's *Armageddon* are only partly seen as fantastic. Robots become scary only when they demonstrate some kind of intentionality. The Martians in Spielberg's *War of the Worlds* instill fear in us because they possess the strength of machines, the sliminess of lower life forms, a high degree of intelligence, and a total lack of emotion.

The fear of predators enhances not only our vigilance, but our capacity for play. Francis Steen and Stephanie Owens (2001) have argued that one of the main evolutionary reasons behind our disposition to play and pretend lies in the survival value of practicing strategies of predator avoidance (and, I would add, practicing good hunting strategies as well). Even very young children enjoy games of chase, and these gradually evolve into more sophisticated games based on fictional scenarios. Horror films may be seen as a vicarious way of playing such games.

Our ability to control our relationship to the environment is geared to a normal, present, and middle-sized world, whereas heroic or demonic agents are often linked either to a cosmic universe or to a tiny biological world and come from the past or the future. The monsters may come from outer space and possess superhuman strength and intellect, or be subhuman zombies that are powerful but possess no intellect or morality. Monsters may also come from the microscopic world, as in those zombie stories where the zombies' strength lies in their ability to contaminate the body's interior. Normally, our controlling actions are directed toward middle-sized external objects, and our struggle against these external enemies takes place over a finite period of time. In dealing with microworlds, however, these normal strategies may fail, and the lack of control options induces fear. Although we have an instinctive hygienic knowledge of the dangers of contagion from viruses and bacteria, it is only recently that we have been able to develop ways of combating this danger, which is seen as instantaneous and irreversible. Similarly, humans and animals have inbuilt fears of food poisoning. Before the advent of modern science, nausea and vomiting were among the few means that humans had to rid themselves of inner pollution. When normal people become infected, as, for instance, in Romero's classic horror trilogy *Night of the Living Dead*, *Dawn of the Dead*, and *Day of the Dead*, there is no remedy but to execute them. Cronenberg's horror stories are likewise often based on the idea of contagion, with people seen as defenseless against this invasion of their inner space. Thus horror films cue and amplify innate hazard-precaution mechanisms.

Spirit and Spirits

The scientific worldview is in many ways only a more sophisticated version of the prescientific understanding of the world that evolved over millions of years in the human struggle for survival. An adequate understanding of causality enhances survival. Commonsense accounts of ordinary causal interactions do not differ that much from scientific descriptions. But in one area our commonsense understanding does differ markedly from the scientific view—namely, in our notion of the psyche and consciousness and their relation to matter. From a scientific point of view, intelligence and consciousness (and life itself) are special, emergent qualities of matter. But popular psychology involves a dualistic, Cartesian understanding of consciousness. In some respects, intelligence, consciousness, and agency are comprehended as purely physical phenomena; thus we acknowledge that consciousness disappears at death and can be influenced in life by chemicals such as drugs. But at the same time consciousness, the psyche, or the soul is perceived as an immaterial, spiritual force, a homunculus-vapor living inside the body, an agency that is the immovable mover of living beings. We conceive our will, beliefs, intentions, memories, and emotions as nonmaterial entities not governed, or not completely governed, by material causation. The idea of free will is a central element in the popular conception of the spirit, and any effort to prove that the mind, too, is subject to material causation elicits strong protest, because this would be to reduce the spirit's free will. The reason the dead lack force and power, according to this view, is that the spirit has departed the body. Where it has not yet completely departed but inhabits an "undead" body, it is liable to be transformed into an evil force. Granted the force of the spirit, it is easy to imagine that it is able to influence the material world either by appropriating another body, as in the numerous stories of people possessed by evil spirits, or by being present but invisible, recognizable only by its doings, as in Lars von Trier's *The Kingdom*. Of course, many modern people do not believe, or fully believe, in such notions, but their popularity in films suggests that such conceptions not only are easy to understand but also powerfully activate our emotions.

One of the reasons behind our conviction that the psyche is autonomous vis-à-vis the body may be that our sensory apparatus is oriented toward the external world, where we are able to see material causality at work. The workings of our brains, on the other hand, are not accessible to sensory perception—the neurons are beyond direct sensation, and all we are able to perceive is the end result: our conscious experience of an exterior world and the way in which we influence that world by letting our immaterial power of will, intentions, and motives control our bodies.

The fantastical power of the spirit is most explicitly presented in stories and films that portray a direct psychosomatic interaction, as when somebody is able—by the sheer force of thoughts and emotions—to influence the environment. As mentioned above, this device is commonly used in fairy tales, but it is also used, for example, by writers like Stephen King. King's novels have been immensely successful and many of them have been made into films, demonstrating that the theme of psychic control over the physical world or over other psyches remains highly salient. The invention of computers has inspired a new variant on this theme in the form of cyberpunk literature and cyberpunk films, such as William Gibson's novel *Neuromancer* and Longo's film *Johnny Mnemonic*, or the highly popular *Matrix* trilogy.

Another powerful reason for our sense that the spirit or soul exists independently of the body relates to memory. Dead people live on in the memories of the living, and these memories are often vivid and charged with emotion. People often talk with the memory image of the deceased, as Private Ryan talks with the dead Captain Miller in the graveyard. Thus, the inner world of imagination and memory is relatively autonomous vis-à-vis the external world, and memories decay in a different fashion than the objects they commemorate. The brain-mind lives in a double niche: the exterior world and the interior world, and it is the task of our often frail reality-status functions to separate those worlds in order to block supernatural beliefs. Conversely, the task of many fictions is precisely to undermine those functions in the frontal brain that evaluate reality status.

Because mental concepts and memories are more permanent than the exterior world, we may feel that the spirit is a force that is independent of the material. As Plato pointed out, sensory impressions are changing and transient, whereas ideas, concepts, and memories provide a permanent foundation. As we will see in chapters 9 and 10, art films seek to create permanent representations of both the autobiographical flow and the deeper meanings of life, and such representations are created mainly by blocking those aspects of film representations that indicate the exterior existence of phenomena. And the blocking of perceptual access to the external world, or motor interaction between agency and world, creates a sense of subjectivity, a "soulish feeling." Plato's notion that ideas are anchored in a transcendental, metaphysical reality, whereas the physical world is merely a bleak reflection of those ideas (the cave allegory) is clearly wrong, just as Jung's ideas of innate archetypal images is problematic. However, this "form idealism" may have a kind of psychological reality. The representation of evil or good in fantasy fiction subsumes and essentializes many different experiences of good and evil, and these ideas are in some sense more real than our experience of singular, concrete instances of good and evil. We may therefore reinterpret Jung's ideas of archetypes as an effort to represent schematization—to describe the psychological synthesis of key prototypes that may be strongly emotionally charged because they subsume many charged experiences.

Fantasy films—especially those of the fairy-tale type—very often possess this kind of prototypical and abstract simplicity. Both in her physical appearance and in her moral habitus, Snow White is created by means of simple features that characterize her as good and beautiful. When they start to draw, children begin with simple, abstract, and prototypical representations: humans with points for eyes, a circle for a head, and lines for nose, mouth, and limbs, or houses consisting of walls, roof, door, and windows. Such representations appear fantastic when made into films, because they blur the distinction between the compressed processes in the mind and memory and the uncompressed exterior world that is characterized by complex specificities and irregular textures. They may thus create spiritual and fantastic associations, because such prototypes or abstractions exist only in minds, not out in the world. Their purity ensures their strong affective impact. In films for adults, such textureless and unspecific characters and objects may also function well in certain contexts, but adults often demand more realistic individualization and complexity. Where adult cinema is concerned, schematization and abstraction are most commonly found in comedy, horror films, or lyrical fiction.

Undead Spirits

If spirit and matter are often seen as two relatively independent forces, it is logical to think it necessary not only to kill an evil spirit's body, but to kill its spirit, because body and soul no longer share the same destiny. In the world of fantasy, there is no direct border between life and death. Rather, existence is divided into three areas: that of the living, where body and soul exist in symbiosis; that of the undead, in which the spirit still exists in a dead body, takes possession of another living body, or exists in a completely disembodied state; and that of the dead, where the body reverts completely to matter and the spirit dissolves. The Dracula films describe, for instance, how the evil Count Dracula's body is killed while his soul continues to haunt the living, until the wise Dr. van Helsing performs rituals involving a cross, holy water, and the piercing of Dracula's undead heart, thereby bringing death proper to the count (figure 5.1). Carl Th. Dreyer's *Vampyr* tells a similar story. Sometimes the spirit-controlling project is more limited, with the spirits merely exorcized from a body that they have possessed, as in Friedkin's *The Exorcist*. Stories about salvation may tell the same story but attach a different value to the separation of body and spirit: the spirit is freed from its material body in order to gain eternal, spiritual life. Both horror films and religious myths often therefore presuppose a double, two-step death, the first stage of which consists in the death of the body, and the next in the death of the spirit or its transportation to some appropriate final destination. Psychologically this means that memories of the dead person cease to be potentially online all the time and are shifted to more or less permanent offline status.

FIGURE 5.1. A central theme in horror films is the disgust caused by death and decay, and the fear of being haunted by powerful and often very biting supernatural agencies. In Coppola's *Bram Stoker's Dracula*, Gary Oldman impersonates the bloodsucking corpse-like undead Dracula, whose face inspires fear and disgust, especially because the sharp razor blade activates hazard precaution. The sound background of the scene is howling wolves, which activate primitive human fears of biting creatures out in the dark. *Bram Stoker's Dracula* © American Zoetrope 1992.

This notion of double death can be found all over the world (Boyer 2001) and underlies a variety of death rituals aimed at preventing the spirit from finding a new body to possess. The Dracula films thus represent one expression of a universal idea. It is characteristic of such stories that spirits are seen to turn evil when they lose their bodies. This may symbolically represent the fact that corpses are sources of infection, but it also offers a causal explanation for deviant mental behavior. Furthermore, as Bowlby (1980), among others, has pointed out, mourners often blame themselves for the death of others and may even believe that the (un)dead are angry with the living and haunt them for that reason.

There is some logic in the notion that if spirits exist independently of the physical world, they can only be controlled by spiritual means: magic formulas or things endowed with special spiritual powers, such as crosses and holy water. We can see, for example, how magic formulas are used to combat evil in *The Exorcist*. A nice 12-year-old girl becomes possessed by a devilish spirit that totally changes her appearance and consciousness, and two priests seek to exorcise the spirit from the girl.

There are obvious problems in representing incorporeal spirits in films. One way to circumvent these has been to present spirits as visible but not tangible, so that they cannot be touched and killed, and can walk through walls and other solid objects. They may not produce any shadows or mirror images. This is paradoxical, since it is precisely shadows and mirror images that are the untouchable elements of normal beings. But spiritual logic seems to define spirits as antibeings; even if the logic does not work globally, it works well enough at the specific level because of the salience of the counterintuitive. Similarly, as pointed out by Boyer and Liénard (2006), rituals are often counterintuitive, like washing clean things, saying meaningless words (abracadabra), or using objects that have no apparent causal powers, such as garlic (except its olfactory salience).

If humans were completely convinced that the spirit was quite independent of the body, rather than an emergent aspect of it (so that the cohabitation of the two was just a matter of chance), the human race would cease to survive, for we would cease to be afraid of exposure to potentially lethal dangers. Thus the belief in the autonomy of the soul must be seen as relative. At the prospect of defeat, the majority of Muslim warriors in Afghanistan surrendered, rather than fighting on, which suggests that they were not totally convinced that they would go directly to paradise if they were slain. On the other hand, not only horror films but many art films show that the notion of disembodied spirits continues to exert a deep fascination. It is a mistake to suppose that the worldview of the average person is totally consistent. Many concepts are produced ad hoc, under particular circumstances, and most people do not feel a deep need to produce total coherence. (Boyer has argued, similarly, that most religions are assemblies of heterogeneous practices, and that coherent religious systems are the invention of theologians.) With increasing mental complexity, there are more hazards of mental noise and mental malfunctions.

Certain tales and films portray the permanence and immortality of the spirit, but others demonstrate its frailty. A recurrent theme is that of the person split into two separate personalities, often with antagonistic moral norms, as in the classic case of *Dr. Jekyll and Mr. Hyde*. A more recent example can be found in the second part of *The Lord of the Rings*, which shows how a moral conflict leads to Gollum's being visually split into two versions of himself, one good and one evil. Such stories of torn souls resemble those of metamorphosis. But whereas in tales of metamorphosis the spirit remains permanent while the body changes (from prince to frog to prince again, for instance), stories of split personalities focus on mental phenomena, which may or may not be accompanied by bodily changes. The brain is modular, divided into many parts, each with its own function; and the synthesis of these parts may break down, perhaps under pressure from conflicting experiences and motives.

One part of Dr. Jekyll has different priorities from his normal self and acts in a different way. It is not always clear whether a given state of consciousness represents a normal variation on the self that may be explained psychologically, or whether it is an autonomous phenomenon that requires supernatural explanation. In Polanski's *Macbeth*, the spirits are clearly projections of Macbeth's fantasies, but it is less clear whether the supernatural phenomena in Roeg's *Don't Look Now* can be explained psychologically or, on the contrary, have metaphysical causes. Although there are at least partial rational explanations for the hallucinatory experiences depicted in Russell's *Altered States* or the brain programming in Verhoeven's *Total Recall*, the sheer intensity of the representation in each case may give the impression that the inner, mental life has an objective existence.

The development of the media over the past 200 years has enabled us to produce increasingly efficient simulations of reality. The creation of video games has inspired cyberpunk artists to represent the spirit being liberated from the body, and joysticks and keyboards have created links to our motor skills so that we are able to test virtual reality as if it were physical. Thus, although mental experiences result from the perceptual impact of the external world on our senses, so that "reality" exists only in our brains, media products have made such mental experiences visible and tangible. Experiments with virtual reality (and hallucinogenic drugs such as those that inspired *Altered States*) strengthen the notion that minds can exist independently of the body and the rest of the material world.

Powerful Corpses

As mentioned above, the conceptualization of the supernatural is very often associated with death and phenomena relating to death. Dracula exists in a space between full life and full death. Frankenstein's monster is created from dead bodies. A certain type of horror film deals with the resurrection of Egyptian mummies, and of course the spirits in Raimi's *Evil Dead* are also linked to death. In Carpenter's *Prince of Darkness* the viewer is confronted with an enormous army of skeletons, and in Rodriguez's *From Dusk Till Dawn* a furious battle is fought between human beings and the powerful undead. The undead derive their power from the fact that as spirits they cannot be fought with traditional weapons. But at the same time they resemble corpses, rotting or decomposing bodies that give rise to negative associations of lethal contamination, and, as Carroll (1990) has pointed out, disgust and revulsion are typical reactions in horror films. Contamination from the undead can take place through a single touch, a single blood-sucking bite, and so on. One of the most basic things known to all humans from experience is that dead bodies no longer suppress the bacteria and viruses that a live body wards off (through the immune defense system, which has only recently been described scientifically). The dead bodies of humans and animals are therefore dangerous sources of contamination, and there is thus considerable survival value in having strong innate feelings of disgust and fear in relation to the dead. It is somewhat paradoxical, however, that horror films emphasize both the notion of the dead body's toxicity and that of the spirit's potency. It is as if the evil effects arise from the spirit's frustration at losing its body, a notion prompted, furthermore, by our mental disposition always to visualize effects in the form of an agency controlled by a spirit. The prevalent notion that contact with the undead and with corpses leads to instantaneous and irreversible contamination seems to indicate a kind of tacit folk knowledge of infection, backed up by autonomic reactions of disgust, vomiting, and so on, which ensure that we minimize contact with possible sources of infection. Thus, the portrayal of the body is quite different in horror stories than in action-adventure films, where death is mostly seen as quite clean, and in tragic melodramas, where the body is revered.

Positive figures, too, may derive their force from death; not until he died and was resurrected did Jesus acquire his full divine power. However, whereas evil spirits get their powers from decomposing bodies, Jesus could be said to derive his strength from what Boyer calls social exchange. Through his death he made a sacrifice of his body, and thus redeemed the rest of humankind from damnation. *The Matrix* is in several respects a variant on this social exchange pattern, where the main character fights and suffers in order to free human beings that have been transformed into an energy source for predatory machines.

In Tarkovsky's *Stalker*, the main characters' access to deep spiritual forces is established in connection with death. Three men, a scientist, an author, and a guide, or stalker, walk into the Zone, an area marked by death and (poetic) decay. The Zone is the only place in the world where the desperate and the faithful can fulfill their deepest wishes. The dead Zone thus purifies the soul and liberates it from the body, and by the end of the film the stalker's daughter has acquired the power to move material things—such as a glass on a table—by means of spirit alone. Thus, whereas from a scientific point of view the spirit, or consciousness, is seen as an emergent aspect of matter, from which it also derives its effects, the spirit in tales of the supernatural is conceived as a powerful essence that becomes diluted within a body, so that when it is freed from the body its power is enhanced and it becomes able to control matter directly.

In most supernatural films (and in religious death rituals), death and the dead are seen from the point of view of the viewers or the survivors. They rarely deal with what would happen in the case of their own deaths, but rather seek to capture their relationship to the death of other people. Death poses a very complex problem for the family and friends of the deceased. At the time of death it is still possible to recognize the deceased, and memories and ideas about his or her psyche do not disappear. The protagonist of *A.I.*, David, spends thousands of years thinking about his dead mother. Our emotional relationship to the deceased does not really alter so long as the dead person still exists in our memory. But at the same time, the dead person is a corpse that decomposes and constitutes a health threat. Mourning and death rituals therefore consist partly in separating the concept of the person, and the emotions attached to it, from the concrete physical body, as in the burial scene in *Breaking the Waves*. In this scene, Jan treats Bess's body as the seat of her identity. But later on, body and soul are separated: Bess's spirit is in heaven, while her body is down at the bottom of the ocean.

A common type of horror story—Siegel's *Invasion of the Body Snatchers* is the paradigmatic example—portrays the experience of seeing one's family, friends, or other familiar people becoming possessed by evil spirits and thus turned into aliens or strangers. In Siegel's film, the body snatchers copy a person's body, but provide the copied version with the body snatchers' own emotionless psyche. The main characters in Siegel's film are constantly confronted with the dilemma that—like people suffering from the mental illness called Capgras syndrome—they are unable to fuse the evidence of their eyes regarding the visual identity of a person with their emotional memories of that person. The neurologist Ramachandran has described patients for whom the neuronal link between the modules for visual face recognition and the limbic system's modules for affective regulation has become disrupted (Ramachandran et al. 1999). Due to this separation between visual perception and emotional reactions, the patients perceive even their closest relatives as strangers, since their perceptions of these relatives and acquaintances no longer give rise to familiar emotional reactions. Stories of being defiled and infected deal not only with relationships to strangers but often also with the metamorphosis of kin, friends, lovers, or children into horrible monsters. They are thus variants on the death story: the story of how humans change into bodies that at the same time exemplify the separation of perception and emotion that occurs in Capgras syndrome. One example can be found in the way sweet children turn into demons in Donner's *The Omen* and numerous other films about children turned into monsters. In chapter 8 I suggest that there may exist mental mechanisms that—due to hate or fear—block normal empathy to enable antagonist actions freed from the impact of normal empathic emotional resonance and mirror effects from facial expressions, and thus create mental states similar to those suffering from Capgras syndrome. However, such stories are also similar to central elements in obsessive-compulsive disorders, in which people are pathologically afraid that they will harm people they love or respect, thus overactivating their hazard precaution system.

The connection between death and emotional or moral decay is indicated indirectly in *The Exorcist*. In the novel on which the film is based, Father Merrin (the character played by Max von Sydow in the film) suffers from an increasing lack of emotion as he digs for dead things in Iraq. The other main male protagonist, the Catholic priest Father Karras, suffers from feelings of guilt because he lacks any tender feelings toward his old mother, who is decaying physically before she dies. The young girl's possession by devils in the film is formally linked to the onset of puberty and sexuality. But there is nothing voluptuous about her; on the contrary, it is the repellent and aggressive elements of the girl that are underlined, so that her development is one of deindividualization and physical decay, bordering on degeneration into pure matter. Thus the emotions that the film elicits arise from the sharp change in emotional attitude from tenderness to disgust, which the girl's mother, the priests, and the film's viewers all share, and which is akin to the emotions felt for devilish children or possessed old people, where attachment and concern are replaced by repulsion and hostility. Similar emotion-shifting elements come to the fore in scenes when beautiful young witches are killed and their bodies are transformed to disgusting, rotting corpses.

Moral and Immoral Negotiations with Devils and Spirits

The concept of social exchange lies at the core of supernatural transactions such as pacts and sacrifices. The importance of social exchange reflects how the exchange of goods, services, and other forms of interpersonal communication is crucial for social life. Giving obliges the recipient to give something in return. Our ways of dealing with other people by means of exchange have provided the model even for our dealings with nature, as we see in the practice of performing sacrifices in order to obtain goods in return from supernatural powers—for instance, that the gods in exchange for sacrifices will give us rain and good crops, health, fertility, or eternal life. A common theme of supernatural tales is precisely that of exchange, often involving suffering, sacrifice, subordination, and prayer. Faust's pact with the devil is a typical example of this type of exchange; another can be seen in the irresponsible forces in *The X Files* that make deals with aliens. A variant of this social exchange theme can be found in Scott's *Alien*, where reckless forces are prepared to sacrifice the crew to gain possession of an alien life form. Even though no formal contract is made, the story is based on the idea of social exchange. Wyler's *Ben-Hur* consists of a series of exchanges: Jesus gives water to Ben-Hur, Ben-Hur returns the favor, and Jesus' death then heals Ben-Hur's leprous mother and sister. The film thus deals with the problem of the unclean, undead body as opposed to the spirit and links this to actions involving social exchange.

A contract may be established explicitly through making deals, invoking or conjuring, as we see in Sam Raimi's films, where witchcraft manuals are abused to invoke supernatural forces. Such films conflate the world of causal-physical powers and the world of human communication and interaction. But contracts can also be established more covertly, as we see in *The Lord of the Rings*. In principle, the contract in this trilogy involves gaining omnipotence through possession of the rings, but becoming subject in the process to the powers of evil and darkness, because to possess or accept a gift from someone obliges one to provide something in return, and to give a gift obliges the recipient. Although this implicit contract may be thought of as a purely metaphorical representation of something psychological-moral, and even though there is no representation of any further layer of metaphysical powers that regulate the contract, the very concrete representation of the forces of good and evil produces a metaphysical, dualistic worldview, in which, for instance, the protagonist has to counteract evil forces through suffering, because to accept suffering is to give a gift of one's well-being that obliges some metaphysical powers to provide something in return, as when Jesus' gift of his life forces God to give something in return, forgiveness of human sins. The trilogy thus institutes laws of moral-metaphysical exchange. Such exchanges with supernatural powers may be beneficial. In *Breaking the Waves*, Bess establishes an exchange that can be seen as a form of atonement: she performs the degrading acts that her husband demands and finally sacrifices her life in order to bring him back to life and restore his ability to walk. The contract between the supernatural agency and Bess is thus respected on both sides. Another salient demonstration of social exchange may be found in Spielberg's *Close Encounters of the Third Kind*. The aliens that arrive on earth possess supernatural technologies. A meeting is arranged in which a cosmic symphony is played in sound and color and humans exchange representatives with the aliens.

Morality, Supervision, and Strategic Knowledge

As humans became increasingly intelligent, their ability to cheat and hide their motives and actions also increased, just as the size of social groups increased, and therefore detecting cheaters became vital (Barkow et al. 1992). Dunbar (1996) has described how social control, for instance in the form of gossip, became increasingly important. Another way of propagating social control has been to invent salient supernatural agencies to supplement the surveillance of neighbors. Very often, there is a moral meaning in the representation of the supernatural and of the contracts established between human beings and supernatural agencies. Moral norms are anchored in such agencies, which supplement ordinary social controls by providing a kind of overall moral supervision, keeping watch on our actions even when we are unobserved by other people. These supernatural agencies have full access to strategic knowledge, that is, knowledge about events and doings that the individual wishes to hide from other people (Boyer 2001). Even those who believe in an omniscient god might not be sure that the divine being would know how many bowls of salad they had in their refrigerators. But they would be convinced that this being would know if they cheated on their partners, stole, lied, and so forth. Macbeth's wicked deeds are monitored by hidden agencies, and the spirits turn against him. The idea of a supernatural supervision of moral behavior might thus be an evolutionary adaptation to group living.

These supernatural forces need not be benevolent. Snake gods such as Satan, the semisupernatural psychopaths in slasher films, the avenging angel Carrie, Dracula, or even Sauron's evil eye are just as effective as positive forces in acting as moral guardians. The evil slasher psychopaths strike when young people are having sex; Satan lures those who sin into eternal damnation; Dracula spots moral weaknesses; and Carrie punishes the evil ones. Thus, the general tendency to fear hidden dangerous agencies, HADD, fuses with moral concerns associated with the wish to detect and punish cheats, and to the fear of being detected oneself. The fear of devilish agents often integrates several subfears: the devilish agents perform moral surveillance; they are linked to death and dead bodies and to the breaking of contracts and prohibitions, that is, rules of social exchange; and the devils are spirits, as in *Evil Dead* and numerous other teenage horror films.

Conclusion

Although our notions of the fantastic and supernatural contain features derived from our prehistory as hunter-gatherers that may look dysfunctional in a modern world, our imagination and credulity are nevertheless intimately linked to the intelligence we have developed through millions of years of evolution. Since fantasy consists in the ability to imagine endless variations of our experience of the external world, from the color of fruit to the concept of causality, it cannot be reduced to a few simple formulas.

Kant saw aesthetics and fantasy as an expression of the emancipation of the spirit from the forces of necessity, since aesthetics involved playing with the notions of purpose and law-boundedness. Research in the humanities tends to follow a narrower, more romantic formulation in which reason and emotion are seen to be in fundamental conflict, so that fantasy is considered the very negation of reason and purpose. This view is untenable, however, since emotion, fantasy, and reason are intimately and functionally linked (Grodal 1997; Damasio 1994). Fantasy presupposes the capacity for hypothetical thought and the ability to produce virtualities, counterfactuals, and it is enhanced by media (language, images, drama, and film) that further liberate our perceptions and experiences from the constraints of our immediate perceptual input. The first phase in the development of sensation and thought consisted in the ability to produce stable representations of the world, but the second phase has included the rearrangement of those elements in imagination, not only as a playful activity, but because this ability to imagine brings practical benefits, in terms of both controlling the external world and dealing with moral and existential problems.

The fascination that fantasy exerts is intimately linked to the development of our rationality and our desire to control our environment. The mental mechanisms that enable us to search for causal laws, and that are also therefore very sensitive to salient deviations from natural laws, provide the cognitive-emotional basis for our fascination with the supernatural and the fantastic. The desire for control is also expressed in fantasies of omnipotence, whether in the form of Chinese fantasy films about flying humans or ideas of achieving magical control through the force of consciousness and words.

However, certain key elements of the fantastic are clearly atavistic because it is linked to a series of primitive fear reactions. The prominence given to invisible or supernatural agencies, the emphasis on the spirit as an immaterial force, and the focus on a cluster of ideas relating to the power emanating from dead bodies and the afterlife of the spirit of dead people are in several aspects out of sync with life in a modern environment and our present scientific knowledge of the working of the mind and brain. Horror stories based on supernatural phenomena may offer viewers a way to practice their control of fear, but they may also serve to enhance paranoia. Ideas of good or evil supernatural agencies that monitor moral behavior and test us with temptation may serve to promote moral behavior, but may also increase our fear and inflexibility in the face of moral problems.

Our scientific understanding of consciousness and agency as an emergent aspect of matter is difficult to incorporate into our ordinary commonsense knowledge of psychology. In popular psychology the spirit lives a life of its own, relatively independent of the body, and the death of the spirit creates problems, especially because of our double fate: dead people live on in the memory of the living while the body itself decays. Although death is mostly viewed from the perspective of the living, certain fictions portray death from the perspective of (un)dead people, as in Shyamalan's very successful film *The Sixth Sense*, Spielberg's *Always*, or Ward's *What Dreams May Come*. In popular psychology the spirit is conceived as having an essence, good or bad, and moral conflicts or existential passages from one important phase to another are therefore common themes of fantasy films.

Modern fantasy films and supernatural films have incorporated many elements from previous periods and from different cultures concerning the fantastic and uncanny. Thus they offer a good example of how, on the one hand, our interest in films is based on a series of innate and therefore universal dispositions, while on the other hand our interest is based on the global cultural development and fine-tuning of a series of functional bundles—such as devils, witches, angels, undead mummies, and so on—that have migrated due to their ability to capture our imagination.

6

Sadness, Melodrama, and Rituals of Loss and Death

This chapter focuses on analyzing the apparent paradox that some films are successful and have social prestige despite the fact that they create a sad mood by presenting stories with a sad ending. The basic hedonic mechanisms cause us to pursue pleasure and avoid pain and displeasure; thus, for viewers to choose to watch films that create sadness, an emotion with a negative hedonic valence, seems a paradox. The chapter focuses on three types of explanation. First, I look at more general mechanisms by which superior goals will temporarily modify aversive reactions to support coping in the service of higher goals. Second, I argue that although such explanations may elucidate negative experiences within the course of a story that ends well, they are not adequate to explain stories with a predominantly sad mood; I therefore argue that viewer preferences for such stories may only be explained as adaptations created during the evolutionary process. Third, I argue that there are two adaptive mechanisms at play: a general mechanism that makes negative events fascinating in order to support information about negative events (supporting learning), and a cluster of more specific adaptations that supports bonding—pair-bonding, male bonding, and tribal bonding—based on rituals of mourning. Rituals of mourning are often linked to scenes that elicit awe and submission to some higher powers (fate or divine forces), and I discuss the biological-evolutionary underpinnings of such emotions and behaviors.

Our fascination with sad stories was already an issue in antiquity. Aristotle provided a vaguely outlined idea called catharsis to explain the effect of watching tragedies: humans have excess passions and witnessing tragedies somehow cleanses the mind of those passions. Many media scholars (e.g., Zillmann and Bryant 1994) have considered the problem of why viewers are attracted to stories that deal with tragic events and inevitable death. Some argue that viewers enjoy sad stories because such stories make them feel better about their own, less miserable lives. Others, such as Mary Beth Oliver (1993), argue on the contrary that viewers, especially women, like watching sad films because they get satisfaction from relating empathetically to other people. These factors may account for some of the attraction of sad stories—we may indeed experience a lightly veiled schadenfreude at other people's tragedies, or take pleasure in our own capacity for empathy—but as general explanations they are not fully satisfying. There are good reasons to believe that viewers of sad films, just like spectators of tragedies in theaters, experience genuine sadness. In the following, I suggest bioevolutionary explanations for this phenomenon, arguing that sorrow and sadness are adaptations linked to (social) attachment. The explanatory power of the biocultural approach is especially evident in relation to sad films, since viewer interest in sadness is difficult to explain without such an adaptive perspective.

Hedonic Valence and Fascination in Film Viewing

The basic principle in hedonic valence (i.e., the value of the degree of pleasantness or unpleasantness of a given experience) is to approach what is pleasant and avoid what is unpleasant, because in general the degree of pleasantness is developed as a guideline for whether a given event is fitness enhancing or not. Rotten food is unpleasant, wounds are painful, nutritious food and attractive partners provide pleasure, and so on. However, simple mechanisms to avoid approach would only work for primitive organisms with a few hard-wired systems of response. A medium-complex environment consists of pleasurable attractors as well as unpleasant and possibly harmful repellents. An animal or a human being wants to find food, but also wants to avoid becoming someone else's meal. To maneuver in a complex environment with stimuli that cause pleasant as well as unpleasant experiences demands more complex mental structures, unless the living being chooses to do nothing, which will not enhance fitness in the long run. Hedonic valence, the mechanism that determines whether a given experience has a positive or negative value or tone, relies on more complex adaptations and functions.

Brokering between negative and positive experiences are the central mechanisms of setting goals and making plans, thereby creating a hierarchy among the experiences. Goal setting is one of the central elements in basic storytelling, if not the constituting feature. Indiana Jones wants the Ark of the Covenant and therefore accepts a series of negative events to achieve his goal. The hobbits suffer through many negative events to destroy the evil ring. Many young men confront dragons to win a princess. The negative experiences in such fictions must keep their negative valence, because otherwise we would not fear snakes or dragons. But the negative emotions are integrated into the positive goals in such a way that the negative events pose activating challenges. Just as mountain climbers suffer hardships and a very high risk of death to climb to the top of Mount Everest, so viewers should, to some degree, be motivated to be exposed to aversive stimuli. If Indiana Jones were not motivated by high-order goals, his hardships in jungles and snake pits would not be quite as enjoyable. And if the police detectives in Se7en did not have important objectives, the disgusting phenomena would not contribute to overall interest.

If a person is confronted with a dangerous or disgusting creature, he or she can choose fight or flight. The emotional reaction and its hedonic valence reflect the person's evaluation of coping options and coping potentials. A person confronting a tiger in the wild might feel fear if equipped only with bare hands, fearful aggression if equipped with a spear, and playful aggression if equipped with a powerful all-destroying laser gun. The arousal triggered by a scene of confrontation with a tiger does not have a fixed hedonic valence; the valence is calibrated relative to coping potentials and goals. It is also calibrated in relation to broader values and concerns. Heroes risk their lives to save damsels in distress, thus placing fear of danger lower than loyalty and romantic attachment.

A narrative is based on creating a hierarchy of valences that motivate action integrating a series of subactivities and goals into an overarching goal. Thus, the goal recalibrates the hedonic valence of the subactivities in relation to that goal (see Cosmides and Tooby 2000). The recalibration of valence systems is not only linked to action films. In art films, physical coping is supplanted with a crisis situation in which the protagonist needs to recalibrate his or her value system. For example, in Ingmar Bergman's Wild Strawberries, the old man is forced by destiny to reevaluate his values.

The main outlay of the basic emotional machinery located in the limbic system is relatively old and simple, and the sophistication of emotions typical of humans (and primates) is related to a radical expansion of the neocortex, especially the frontal lobes (see Goldberg 2001). Such higher neocortical processes modify the basic and primitive limbic functions. Much of this expansion of the frontal lobes deals with how to control actions through more sophisticated responses, for instance, by calibrating the punishment-reward mechanisms in the orbitofrontal cortex (Kringelbach and Rolls 2004). This can further be done, for instance, by setting long-term goals and by making hierarchies and compromises between different concerns and their emotional support. Central to many films, especially the so-called dramas, are deliberations that attempt to set priorities between different concerns.

Even if the arousal created by the confrontation with negative phenomena needs to be negative, there are built-in mechanisms that elicit pleasure out of confrontations and motivate people to cope, the dopaminergic reward system that Panksepp (1998) calls the seek system, which developed to motivate us to seek resources such as food or mates. Goal-oriented coping releases dopamine—a pleasure-creating neurotransmitter—in the brain to support the coping effort. Part of the arousal caused by a disgusting monster may be transformed to positively valenced emotions if the viewers simulate protagonists that have sufficient coping potentials. The pleasure of shooting down the vampires in *From Dusk Till Dawn* is that much greater because they are very disgusting. In this way, the arousal created by disgust can be transformed into the positive arousal created by aggressive coping. This makes functional sense because a simple system of hedonic valence in conjunction with approach-avoidance mechanisms would have created obstacles to efficient control. It may be vital to prepare mentally to boost the effort to deal with negative phenomena.

The idea that such mechanisms for mental boosting exist has gained support by some experiments involving video game players. The brains of video game players release large amounts of dopamine—a pleasure-creating neurotransmitter—during play that requires challenging motor control (see, e.g., Koepp et al. 1998). Psychologist Niklas Ravaja and his colleagues (2006) have shown that there is a difference in hedonic valence that depends upon whether an intermediary failure is part of an active coping situation or whether the player watches a taped representation of his or her own performance. In open coping situations, even short-term failures may create positively valenced arousal in the video game player; whereas the arousal is negative when the player is seeing a replay of the failure to cope. Under those circumstances, the player has no active coping potentials.

The film equivalent to pleasure by coping would be that the viewer might have vicarious pleasures connected to protagonists in dire circumstances but with coping potentials. This modifies Zillmann and Bryant's (1994) description of the pleasure connected to painful experiences in film. Zillmann argues that the pleasure is solely derived from the positive outcome: "Great enjoyment rides on the back of great distress" (452). This point of view, however, disregards the mental mechanisms that motivate agents, including viewers, to continue in a stressful environment. Part of the pleasure exists before arriving at goals, like the pleasure-producing dopamine release described by Koepp et al. (1998). Achievement of big goals might be pleasant, but also may provide a feeling of emptiness just as intense coping, even in adverse circumstances, may provide pleasure. Even if coping in films as in real life is goal-directed, part of the pleasure is derived from the process leading to the goal.

The 19th-century German psychologist Wilhelm Wundt argued that the relationship between arousal and pleasure could be described by the so-called Wundt curve. Increasing stimulation and arousal led to increasing pleasure to a point after which increasing stimulation would lead to decreasing pleasure and ultimately to unpleasure and pain. Berlyne (1971) has used Wundt's ideas to propose a bioaesthetic "workout" theory of how aesthetic works stimulate the brain by dynamic variations of stimulus complexity. One also may get pleasure out of an increase of arousal followed by a quick decrease, the so-called arousal jag. Alan Rubin (1994) has employed "uses and gratification" theories of media consumption. Viewers use media products to regulate their level of arousal. Stressed people want calm programs, whereas unstressed people want action. Thus, the relation between hedonic valence of parts and of goals is complex, because negative elements are also challenges. Young people, especially young men, often seek sensation through horror stories such as Quentin Tarantino's *Kill Bill* to increase the level of challenge, whereas older people often avoid high levels of challenge.

Grief and Sadness as Separation Anxiety and as a Reaction of Surrender

Sadness is a negative emotion linked principally to separation, and as such it is the opposite of positive emotions based on attachment. The evolutionary roots of sadness are those mechanisms that attach mothers (parents) to offspring and vice versa (Panksepp 1998; Bowlby 1980, 1982). These mechanisms are central for all mammals. Young animals and children need the care of their mother to survive; therefore separation evokes severe distress. These attachment mechanisms have later been reused to support a wider range of attachments: pair-bonding, kin bonding, and tribal bonding, as I discuss later in detail.

There are two main phases in such separation anxiety. The first phase consists in emitting sounds of distress aimed at attracting the attention of the caretakers, as when children are crying. The second phase consists of a deactivation, eventually with weeping and only intermittent cries of separation anxiety, and this deactivation may serve as energy conservation when the lost ones have to survive for some time in isolation from the caretaker. We notice that the situation of being lost as a small child or young animal has two components with rather

opposite action strategies: on one hand the separation anxiety that motivates vocalizations and even an effort to approach the lost parent, on the other hand fear
that motivates freezing and blocks vocalizations that might attract predators.

We may thus distinguish between a more active form of separation pain
that has different forms, like anger, grief, and emission of separation cries; and
a more passive form of separation reaction: sadness and depression, whose vocal
form is weeping. In terms of its biological underpinning, the active form of
distress is a sympathetic reaction supporting coping, whereas the passive form,
sadness, is a parasympathetic reaction, and such reactions lead to the relaxation of coping tendencies, a deactivation in the motor-related prefrontal cortices (Damasio 2003). Measurements done on children watching the death of
Bambi's mother showed that they were experiencing parasympathetic reactions,
whereas students watching the shooting of Kennedy showed sympathetic reactions that may support emotions such as anger (Averill 1968). As a first approxi-
mation to the effect of sad melodramas, we may hypothesize that such stories
focus on transforming active grief to passive sadness.

Frijda (1986) has pointed out that weeping centrally expresses helplessness
and in that sense is a surrender and detachment response, a giving up of coping.
Weeping has strong affiliation to laughter, and it is often difficult to hear whether
someone is weeping or laughing; it activates several of the same brain mechanisms, and both reactions consist in exhaling air with lungs and larynx. People
may weep for pleasure, and sometimes dire situations elicit hysterical laughter.
However, the two detachment responses have two different origins: laughter is
rooted in the evolution of mammalian playing (Provine 2000), whereas crying, as
mentioned, is rooted in separation reactions. Tan and Frijda (1999) have analyzed
how sentimental film melodramas evoke (happy) tears when the separation of
main protagonists reverses into reunion and reattachment, as in Fleming's *The
Wizard of Oz*; when the justice in jeopardy comes to a happy end, as in Disney's
Pocahontas; or when the film portrays situations that are awe-inspiring and evoke
helplessness and surrender.

Tan and Frijda analyze stories that evoke happy tears, whereas stories like
Romeo + Juliet or Michael Mann's *The Last of the Mohicans* are crafted to evoke sad
tears. Thus, even if the fascination with sad or tragic films shares some of its effect
and motivation with films that deal with attachment in jeopardy (like many of
the films analyzed in chapter 2), sad films have no final reversal to reattachment;
the stories end in a permanent separation. Such tragic films make attachment
highly salient, perhaps more so than films with happy endings. Tragic stories like
those of Tristan and Isolde or Romeo and Juliet have been remembered better
than stories with happy endings because the extreme sadness expresses attachment in the negative, as a strong psychobiological craving. Frijda (1988) has stated

that there is a law of hedonic asymmetry which says that the pleasure of positive experiences is more short-lived than the pain of negative experiences. The sad stories may therefore provide an additional salience and emphasis on attachment dispositions by the very fact that they eternalize a painful urge to bond.

Sad films might further rely on some fundamental mechanisms that mold and alleviate negative situations. An example of mechanisms that mold and alleviate fear and loss may be found in the sublime experiences linked to loss by using the freeze reaction that is built into all mammals when confronted with dangerous fear-inducing situations. Freeze reactions in humans are often concomitant with shivers and chills that, besides being linked to piloerection or gooseflesh, is a way of keeping up body temperature by supplanting normal heat production with such involuntary muscle contractions when forced to immobility. Such chills are, however, also a very common way of reacting during aesthetic experiences. This has especially been studied in relation to music. Neurologists Jaak Panksepp and Günther Bernatzky (2002) point out that such shivers are prominently induced by bittersweet music that expresses unrequited love and music that expresses patriotic pride through the commemoration of lost warriors (see also Sloboda 2005). This is very much in accordance with prominent situations in sad film scenes and also accords with Tan and Frijda's (1999) emphasis on awe as a means of creating helplessness and surrender. It further resonates with the aesthetic ideas of Edmund Burke and others that sublime experiences might somehow be related to fear.

Panksepp and Bernatzky further analyze how a central element in this chill reaction might be rooted in some fundamental similarities between the acoustic properties of chill-evoking music and the separation calls of young animals. These calls represent a mix of longing for a reunion and pain, and Panksepp and Bernatzky point out that animal experiments suggest that the pain of the lost, distressed young animal is somewhat alleviated by secretion of oxytocin and prolactin. Listeners seek out sad music just as viewers seek out sad films that often have sad music as a very prominent element in the saddest scenes. According to Panksepp and Bernatzky, sad listeners or viewers might get some emotional relief out of such experiences. This would parallel the way in which laughter alleviates painful experiences by a combination of blocking of action tendencies and activation of limbic pleasure centers (Provine 2000).

Thus, central to tragic endings is that they articulate processes of surrendering and helplessness, and that such tragic scenes are often sublime. There is a good functional reason for that, because it is easier to give in and surrender if the cause and the circumstances of the negative result are bigger than life. The end of *Close Encounters of the Third Kind* illustrates these sublime mechanisms beautifully, although the occasion is one of cosmic reunion. The spaceship approach is in principle fear-evoking, and the humans are reduced to total helplessness, at the mercy of the all-powerful aliens. The acoustic and visual input is overwhelming, and the onlookers can only respond with awe, tears, and submission. Similarly, the death scenes in *Titanic* are larger than life.

Sadness as Bonding Emphasis

Separation and distress may be portrayed from the point of view of the distressed, the caller, although such calls of separation of course also have a profound effect on mothers (parents), who are biologically motivated to respond to signals of distress. Tragic films are, however, also very much focused on situations of loss and separation caused by death based on adult bonds, and this grief or sadness is not only experienced from the point of view of the persons that die but also or mainly from the point of view of those that have strong bonds to the dead, as in Cameron's *Titanic, The English Patient*, or *Saving Private Ryan*. The Romeo and Juliet story as play or as film even masters this process in double so that both hero and heroine survive but decide to commit suicide when confronted with the grief of separation. The viewer may feel grief in resonance with Romeo and Juliet, but the end result may probably be that viewers feel sadness over the death of the two lovers, just as the viewers participate in Private Ryan's sadness at the grave of Captain Miller. Similarly, the viewers participate in Hawkeye's, Cora's, and Chingachgook's sadness at the grave of Uncas and Alice in *The Last of the Mohicans*. Such death scenes or grave scenes clearly implicate viewers in an activity of mourning. Sadness is contagious; thus Harrison et al. (2006) have shown that sorrow is transferred intersubjectively through the low-order effects of facial expressions, much as occurs in the case of mirror neurons, so that someone observing a sad person with contracted pupils will tend to contract his or her own pupils in response. Similarly, the contagious effects of melancholy sounds have been discussed earlier. The fact that this contagiousness appears to be hardwired supports the idea that sadness fulfills important social functions by creating emotional resonance within a social group and helps to explain ritual sadness, such as an audience feels when watching a tragic ending. Therefore, tragic films that are larger than life, such as *Titanic*, support a ritualistic audience experience of sublime bonding.

Burial and mourning rituals are some of the central human rituals. To ritualize sadness is a central element in most cultures: indeed, the development of such burial ceremonies was an important constituent of the cultural explosion some 40,000–50,000 years ago in the Upper Paleolithic, which triggered the sudden rapid development of human culture (Tattersall 2001; Mithen 1996). The graves and grave gifts were often very elaborate, and enormous resources have been used for grave making, with the Egyptian pyramids as the prime example of such efforts. Religion is intimately intertwined with the question of death, and often religious institutions are burial grounds. Burial grounds are special places of bonding, because they constitute a virtual society of the living and the dead. This is very explicitly formulated in the mourning ceremony in *The Last of the Mohicans* where Chingachgook describes how Uncas has gone to the rest of the tribe, which now consists of one living person, Chingachgook, and a group of "undead" Mohicans that live in the world of the Great Spirit. The importance of bringing back the dead soldiers from Vietnam to the United States in *We Were Soldiers* grows from similar ideas of a virtual tribe consisting of the living as well as the dead. That sad films often enjoy greater respect than happy films may reflect the way in which sad films are rituals of social bonding and that, as I analyze in more detail later, sad films express conflict-reducing submission to tribal values and their eventual metaphysical dimensions. That rituals of bonding linked to sadness have emotional costs (as well as eventually the economic costs of making tombs or grave gifts) might even be an advantage because, as argued by sociologists of religion, rituals linked to social bonding are often costly for the participants. They are hard to fake in order to prove the sincerity of their commitment (see, e.g., Sosis and Bressler 2003). Alcorta and Sosis (2005) have further argued that religious rituals and symbols became increasingly important in prehistoric and historic time, driven by the need to create bonding systems in increasingly large groups of unrelated persons that were the result of population growth, and that rituals are especially intense in groups that must engage in high-risk cooperative endeavors such as external warfare or long-term sharing of scarce resources. This fits well with the prominence of sad rituals in heroic films. The prominence of music further resonates with Steven Brown's (2000) emphasis on music as linked to group bonding originating in group rituals.

The offspring-mother bond has been generalized through a process of evolution. Even if some sad films focus on simple mother-child separation or pair-bonding separation, many sad films are linked to tribal bonding, including the large group of films that relate to bonding with dead warrior comrades (whether in Homer's *Iliad* or Spielberg's *Saving Private Ryan*) and films that, like *The Last of the Mohicans*, mix tribal bonding with kin bonding, parent-child bonding, and pair-bonding. James Averill (1968; see also Izard 1991) has argued that grief, as a painful response to separation and loss, is a biological reaction: an evolutionary adaptation to secure social cohesion in humans and other primates, for whom group living is vital for survival. Burial rituals occur universally in human societies and play a key role in defining individuals as part of a community. As pointed out by many scientists, one of the distinctive features of humans is their ability to cooperate in large social groups, what Boyd and Richerson (1998) describe as human ultrasociality. Thus the evolution of those sociobiological mechanisms that enable humans to behave in a relatively cooperative or even altruistic fashion is central for understanding culture and cultural products. The first step in this process has been to develop bonds between individuals. The attachment between mother and child is biologically and evolutionarily the fundamental bonding mechanism, just as oxytocin, as discussed in chapter 3, is the central neuropeptide regulating pair-bonding. However, human evolution has consisted in making humans increasingly social animals. In chapter 3 I discussed how demands stemming from the increasing resources needed by children born at an immature stage led humans down the same road that birds had taken previously to forge pair-bonding. The next evolutionary step was the development of kin bonding. In one of the centerpieces of evolutionary theory, W. D. Hamilton showed that it might be possible to explain kin altruism in humans and some primates because kin share DNA, and it is therefore advantageous for one not only to help and invest resources in one's own offspring but also to invest in, for example, brothers and sisters or nephews (see Buss 2005, chapter 18).

Peter Richerson and Robert Boyd (2005; see also Boyd and Richerson 1998) have argued that one of the defining features of human culture is that it enables a certain feedback to biology. The pressure for and advantage of forming larger groups did create cultural forms that had feedback on biological selection, like the exclusion or killing of defectors and the provision of advantages for those that complied and forged strong social bonds. They thus argue that tribal bonding is one of the key examples of how culture interacts with biology. Because the tribe is probably the most complex level of the social bonding systems that has some innate biological underpinnings, I will use the word *tribe* and its derivatives to cover such terms as nation, empire, and ethnic affiliation, just as the function of religion is often to constitute tribelike social formations.

A central element in tribal bonding is the bonding of warriors, and Robin Fox (2005) has outlined the history of male warrior bonding in epic literature from the Sumerian *Gilgamesh* onward. The list of films that portray the altruistic behavior of men that forms male bonds, as a strategy of mutual help when fighting, is endless, not only in tragic buddy films like George Roy Hill's *Butch Cassidy and the Sundance Kid* but also in all kinds of war films. Thus, such kinds of bonding rely on a double, interacting stream of culture and biology, because, as stated by Richerson and Boyd (2005), genes and culture coevolve. The steady stream of films dealing with male bonding and tribal bonding is part of the cultural underpinning of tribal bonding. Even films like *The Deer Hunter*, which has an antiwar attitude, also have a strong positive valorization of ethnic bonds and war buddy bonds.

The formation of tribal units was, according to Boyd and Richerson (1998) and others, concomitant with a series of cultural innovations from the Upper Paleolithic onward that was aimed at increasing the cohesion of the tribal group. Special dress, language, and style in the creation of artifacts were some of the means of emphasizing tribal cohesion (see Alcorta and Sosis 2005 for a discussion of the importance of group emblems and symbolism to underpin group cohesion). One of the central elements in the formation of tribal identity has been the invention of religion as a distinguishing mark of a given tribe. The relation between the tribe of Israel and Yahweh is the prototypical example of how religion enhances tribal identity, just as present-day revivals of fundamentalist Islam express a regrouping of tribe formation. David Sloan Wilson (2002) has described how religion has enhanced solidarity within tribelike social groups.

Thus, sad films are often supported by a cluster of bonding-related themes, including themes related to tribal bonding and religious affiliation.

Aggression, Dominance, Submission, and the Sublime

The development of an extended altruism is intimately linked to an enhancement of aggression in relation to rival groups or rival tribes. A great many films, especially those that deal with war or other grand themes, link a story of individual bonding to the fate of the tribe. Thus melodramas such as *Gone with the Wind*, *The Godfather* trilogy, or *The English Patient* link problems of tribal affiliation to problems of individual bonding in combination with uninhibited aggression. In the animal kingdom, mortal combat between members of the same species is relatively rare: killing is centrally something animals do for predation or as a protection against predation, and fighting between members of the same species is mostly ritualized male fights for mating rights, where the fighting stops when the relative strength is calibrated. However, *Homo sapiens* belongs to those species that engage in mortal fights with conspecifics. Konrad Lorenz (1966), Averill (1968), and Eibl-Eibesfeldt (1979) have observed that strong bonds of attachment are manifest only in very aggressive species that also depend vitally on cooperation in their fight for territory, like wolf packs or rat packs.

A high level of aggression creates problems for the internal cohesion of the group. One of the vital means to reduce this intraspecies aggression is to create a hierarchy within the group, supported by mechanisms of dominance and submission, so that an acceptance of location in the pecking order may diminish aggression. Submission is centrally elicited by fear and may lead to behavior emulating that of a child in relation to an adult and to a general deactivation.

Gilbert (2005) has argued that not only loss of attachment but also loss of social control (an extreme form of submission) leads to depression. The submissive behavior is centrally to give up active, physical agency, except to obey orders from a dominant agency. However, as Atran (2002) has argued, even dominant persons often demonstrate symbolic submission to powerful counterintuitive agents and thereby emphasize the need for submission in order to have social cohesion.

Mourning ceremonies, especially those made to provide last respects to a comrade in arms, are central examples of ceremonies of submission. Social bonding might, in principle, be based on tit-for-tat, a social exchange where favors are returned at a later point in time. It is, however, obvious that Private Ryan cannot really repay Captain Miller, who died to help him, at a later point in time. The way in which Private Ryan repays him is by enacting a ceremony of sad submission, just as the way in which a tribal unit repays dead warriors is by making ceremonies that honor the dead, enacting submission so that even the highest ranking living person shows acts of sad submission to the dead, and promises they will have eternal life in the memory of the living. Graveyards and memorials are places for tribal submission to guarantee bonding over time and across the life-death barrier. The story told in *Titanic* by the surviving Rose DeWitt worships Jack Dawson, who saved her life, and emphasizes her lifelong bonds to him, in the context of the sublime underwater graveyard that holds his body and the bodies of many other passengers and crew members.

In the previous chapter I discussed how Christian devotion, including film versions such as *Ben-Hur*, centrally focuses on social exchange by means of sacrifice. The existence of counterintuitive agents like gods, fate, and so on may enhance the process of submission and bonding, but such counterintuitive agents are not necessary for such experiences of submission. The basic emotion of sad submission is elicited by a confrontation with the sacred that is something, a place, a process, an agent, or a thing, that inspires absolute fear in the form of awe and submission. That something is sacred means that it should cause absolute submission because it is connected to all-powerful forces. The core of submission is to persuade the powerful forces to show some kind of clemency, and therefore submission is a kind of fear containment.

Death scenes are predominantly visualized in a sublime, submission-inspiring fashion, and, as previously pointed out, some sublime, chill-evoking music is played that causes tears and freeze reactions. In chapter 5 I discussed how the fear of dead people in horror films is underpinned by the fear of possible contamination from the dead body. However, sad tragedies and melodramas take another tack in relation to dead bodies than horror films in two dimensions. First, the body is pure and sacred, an object of sad submission. Second, death in sad films blocks action tendencies. Even if horror films may cause quasi-paralysis freeze reactions in viewers and characters, the predominant mood is a wish for action and confrontation that also characterizes the endings of most horror films. In contrast, sad stories like *Titanic* couple sublime awe, a fearful situation larger than life, with an emphasis on bonding. The difference might be described as the opposition between "possession denied" and "possession accepted." The anthropologist Maurice Bloch (1992) has written extensively of different ceremonies in which people accept possession by other beings, and even called one book *Prey into Hunter*, describing how people performed ceremonies that made them into prey for some supernatural beings. Religious sects preach how to give in to Jesus, how to suspend one's own agency. Rose DeWitt is still "possessed" by Jack Dawson, and although *The Last of the Mohicans* in some respects is a violent goal-directed film that ends happily because Hawkeye and Cora are united and free, nevertheless Michael Mann rekeyed the ending into a situation in which the living are only sad vessels for the memories of the dead in a sublime gesture of submission.

The Last of the Mohicans is typical of the way in which sad films as a whole counterbalance the two opposite tendencies of the bonding species that Lorenz (1974) points out: aggression and bonding. (Lorenz even provides numerous bird examples of how, e.g., courtship among aggressive species varies between aggression and infantile displays of submission, and he calls this relation between bonding and aggression a rebound phenomenon.) Similarly, the foil of Romeo and Juliet's love is the fierce aggression that splinters Verona into two warring subtribes. The love story in *The English Patient* takes place against a violent World War II background, where the sad funeral ceremonies of dead warriors are preceded by violent battles. The male bonding in Cimino's *Deer Hunter* is grounded in the men's Eastern European and hillbilly background but blossoms in their confrontation with the Vietnam inferno. Violence provides the emotional background for the fear-rooted experience of sublime awe. Lurie's *The Last Castle* combines aggression and rebellion with total submission to "legitimate command" and sublime worship of the tribal emblem, the Stars and Stripes, and a lieutenant general played by Robert Redford who makes a gesture of social exchange (dying for the other prisoners) and submission by dying when hoisting the flag.

Even in a nonsad film about sublime submission, *Close Encounters of the Third Kind*, the actions leading up to the sublime awe and submission activate fear reactions that feed the final sublime awe, just as the basic spaceship situation activates a rich background of fear of super-powerful extraterrestrials, even though they release "dead" American hostages and even though they resemble newborns and are thus as cute as E.T.

The sad, sublime death ceremony is consequently often Janus faced: on one hand, it points to bonding in a community of the living and the dead; on the other hand, it seems to be a kind of effort to control mortal violence by showing submissive remorse.

By creating social cohesion and bonding through empathy, sorrow and grief thus act as an important counterweight to aggressive coping strategies. If aggression and active coping were the only mental mechanisms available, group living would be extremely difficult. Additionally, active coping is not the only fitness-enhancing strategy. Passive acceptance, of the kind we see in both tragic narratives and comedy, can also be seen in some cases to enhance our survival. Where a situation cannot be remedied, active coping may be a waste of precious energy, and it may therefore be fitness enhancing to balance stories of triumphant victories over fate with ones that tell of resignation and acceptance of failure. Indeed, the positive goal in tragedy and melodrama may be precisely to accept and come to terms with situations that are impossible to reverse, and in which attempts to do so may be costly or lead to dire consequences, and to emphasize the need for social bonding, eventually molded by a social hierarchy.

In numerous (although not all) sad stories, the level of emotional engagement is furthermore elevated by creating violent and often unsolvable conflicts between different types of bonding. Even if offspring bonding, pair-bonding, kin bonding, and tribal bonding have evolved slowly from the same dispositions and are supported by similar biopsychological mechanisms, they do of course often conflict. When Sophocles's Antigone wants to live up to her kin bond to her brother by providing him with a proper burial, she is in conflict with tribal authority, just as conflicts between pair-bonds and kin bonds to parents is the prototypical love conflict. In Sophocles's *Medea* as well as Lars von Trier's remake, Medea is first torn between her loyalty to her kin and her pair-bond with Jason, and later, her wish for revenge leads her into sacrificing her and Jason's children to break even. There is no fixed system that determines what kind of bond has priority over other bonds, although Medea's sacrifice of her children motivated by pair-bonding might be universally perceived as perverse in relation to the evolutionary priority of the parent-offspring bond. Conflicts between types of bonds increase the sadness of the conflict because they make the tragic conflict unsolvable and the tragic outcome inevitable.

Submission and Social Exchange in *Saving Private Ryan, Hero,* and *Pan's Labyrinth*

Sad films orchestrate different kinds of bonding and advocate submission, even in the form of social exchange by deadly sacrifices. The personal sacrifice emphasizes the importance of the tribe vis-à-vis the individual. Thus in Ridley Scott's

Gladiator, Maximus's self-sacrifice demonstrates not only his capacity for violence but the value he places on Rome and democracy. Moreover, subjective inserts in the story link his death to his attachment to his dead, victimized wife and son, so that his redemptive act is seen to relate to the private as well as the public realm. Maximus's loyal attachment to his brothers in arms is also emphasized. In Ridley Scott's *Blade Runner*, Roy Batty sacrifices himself to prove that replicants are able to show higher feelings, and in *Saving Private Ryan* Captain Miller sacrifices himself for the sake of his comrade Ryan. Although many of these self-sacrificing characters, like Maximus or Batty, are also ultraviolent, the heroes of tragic films may also be passive victims. In *Ben-Hur* Jesus sacrifices himself to save humankind, and in the process also saves Ben-Hur's family. Like Romeo and Juliet, the black mother in Sirk's *Imitation of Life* is the victim of warring subclans, the black and the white, which disrupt the mother's relationship with her daughter. The daughter accepts her attachment to her mother only once her mother is dead. In the context of racial conflict, the mother is seen as a symbolic victim and her death as a form of sacrifice, so that the viewer is drawn to participate in a healing, sorrowful burial ceremony that advocates acceptance and reconciliation.

An intriguing mix of emotions linked to attachment, sadness, burial ceremonies, and social exchange may be found in *Saving Private Ryan*. The global theme of the film consists in the subordination of the individual to a tribal identity: the first frames of the film show a bleached version of a tribal symbol, the American flag, and the central symbolic field of the film is the burial ground for those killed on Omaha Beach during the invasion of Normandy. A survivor, Private Ryan, returns as an old man to the cemetery to pay his respects to Captain John Miller, the head of a mission sent to take Ryan out of the invasion battlefield and back to his mother, because she has already lost three sons in World War II. Thus a mother's private sorrow at losing her son is set against the tribal need for solidarity in war and submission to the hierarchy of command. At the ceremony in the cemetery, Private Ryan is surrounded by his family and all are strongly moved; thus the sense of kinship is reinforced by their shared sadness. The main part of the film consists in numerous scenes of fighting and aggression, but it also tells the story of Miller's effort to rescue Private Ryan and contains scenes that demonstrate intense feelings of solidarity among the soldiers. In a key scene, Ryan refuses out of patriotism and solidarity to return to his mother and desert his brothers in arms. So the film excels in the paradoxical juxtaposition of values: those high up in the military hierarchy place greater value on a mother's feelings than on tribal solidarity, whereas Private Ryan, although a good son, opts for solidarity with his comrades. The film thus has it both ways, solving the deadlock by having Captain Miller sacrifice himself for Ryan's sake in an act of tribal bonding by the social exchange of life.

Yimou Zhang's tragedy *Hero* presents a similar mixture of sadness, aggression, and acceptance within a framework of social exchange. Before discussing the film itself, it may be useful to look at its biographical-historical background. Zhang's father was an officer in the Kuomintang army, his brother fled to Taiwan, and Zhang himself was forced during the Cultural Revolution to work in the countryside. *Hero* is about the unification of China through the dictatorship of the king of Qin. However, it also resonates with recent Chinese history and the way in which the Communist Party unified China through oppression. Clearly, the rebels' acceptance of dictatorship to put an end to bloodshed resonates, too, with Zhang's forced acceptance of Communist rule for the sake of peace. Thus I imagine that Zhang's intention in the film is to articulate a sorrowful resignation that rests on sublime tribal feelings.

Hero belongs to the *wuxia* tradition, the Chinese genre that has affinities to cloak-and-dagger stories and chivalric tales. All these stories focus on aggression through swordplay, but also on codes of honor that set certain limits to aggression. The film describes a crucial moment in the third century B.C. when the king of Qin (a region within what will become China) tries to conquer the rest of China and seeks to position himself as emperor. Four people—two men and two women—who belong to other ethnic groups that have been suppressed by the king of Qin, and whose relatives have died at his hands, decide to kill the emperor. Part of the plot consists in their feigning that one of them, Nameless, has killed the others in order to gain access to the king. However, the two men become convinced—at different points in the story—that it is necessary to bow to the king's rule in order to put a stop to the killing in China. Nameless is executed but gets a martyr's burial because he refrained from killing the king. A close-up of the king of Qin shows his sad face when he has to submit to the law and give the order to kill Nameless because of his unlawful intention to kill the king. Another rebel, Broken Sword, is killed by one of the female assassins, Flying Snow, who is also his lover. She kills herself simultaneously by pressing her body against his and letting the sword pierce both of them in a *Liebestod* that may evoke a Freudian blush in the viewer.

The film thus presents three conflicting types of behavior underpinned respectively by aggression, attachment, and submission. The aggression is expressed mainly through swordfights, generally conducted by three people, and through military operations in which thousands of anonymous men fire arrows at one another. The aggression may be motivated by the search for justice, revenge, or power. The second type of behavior consists of various kinds of bonding: male bonding among the confederates in the rebellion, and the erotic bonding between Broken Sword and Flying Snow. Finally, a third type of behavior involves (feudal) submission and allegiance. Death in the form of the *Liebestod* between

Flying Snow and Broken Sword becomes the supreme symbol of attachment and submission, intimately linked to social exchange.

The theme of submission is linked to that of imperial power and expressed in a sublime relationship to the emperor, who embodies China (figure 6.1). The king is—quite unhistorically—portrayed as living in a palace that resembles the Forbidden City (which was not in fact built until over 1,500 years later), and which thus provides a sublime backdrop to the action and evokes a rich complex of associations. The film ends by showing us the Great Wall of China, which supposedly concluded the emperor's work in creating Chinese unity. The sublime aspects of his position are emphasized by numerous elements of mise-en-scène that further enhance the superhuman, sublime dimensions of the imperial domain as a symbol of Chinese power. The theme of submission is also linked to that of calligraphy: submission to the discipline of learning the mysterious system of Chinese signs, which represents the supreme symbol of Han Chinese tribal identity. The sign system is thus intimately associated with the main characters' tribal identity, just as the Bible, the scriptures, may be seen as a central aspect of Jewish

FIGURE 6.1. Tragic dramas are often linked to representations of sublime submission to some higher principles like gods, destiny, or nations to emphasize bonding. In Yimou Zhang's *Hero*, submission is made to the king of Qin (Daoming Chen), who in a quasi-supernatural way represents Chinese nationhood. The importance of submission and bonding is emphasized by a series of martyrdoms that are hard-to-fake signs of submissive devotion to the Chinese tribe and also devotion to romantic pair-bonding. *Hero* © Beijing New Film Picture Co. 2002.

or Christian tribal identities. The student of calligraphy must focus especially on the sign All under Heaven, which symbolizes China and unity.

The key acts of submission are self-sacrifice and death, which evoke powerful feelings of sorrow. Indeed, the story consists of a series of events in which one or other character sacrifices himself or herself for some higher goal. A crucial moment occurs when the insurgents feign their own deaths at the hands of one of their confederates in order to promote the project of assassinating the king. However, Flying Snow also sacrifices her love for Broken Sword out of political conviction, and at the same time sacrifices herself in the operatic scene in which she and her lover are united in death by the same sword. The king accepts the need to execute Nameless in submission to the law, but at the same time develops sympathy for him and arranges a heroic burial ceremony in his honor.

The higher goals at work in this film are concrete cultural constructions: the affiliation to China, the emperor, or other sources of tribal identity are presented concretely and historically. However, the construction of tribal identity draws on innate emotions and dispositions: the sorrow associated with death; awe and the related sense of the sublime; the desire to bond, whether fraternally with warpath friends (Fox 2005) or erotically; and feelings of acceptance and submission. Death cults play a central role in constructing tribal identities by confirming their participants as members of a transindividual community. On the story surface, the protagonists' submission to the king does not make much sense; the king is a cruel dictator, and they have no ideas about a future powerful Han China. Only at the level of innate dispositions to provide counterintuitive power to social exchange by sacrifice and innate dispositions for submission to tribal values (selected by evolution; see Richerson and Boyd 2005) does the film make sense.

The arguments for the universality of emotional activation due to a complex of bonding, counterintuitive powers, social exchange, and self-sacrifice may be further strengthened by looking at a recent Spanish film, del Toro's *Pan's Labyrinth*. The film is set in the aftermath of the Spanish civil war, in 1944. Rebels and Franco soldiers are still fighting cruelly. The heroine is a 12-year-old girl, Ofelia, who has lost her father and who during the film loses her mother: she dies while giving birth to Ofelia's little brother. The brother's father is Ofelia's new stepfather, an extremely brutal fascist officer. Ofelia is approached by supernatural beings, including a faun, who tells her that she is a princess and can return to her subterranean kingdom and gain eternal life if she succeeds in performing three tasks. The first two tasks involve submission and confrontation with disgust and death. The third task also focuses on submission to the supernatural beings, to the faun. Ofelia can gain eternal life by sacrificing her little brother. The alternative is that she sacrifice herself and accepts being killed by the evil Franco stepfather.

To submit to this third demand would be a selfish social exchange: she would sacrifice her brother and get eternal life in return. The alternative, to let herself be killed, is a total submission to moral values and kin bonding, without any personal benefit. She chooses to submit to her kin bonding and higher moral values by sacrificing her life to save her brother. In a dream sequence, Ofelia is united with her father and mother in a supernatural-subterranean world, deep in that ancient tomb or death world whose entrance is the setting of her death. Her death somehow symbolically alleviates the violent civil war conflict, the tribal conflict. In addition, the brother, son of a Franco officer, will be brought up by the rebels.

Now, the main reactions of viewers are probably sadness and resignation. The viewers may feel sadness because of the cruelty of the civil war and the death of Ofelia. Viewers may furthermore feel sadness because the metaphysical powers, exemplified by the faun, are unreliable and sometimes cruel, and because the story is ambiguous concerning the reality status of the supernatural world, which makes actions and calculations difficult. Sometimes the supernatural agents are shown as effects of Ofelia's imagination; other scenes only make sense if the supernatural beings are real. The world shown is marked by cruelty and loss. However, despite the ambiguity of the metaphysical forces, they are visually real; somehow the whole burial ground setting evokes ideas of a metaphysical community of the living and the dead that controls a fundamental universal justice. It is in relation to this metaphysical community—the history of the Spanish people—that Ofelia's sacrifice has healing powers for the conflict-ridden nation. She is actually united with her ancestors, primarily her parents, and maybe especially her father. Thus, the effect is also one of fatalism and acceptance of the negation of agency, and the primary model is infantile acceptance of omniscient parental guidance: the father and mother are shown as being high up on bigger-than-life thronelike pedestals. That submission and acceptance are linked not only to subjection to alpha agents but also to the parent-child relationship is not so surprising, especially in a Christian environment in which there is a direct mapping of God's role as superagent to his role as father.

That the main characters in *Hero* and in *Pan's Labyrinth* actively or passively accept death and implicitly are parts of tragic bonding ceremonies only makes emotional sense to the extent that such acts of social exchange by submission and sacrifice rituals rely on innate dispositions. The actions in the stories do not make sense from a limited survival perspective, only from a perspective that has ingrained preferences for metaphysical exchange acts in relation to key interpersonal relations such as kin and tribe. Despite different cultural settings, the core themes have a similarity that cannot be explained by cultural influence, although such core themes may travel.

Fascination as Mental Adaptation

As we have seen, our interest in sad films is not easy to explain purely from considerations of hedonic valence; that is, from the assumption that the pursuit of pleasure and the avoidance of pain are the sole motives behind our actions as viewers or those of the characters in the films we watch. Although our basic action control rests on simple mechanisms of pleasure and pain, so that we are motivated to seek out pleasant experiences and avoid unpleasant ones, such mechanisms have been modified by a series of adaptations. There are mechanisms that allow us to navigate in a hedonically complex environment of positive attractors and negative repellents by making priorities: I confront the dragon in order to save the princess; I decide to become emperor of Rome and accept the suffering involved. Confronting and coping with pain releases pleasure-creating dopamine (Koepp et al. 1998), which diminishes the negative feelings involved and may even create positive ones. Our fascination with sad stories moreover raises the question of the relationship between existential relevance and hedonic valence (i.e., the judgment we make as to whether a given experience is positive or negative). Likewise, the link between sadness and individual or tribal bonding points to mental adaptations that cannot be explained on the individual level as simple modifications to the approach-avoidance behavior of a single agency. Children's fascination with stories in which attachment is put in jeopardy or in which the characters fall prey to evildoers or other activations of hazard precaution systems indicates that existential relevance is an important element in fascination. I therefore define fascination as the mental-affective propensity to seek out information that is, or is felt to be, highly relevant to our lives, irrespective of whether we experience pain or pleasure in the process.

This suggests further aspects of the relationship between mental representations—those used, for example, in fiction—and the way in which we would react if the content of these representations were implemented in reality. If our mental interests and fascinations were controlled by exactly the same mechanisms that control our behavior in real life, there would be a strong inhibition against using our mental abilities to deal with negative phenomena of high existential relevance. We would be caught in a Freudian universe in which all phenomena that created negative feelings would be denied access to consciousness. It is therefore more logical and more in accordance with our earlier observations to suppose that our interest partly depends on the existential relevance of any given event. Negative events such as fatal accidents create headlines, and it is logical that such events may in some cases interest us more than positive happenings, since evolution has adapted the mind to pick up any information that may help us avoid negative events in real life. Our interest in tragic stories may thus be determined by multiple factors: by our fascination with picking up information on crucial negative phenomena; by our disposition in some cases to cope through acceptance; or by our innate desire to reaffirm bonding, albeit in negative form, whether the bonding is romantic, as in *Romeo + Juliet*, or tribal, as in *Hero*.

The game of hide-and-seek, as we saw in chapter 2, provides a basic example of the relationship between fascination and existential relevance. The fact that we sometimes agree to play the hunted prey ourselves, or are fascinated by the spectacle of the hunt—whether in children's games or in horror stories, thrillers, or action films—shows that the pleasantness of an experience in real life is not a good indicator of the fascination it exerts. It is unlikely that our common fascination with stories of pursuit by evil monsters only reveals hidden sadistic or masochistic tendencies. Clearly, the mental mechanisms that we call fascination have served some evolutionary, fitness-enhancing purpose, enabling us to seek out, process, and cope with vital information even if it is unpleasant, although it is problematic whether all those mechanisms are fitness enhancing in a modern world, say the interest in hunter-prey scenarios or the fascination with stories of social exchange by means of sacrifice and submission to higher powers.

That there are innate mental mechanisms that explain why viewers may be attracted to sad fictions does not mean, of course, that film viewers consume an equal amount of positive and negative information; there are more comedies than tragedies, so "all's well that ends well" is the dominant principle. But it is worth remembering that comedies often deal with very painful, embarrassing, and shame-evoking events that are rendered acceptable only by our innate capacity for laughter, which serves to diminish the felt reality of phenomena (Grodal 1997) and activates the nucleus accumbens pleasure center. Sadness and laughter are two very different innate (parasympathetic) adaptations that both serve to process strongly negative events.

Part II

Narrative, Visual Aesthetics, Brain,
and the PECMA Flow

Introduction to Part II

The PECMA Flow

The PECMA Flow: A General Theory of the Film Experience

Our embodied brains shape our experience of film, and central features of the film experience and film aesthetics are determined by the basic architecture of the brain and the functions it has evolved to serve. We watch movies with our eyes and ears, and our senses have not evolved in order to be abstract processors of information, but to provide information as background for motor actions that can implement the preferences of our embodied brains—preferences that are expressed in our emotions.

As Merleau-Ponty (1962, French original 1945) was the first to point out, our intentionality is founded on the way in which our motor system is directed toward acting in and on the world. Recent theories within neurology likewise emphasize the fact that vision and consciousness are ancillary to the motor system, to praxis (Noë and O'Regan 2001). Audiovisual experiences are therefore intimately related to the types of action they afford, and central aesthetic phenomena are linked to manipulations of the way in which what is seen or heard prompts action or—as happens in film—prompts vicarious actions in diegetic worlds. Consciousness works in such a way as to highlight perceptual information, whereas the emotions and motor dispositions for action (the anchoring of perceptual information in embodied brains) are more diffuse, existing in our consciousness, for instance, as positive (approach) emotions or negative (avoidance) emotions, or in the form of interest and muscular tension. These feelings are sometimes attached to objects (e.g., a delicious apple) and sometimes to the experiencing agents themselves. In order to understand visions of the world in real life and on film, we need to reconstruct the invisible embodied brain and its feelings, to see how it supports and motivates visual and aural perceptions, and to understand how its construction molds what is experienced. Our senses are directed outward, toward the outside world, and we need to analyze the way in which our visions are determined by our invisible inner embodiedness, and to see how emotion is linked to motion. An embodied approach presupposes that human experiences are intimately linked to the concrete specifications of the embodied mind, in contrast to a semiotic model that presupposes an abstract language approach to interpretation that does not specify how emotions, cognitions, perceptions, and actions are part of a psychophysical totality (for a critique of the abstract description of language, see Barsalou 1999).

In 1997 I published a general theory of the film experience in *Moving Pictures: A New Theory of Film Genres, Feelings, and Cognition* that I will summarize here and update to clarify the relation between culture and biology (see also the updates in Grodal 2006, in press). The theory describes how the film experience relies on a processing flow that follows the brain's general architecture, namely a flow from perception (ear and eye), via visual and acoustic brain structures, association areas, and frontal brain structures to action (motor activation). The flow involves not only an abstract computer-chip-like processing of data, because the human biocomputer is an integrated system of perceptions, emotions, cognitions, and muscular activations. I have therefore named the model the PECMA flow model (perception, emotion, cognition, and motor action; see figure II.1). When we watch a horror movie, for example, our hearts beat faster, we get an adrenalin flush, our muscles tense, and our fear focuses our perceptions of sounds and visual stimuli. The experience can only be fully described in terms of the interaction of the PECMA dimensions.

The PECMA model therefore highlights how our basic human experience, and the canonical film narrative, are aimed at molding and controlling (narrative) actions, and how the basic architecture of our brains and bodies reflects this purpose. From a functional point of view, the senses are designed to pick up information which may in turn prompt actions that implement the preferences of agents, as expressed in their emotions. Emotions are tendencies to action (Frijda 1986), guiding the body in what to approach and what to avoid. Emotional states are supported by the autonomic nervous system, which controls the activation

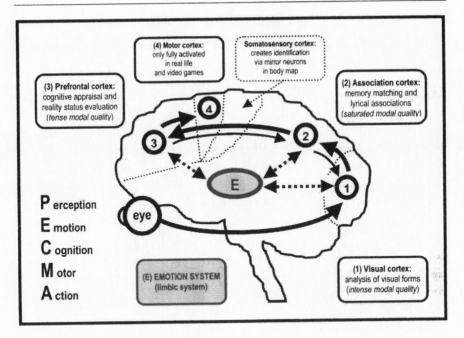

FIGURE II.I. The PECMA flow model.

of the whole body through two subsystems, the sympathetic, which supports action, and the parasympathetic, which supports relaxation and food intake.

The emotional systems of the brain are located in old (subcortical) parts of the brain, especially in the lower central part of the brain, often called the limbic system (or the old mammalian brain), and some adjacent areas in the (reptilian) brain stem and cortical areas in front of the limbic system (see Damasio 1994, 1999; Panksepp 1998; Ledoux 1998, 2002; Kringelbach and Rolls 2004). Here we find centers for fear, sexual urges, and so on and centers that link emotional tags to experiences when they are stored in long-term memory and that reactivate the tagged emotions when memories are retrieved or matched with incoming experiences. The emotional and perceptual processes are therefore intertwined in film viewing.

Large parts of the primary processing of visual information take place in innate, sealed modules that are totally impervious to cultural influence and learning, as we can easily see in illusions such as false contour lines or Müller-Lyer's illusion. When it comes to the identification and emotional labeling of visual information and the development of associational networks, culture and personal experiences play a much greater part. The identification of course depends on previous experience, but so too, to a great extent, does the emotional valence attached to the information (and, as we shall see, this emotional valence also depends on cognitive evaluations of coping potential, e.g., one's potential to cope with tigers or enemies).

The emotional system has innate biases. For evolutionary reasons, our emotional systems are constantly on the lookout for other agents: even modern humans fear snakes, sharks, and tigers more than cars or cigarettes, although the latter kill hundreds of thousands of people globally every year, whereas very few humans die as a result of attacks by wild animals. Our hormonal systems may facilitate the activation of tender feelings when we see Bambi on the ice, because we have a hardwired disposition to tenderness toward helpless youngsters. Hardwired erotic dispositions are easily activated in men by the sight of young women, and fear is activated in all of us by the sight of sharp teeth or "evil" watching eyes.

The PECMA flow can be described in a bottom-up fashion, but I will later point out the top-down aspects as well. For the sake of simplicity, I have described the flow in distinct phases, as presented in figure II.1.

The eye receives light (data) from the world or the screen. This light-induced information flows to the visual cortex in the rear of the brain. Here, the neural systems seek to transform the data received into information that is of interest to humans: analyzing millions of data for contours, colors, orientations, depth cues such as shadows, and so on that may provide the material for later identifying possible objects—humans, houses, trees, cars, and so forth (see Zeki 1993, 1999; Solso 1994). Some so-called abstract films offer an input in which the significant forms cannot be matched with normal objects and may provide an intense perceptual pleasure that cannot be accorded any specific meaning. However, as the brain is preset to provide information about realistic worlds consisting of spaces and objects, unmatched significant forms will create a feeling of meaning (often called excess or third meaning; Barthes 1977; Thompson 1988). This is not to say that there necessarily exists some hidden meaning that could be excavated; rather, the feeling of significance arises simply because the brain's sense-making machine is switched on. Aesthetics often rely on the playful use of the brain's innate specifications.

However, the typical film is not an abstract one and the typical film therefore supports the idea that incoming visual data are matched with some images or image schemas stored in adjacent association areas in the temporal and parietal lobes (the brain areas between the ears and at the top rear of the brain). Each time parts of the visual cortex find some significant forms, the findings are subliminally reinforced by positive emotional responses from the limbic system (see Ramachandran and Hirstein 1999b). The brain thus tries to identify possible objects by matching these significant forms with the vast number of memories. If, for example, the visual cortex isolates a moving object with black and yellow stripes, the association area will provide a match—tiger—and, because memories are always stored with an emotional tag or marker that indicates how to relate to the object, a tiger match will typically evoke a state of frightened alertness. That memories are always stored with an emotional tag is due to the basic function of memory: to provide quick guidance for what appropriate action to take when the memory is later reactivated by seeing something similar. We have millions of stored memories that tell us who are our friends, who are our enemies, what is dangerous, what is delicious, and so on (see Damasio 1994, 1999; Panksepp 1998; Ledoux 1998, 2002). So when we make a match while viewing a film, whether the match is tiger or handsome man, our emotions are automatically activated via links between memory files and the limbic system.

Mostly we do not see only one object; we see a sequence of several objects and phenomena that activates networks of emotion-charged associations. If films allow for matches with stored memories but do not support a narrative, we will get lyrical-associative feelings of the kind induced by some music videos, certain art films, and subjective episodes in mainstream films. The feelings evoked have moodlike qualities that I call saturated; they are strong but unfocused. There is no clear goal that might provide an outlet to such feelings through narrative action. The saturated emotional charge of the associative networks therefore fuels the brain's hermeneutic machinery and provides feelings of deep meaning, for instance when we are watching some art films. The feeling of deep ungraspable meaning need not correspond to deep, buried meaning in the film. Sometimes, indeed, the opposite is true. Lynch's or Resnais's films, for example, use all the mind's blind spots to send the viewer on a quest for meanings that can never be fully found because the images and scenes are underdetermined. Similarly, films with supernatural themes may play with the brain's sense-making hermeneutic machinery by presenting paradoxes and counterintuitive events. The feeling of deep significance is similar to experiences during a special kind of epilepsy in which especially the temporal lobe and its long-term memories are strongly activated in conjunction with limbic systems. This very often provides feelings of deep meaning—for instance, religious experiences or out-of-body experiences (see Ramachandran et al. 1999; Atran 2002). Ramachandran and Hirstein (1999a) have further argued that the temporal lobes are the central locus of the qualia of consciousness (i.e., the conscious qualities of sensory experience) because it is here that perceptual input is matched with memories and emotionally reinforced by limbic structures and thus hyperactivation will lead to extreme vividness and also feelings of truth. Thus, if some types of film arrest the PECMA flow and overactivate the association areas, they will provide similar experiences of deep significance. There is no clear goal that might provide an outlet to such feelings linked to images and sounds through narrative action.

The next step in the flow is to link objects and spaces to a living agent that has preferences and action potentials in a given setting, a narrative scene. Brain scans have shown some of the brain regions that are central for verbal narratives (see Mar 2004; Vogeley et al. 2002; Young and Saver 2001; Hasson et al. 2008), and they are predominantly located in the temporal and frontal lobes, the temporal-parietal junction, and limbic structures such as the hippocampus and amygdala. The regions have functions such as the understanding of (other) minds and their intentions, including pretense (German et al. 2004), the ordering of events in time, cognizing plans for motor actions motivated by emotional concerns, and simulating possible consequences of actions including emotional consequences. The frontal lobe is the executive part of the brain (see Goldberg 2001) that controls the premotor planning of actions and the motor implementation of actions. Those mental functions that support narratives are central to how human action is planned, controlled, and executed, motivated by subcortical structures; and the executive functions are important for inhibiting response—for instance, on fictional film inputs or imagined scenarios (Goldman 2006). Those inhibiting functions develop in children in tandem with their ability to understand pretend behavior and false belief.

In natural conditions, visual information is not just abstract information; it is information of relevance to an experiencing person who has certain specific interests and certain abilities to implement his or her preferences. In narrative films, shots of doors, lions, food, or pistols provide not simply disinterested information, but information that derives its interest and relevance from its relationship to the main characters and their emotional state, which in turn expresses their preferences, their action tendencies. Present, "online" perceptions and correlated emotions point to possible future actions: escape through this door, approach this person, or get to this goal. The emotional-conscious experience is thus colored by, or modalized by, muscular tension because it is the muscles, whether in the arms or legs or in the speech organs, that implement our preferences, and thus this muscular intentionality colors the experience. Mirror neurons in the premotor cortex may play a major role in prompting action tendencies in viewers that mirror the actions and intentions of the characters. In mental simulations such as film viewing, the modeling of actions in the premotor areas, of course, does not lead to actual motor actions; the motor centers are only resonating, not executing.

The tension may be transformed into relaxation when the goals are implemented. This applies when the major goals are reached, but the achievement of one subgoal or sub-subgoal will simply change the perceptual and affective setting so as to make a new subgoal or sub-subgoal urgent, and thus we get a continuous flow: PECMA-PECMA-PECMA . . . Thus motor action is the final step only in terms of brain-body architecture. In real life the flow does not need to begin with perception: a person may remember that he wants x and this will initiate a new direction of the flow. In films, however, it is the perception of activities on the screen that cues the viewer's simulation of the flow, even though the flow in the diegetic world may be initiated in the interior of the protagonist's mind.

A variation on the canonical tense narrative relates to the embodied brain's safety valves: the parasympathetic branch of the autonomic nervous system that is responsible for relaxation. The active coping that is typical of most narrative films is supported by the sympathetic nervous system and by neurotransmitters such as adrenalin. But important genres of film—such as comedy and passive (tragic) melodrama—rely on innate bail-out mechanisms like laughter and tears (see Grodal 1997; Provine 2000).

The PECMA flow and its relation to the architecture of the embodied brain provides a series of aesthetic options: to cue an intense focus on perceptual processes; to evoke saturated emotions linked to affect-charged associations; to evoke tense, action-oriented, and goal-oriented emotions; to elicit relaxation through laughter by blocking goal achievement in an active setting; or to elicit sorrow and tears by blocking such achievement in a passive setting. A film may continuously orchestrate these options and shift experiential focus, or it may focus on one option, for instance tense action or mood-saturated lyrical associations. The film experience is in some respects larger than life, because the flow and focus may change quickly during the 90 minutes and compress experiences that in real life would take hours, weeks, or months. Thus the perceptual, emotional, and existential experiences involved in watching films are intensified by the fact that rapid change provides salient contrasts, for instance in the characters' emotions or in the weather or the diurnal cycle, and are often heightened still further by the temporal flow in the music. PECMA cycles exist on many levels that are often integrated in a hierarchical fashion: a superior goal (say to win the princess) may consist of various subgoals (kill the dragon) that may again have subgoals (get magic sword) with further subgoals (grasp sword). In chapter 7 I analyze in more detail the way in which narratives may focus on different levels.

A mini PECMA cycle may exist as an isolated fragment and may be activated vicariously. Contrary to what happens with action sequences in real life and in interactive simulations such as virtual reality and video games, the motor aspect here is only simulated: the viewer can only mentally simulate the motor actions of the protagonists in the premotor cortex, which plans actions executed by the motor cortex (the simulation may, for instance, be induced by means of the mirror neurons; Rizzolatti et al. 2002), whereas the perceptions are similar to those of real life. But we are predisposed to engage cognitively and emotionally in hypothetical actions, because evolution has developed increasingly sophisticated ways of considering alternative strategies for action—such as fight or flight—before deciding on a preferred course and carrying it out. The consideration of options takes place by means of different forms of imagination and mental simulations. Fiction relies on this ability to engage affectively and cognitively in hypothetical scenarios. The quality of our understanding is enhanced by witnessing and learning from the actions of others (Bandura 1994).

Top-Down Flows: Cultural Priming and Evaluation of Reality Status

In the above description of the flow experience, I have emphasized the bottom-up aspects of the process, in which the eyes and ears feed emotions, cognitions, and actions. However, the flow system also has vital top-down and feedback components (Edelman and Tononi 2000) that are important for understanding the relation between the innate and the culturally acquired aspects of experience. The procedure of matching input to stored memories and schemata may be described as a top-down procedure, insofar as matching presupposes previous learning, as does the evaluation of possible actions and the evaluation of a given protagonist's coping potential. The bottom-up flow is therefore supported and constrained both by the architecture of the brain and by previous learning.

Here I will focus on three top-down aspects that are vital to the film experience: cueing attention, molding emotion, and evaluating reality status.

Sensory information is continually fed into the sensory systems, but only a fraction of that information will get focal attention. At a cocktail party, you may engage in a conversation and block out all other acoustic information. However, nonconscious mechanisms monitor the blocked-out information, and when your name is mentioned elsewhere in the room you suddenly prick up your ears (the so-called cocktail effect). When you use your eyes, most aspects of the field of vision go unnoticed, and by means of a little-understood mechanism you are able to focus your attention on different aspects of what you see by switching on additional neurons in that field in the visual cortex and integrating these within a larger network (Noë and O'Regan 2001; Churchland 2002, e.g., 143–148). Such features of selective attention are part of a top-down flow (Bundesen et al. 2005), and although the attention does not alter the basic features of the sensation (color and shape are processed by innate mechanisms in sealed modules, for example), the priming and cueing of your attention is certainly influenced by your knowledge and individual and cultural background. Through their use of camera direction, action, resolution, and so on, filmmakers can strongly influence the viewer's attention, but the viewer's cultural and individual competencies also influence the way in which he or she focuses attention.

The basic architecture of the emotional system is universal and innate, but one of its roles consists in providing flexible motivation and intelligent execution of preferences. When Indiana Jones confronts the Arab swordsman in *Raiders of the Lost Ark*, he might have felt fear had he been unarmed, or vigilant self-assertion had he possessed a sword and been a good fighter, but in fact he ends up putting on a show of cool superiority because he has a pistol and is therefore able simply to shoot the Arab swordsman down. Thus, his cognitive evaluation of his possible actions provides flexibility, influencing his emotions in a top-down fashion and thereby determining his final choice of action. The viewers start out ignorant of Indy's equipment and intentions and will therefore move quickly through different emotions as new information emerges and their evaluation of Indy's coping potential changes accordingly. Romeo and Juliet must choose between their mutual love and their attachment to their families and clans, and both love and attachment are supported by innate emotions, so that their choice of romantic love is a top-down decision. A poisonous snake in a solid cage normally induces less fear than if it is free to attack. Thus, emotions are multifaceted states that are determined not only by the perceptual input and the innate architecture of the brain but also by a given agent's coping potential and previous emotional experiences as stored in long-term memory, so that frontal lobe cognitive assessments provide top-down feedback on emotional experiences. The assessments of the protagonists in a film do not need to match those of the spectators. Such assessments do, however, presuppose a narrative scene, and if by various means the film blocks coping potential, saturated feelings and moods will reappear.

The ability to evaluate the reality status of sensory input is vital in real life as well as in film. Quite different types of experience activate some of the basic perceptual mechanisms, and reality status mechanisms in the mind must keep track of the different types of reality. Dreams, memories, films, mirror images, and hypothesis making of all kinds—from viewing fiction or looking at realistic statues to entertaining ideas about how to redecorate one's living room—may all activate the same perceptual mechanisms; for example, those brain modules in the visual cortex that analyze shapes and colors. Reality status mechanisms then continuously try to monitor and tag these experiences, determining that this one is a dream, that one a hallucination, this one a plan, that one a memory. The tagging may be presented in consciousness in terms of degrees of vividness in order to simulate the brain's tagging of reality status by vividness: online reality as provided by perceptions is often more vivid than offline imagination such as memories or plans, but they may also be tagged by higher order abstract evaluations. During film viewing, the "stupid" robot neurons in the visual cortex are bombarded with often strongly emotion-evoking images, and it is only further along in the PECMA flow that a special brain mechanism will evaluate the reality status of these images in order to control our responses to the images according to their reality status. Such assessments will rely on individual capacities and cultural backgrounds, but salient and emotion-charged moving images strain the control mechanisms used in these assessments. Contrary to the common credo that fiction demands a suspension of disbelief, it actually demands a modification of belief or a suspension of belief so that film viewing does not produce full-scale illusions. Our brains were not constructed for film viewing, for a world in which it is possible to be exposed to very salient and complex moving images; thus even as we watch fictional films it remains true that seeing is believing, because to believe incoming information is, as previously mentioned, the default mode and to disbelieve demands a special effort (Gilbert et al. 1990).

The general principle behind reality status evaluation is that it serves those decision-making mechanisms that give a green light for action. The mind-brain tries to indicate whether a given mental experience provides a sound basis for action or not, in the same way and often with the same means as film directors use when they cue viewers to distinguish between memories, online perceptions, hallucinations, lyrical daydreaming, and so on (see chapters 9 and 10). A change in reality status will cause a change in emotion: a past danger, for example, does not demand the same type of action as a present danger. Reality status is often therefore experienced as a feeling, such as the feeling of vertigo that warns us to be careful with acting on what we see, or the feeling connected to sublime vistas that reflect a lack of action potential vis-à-vis phenomena bigger than life. Film and other types of fiction do not merely simulate the different types of reality; they also enhance our understanding of these different types.

A possible evolutionary root for reality status evaluation mechanisms is the act of playing (Steen and Owens 2001; Panksepp 1998; Björklund and Pellegrini 2006). Playing demands that the participants mark the behavior as special, such as the play face of chimpanzees, which is similar to human laughter (Provine 2000). Additional mechanisms may be linked to the human abilities to make theories and models of other minds (Leslie 1987; Baron-Cohen 1995). Leslie has argued that when trying to understand other minds we take a metaposition or a decoupled position, because the modeling does not claim that what is modeled is true. At two years of age children understand pretend behavior, say when a grownup pretends that a banana is a telephone or a child pretends that a shoe is a car driving and making engine noises. At a later age, children are able to understand that other people's minds may be different from their own. The classical experiment to show this is to put a doll in one box in the sight of an adult and a child, and then switch the doll to another box when the adult is gone but the child is still watching. When the adult returns, the very small child or the autistic child thinks that the adult knows the same thing as the child does, but an older child is able to understand that the adult still believes that the doll is in the first box. To have a theory of mind therefore consists in the ability to model the minds of others and to model behaviors and psychological activities that have a special reality status (e.g., being a misunderstanding, being false, or being a pretense). Playing, acting, pretending, laughing, or modeling other people's minds and story comprehension all demand skills that modify or decouple the reality of events. As mentioned previously, story comprehension strongly activates the same mechanisms as used for theories of mind.

Thus, the forward or bottom-up thrust of the PECMA flow is modulated by top-down processes that reflect the way in which cognitive assessments and knowledge modulate our experience. In some respects we feel this modulation more keenly in the cinema than in ordinary life because of the swiftness with which films often cue changes in perceptions, emotions, reality status, and action.

The neurocognitive theory resembles postmodern theory in certain respects: it assumes that there is no fixed mental center, no homunculus who operates the central controls in the mental machine, but many different forces that may conflict or accord with one another. According to Gerald Edelman (Edelman and Tononi 2000) and others, consciousness consists in the functional integration of different regions of the brain through very complex systems of synchronization and interaction. At any given time (to use the model put forward by Baars 1988), a central topic may be broadcast to all those parts of the brain that are relevant to the task in question. Because it has very limited capacity, consciousness deals only with the broad picture and with phenomena that may require a choice. The Freudian unconscious of repressed desires and traumas represents only a small part of the unconscious, most of which works in concert with conscious intentions and goals. The fact that our consciousness and intentions are influenced by unconscious factors has been interpreted to mean that consciousness plays no role whatsoever. In evolutionary terms, this makes no sense. Consciousness probably evolved as a means to exert central control over an increasingly vast range of nonconscious processes and thus to enhance the ability to consider alternative strategies for action (Baars 1988). Conscious processes are not perfect, but it does not make functional sense to argue from this that only the nonconscious processes are important, so that our conscious thoughts and intentions are only a form of false consciousness that veils a fragmented, decentered subject.

Thus minds may have intentions and goals even if there is no "little man," no homunculus overseeing what the rest of the cells are doing. Central consciousness cannot really control what is happening in the different regions of the brain; internal communication is based mainly on self-organizing mechanisms. But central consciousness can reject suggestions and results issuing from the different parts of the brain. The embodied mind is tuned by the interaction of biology and individual socialization. However, in contrast to postmodern theories in which humans are seen as abstract interpreters, the neurocognitive theory argues that the embodied mind is designed to act and interact with the surrounding social and physical world in given situations. This interaction is often influenced by certain constraints (laws, obligations, or reward-punishment systems, for instance; Kringelbach and Rolls 2004) that will create more or less fixed identities, that is, consistency over time. The neurocognitive theory also resembles aspects of Freudian theory insofar as it emphasizes that the inner world and its many different forces involve a number of unconscious aspects. But contrary to Freudian theory, neurocognitive theory presupposes that many of these forces serve functions in relation to current needs and problems and are not merely determined by childhood traumas. The molding and negotiation of different needs in relation to each other take place at the individual level, but are influenced by institutions like film.

Biology influences not only the way that we experience the natural world that shaped it, but also our experience of the virtual audiovisual games that modern technology affords. Although films often mimic the way in which we experience the world outside the cinema, they need not do so. In the cinema the world may freeze and time may be arrested in its course. However, these recent manufactured effects do not create a cultural world that is totally unbound by biology. The film experience of a frozen world takes place against the background of perceptual mechanisms that presuppose that worlds do not freeze. Each time we experience a freeze frame against a background of moving images, we will have a feeling of unnaturalness. We do not need to learn to watch a freeze frame: the experience is not comparable to that of learning a foreign language—to learning, for instance, that *chien* has the same referent as *dog*. People do not need to learn to experience films any more or less than they need to learn the world in order to experience the world (Messaris 1994; Grodal 1997).

The main experience of the PECMA flow is projected on an exterior world. The perceptions, emotions, cognitions, and actions are perceived in connection with the distal source in the world or on the screen, not in the proximal-interior brain activation that is mostly inaccessible to us. Only indirectly, by means of theory and brain experiments, do we have access to the working of our own minds, and therefore brain science is indispensable for understanding the film experience that takes place in our minds, although we mostly only perceive the screen part of the experience.

The following chapters use the PECMA model to deal with different aspects of the relation between brain and film experience: chapter 7 discusses brain and narrative; chapter 8, brain and character simulation; chapter 9, brain and art film narration; chapter 10, brain and subjective experiences; and chapter 11 covers how the experience of realism is a feeling that is aimed at guiding actions and thought actions, and how the feeling of realism during film viewing is often very different from what is actually real. Chapter 12 sums up some of the main arguments and perspectives of the book. An appendix exemplifies the PECMA model through the films of one filmmaker, Lars von Trier, and shows how he grapples with representing subjective experiences on film.

7

Stories for Eyes, Ears, and Muscles

The Evolution of Embodied Simulations

In this chapter, I aim to show how storytelling represents an innate mental capacity to synthesize an agency's perceptual input, its emotions, and its output in terms of action. Insight into the architecture of the brain and the PECMA flow may clarify our understanding of stories. I further describe the way that different media—language and oral storytelling, drama, written stories, film, and video games—use different aspects of premediated mental storytelling. I discuss how the narration of unique events relates to games and to story consumption as a game based on repetition. Finally, I discuss the relationship between storytelling interactivity and linearity and show that there are a number of psychological and motivational reasons why nonlinear storytelling is difficult, and why many so-called nonlinear formats consist in fact of sets of linear stories.

It is common to describe representational structures by considering their manifestation in various media. Key concepts such as narrative or point of view are explained by reference to the media in which these structures commonly appear. Some researchers, for example, define narrative by referring to literary works; others (Laurel 1993) describe film or video games and other computer applications by reference to the theater and dramatic structures. Such descriptions have certain advantages, but also certain problematic consequences, because they define concepts such as story or narrative only in relation to their realization in the media, rather than in relation to unmediated real-life experiences and those mental structures that support such experiences. In my view, media representations are better described as various realizations of basic real-life experiences. As early as 1916, the Harvard psychologist Hugo Münsterberg (1970) showed how the film experience might be described as a cued simulation of key mental and bodily functions. Such an approach offers many advantages in analyzing the nature of stories independently of the media in which they are manifest, because it makes clear that even the various formal aspects of stories represent cues for simulating processes, rather than signs that we are supposed to read. In the following, I describe the phenomenon of storytelling by analyzing the link between nonmediated types of human story experience and different mediated story forms such as oral narratives, drama, printed narratives, films, and computer games.

Before proceeding further, let me provide a definition of *story*. A story is a sequence of events brought into focus by one or a few living beings; the events are based on simulations of experiences in which there is a constant interaction of perceptions, emotions, cognitions, and actions. An example: Harry sees the dragon coming. He is upset, thinks that he needs to grasp his sword; he does so and he kills the dragon. The experience of stories is based on central embodied mental mechanisms as discussed in connection with the PECMA flow in the introduction to part II. We experience stories as representations of exterior worlds and they may be described as such, but at the same time they represent internal physical and mental processes that have to follow the innate specifications of the body and brain.

The story mechanisms in the brain provide the superior framework for our experience of events by integrating perceptions, emotions, cognitions, and actions (see the two sections in the introduction to part II and its description of the PECMA flow). Story mechanisms developed in humans as a means of integrating complex mental data and complex goal-related actions (Dennett 1991). When we go to the supermarket, for instance, a microstory in our mind tells us that we have left home because we want to buy various goods, that we are now at the entrance to the mall, and that we will find the grocery store if we make a given sequence of maneuvers. The microstory thus orients us in space, describes our desires and projects, and guides our motor actions. Damage to certain brain structures that play a key role in narrative may lead to confusion: Where am I and why? Where should I go next? And so on. The story includes a quest and the motive for pursuing it. A medium-length story—somewhat longer than the one outlined above—might be as follows: I met Linda. We had some lovely days in San Diego. She disappeared, but I want to find her again. A macrostory might tell the tale of my life up to now, including the way that the past has set up certain agendas for the future (cf. the question of autobiographical consistency in art film, discussed in chapter 9). In such stories there are actors and settings, actions and happenings, not because such elements exist in mediated representations (novels, dramas, films, or video games), but because such things are important for my experience of, navigation in, and interaction with the world. Stories are based on innate mental functions that match the ecological niche of humans; they are not merely social or media constructions. Although the basic story structure (agency, setting, actions, etc.) is based on functions shaped in our embodied brains by evolution, we may of course interpolate both real and invented material in our stories, and learning mediated stories may enhance our ability to structure nonmediated events.

Human motivations exist in a nested hierarchy. There are high-order goals of the kind that feature commonly in folk tales—getting married, for instance, or becoming king, or high-order existential goals such as survival (the goal in much horror fiction). High-order goals may entail lower goals, such as courting the princess or fighting the dragon, and the latter may presuppose acquiring a good weapon, such as a magic sword or laser gun. Such goals presuppose that you sleep and eat, and at the most basic level what is involved are simple muscular movements and elementary perceptions. The representation may focus on high-order goals and motivations, because such goals are emotionally activating, and to a varying extent recruit nested activities. Some scholars believe that such high-order dramatic events are essential to the definition of stories. However, realism or modern high art narratives may focus on low-level events: take, for example, kitchen sink realism, stream-of-consciousness narratives, and Sarraute's tropisms. Video games may involve certain high-order motivations, but for a number of reasons such games often focus strongly on the execution of low-level (sub)goals such as simple navigation and handling processes: what video game theoreticians call the game play.

The nested hierarchy relies on goal setting, which orients emotions and action strategies. The story experience is not only driven by a pull from the goal, but may also be driven by a push from the immediately given narrative situation, especially if this is a negative one. This problem is highlighted in the problem of suspense as analyzed in, for instance, Vorderer et al. (1996), especially in relation to what happens when people view a film several times and thus know the outcome. Carroll (1996a) convincingly argues that the stimulus from a given suspenseful situation, say a woman threatened by a chainsaw, will exert a strong emotional influence irrespective of our knowledge of a positive outcome from previous viewings of the same film. This is yet another example of how early phases of the PECMA flow may be cognitively impenetrable (Pylyshyn 1991) even in its emotional effects; that is, the emotional force of the situation is relatively immune to high-order knowledge, like reality status information and knowledge of outcomes.

To describe story in terms of a functionally nested hierarchy of PECMA segments may clarify some of the problems and ambiguities in narrative models based on the story-discourse distinction (similar to what Bordwell [1986] discusses as *fabula-syuzhet*). The story-discourse distinction is rooted in the structuralist model of system and manifestation: story is understood as an abstract logical system that has a canonical form, that is, a temporal progression from beginning to end. The story system may be transformed into or manifested in a multitude of different concrete realizations, discourses. The easy version of this theory is that the story consists in a short verbal presentation of the plot of a film, whereas the actual film is one of infinitely many discursive variations on that story. The seminal analysis of story-discourse problems was made by Gerard Genette (1983, English translation) as a tool for describing complicated modern novels such as Proust's *In Search of Lost Time* and also translated to film studies by Chatman (1978). Genette thought that five parameters were important in describing how the discourse relates to and possibly rearranges the story:

1. Order: the temporal order in which the story elements are presented in the narrative discourse
2. Frequency: how often story elements are repeated in the discourse
3. Duration: the degree of temporal condensation or expansion as measured in the relationship between the time span represented and the time taken to represent it
4. Voice: the position of the narrator in relation to the narrative
5. Mood

I will not comment here on (4) and (5).

To describe the story as a canonical PECMA flow based on functionally nested PECMA segments enables us to explain why the so-called linear canonical story is not some arbitrary or ideological invention, nor simply an expression of a certain narrative-aesthetic logic, as structuralist narrative theory implies, but rather a reflection of basic features in the brain's innate architecture. Canonical stories mimic the way in which actions in the world take place in time, and canonical order reflects this. The PECMA flow model describes how the fundamental narrative flow is based on the way in which incoming perceptual (story) information relevant to some vital concern of the protagonist activates emotions in the viewer that are linked to the protagonist's preferences. The emotional activation of body and brain informs the viewer's engagement in the film, as he or she identifies with and seeks to solve the protagonist's problems, and it gives rise to mental simulations of motor actions relevant to the protagonist's concerns and preferences. The basic story experience consists of a continuous interaction between perceptions (I see a monster approaching), emotions (I feel fear, because I know or sense that monsters are dangerous), cognitions (I think that I'd better shoot the monster), and action (the actual motor act of shooting that changes the motivational emotion—fear—into relaxation). The flow model also explains the experiential consequences that follow from tampering with canonical order—for instance, evoking distance or causing lyrical saturation (Grodal 1997) by blocking the normal emotional development from evoking an emotion to its narrative outlet. Functionally, the question of what Genette calls frequency is a subproblem of the question of temporal order, because to repeat a story element several times is a violation of the canonical order.

Moreover, it is evident from the description of functionally nested PECMA segments that there is no canonical format for duration. A verbal story may be told on a high level of abstraction and thus with a high degree of condensation, but all forms of stories—whether verbal, film, or video game—may be told with many different resolutions, some very condensed, others highly detailed. To claim that stories exist only at a certain level of abstraction does not make sense. It is therefore often difficult to distinguish, in terms of duration, between story and discourse. For this reason, too, Bordwell's distinction between *fabula* and *syuzhet* (similar to story/plot) cannot be upheld except in relation to narrative order, because in a canonical story there are no clear distinctions between story and *syuzhet* elements.

However, it is clearly an important, different task to describe a given story from the point of view of the story maker and to describe the story maker's craft and design intentions (see Grodal 2004, 2007), and discourse analysis is often such an analysis of craft and design. Bordwell's (1986) descriptions of narration are to a large degree such highly important descriptions of design, not descriptions of the experience of narrative. What are challenges from a description inside the story world may from a design perspective be means to create suspense; what is lack of information from an inside perspective is from a design perspective a withholding of information. Furthermore, some stories motivate, say, the withholding of information, whereas other stories flaunt the fact that the filmmaker controls the stream of information. Some filmmakers, especially of art films, are more interested in letting viewers experience craft than story (Grodal 2004), just as many viewers of art films are primarily interested in craft.

Until the invention of moving pictures, the verbal form was the most common external medium for storytelling. Perhaps for this reason, the vocabulary used to describe story phenomena consists primarily of words that refer to verbal storytelling: narrative, narration, author, enunciation, and so on. This has led certain theoreticians, among them Marie-Laure Ryan (2001), to the erroneous conclusion that story is principally a verbal phenomenon, because they conflate the story experience with the verbal retelling. In principle, Ryan follows Jakobson's (1960) prudent semiotic definition of stories as phenomena that can be manifested in many forms and that are not defined in relation to any one medium, and her general description of narrative avoids a series of linguistic traps. Nevertheless, she gives pride of place to the verbal form of storytelling. Thus she argues that video games embody a virtualized or potential dramatic narrativity because these games offer virtual stories that could in principle be verbally retold even if they never are in practice. But this conception is paradoxical, because it implies that we cannot experience stories unless or until they acquire linguistic form; thus films would become stories only once we had made a verbal résumé of their plot. In contrast, Barsalou (1999), Zwaan (2004), and others have described how language is mostly cues to embodied mental simulations of the perceptual and motor experiences so that words are just cues that activate brain regions dealing with perceptions, emotions, body images, and actions.

In fact, the story experience need not have any verbal representation, for the ability to hold the story (including possible future elements of that story) in our consciousness—an ability that is important for prolonged action patterns—is independent of language: we can perform this holding operation at the nonverbal level of perception-emotion-action. Thus Antonio Damasio (1999) describes core consciousness as a wordless storytelling and proceeds:

> Movies are the closest external representation of the prevailing storytelling that goes on in our minds. What goes on within each shot, the different framing of a subject that the movement of the camera can accomplish, what goes on in the transition of shots achieved by editing, and what goes on in the narrative constructed by a particular juxtaposition of shot is comparable in some respects to what goes on in the mind, thanks to the machinery in charge of making visual and auditory images, and to devices such as the many levels of attention and working memory. (188)

This mental film is not of course silent; there is the constant voice-over that doubles experience with a phonological stream of words, that is, an inner monologue. A verbal voice-over or inner monologue may strongly enhance our cognitive analysis of a given experience and make it easier to manipulate that experience—for example, to compare it with other experiences or to imagine possible consequences. But the inner monologue may also mask part of the salience of the perceptual-motor experience. Fauconnier and Turner (2002) have described the prelinguistic basis of experience. Damasio could have pointed out that in several respects three-dimensional video games of the shooting variety or some types of virtual reality come even closer to our core consciousness, for not only are we able to see and feel in these games, but we are even able to act upon what we see in the light of our concerns: our (inter)active motor capacities allow us to shoot at what frightens us or approach what arouses our curiosity. Video games and certain types of virtual reality are the supreme media for the full simulation of our basic first-person story experience, because they allow the full experiential flow by linking perceptions, cognitions, and emotions with first-person actions (although video games have problems with "passive experiences" due to their motor bias; see Grodal 2000). The motor cortex and muscles focus our audiovisual attention, adding a sense of muscular reality and immersion to our perceptions. Even visually crude video games such as Pac-Man offer a strong sense of immersion because of the way they activate elementary links between sight and motor action. Inventing stories and creating art in general involves selecting aspects of our total potential consciousness and the supporting unconscious levels of activation. Different media draw on different aspects of consciousness to provide salient experiences.

An embodied-brain approach to the experience of story allows us to characterize verbal storytelling as a media-specific variant of the story experience. Many language-based descriptions of films and video games give detailed accounts of their stories, ignoring the fact that semantic meaning is based on concrete perceptions and motor patterns, not on an abstract semantics kept in place by verbal signifiers. Humans probably acquired language only relatively recently (Tattersall 2001; Fauconnier and Turner 2002), whereas the basic mechanisms to structure actions and events that are involved in story making may have existed for millions of years. Language has certainly played an important role in communicating human stories and has been a superior tool for the retrieval and complex manipulation of basic experiences (see Corballis 1991; Damasio and Damasio 1993; Fauconnier and Turner 2002). Furthermore, language enables us to tell stories at a very high level of abstraction, whereas audiovisual storytelling involves a much more concrete, uncompressed level of representation of the kind that may have filled our prelinguistic consciousness. But a purely linguistic model may seriously impede our ability to describe media such as film, pantomime, and video games that rely on a series of nonverbal skills, including our ability to perceive, feel, and act.

Stories are not the only means by which we experience the world. We may approach it through analytical reasoning of the kind used in writing an essay; we may have thematic-categorical principles of organization or principles based on a network of lyrical associations (Bordwell and Thompson 2001; Grodal 1997). Novels, films, or video games may be full of nonnarrative material such as philosophical reflections, descriptions unrelated to the narrative core, or lyrical sections.

The Evolution of Representations of Experience through the Evolution of Media

The basic story format is what we call the *canonical story* (Bordwell 1986; Grodal 1997), that is, a story with one (or a few) focusing characters which—as Aristotle noticed—unfolds over linear, forward-moving time, from beginning through middle to end. A canonical representation not only accords with the way in which we experience unmediated reality as a series of events occurring over time; it is also the easiest form to remember and represent (Mandler 1984). People will tend to reproduce a story in canonical fashion even if they first heard it noncanonically, that is, heard it with temporal rearrangements. Thus our innate mental machinery seems to take the canonical story format as its baseline. It is important to point out that the basic story experience must be described as taking place in the present: the person experiencing the story is situated in a present anchored in the memory of a past, which in turn gives rise to and informs cognitions, emotions, and actions directed toward the future. Furthermore, the nucleus of the story experience is that of the first person, because from an evolutionary point of view third-person perspectives, even down to the level of motor activation, are expansions of a first-person perspective. We infer how other people experience things by extrapolating from our own experiences; for instance, by using the so-called mirror neurons (cf. the discussion of character simulation in chapter 8). Film theory has uncritically adopted and adapted the literary idea that stories are by default third-person narratives experienced in the past, despite the fact that events in films in principle take place in an experiential present similar to that described by Damasio as core consciousness. Sound and images are directly available to the viewer in that present; markers of the past exist only in language, so that in visual communication "pastness" can be conveyed only by special devices such as those used in short flashbacks (special tinting, out-of-focus shots, and so on). A film does not need to say "Henry saw a bear approaching"; viewers directly see the bear and where it is heading.

Media representations of experience have led many academic theoreticians to give misleading accounts of stories. They tend to focus on story mediation, leaving out those aspects of stories that the French structuralists called *l'énoncé*, the story as such, in order to define *story* as a discursive phenomenon (*l'énonciation*). As mentioned above, discourse analysis was developed as a tool to describe complicated modern novels. For Genette (1983), as for most film theoreticians dealing with discourse, the central question was how rather than what: How does the novel deal with the story? as opposed to, What are the central mechanisms and features of stories? This approach is implicitly based on storytelling as retelling, because the rearrangement of information is the phenomenon at issue.

By contrast, theoreticians of creative writing—such as Syd Field (1984) in the very influential *Screenplay* or Robert McKee (1997) in the more ambitious *Story*, which aims to describe mainstream, popular storytelling—tend to deal with the "what" questions. Some of their analyses—for instance, those regarding plot points or turning points—deal with dramaturgical considerations that may not be present in the minds of viewers. However, most of their discussions deal with aspects of content that both viewers and storytellers regard as definitive, such as problems relating to how the main characters are portrayed, how the story lines are constructed, and so on.

The first media representation of the brain's story experiences occurred when language was invented. This must have led to several changes and additions to our mental narratives, understood as the cortical mechanisms that order and control our experience of life and action. Linguistic representations stabilize these experiences and make them easier to recall and to manipulate. Language is able to create abstract higher order categories and to generate condensed representations and mental associations. Moreover, a central purpose of language is to render stories in an intersubjective form and thus refocus the story from a primarily first-person experience (albeit one in which others are perceived in the third person) to an experience that also includes a third-person perspective, that of the storyteller in relation to his or her retold stories of past experiences, or his or her retold stories of others' experiences. Verbal representations enhance the already existing possibility of providing stories with a third-person perspective, because even if the story concerns one's own experience, language enables us more easily to relive past experiences out of their direct perceptual context. Thus even first-person autobiographical narratives are constructed by a storyteller who has a temporal and possibly a spatial distance from the time (and space) represented in the narrative. The stable, intersubjective representation afforded by language creates a filter of arbitrary symbols between perceptions, emotions, and actions on the one hand and, on the other, their existence in communication. Language enhances our ability to describe fictitious events, because although the ability to imagine a story is functionally linked to the mechanisms that enable us to imagine different possible future actions, language goes one step further in removing all constraints on the veracity of stories. Stories experienced through vision (before paintings, film, and television) represented what existed and thus had strong indexical links, because they were the visual imprint of reality. However, in language (or even in paintings) it is just as easy to lie or to fantasize as to tell the facts (see Fauconnier and Turner 2002). This has led many scholars to assume a link between story and fiction, whereas in fact story structures have no fixed reality status: they range in truth value from total fantasy to crude realism and documentary representation.

Most oral narratives were—and are—canonical, because the limitations on our memory and cognitive capacity make it difficult to accommodate any radical alteration in the temporal order (Mandler 1984). Thus, even where oral stories are concerned, the distinction between story and discourse is of limited value, because one of the main practical uses of the story-discourse distinction has been as a tool for describing texts with a scrambled temporal order and for comparing several versions of the same story. But if there is no scrambled temporal order and no alternative versions exist, the only use that one can make of the story-discourse distinction is to consider the degree of story compression and the focus on important events. A notable feature of oral narratives, and one that many have identified as a defining feature of story as such, is that they tend to deal with highly salient themes—love, conflict, death, and so on—and leave out more trivial events. But to define story as a compressed narrative that focuses on the high-order experience of key existential situations and excludes the representation of trivial events proves problematic.

Prelinguistic mental narratives probably involved a high degree of selectivity in choosing the aspects of a given experience that would feature in the story: some aspects of the experience were probably more important than others. Thus the tendency to compress a story and focus chiefly on salient events reflects an aspect of the mind's general functioning, in which priorities are made for access to the limited space of the working memory. Joseph Anderson (1996) has described the important role that superior structures play in the comprehension of detail. Compression may thus be seen as a protodiscursive phenomenon, because it is not really possible to distinguish between a story "as it really happened" and its presentation. What is compressed in a given story depends on the story's purpose.

By enabling us to assume a third-person perspective, verbal representations also greatly enhance the experience of stories that depend on certain third-person emotions, such as sympathy. The most fundamental emotions—love, hate, jealousy, curiosity, sorrow, and fear—can only be fully experienced in the first person (see chapter 8). But the assumption of a third-person perspective enables us to simulate these emotions and modulate them through sympathy, as, for example, when we pity the tragic hero or admire the superhuman. First-person emotions are dynamic in the sense that they stimulate us to action, whereas third-person emotions such as pity or admiration, though they too may motivate action, tend to be more static dispositions. Certain theoreticians have argued that emotions based on sympathy are more valuable than first-person emotions (especially those involved in active coping), and that they feature more prominently in stories. Thus, for instance, Marie-Laure Ryan (2001) uses this emotional valorization as an argument against video game stories and, in some cases, virtual reality stories because such stories tend to focus on first-person emotions, whereas novels, for example, excel in evoking sympathetic involvement. However, it is highly problematic to use the ranking of emotions in Maslow's pyramid of needs as the criterion for deciding whether something counts as a story or not. From an evolutionary perspective, first-person emotions such as the urge to explore and fight (based on the sympathetic nervous system), or those associated with sex, food, and laughter (linked to parasympathetic reactions) have played a more fundamental role in stories than emotions expressing sympathy, linked to historically later phases in the development of storytelling.

The invention of dramatic representation expanded the story experience still further. The dramatic form (re)infuses the story representation with online perceptual qualities. The actors are physically present and some dramatic representations rely on sets and props. Although the spectators may mentally identify with the protagonist, they view the representation from a third-person perspective (both because they sit at a physical distance from the stage, and because actors are seen phenomenologically from the outside). The physical constraints on dramatic performance mean that some stories are better suited to dramatic presentation than others. Verbal narratives have no difficulty in representing movement over vast spaces or sudden jumps in time, in handling complicated props and describing complex actions, or in accelerating and compressing time. Drama is confined to a more limited space and to the representation of a few temporally contiguous scenes. But it is well suited to representing personal interaction associated with emotionally laden events, from courting to jesting to tragic death. Theater has prompted a series of ancillary techniques, from the art of making sets to the art of structuring events and characters.

Dramatic representations mostly take place in the present tense, and thus provide an additional challenge to the belief that a core element of stories in general is their pastness. There are good emotional reasons why the present tense experience is central to the story mode. In order that our curiosity be awakened and our desire for action stimulated, we need to have the sense that the story's ending is still open and undecided. If we know for certain that the hero is going to fall into the pit, there is no reason to feel fear or to simulate active coping in order to avoid the danger; all we feel is a distanced pity. Similarly, there is not much suspense if we know for certain that the hero is going to win the heroine. Earlier in this chapter, I discussed how many viewers are excited by suspense films that they have seen many times (see also Vorderer et al. 1996), and you might think that this contradicts the need for uncertainty. However, as argued, this proves that if a given situation is salient enough, even previous viewings cannot make the experience past and mediated, and even knowledge cannot control the emotional urge that is cued by the salient situations.

Although tales are told in the past tense, the listener will take that past point in time as the focus of presentness and construct an open future. The problem with certain types of strongly narrative video games is that it is difficult to simulate such stories in dynamic real time, and this deprives the player of the vivid sense of experiencing the story in the present tense.

The dominant present tense of drama may be somewhat blurred by the fact that some dramas, such as the most famous of the Greek tragedies, are based on stories that are well known in advance, so that the viewer may already know what is going to happen and may be curious only to see how it will be enacted. Tragedies and melodramas represent a special type of story because they rely on passive emotions, the acceptance of loss, or on third-person emotions. In such stories, the sense of pastness, the knowledge that the die is cast and the outcome fated, plays an important role in blocking the present-tense experience that would make it more difficult passively to accept the painful and inevitable. The fact that the characters' fate has already been decided blocks the active coping mechanism and thus the temporal active directedness that is the hallmark of the present tense, and this eases the transition from first-person to third-person emotions (see chapter 10 and appendix), including such action blockers and agency blockers as sorrow and crying, which are typical of passive melodramas (Grodal 1997). However, to create a feeling of pastness in films and theater is an uphill battle that demands that the feeling of pastness is continuously cued; else the viewer will return to the default mode, the present tense. Comedies, another ancient dramatic form, do not usually need or presuppose this pastness.

The invention of writing and print enabled us for the first time to present our stories in a written form. By fixing the story in an external storage medium, written representations overcame some of the memory constraints of oral stories. The written medium is able to accommodate complex narratives, including discursive rearrangements. It may emphasize the pastness of the experience, and at the same time enhance the sense that the story is fixed, because the beginning, middle, and end already exist physically in a fixed form. But this does not prevent us from reading such stories in a simulated present and feeling that the outcome of a given narrative is undecided; the medium merely emphasizes the fixity of the story (and often the third-person perspective). In the 20th century, film and TV fiction became the prime vehicles for basic storytelling, whereas high art literature increasingly laid weight on the discursive dimensions of the story, using complex narrative strategies or adding nonnarrative material such as philosophical reflections. Mainstream literature, however, still tends to adhere to reasonably canonical storytelling.

The invention of film created a new medium for the simulation of fundamental story experiences. Like theater, film enables us to present events in a direct perceptual form. In some respects, the screen does not have the same intense physical presence as the stage, but at the same time it is free of some of the constraints of theater. Films make it possible to move freely through time and space and to cue and simulate an experience that is close to first-person perception, either directly, through subjective point-of-view shots or by shooting from positions close to the characters, whereas the theater imposes a fixed and distant perspective on the viewer (Balazs 1970). The focusing and framing of the characters, objects, and events simulate and cue our attention. Moreover, film can represent various aspects of reality with photographic verisimilitude. Since it is an audiovisual medium, film's dominant temporal dimension is the present tense: we witness the events in the story directly. It is possible to present parts of the story in the past tense, but this is not the norm as it is in written stories. The natural focus of the film story is on the now, with an undecided future that has to be constructed by the actions of the hero. There are also strong emotional reasons for keeping largely to the present tense, because present-tense narratives prompt the emotions associated with active coping (hate, fear, love, desire), although the medium also excels in presenting passive emotions.

The dominant mode of representation in film is canonical, because film viewing often takes place under strong time constraints that strain the viewer's cognitive capacities (Bordwell 1986). In mainstream cinema, these mental limitations deter filmmakers from too much narrative complexity. This does not mean that films never use the more complex forms of representation associated with written narratives; art films, in particular, often do so by introducing explicit narrators and discursive rearrangements. But in mainstream cinema such devices are used mainly for specific purposes (explicit narrators, for example, are generally used to create passive effects, while discursive rearrangements serve mainly to introduce subjective dimensions such as flashbacks to childhood experiences).

Computers present the newest medium for story simulation. By contributing an interactive motor dimension to the story experience, computer media have added a powerful new dimension to the simulation of first-person experiences. The motor links involved are still primitive compared to the capacities used in our physical interaction with real-life environments (in this context, speech is also a motor act). However, whereas with earlier media the eye and ear activate only the premotor cortex, computer simulations activate the full motor cortex and muscles. Like the cinema, the video game screen predominantly simulates perceptions of spaces and objects that are present to the senses, but in this case the people and objects on the screen can be influenced by the viewer's actions. In some respects, as we have seen, video games are the medium that comes closest to the basic embodied story experience (for a discussion of video games, narratives, and agency see also Grodal 2003a; Gregersen and Grodal 2008).

The interactive aspect of video games also raises a series of problems that did not arise with the earlier media, but resemble those involved in interacting with real-life phenomena on a first-person basis. The reader or viewer of traditional mediated stories needs only to activate certain general cognitive skills, including the ability to form expectations. Indeed, the story will proceed even without such expectations. The computer story, by contrast, develops only through the player's active participation, and in order to develop the story the player needs to possess a number of specific skills, from concrete motor skills and routines to a series of planning skills. This new form of activation thus intensifies the problem of mental capacity, and the increased demand on working memory space also increases the player's degree of immersion (Murray 1997).

In the earlier media, the development of the story is controlled by the author or director. Following the protagonist through space (imagining, for instance, that a character somehow gets from his apartment in Berkeley to Golden Gate Bridge) requires only somewhat vague mental models; detailed cognitive maps and eye-hand coordination are not necessary. In order to understand what is happening when John Wayne shoots an opponent, we need only a crude model of the actions involved, not a precise motor program for grasping the gun and aiming precisely. But in order to be able to play video games with similar scenes, we often need quite detailed cognitive maps and motor skills, and may therefore require extensive training. One of the reasons video games are called games is precisely that they involve the repetitive training in coping skills that is a distinguishing feature of game playing. Video games therefore face the challenge of combining a high degree of interactivity and a high level of story compression. For this reason, many video games provide the compressed information in a filmlike fashion in the noninteractive "cut scenes," whereas in the key interactive scenes the stories are often expanded, giving the opportunity for more detailed action than can be found in other media.

A central aspect of game playing is that the problem solving it entails requires extensive training of basic motor skills and eye-hand coordination. Such activities take up a lot of time, not least in the earlier phases of life, in performing routine jobs, and in sports, and everyday life is full of practiced, skillful activities that nevertheless rank low in the nested hierarchy of goals and actions. Such activities may often be very gratifying for those that perform them, but they are much more difficult to communicate to other people than higher order goals and activities. A short story about how a future prince killed a dragon and won the princess is easy to communicate, whereas most people will not be interested to hear the details of how you managed to do a very practical job or how you improved your eye-leg-arm coordination to become a good skier. Modernist novels or films that provide very circumstantial descriptions of basic activities are often considered dull by people who prefer more conventional stories that focus on higher order goals and include fewer everyday details. Video games thus represent a new form of storytelling that integrates high-order goals with low-level muscle- and attention-training stories, in a medium that allows for the mass production of such experiences. As suggested above, the repetitive training aspect of video games is one reason that they are referred to as games, even though the activities involved are mostly framed by higher order goals that provide the superior motivation.

Play, Game, Narrative, and Fiction

Narratives and games seem to be related and may sometimes even be two different ways of describing the same phenomenon. The term *game* is a very loose one; Wittgenstein used it as a prime example of a category based on family resemblance, while Lakoff (1987) used the notion of family resemblance to describe categorizations based on prototypes. There are no necessary and sufficient conditions for belonging or not belonging to the category games, only a loose network of interconnected resemblances. Several video game researchers have used Roger Caillois's (1958) categorization of games as a tool for characterizing games in contrast to narratives. Caillois divides games into four types: Agon (competition), Alea (chance), Mimicry (simulation), and Ilinx (vertigo). Mimicry may be used in play but is also a key feature of film and theater. Both Ilinx and Agon are central elements in many action films. Alea plays a prominent role in lotteries, for example, but is not a typical feature of either visual fiction or of video games, even though most events in this world of course contain an element of chance.

It is more rewarding to embark from a more general definition of *play* and then describe games and fictions as special forms of play. The ability to play is an innate feature of all mammals (MacLean 1986; Panksepp 1998; Björklund and Pellegrini 2002). To play means to perform an activity for pleasure, not out of necessity, although play has survival value insofar as it trains us in important skills, from motor skills to imagination and hypothesis forming (Pellegrini et al. 2007). Cats play fighting or hunting, and although their playing may enhance their skills in real-life fighting or hunting, their intentions in the play situation are not the same as they would be in a real fight or hunt: their claws are withdrawn. Humans play cops and robbers, perform plays, or take part in soccer or monopoly games, but these remain forms of play so long as they are not carried out with real-life intentions: so long as the players do not aim to kill each other or risk their fortunes. Thus the reality status manifested in a given play activity is a defining aspect of the concept of playing.

In some (realist) fictions, the fictive playfulness of the action is only a general prescript that prevents the viewer (or actor) from confusing the fiction with reality, but in several respects such fictions are consumed as if they were real. Other fictions are overtly playful. Some are fantasy stories that delight spectators or readers by violating the laws of reality. Others—notably comedies—prompt spectators to see the action as playful. Thus situation comedies like *The Cosby Show* clearly signal that the characters in them, like circus artists, are going to enact an artist performance designed to please the audience, and this sense is enhanced by the laugh track on the show. The more the "fourth wall" of the theater is negated, and the more the actors communicate not only with other people in the diegetic world but also with the spectators, the more we will be inclined to think of their activity as a performance, a game. Such comic shows never come to any final conclusion because in the next episode the action will start all over again; likewise we know that Laurel and Hardy will never develop as people but continue forever repeating the same stupidities. Thus (realist) fictions often claim serious intentions, whereas games and shows overtly acknowledge that their intentions are playful.

A central element in the playful activities that we call games is their repetitiveness, because repetitive (reversible) actions are somehow felt to be less serious, less real than those in tragic stories that represent irreversible processes. A sophisticated viewer of, say, a tragic Western might see the film as a game, as less real and serious than it appears, because he or she recognizes in it a formal structure consisting of elements that could be repeated in other Westerns. Thus we might define games as a special kind of playfulness characterized by a virtual or actual element of repetitiveness, linked to a conscious feeling that the activity consists of exploring some pattern-bound, rule-bound possibilities (narrative schemas, comic schemas, etc.). The repetitiveness may diminish the degree of seriousness felt by viewers or participants. Although some activities may give more scope for playfulness than others, playfulness depends on subjective attitudes and skills as well as on objective factors. Just as a Western can be enjoyed both as a serious simulation of reality and as a game that follows certain prescribed patterns, so a video game can be played in both a serious-realist and a playful mode. The ease with which we can start a new game is certainly an indication of playfulness, but there is a trade-off between the depth of involvement and the degree of playfulness. David Bordwell (2002) has described a group of films that try out different options, different futures, thus telling stories that wind back to a possible point of bifurcation. The viewer's experience of such films may often change from the mimetic to the playful. Spectators watch the first version of the narrative in a more serious, existential mood than the versions that follow, because by versions two and three they are aware of the filmmaker's playful intentions, as in Tom Tykwer's

Lola rennt. However, if the film's use of multiple futures is based on some super-natural premise, as in *Groundhog Day* or *Terminator 2*, the viewer may accept alternative versions with the same kind of existential involvement, because they are no longer seen as playful repetitions but as consequences of supernatural laws (see the discussion of ritual in chapters 5 and 6). The lack of depth of involve-ment may, however, be an advantage if the purpose is to try out roles that conflict with our normal identity-defining behavior (as when we play at being monsters, killer-drivers, angels, or devils). Here, the role-playing playfulness may function as an excuse for exploring suppressed or virtual aspects of ourselves.

Mediated fictions are mostly enjoyed perceptually from a third-person per-spective that in some cases is simulated mentally from a first-person perspec-tive, whereas many types of play are not only spectator sports but can also be enjoyed—even in their motor dimensions—from a first-person perspective. Fic-tions are about the concerns of anthropomorphic beings, whereas some kinds of games, such as solitaire, lack an anthropomorphic dimension. Moreover, from a first-person perspective most kinds of play are repetitive in nature, although competition may give rise to distinct events. Thus the spectators' experience in watching a big professional soccer game resembles that of watching a drama in the theater, though the players themselves may lose their sense of playfulness because their pay, honor, or job may be at stake in the game and their motivation is therefore serious. Whether a given game represents a unique event or part of a repetitive series depends on subjective, experiential judgments: players of all kinds of games or consumers of stories may experience the game or story on the superior level of pattern repetition, or focus on the unique variations of a genre or a game world (in structuralist terminology, they may have either a system-based or a manifestation-based experience). Film buffs may be more prone than the naive viewer to see genre films as a game.

Stories and games are prototypical categories (or, in Wittgenstein's terminol-ogy, categories based on family resemblance). They bleed into each other and can-not be sharply delimited from other categorizations. Thus, shooting and adventure video games, which are based on intelligent agencies acting in time-space, resem-ble the prototypical story, whereas other games—such as Tetris—are less closely linked to stories. Similarly, some film forms like parodies or some types of metafic-tion signal playfulness, whereas other forms signal a nonrepetitive commitment.

Linearity, Nonlinearity, and Interactivity as Agency

I noted above that, unlike the reader-viewer of mediated stories (and other texts), the user of video games and related phenomena such as hypertexts needs actively to develop the story. This development is often described by means of certain 'hyped' terms such as *interactivity* and *nonlinearity*. Such terms often return with a vengeance to noninteractive narrative forms that are considered to be rigid and dictatorial, although some may be reinterpreted as allowing the reader-viewer actively to create the story (see Barthes' 1974 description of the "writerly" text). The use of the word *interactivity* very much focuses on ideas of being in control as opposed to being passive victims of incoming information.

The media theoreticians Bordewijk and van Kaam (1986) have attempted to construct an objective typology of different types of communication. Traditional one-way media such as television are "transmissions." Information that is produced by a "center," but the distribution of which is controlled by the user (as in the case of a database or video game), is characterized as a "consultation." The true interactive forms are the telephone, e-mail, chat groups, and so on, because only these media formats enable the user to both produce and distribute information. But such a description clearly violates normal language. We do not consult Doom in order to find out what information the producers of that game have provided: we play the game in order to get an experience that simulates the way in which we might act in a hypothetical world. Our primary model is the way in which we experience interaction in the real world.

Both in the real world and in simulated worlds, our influence is limited by the general design of the world in question: we follow roads, tunnels, or career tracks, and obey rules, but within a given framework we may alter certain elements, take different roads, build houses, and so on. The only necessary condition for experiencing agency is that our actions make a difference. Our experience of agency is not limited to motor actions; active visual attention creates a sense of agency provided the agent feels that she or he is in control of that attention, and thus film viewing may provide the viewer with a strong sense of agency. But we may also feel that our eyes are passive victims of films or worlds that dump unwanted visual material on our retinas.

A key element in creating the sense of agency and interactivity lies in the ability to change our experience. In real life I may have a sense of agency by going to Italy and altering my experiences in that way; this might be described as "exploring the database Italy" and it does not change the world itself in any significant way. The database Italy is pretty much the same after my visit, but I nevertheless experience agency in my power to change my own mental states through navigation, just as I may have a sense of agency in watching a film motivated by interest. When I wander around in a mystery, adventure, or shooting game, I cannot change the fundamental layout of the game world, just as I cannot change Italy by my visit. Thus interactivity is not primarily about changing a given world but about changing the mental states of the experiencer, whether that occurs through changing certain objects in the world or by altering his or her point of view or experience. The term *interactivity* is often used in a hyped fashion in which the essence of interactivity is seen as the possession of free, demiurgic powers to (re)create the world. Instead, we should understand interactivity as the creation of experiences that appear to flow from one's own actions, including the ability to devote attention to phenomena.

Our experience of our scope for interaction is not constant over time, but influenced by novelty-habituation cycles. When we embark on a new form of activity or start exploring a new environment, we may feel that we have many options that depend on our own choices. However, as we learn more about the given activity or environment, we acquire an increasingly clear map of our options and may even come to feel that we are simply alienated robots, following the commands of society or our own fixed compulsions. Likewise, when we watch our first genre film we may think that the characters have unlimited possibilities in a live world, but once we have watched 1,000 crime fictions we may start to feel that we are simply watching automatons going once again through the same old drill. However, we may also increasingly take metapositions and analyze the design and the craft of the given instantiation of a general pattern. Aesthetic experience therefore develops over time. When we start on a new aesthetic activity, we may feel that there are many different routes to follow and that the story line or melody may proceed in many different ways. This experience applies not only to individual works: a given narrative world such as the Western or film noir, a given narrative, or a given melody may appear to offer scope for numerous variations. But when we gain greater mastery, we not only start to see the given story world as a series of potential routes; we also start to create a total map of that world and realize that we have only a limited set of options. Connoisseurs enjoy works at this level: they review the possible options and enjoy observing how the artist chooses among them. Such experienced viewers or players are more likely to experience the artwork as a message from the artist or producer, because they can see the design and artistic intentions as a choice between options. Observing fictions and games as forms of communication spoils certain types of fun but creates other connoisseur pleasures. The connoisseur watching *Psycho* may ask the question, "Will Hitchcock kill this woman?" instead of simulating her destiny as a real-life event. Similarly, in some cases the pleasure of game playing lies in simulating an experiential flow, while in others the pleasure consists in gaining insight into the creator's intentions. Our experience of basic mimesis is one of naturalness, "it has to be so." By contrast, our experience of art as style is based on our insight into the way in which a given artist realizes specific intentions that are only fully understandable as a choice selected from among several possible options (Gombrich 1968), and this demands expertise. The metaphors "art as an experiential route" versus "art as a map and as a system" sum up the two poles in the aesthetic experience (novice-master) and may perhaps also cover the way in which texts can be experienced either as mimesis or as art.

The term *nonlinear* is closely related to the question of interactivity, because many scholars within the humanities take nonlinearity to be a key aspect of interactivity and supreme agency. The term is heavily loaded with associations emanating from different strands of postmodernist-deconstructionist thinking, including those derived from Derrida. According to this philosophy, linearity is a product of Western, metaphysical "logos" (causal) thinking, and is enhanced by the linearity of alphabetic writing. These ideas often carry the patronizing implication that non-Western people are more illogical than Westerners. The computer hype version of nonlinearity consists in claiming that computer media have the potential to emancipate us from these metaphysical and ideological constraints.

However, linearity is not a product of Western metaphysics but is based on fundamental features of the world, action, and consciousness. An experiential flow—unless totally unfocused—is a linear process in time. At the same time, linearity is a mental representation of an essential feature of the world, namely that it exists in time, and that time is experienced as linked to irreversible processes. Such processes are represented mentally by concepts such as cause and effect. The sun begins to shine and the snow melts. The arrow pierces the heart and the person or animal dies. The man enters the tunnel, goes through, and emerges on the other side of the mountain, and so on. Lakoff (1987) has shown how such causal links are universally represented by source-path-goal schemas. Our whole conceptual machinery is based on such linear processes and on concepts of causality that we share even with animals. Linearity and causality in science are only sophisticated versions of innate mental mechanisms that developed because of their survival value. Actions are causes that make a difference, that have an effect, and it would therefore be difficult to construct a story that was not based on some kind of linearity and causality, for it would mean that the actions in the story would make no difference.

A given effect may have different causes: the street may be wet because of rain or because a city water wagon has passed. We may construct video games consisting of different paths that intersect each other at certain points. In one of the story lines we may arrive at a given space after following a path that simulates rain, while in another story line we may arrive at the same space by another path, after witnessing a water wagon showering the street. Thus by offering several linear trajectories to the same point, we may create ambiguity, offering one effect from several possible causes (seen from a system point of view, as in the deliberations of possible motives and causes in crime fiction, including representations of alternative possible scenarios). It is evident, however, that because a given effect cannot have an unlimited number of different causes, there can only be a finite number of causally motivated criss-crossing paths (see Ryan 2001). A hypertext such as a computer story in which all the scenes of the game were connected by a complex web of links would have to be fairly primitive, or have only insignificant effects. It would be impossible to figure out hundreds of different paths crossing in hundreds of different scene-nodes that allowed for significant processes and actions irrespective of the concrete trajectory taken in the web of links. Thus such "alinear" hypertext web structures give rise to association-like phenomena (similar to those created by dictionary cross-reference links, lyrical associations, literary allusions, etc.) that derive their significance from the accumulation of associations. But complex hypertext-like networks do not give much scope for narrative actions that rely on causality, a certain time direction, and some degree of irreversibility. Networks of (lyrical) associations and linear (narrative) trajectories are linked respectively to two different types of emotions: on the one hand, the unfocused emotions that I have called "saturated" (Grodal 1997), and on the other "tense" emotions, such as aggression, that motivate action and require a linear-causal setting. Media cannot change our innate cognitive and emotional architecture, only give rise to products that may activate and enhance different aspects of the innate specifications.

The reason for having multiple choices and multiple possible story lines is to simulate the feeling of (relative) freedom of choice that we may have in real life, or to fulfill a utopian-romantic wish for a virtual world that liberates us from the restrictions of the real world. From this point of view, then, the creation of several alternative routes simulates freedom. We may, for instance, follow a path that requires us to kill a dragon in order to proceed to the princess, whereas the trial we encounter on another path to the princess may consist in solving a riddle. But choices based on path bifurcation and path separation also entail certain constraints on significance, because if one path involved the hero losing an eye, while the other did not, the two paths could not meet (except in those supernatural stories that are able to undo everything by miraculous means). If choice is created only by combining several alternative paths leading to different goals, then what we have is really a collection of linear stories. They merely serve to make explicit what is implicit in other story forms, namely that our comprehension of the story is based on the understanding that, as Bremond (1964) observed, the story represents a series of forks or choices between alternatives. We may go left or right, the hero may win or lose the battle, and so on. In conventional stories, these options are only virtual even in the second reading or viewing, whereas a computer story may be constructed in such a way that what was only virtual in the first game is chosen and actualized in the second.

Thus we may conclude that stories are essentially linear in their realization. First, our experience of all texts, even hypertexts, is linear, just as a taped recording of our hypertext activity, our Net surfing, or our consultation of an electronic dictionary with links between articles and terms would be linear. Second, the story as a sequence of significant events is linear because a significant story relies on causality, on irreversible processes, and on the choice of a trajectory of action. Freedom is the transient feeling that precedes a choice. This insight may be blurred by the fact that a given story world may allow for different stories and different choices of paths (and in computer stories, different player performances). However, we need to distinguish between the experience of the story and the objective scope of the story world, because a given story world or game world may give scope for one or several story experiences (Bordwell 2002). A large collection of Westerns or crime fictions might constitute a kind of Western world or crime world in which each individual film would be one of the potential stories made possible by that world. However, our awareness that a given game or story world offers one or several potential stories is not an alinear experience but a metaexperience, one that allows us to have a mountaintop panorama or map of that world and its different linear routes. In psychological and experiential terms, we might say that our visual perception is a two- or three-dimensional field supported by a multidimensional and atemporal web of associations, but that our actions are based on linearity and time and the basic narrative mode is therefore linear.

It might be objected that this view is contradicted by stories involving a very scrambled narrative or a fundamental rearrangement of the canonical narrative order. However, what we need to consider is the sense in which the underlying canonical story is important to the narrative. I would argue that such narratives are based on saturated associative networks that are linked to the linear discursive surface. When it is impossible on first viewing to reconstruct a canonical narrative, as in the case of Resnais's *Last Year in Marienbad* or Nolan's *Memento*, instead the viewer experiences a linear, loosely organized narrative with weak causal links.

Conclusion

Narrative mechanisms are central for human meaning making in general. They are supported by a series of mental functions, predominantly located in the frontal lobe but also in the limbic system and brain stem. The nonmedia use of narratives serves to provide a framework for agency by planning and controlling actions and by welding together plans, goals, and motivating emotions in a PECMA flow, although motor implementations only take place in full in video games. The narrative actions are supported by mechanisms for keeping track of the past as a background for motivation. The default mode of narrative is therefore a linear time and a presence in time-space of some agencies that have goals or interests that point to the future. Different media afford representations of different aspects of such experiential sequences.

Basic narratives such as orally transmitted narratives are simple due to memory constraints, whereas stories supported by external storage media such as writing, film, and computers can be more complicated, although media such as films are constrained in making complicated deviations from a basic canonical mode by the fact that—contrary to books—viewers' processing capacity needs to match the continuous audiovisual stream (although "interactive" media like tape and DVD provide freedom to control viewing speed).

There are two basic modes of processing narratives, a serious mode and a play mode. The serious mode is linked to an irreversible time in which consequences are final, whereas the consequences may be undone and actions repeated in the play mode. The serious mode is supported by what Panksepp (1998) calls the seek system, although its reality status is modified by what Panksepp calls the play system. A special variation of the play mode is comic fictions in which laughter (change of reality status) further wipes out the seriousness of consequences. Viewers may also view films made in a serious mode from a distanced position as games made by filmmakers, and in such viewings the focus is on craft and an expert understanding of the options and choices made, not on simulating an immersed experience (that will be the focus of chapter 8).

Besides the linear structure typical of representing irreversible action in time, the brain has another mode: the associative atemporal linking of phenomena. It has—erroneously—been argued that the linear mode is a special Western form, and that broken narratives or hypertexts are such unideological forms. However, linearity and associative principles are two basic brain modes, the first linked to the embodied action in time and space, the second linked to the makeup of our interior neural networks and to the three-dimensionality of space.

8

Character Simulation
and Emotion

In this chapter, I analyze the way that viewers simulate film fictions and show how simulations of characters and fictitious worlds are central to the film experience. I thus elaborate on the simulation theory that I presented in *Moving Pictures* (Grodal 1997) and argue that films cue different engagement positions in relation to characters, from immersed emotional simulation to distant observation. I go on to argue that the problem with many rival theories of film viewing derives from erroneous ideas of how we experience everyday life.

A number of film theories claim explicitly or implicitly that film is experienced solely or mainly from the point of view of an observer. This applies, for instance, to Noël Carroll's theory of emotions (Carroll 1988, 1998). Carroll states that when we watch a fiction film our emotions are "similar to [those] of onlookers or observers, not participants" (1998, 260). He goes on to say, "We do not become the character or acquire her goals. The character's emotion does not transmigrate into us. Rather, our pre-existing dispositions to certain values and preferences are mobilized by the text's providing an affective cement that fixes our attention to the text and shapes our attention to ongoing situations" (269). Thus according to Carroll the viewer will rarely share the goals, emotions, and perspectives of the characters on screen. When watching Spielberg's *Raiders of the Lost Ark*, for instance, the viewer does not—if we adopt Carroll's line—temporarily take on and simulate Indiana Jones's goal of reaching the Ark. Similarly, viewers of Spielberg's *E. T.* do not experience in themselves E.T.'s strong urge to go home. Carroll's conception of film viewing seems to be the following: Cognitively I observe, say, the distress of E.T. My "pre-existing dispositions to certain values and preferences" will focus my attention on E.T. and his distress. My thoughts and values may induce me to feel pity for E.T. and hope that he will get home. But the experience is radically different from what E.T. is supposed to feel and experience.

Theorists who take this observer view reject the notion that the film viewer often simulates the characters' emotions, thereby dissociating themselves from the psychoanalytic approach to film. But I argue that these observer theories are unable to provide an account of our experience of fictitious events and their emotional impact. Such theories, indeed, often claim that the viewer is a distant observer, following Bullock's classical idea that art demands distance (Currie 1995; Carroll 1998). Thus observer theories often give impoverished descriptions of the film viewer's experience, focusing mainly on emotions such as pity, admiration, or fear for the protagonist—emotions shaped by the viewer's distanced relationships to other people. They implicitly rule out feelings arising from the viewer's own immersed experience of first-person emotions such as love and fear. As I will show, what distinguishes an immersed from a distanced experience is that the former involves the simulation of action-motivating emotions seen from the perspective of the characters in the film. The question of action is central to our understanding of emotional responses both to film and to real-life phenomena, because emotions represent action tendencies and dispositions. Similarly, the simulation of fictitious worlds is essential in prompting action tendencies. As Zillmann (1991) points out (following McDougall), empathetic simulation is adaptive only if it promotes behavior directed at lessening the model's misery. This explains why empathetic simulations entail action tendencies aimed at transforming a given situation.

Simulation and Film Viewing

Simulation is here understood as a metaphor derived from the world of computers, where computers calculate complicated relations that simulate either thought processes, aspects of the world, or the interaction between thought processes and the world. A good example of a simulator is the flight simulator used for training pilots, in which the pilot is placed in a naturalistic cockpit and all the instruments are hooked up to a computer. In a good flight simulator, it might only be the trainee's knowledge that this is not a night flight that separates the simulation from the real thing. Such simulators have been imitated by the creators of video games. In the flight simulator, you might say that the trainee simulates the psychological and practical processes that he should perform as a real pilot; in video games the player interacts with a fictitious world. The simulator machines provide simulations of real actions and the trainees or players participate in such simulations.

Both in psychology and in film studies, such computer simulations are used as metaphors for a series of phenomena—for instance, imagination, fiction, or thought processes—but also for the way in which, for instance, a screen or a monitor may simulate aspects of the world. Before proceeding to the question of character simulation in film, I will clarify some general problems in relation to the use of the word *simulation* and clarify my use of simulation as distinct from imagination, contrary to a tradition within aesthetic philosophy (e.g., Currie 1995).

One use of the term *simulation* in relation to film studies is as a metaphor for the term *imagination* as done, for instance, by Currie (1995). The basic sense of imagination as used to describe the imagination of poets would be that the poet's mind reactivates different images from his or her memory files in order to, for instance, create a story world. Currie compares such a use of imagination to a computer that is working offline, disconnected from the Internet (the outside world), and calls such imaginations simulations. This may be reasonable: the senses, eyes and ears especially, are not hooked up to the exterior world, and some mental mechanisms trigger those visual and acoustic cortices that normally process information from the exterior world. Such simulation is part of the vital processes by which our minds continuously run all kinds of hypothetical scenarios for various reasons such as planning future actions, playing, or fantasizing.

Then Currie also uses imagination and simulation in parallel with what viewers are doing when they watch a film. Currie claims that what the viewer of film is confronted with is iconic signs that tell us what it is appropriate to imagine. This is a curious formulation, because only extreme semioticians would claim that when we are in real-life situations we are confronted with iconic signs that tell us what it is appropriate to imagine. We do not imagine the real world; we see the real world by means of our eyes and those brain structures that analyze the visual input. We use exactly the same eyes and brain structures when we are watching films and watching the real unmediated world. There is an element of qualified construction when we see the real world or when we see a film, as numerous perceptual psychologists have shown (see Rock 1995), but saying that the brain constructs the world out of sensory inputs is not the same as adhering to solipsism. The people that produce and transmit a film make a simulation of some happenings in the world; for instance, they make a profilmic event in which Michael Douglas walks through San Francisco and pretends to have some intentions, say, to kill somebody. They also make a film recording that when shown will provide the viewer with a simulation of the profilmic event. Similarly, viewers participate in media simulations when they watch the evening news or watch a film; however, they do not imagine what they see. In respect to their viewing process they are online, although they are offline with respect to action and tactility.

The film experience is therefore determined by several interlinked simulations, each with a set of reality status problems. The filmmakers and the communication systems (theater, screen) provide audiovisual simulations of events, the content of which may be fictitious simulations, and the film viewer may to varying degrees resonate with or simulate the events portrayed.

There are probably two reasons why Currie and others use the word imagination in relation to film viewing. The first is a historical one: theories of imagination have their roots in efforts to describe how poets invent things by imagining, running their mental apparatus offline, and this spilled over into descriptions of how readers could make images out of verbal signs even if this process is not quite offline: the readers get input from the book. Film is then described by the same tools, although a standard film directly cues our perceptual apparatus with a little help from our stored images, as also our perception of the real world is aided by our stored images, concepts, and so on. The film simulates some events and scenes that are offline from reality, and viewers see that simulation. The consequence of using the word imagination in the way that Currie and others do is to blur the distinction between experiences activated by inner mental functions and experiences cued by exterior stimuli. The second reason connects to the way in which discussions of the relation between mediated and unmediated access to reality has been mixed with the problem of the reality status of what is presented or represented in audiovisual media. The audiovisual data that activate our eyes and ears are positive exterior facts that trigger our brain. These data and their (preliminary) representation in the brain may have a real and true foundation in some external reality or they may not, and these data may be mediated or unmediated; that poses a series of other problems. We may see a film that triggers our visual system into seeing a vicious troll, and the seeing is online. The troll is not real for two different reasons: because it is an audiovisual simulation of a troll that has no tactile qualities, and because trolls do not exist; they are fantasy creatures. Thus, our total brain processing of audiovisual data in real worlds as well as in relation to audiovisual media consists in different processes: the processing of the visual data to find what they represent and the higher order cognitive evaluations of their reality status in frontal parts of the brain. Are they physically present, are they an audiovisual simulation, are they a documentary, a fantasy event, an animation, are people sincere, or are they pretending? To analyze the reality status of a given set of stimuli demands a continuous series of complex evaluations (cf. the description of reality status evaluations in Grodal 1997 and the introduction to part II).

The salience and impact of the primary processing of audiovisual data are partly independent of the reality status evaluation because the light-transmitted audiovisual data trigger basic visual and limbic centers whether their source is a film or the real world due to the cognitive impenetrability of the low-level perceptual modules (as also presupposed by Currie). If a man sees a picture of a naked woman, he may be strongly aroused because the visual cues trigger desire centers even if the higher reality status evaluators have a clear understanding of the fact that this is only a partial, visual simulation of a woman. If somebody says that there is such a thing as God or an angel or even make an image of God or an angel, this provides a set of positive acoustic or visual facts, and thus they exist in the brain, even if some higher order evaluation in the brain denies the reality of such facts (see the discussion in chapter 5 of how the default assumption in relation to incoming data is that they are true, while disbelief demands an active process of disconfirmation). My description parallels in several respects Carroll's (1990) thought theory of fiction: thoughts about events and agents may have real emotional impact because even if the events and agents are not believed to exist, they are entertained in the mind as nonasserted thoughts and ideas. The difference is that for me, images, sounds, and words are claims of existence because they simulate the world, although our reason most of the time successfully controls their reality status.

However, to delimit the impact of such incoming data is often an uphill fight because many such representations are mind-grabbers. As the example of religious beliefs demonstrates, suspension of belief is often difficult, and thus suspension or control of belief is the central problem in relation to fiction and supernatural phenomena, not, as has been traditionally argued, the suspension of disbelief in relation to fictions or religions.

The fundamental architecture of the brain was made at a time when incoming data were essentially true, so that reality status evaluation was a secondary process and the later cultural development of visual (and acoustic) simulations made it necessary to contain the impact of such simulations by higher order cognitive processes. Thus, whereas Currie, Carroll, and others are focused on explaining how and why we may be engaged in phenomena that are nonexistent and fictitious, I focus on explaining by what mechanisms we may control our engagements with audiovisual data facts that have a nonnatural reality status. We partly react to, say, monsters on film—our muscles may become tense—but adults do not run out of the cinema when evil monsters appear, although many people avoid films that are too mind-grabbing. Viewers may be desensitized by habituation to film events or real-life events. An insight into the processing procedures provides simpler descriptions than those based on imagination because brain-centered description can distinguish between the perceptual-emotional engagement in the incoming audiovisual data and their reality status.

The problems involved in constructing a coherent picture of what is happening in a film are not necessarily different from those involved in understanding what is going on in the real, nonfilm world, just as a pilot performs the same operations when using a simulator as when flying a real airplane. Film viewers see the people and landscapes in the film and do not merely imagine these phenomena, even though they are "output-offline": unlike the players of video games, they cannot influence the film. At the same time, the viewers are explicitly or implicitly aware that what they are seeing is images transmitted by photographic processes or made by computer animation, so their reality status modules tell them that they are offline as far as interacting with that staged reality is concerned. Because viewers do not simply imagine, but see and hear the film, the distinction often drawn between acentral and central imagining (see Smith 1995) cannot be applied so categorically when it comes to film viewing. Viewers' film experience varies, depending on the film input, its salience, resolution, and so on, and depending on their cognitive and emotional state and their evaluation of the reality status of the cued representation and its elements. Just as the performance and experience of a pilot trainee in a flight simulator may vary according to the type of simulator and the trainee's skills and degree of emotional involvement, so the mental resolution of the viewer's film simulation varies. Viewers may be fully engaged in the way that Csikszentmihalyi (1990) described as a flow experience, or their experience may be more or less distanced.

Self-Other Identification: Theory of Mind

Viewers of fiction films simulate the events of the film in relation to the experiences of some living beings. A central question is therefore how these characters influence the way in which we simulate films. Within psychology, there are two rival theories concerning the way we perceive other people and their minds. One is called the theory-theory or the theory of mind that I discussed in the introduction to part II; the other is the simulation theory. According to the theory-theory, our understanding of other people's minds is a special cognitive activity based on a third-person perspective (Leslie 1987) that is especially based on structures in the frontal part of the brain (Gallagher and Frith 2003). Just as we understand physical relationships by constructing theories, so we construct theories of other people's minds, often called by the abbreviation TOM (theory of mind). Sufferers from autism are not able to develop such theories, and are therefore unable to understand other people (Leslie 1987; Baron-Cohen 1995).

According to the alternative theory, simulation theory, people try to understand others from a first-person perspective by running a simulation: if I were in that situation, what would I think or do? Such a simulation does not need to be a copy of the mental processes of the characters, only that the viewer resonates with the characters' cognitive, emotional, and situational experiences. The discovery of so-called mirror neurons has lent new credence to this theory. Mirror neurons are neurons that fire not only when, for example, a monkey plans to grasp something, but also when it witnesses other monkeys grasping. So (part of) the brain mirrors and simulates the acts of others (Gallese 1998; Rizzolatti et al. 2002; Goldman 2006). Furthermore, studies of children have shown that they start performing simulations of other people at an early age (Bråten 2002) and that there is a close connection between the ability to feel specific emotions and to interpret the emotional content of the facial expression of others (Goldberg 2006). Via mirror neurons, the facial expressions' emotions resonate in the onlooker (van der Gaag et al. 2007), and that explains the emotional contagion emanating from close-ups.

However, the theory-theory and the simulation theory do not necessarily exclude one another: in the developmental process, imitation and simulation precede the more sophisticated understanding of other minds presupposed by TOM. A simulation may be cognitive as well as emotional, and the notion of identification with others implies that the experience of another agency involves a kind of simulation of the self. According to Panksepp (1999), the self is located in subcortical systems that generate primitive self-centered emotions and motivations such as pain, fear, anger, separation anxiety, and sexual and maternal urges. The self is linked to motor-related processes and acts as a motivator for voluntary actions. A key aspect of identification with a given character, be it Lassie the dog or Little Red Riding Hood, is that the viewer's basic self-system is activated.

If simulation were the only means to access other minds, this would clearly create problems. In situations where the viewer's knowledge is different from that of the protagonist (as, for instance, in the previously mentioned example of a child knowing that a doll has been moved to another box, with another person who does not share this knowledge), a simple simulation is not sufficient; there needs to be a decoupled understanding and intuitive modeling of other minds. Furthermore, it would clearly be impossible to understand an agent with whom the embodied self was in conflict: you cannot at the same time simulate both self and other—for instance, hero and opponent—by means of mental processes in which emotions and action tendencies are intimately intertwined.

Thus, for example, it would be impossible in this case to simulate the hatred that the opponent feels toward the hero. Fortunately, it seems that we possess the ability both to simulate and to perform third-person TOM-based calculations. Vogeley and Newen (2002) have measured brain activation in people reading four different types of stories: (1) a nonfocused story told in the third person but involving one agent and focusing on physical acts; (2) a story focusing on the experiences of a first-person agent; (3) a story in which a person marked as having first-person status is in conflict with another person; and (4) a story in which two people presented in the third person are in conflict with one another. The first two stories activated the brain in ways that resembled the activation of the self described by Panksepp, while the activation in types (3) and (4) appeared to fit with the TOM account. Furthermore, the study bore out the predictions that would follow from the PECMA model: types (1) and (2) activated not only the emotion centers of the brain but also those involved in premotor activity because self-based simulations activate action tendencies.

From the point of view of the experience of fiction, it is interesting that story type (1), which described the physical activities of a single agent in third-person language ("he"), nevertheless seemed to evoke a reaction compatible with simulation theory (even though the person in the story was a burglar). The strong presence of a single agency involved in a physical activity engaged the (primitive) self-centered emotions and premotor action tendencies. The reason for this is probably that the third person "he" was experienced in this context as an unmarked indicator of agency, evoking the same type of emotions and action tendencies as an "I," whereas in descriptions of a conflict between self and other, as in the phrase "I hit him," the third person has become an object and as such ceases to activate first-person experiences of agency.

One might therefore hypothesize that the basic, default mode of experiencing others consists in a simulation in which emotions and action tendencies derived from the self, that is, first-person emotions, are activated. Panksepp emphasizes that the self is much more closely linked to the body-emotion-action system than to perception, and this accords with the findings from Vogeley and Newen's study, in which a story told in the third person evoked simulation, because this is the easiest and most basic mode of interpreting the actions of others. If linguistic markers such as the use of the third person or the past tense are unimportant compared with, say, an action-oriented forward narrative drive, they are simply ignored or recede into the background.

As I discuss in more detail later, films are often able to engage us on a first-person basis even when we witness the action in some respects from a third-person perspective. However, more complex situations may evoke a different kind of mental modeling, and this will also be reflected in the types of emotions that are activated. If, for example, the viewer is attached to a hero-protagonist but is also confronted with the task of understanding the villain, a direct simulation of the villain would not only activate a cognitive understanding of his actions but also evoke his emotions, and this would be confusing. As we saw in chapter 4, an intriguing villain such as Hannibal in *The Silence of the Lambs* may lure viewers into an identification-based simulation. But even one's relations to oneself often involve a second- or third-person perspective, a TOM-like reasoning, as when people scold themselves for faults, command themselves to pull themselves together, and so on. Large parts of the frontal cortices work to modify or block impulses and create a distance from them. Similarly, our relationship to the main characters in a film will vary according to the situation.

Our experiential flow is, however, not always strongly identified as belonging to us. We may look at a landscape, objects, or people without experiencing any emotions or action tendencies that require us to think of an "I" confronting other things or beings in the world. Our periods of emotional engagement with ourselves and other people are interspersed with periods of disinterested observation.

Roles and Imitations

Central to observer theories of film viewing is a strong distinction between observing something from the outside and experiencing something from within a character: between being an observer and being a participant. However, one of the most fundamental ways in which humans develop is by imitating and simulating the behavior of other humans and other living beings. I learn how to be a professor, a lover, a driver, or a hunter by vividly simulating and copying other people, including their cognitions, emotions, behavior, and goals. Furthermore, most of my personality consists of the different roles that I have learned by simulating other people, and I have acquired aspects of several of these roles by watching films. When I simulate a film character, I do not give up my own personality and become the other; I live out a potential role that I have acquired or am in the process of acquiring by observation and by integrating a first- and a third-person model of myself. The emotions generated by the self are basic and unspecific, and provide a sense of unity and continuity in one's life despite changing life situations and the enormous differences between one's qualifications as a child and as an adult. Such feelings fuel our emotional agency even when we watch a movie about Lassie or E.T., and when cued appropriately the self may prove extremely plastic, especially in fictitious-hypothetical situations. Some viewers, to be sure, have more flexible moral boundaries than others. Moreover, as I discuss later, art films often portray people who are in search of an identity based on consistent values.

The ability to learn by simulation is central to our cognition. Indeed, simulation is a two-way street: as cognitive learning theories have pointed out, we watch other people not only in order to learn how and why they behave as they do, but also to learn how to behave ourselves. Albert Bandura (1994, 66) has commented that "if knowledge and skills could be acquired only by direct experience, the process of human development would be greatly retarded." But most learning processes can in fact take place vicariously, by observing other people and performing a "first person" simulation of their doings. Furthermore, Tomasello (1999) has pointed out that children only get a full understanding of themselves when they are also able to understand themselves from a third-person perspective. Important aspects of my self-understanding are based on also understanding myself as an agency from the outside, as being similar to people that I watch from a third-person perspective, and central social emotions such as shame, embarrassment, or pride are based on taking a third-person perspective on oneself.

In film viewing as in real life, I cannot simulate all roles simultaneously: some roles conflict, as is the case, say, for lecturing and courtship. Some of my possible roles and role dispositions may never be enacted in real life because no suitable situation arises: I perform only those roles that are relevant in a given situation. Likewise, when I simulate a film character, I simulate only those aspects of the role that are cued by the film. Simulating the experiences of a given film character does not create ego confusion, because I am nonfocally or focally aware that I am simulating a character in a diegetic world. Focal awareness diminishes the degree of my immersion: if, for example, I simulate a charming, successful con man I will be aware that this role is acceptable only because I am dealing with a fictitious world, in which the comic toning given the character allows me to be a bit immoral.

The set of features or set of agents that my "self-feelings" comprehend varies continuously, expanding and contracting according to the circumstances. I can watch a soccer match between a Danish and a British team and feel strongly nationalistic, whereas in another situation I may be partisan toward my department as opposed to other departments, my family versus other families, myself versus my partner, and so on. I may suddenly conceive a hatred for all human beings because they shot Bambi's mother, and therefore invest all my self-feelings in Bambi. Thus the focus and boundaries of our feelings of self—feelings that orient us in our actions—are in constant flux, driven by context although limited by our overall values.

The incentive to mimic the roles and situations of other people is even stronger when watching a film than in real life, because, as Carroll (1988, 1998) has pointed out, films are often strongly prefocused, in the sense that the director uses technical and narrative skills to influence or even control the viewer's experience. Key cinematic scenes are constructed in such a way that we are compelled to simulate the perceptions, emotions, and actions of the characters. And this process is not merely abstract and cognitive: it is simulation in the flesh.

The Other as Object and Empathy Antagonism

Our relations to other people do not always involve simulation, and by no means always involve empathy. In real life, certain people are antagonistic to our interests, just as the villains in fiction are antagonistic to the hero. Villains are agencies, but we may treat them as physical objects or use all our general knowledge of living beings in order to hurt or even kill them. As Mithen (1996) and Dunbar (1996) have pointed out, our ability to understand other people is probably developed not only for social purposes but also to understand prey animals (and enemies). Thus in confronting a perceived villain it is important precisely to block emotional empathy or simulation: if a potential victim, confronted by Dracula, allowed herself to be momentarily misled by Dracula's evident pleasure at the sight of a human meal, she might lose the ability to pursue her vital interests. The horror of some of the Dracula scenes consists in seeing potential victims seduced into giving up their own interests and accepting Dracula's bite. Jack Nicholson's smile in *The Shining* evokes a fear that is probably all the greater because protagonists and viewers need to block the simple empathetic mimicry that would implicate them in Nicholson's pleasures.

Many films with a very basic morality may even evoke a total reversal of the normal mimicry of other people's facial expressions. Thus both protagonists and viewers may take pleasure in seeing a villain tortured and moaning in pain, just as some viewers are aroused by slasher films that implicate them in the point of view and emotions of the slasher (Clover 1992). Probably there exist certain basic mental mechanisms that serve during angry confrontations to block the normal transfer of empathy-based emotions; thus Lamm et al. (2007) have by means of brain scans shown how humans' responses to the pain of others can be modulated by cognitive and motivational processes, so that empathy decreases with increasing focus on self. Given that humans have been selected, in the course of evolution, not only by their ability to feel sympathy for their fellow tribe members, but also by their ability as hunters and warriors, capable of defending their interests in the competition for limited resources, it makes sense, alas, to think that, just as we have innate capacities for empathy, so we also have blocking or distorting mechanisms that prompt us to take pleasure in the cries of an enemy and which are aroused by strong stimuli even where these evoke fear (Larkin et al. 2002).

Thus, full identification with or full alienation from the self or the other represent the extreme positions. Our relationship to the characters in a film will therefore vary during the film within a spectrum that goes from the maximum activation of primitive self-feelings, via a broad spectrum of empathy feelings and more or less distanced emotions, to the activation of primitive antagonism and hatred.

Self-Experiences and Point of View

The question of (distant) observation versus immersed simulation is linked to the question of point of view. Clearly, the way in which we experience the world, whether in real life or on film, depends on our optical point of view, anchored in our empirical body and mind. But, as Marr (1982) has argued (presenting a view subsequently elaborated by, among others, Crick and Koch 1993), the visual input we receive through our eyes is only the raw material for constructing object-centered representations. In a similar vein, Husserl and other phenomenologists emphasize that we experience full three-dimensional objects; our minds not only experience the given point of view of an object, we also tacitly experience the full object, which enables many different views (Gallagher and Zahavi 2008).

Our basic attitude to the world implies that it exists independently of our subjective point of view. Often we pay no attention to the point that anchors our point of view; what we attend to is (a part of) the world, a scene that exists in our minds as something given and objective. Indeed, it would often be uneconomical to attend to our optical point of view, since the world is much more constant than our potential perspectives on it. I call this object-centered comprehension. In a scene with fast cutting from many different angles, it would be impossible to reflect on the exact location of the camera. Viewers soak in the information to expand their knowledge of the object. When we are watching John Wayne riding through Monument Valley, we continuously try to model the figure Wayne in relation to the (back)ground (Monument Valley), and shots from different angles are input to this modeling. What we attend to when watching films is also visual information that is salient and relevant in relation to the concerns and goals depicted in a given scene. If a film portrays a character whose concerns we share, our mental and bodily activation results from the salience of the audiovisual information about him or her. A particular optical point of view may enhance salience, but a great many other factors may be equally important in determining what is salient in a given scene. Thus the viewer will use all the available information in order to decide on his or her focus of concern. In general, this focused concern will correspond to what is popularly called character identification, which could also be called agency simulation.

Because our minds partly experience the world in an object-centered fashion, our concerns will be shaped by the coordinates of the diegetic world in combination with its most salient concerns. In Kubrick's *The Shining*, a crucial scene portrays the mad Jack Nicholson character attempting to break into the bedroom of a flat where the Shelley Duvall character and her son have sought shelter. The viewer's attention is immersed in this world and is focused on simulating the Duvall character's situation. She and her son try to escape through the bathroom window; the son succeeds, but the window is too small for her, and she therefore changes plans, grasping a knife in order to confront the intruder. The different optical points of view provide only the raw visual input that enables us to experience her concerns, her emotions, and her action potentials. Even when we see things that she cannot see—for instance, shots of Nicholson—we use this information as raw material for simulating her emotions and action potentials. In other words, our attention is tuned to the diegetic focus of concern, rather than the various optical focuses of the film's information-providing shots.

Our capability of watching films is linked to our ability to model and simulate ourselves seen from the outside. We ordinarily have less visual access to ourselves than to other people. On one hand we experience ourselves as an inner essence, consisting of will, consciousness, and so on, but on the other hand also as a physical object in space, the body as seen by third-person observation (see Tomasello 1999). Ideas of metamorphosis in fairy tales and ideas of spirits of dead bodies are based on this fundamental Cartesian dualism in our thoughts, which is also expressed in all those sentences in which we split ourselves up into an I (powered by basic self-feelings) and an object, as in "I hate myself." To have a full understanding of oneself as a visual body in space, the self-experience that derives from within our embodied mind somehow has to be molded into a self-image that we construct on the basis of our observations of other people. Lakoff and Johnson (1999) have made a very thorough analysis of this double self-understanding of mind and body (subject and self) and, for example, pointed to how films like *Invasion of the Body Snatchers* exemplify this fundamental dualism. In film viewing, we are the body snatchers by letting our self-feelings power some of those characters that we watch. In the cinema, our minds give up control of our own bodies, which are quietly placed in seats in dark rooms, and what enter the eyes are emotionally charged audiovisual data of relevance for the bodies and minds of characters.

The distant observer theory would assume that the typical film activates a kind of focal consciousness about the position from which a given world is optically shown. The viewer is assumed to be constantly or almost constantly aware of his or her role as witness to the diegetic world. This positioning of the viewer elicits cognitive and emotional reactions to the fate of the protagonists. That the viewer is often fully or subliminally aware of his or her position vis-à-vis the film is obvious. But attending to this will often be a much more complicated mental procedure than directly simulating the character's concerns from a point of view within the diegetic world. A keen awareness of the viewer's own concerns in relation to the character will compete with the scarce mental resources available for simulating the diegetic events. And, more important, the viewer has absolutely no way concretely to influence the action in the diegetic world. Only the characters in the film can rescue the baby attacked by wolves; the viewer in the cinema is helpless. However, if the narrative makes it possible to simulate rescue options, we will feel far more involved than if we merely feel pity for the victim.

Our ability to experience visual fiction from an immersed position is enhanced by a peculiar aspect of our brains and consciousness. The neuroscientists Milner and Goodale (1996) have discovered that our brains have two different pathways for processing perceptual information. One pathway, the dorsal stream, functions nonconsciously. The dorsal stream controls the actual execution of our actions, such as the way our hand grasps a glass of wine. Thus, the control of our concrete motor interaction with the world lies outside our consciousness. Players of video games may indulge in training the nonconscious (dorsal) procedural knowledge needed to maneuver in a virtual world. The other pathway, the ventral stream, also processes perceptual information, but with a more general purpose: to support planning, choice, and general orientation and motivation. Thus our conscious experience is more disembodied and abstract than many of the nonconscious mechanisms that control our action, and it has a filmlike quality in the sense that it is sealed off from the practical aspects of interaction. The ventral stream and the working memory thus perform functions that are highly compatible with those performed during film viewing. Viewers gain access to perceptual and emotional information; they ponder over or simulate possible actions; but they have no actual control over what happens. The lack of full motor control constitutes the difference between film and computer games; in the case of games, the visual feedback from motor actions provides an additional dimension of immersion.

Distant viewers mainly perform mental actions that "cross over" from their world to the diegetic world, as when they feel pity for the protagonists. They do not simulate actions defined within the diegetic world by the concerns and coordinates of the characters. Many of Carroll's examples are therefore drawn from moments when the diegetic world is fading, often at the end of a film. When a melodrama ends, the film action stops, and the viewer may feel pity for the characters. But this transformation of emotions from character simulation to viewer-centered feelings such as pity is a direct result of the fact that character simulation is no longer possible. Once the film ends, we cease trying to simulate, from the protagonist's own perspective, the various ways he might avoid his fate. Once the protagonist is dead, or if we have arrived at narrative closure, no further character concerns are available. Thus, viewer-centered emotions will come to the fore as the potential for diegetic action diminishes, and films have a series of optical procedures to facilitate such a change from intimacy to distance at the end of a film, like using a crane up, a fade, a long shot, or other devices that produce distance.

Object-centered representations provide us with much more flexible means for the immersed simulation of character concerns and character perspectives. Even though we look at the Duvall character from an optical position outside her mind and body, we can simulate aspects of her experience from the inside. A point-of-view shot may enhance the salience of the characters with whom we empathize. But, as Nick Browne (1982) has pointed out, our simulations are often based on global evaluations, and these may or may not match the optical point of view. Indeed, strong social emotions such as shame or the feeling of being loved are based on understanding oneself from the point of view of others. A key element in *Bridget Jones's Diary* consists in the shame and embarrassment that Bridget feels when she imagines how she looks in the eyes of others, and which we as viewers feel on her behalf. Through TOM activities Bridget and the viewer reconstruct other people's experiences of her, and these influence her emotions and those of the viewers empathizing with her.

Our immersed simulations are facilitated by the fact that, unlike in real life, the simulation of others does not generally conflict with our empirical interests. In real life we may often shun a full simulation of the people we observe because their interests are in conflict with ours, or because we envy their success, whereas in film viewing there is no such conflict or rivalry, since the viewer's real-life interests are not defined in the diegetic world. In the diegetic world, the viewer can often receive the full emotional benefit of identifying with the character's achievements. However, general interests such as class, gender, or ethnic affiliations may impede or block our identification with characters who have different interests from our own, or ones that are antagonistic to ours. Arab viewers may find it impossible to simulate American film heroes shown fighting Arab terrorists. The degree of one's immersion both in fiction and in real-life events fluctuates with the ebb and flow of one's own concerns. If I have no personal concern in a given situation, my mental state will be that of an impersonal observer, and the same applies during those intervals in a film when there is no single strong concern.

Thoughts as Simulations

Observer theories are based on the assumption of a clear division between abstract thoughts and immersed, concrete simulations. Those who adhere to an abstract theory of mental experiences may suggest that on seeing Shelley Duvall in a dangerous situation, the viewer will, in some abstract way, register her situation. But this kind of abstract, distant comprehension is untypical of most viewers' experience. To understand the character's situation in depth is to simulate his or her dilemma with eyes, bowels, heart, cognition, and muscles. The idea of abstract comprehension also underemphasizes the importance of salience. Our emotional and cognitive reactions are intimately linked to the way in which salience (for instance, visual salience) directly impacts on the emotional and cognitive relevance of a given experience.

Traditional psychology has distinguished between perceptual and emotional phenomena on the one hand, and cognitions such as thoughts on the other. The fact that our thoughts may take an abstract linguistic form disposes people to think that the experience of such thoughts is also abstract. But very often the content of thought consists in tacit simulations of perceptual, emotional, and enactive processes. Typically, our understanding is based on reactivations—simulations—of experiences, even when such experiences are verbally cued. This also implies that it is impossible to draw a hard-and-fast distinction between perception and cognition. Perception "is" cognition, and higher cognition is ultimately based on simple forms of perceptual and motor cognition.

Take the following examples: when we speak about a given item, say a cup, we might assume that the semantic content of the word *cup* would exist in a linguistic form somewhere in the brain. But as Damasio and Damasio (1993) have shown, the semantic content exists in the form of percepts that are simulated, or rerun, in the brain. So when I say "a cup," my mind simulates some of the sensuous and motor aspects of the cup. My visual cortex and certain associated areas are activated, and my comprehension of the word thus depends on visual simulation, although this simulation is not usually directly accessible to consciousness: we feel that we have understood the word, but on the whole we do not visualize a cup. Similarly, when we use some of the basic mental metaphors studied by Lakoff and Johnson (Lakoff 1987; Johnson 1987), such as understanding life as a movement along a path, certain premotor neurons are probably activated. Higher mental life is based on an abstract simulation of more primitive schemata, such as—in this instance—moving along a path, being confronted with obstacles, and so on.

Another example: when we see somebody grasp a thing, we simulate, or activate, part of the grasping process; thus the neurons in our premotor cortex that are involved in planning to grasp something are activated when we witness this action performed by someone else. Although the simulation does not usually spill over to the motor cortex (which would cause us actually to make a grasping motion), our comprehension is based on a simulation of the act in our premotor cortex. This effect has been analyzed by the neurologist Gallese (1998), who identified mirror neurons in this context. Mirror neurons also exist in the sensory cortex, which maps the different areas of the body. Thus when we see a man being hit in the stomach, the same neurons that would anticipate such a blow to our own body will also reflect the other person's experience of being hit. To understand is to simulate, even down to the level of understanding that other people grasp or are hit or touched.

A third example: to feel an emotion experienced by others involves an appropriate physical response and a cognitive-motor appreciation of the emotion in question. The mechanism involved in understanding ourselves also serves in our understanding of others, not only from a distanced perspective but in the sense that our bodies and brains simulate key aspects of their situation. Thus it is through our simulation of the Duvall character in *The Shining* that we comprehend her situation (figure 8.1). We may then, for various reasons, dissociate ourselves from her; for instance, by laughing at her or feeling pity for her sufferings. But such a distancing is a secondary reaction that blocks our full understanding; it resembles the reactions of mentally ill people who show no emotional response to possible bodily harm or even death. Duvall's situation can only be fully comprehended through a state of immersion, in which we share her fear and simulate her action tendencies—simulate, for instance, her effort to escape from the bathroom and to allow her son to escape, and, later on, her plan to stab the Nicholson character with a knife. Our simulations are enhanced by the fact that the filmmaker, Kubrick, has provided us with ample information about the character's situation, her emotions, and her goals. It is only through such immersed simulations, in which the feelings and action tendencies prompted by events on screen are closely integrated with one another, that a film is able to induce fundamental emotions such as fear.

The same applies to our experience of a love story. As distanced observers, we might think that Richard Gere and Julia Roberts were attractive people. A distant observation of this kind may even evoke saturated, fetishistic feelings of the kind that film fans display toward photographs of their favorite stars. But if they are to be emotionally stirred by the film, viewers must not only experience the pleasure of watching attractive characters but also be prompted to simulate their action tendencies. To feel the full glow of love, we must experience the desire to come close to the characters by simulating how they approach one another in the diegetic world. The reason that films are able to evoke strong passions is precisely

FIGURE 8.1. The face is the most important cue for understanding intentions and emotions of other minds, and the emotions resonate in the viewers via innate resonance systems (mirror neurons). Here Shelley Duvall, Danny Lloyd, and Jack Nicholson emit emotional signs. The viewer is aligned with Wendy Torrance/Shelley Duvall, emphasized by the gaze of the son, and the viewer resonates with her deeply worried curiosity, amplified by the impact of the anger emanating to the viewer from Jack Torrance/Jack Nicholson's face. *The Shining* © Warner Bros. Pictures 1990.

that they give viewers the opportunity to simulate the actions motivated by such emotions. Distanced observation can be practiced on photographs or stills, but only moving pictures give us the chance to simulate strong passions because they prompt action and change and, as Frijda (1986) has shown, emotions consist precisely in action tendencies.

Distant observer theorists might object that we cannot really act out what we see in films; our mouths are for the most part closed, our bodies confined by our seats in the cinema; we remain seated while all the action takes place up there on the screen. We cannot reach out to touch Richard Gere or Julia Roberts: only the Richard Gere character or the Julia Roberts character can touch one another. However, the film takes place not only on the screen but, crucially, in the various parts of our brains, including our working memory, that support our consciousness. And during the peak moments in a passionate film story, our working memory becomes overloaded. Our consciousness does not have the capacity to attend fully both to an immersed simulation of what is happening in the film and to our thoughts as distant observers. In such situations we therefore focus most of our attention on the information we receive from the diegetic world. Our conscious mind absorbs visual images of Julia Roberts or Richard Gere plus messages of excitement from our bodies and action tendencies from our motor neurons. These messages are relevant to the diegetic world, not to the world we live in. We therefore get additional gratification by simulating the characters' action tendencies and experiencing their emotions. This presupposes, of course, that the viewer's ideas of what to do in the protagonist's situation more or less coincide with those of the protagonist. Strange behavior on the part of the main character creates distance.

Sympathy

There are different definitions of the words *empathy* and *sympathy*. I use *empathy* to describe simulations of other agencies that at least to a certain degree involve emotional action tendencies, say vicarious fear or shame, whereas I use *sympathy* to describe what happens when an agency such as a film viewer is emotionally touched by the fate of another agency, feeling, for example, pity or admiration for him or her. In the case of sympathy, the first agency treats the second as object, in the sense that the sympathy emotions express action tendencies directed at the other agent—for example, to help or submit to him or her. However, empathy and sympathy bleed into each other, which is the reason that differing definitions have been offered.

Clearly, the emotions deriving from empathetic first-person simulations of film characters are not the only ones that we experience as we watch a film. As Ed Tan (1996), among others, has pointed out, sympathy is an important element in film viewing. The capacity for sympathy must originate in the survival value attached to caring for the well-being of other members of the kinds of small groups in which our primate and hunter-gatherer ancestors lived. Sympathy is a strong motivator for parental care of children, for food sharing among the tribe, for helping others to combat enemies, and for expressing care in situations of distress and misery. First-person simulations presuppose that the action tendencies and emotions activated by the simulation are shaped according to the point of view of the person or being in whose situation we are imagining ourselves. By contrast, sympathy presupposes not only that there are strong emotional links between the person sympathizing and the object of sympathy, but that he or she experiences the emotions from a position outside the object of sympathy. This distance is revealed in the action tendencies prompted by sympathy—for instance, the impulse to care and comfort someone in distress. In *Free Willie*, the boy Jesse relates to an orca whale, Willie, partly through simulation, especially since he feels that Willie, like himself, is trapped in a bad situation. But at the same time he experiences other emotions from a position outside that of the whale. Thus the boy feels sympathy for the trapped creature, and this motivates him to take care of Willie and eventually set him free. Most viewers of the film, like Jesse, will simulate aspects of the whale's situation but at the same time feel a strong sympathy both for the whale and for the boy. Their emotions will express action tendencies toward care for Jesse and the orca, action tendencies that stem partly from their position as outsiders.

To a certain degree, sympathetic emotions are based on a form of first-person simulation. Viewers watching the snake pit scene in *Raiders of the Lost Ark* may not simulate the scene in depth from a first-person perspective; thus, rather than simulating the protagonist's fear and related action tendencies, they may predominantly feel pity for Indiana Jones. Their first-person empathy-based simulation is thus transformed into sympathy. The first-person simulation of fear may therefore compete with the viewer's ability to experience sympathy. If you feel sorry for yourself, you may be less motivated to do something about the situation that has given rise to this negative experience because there may be an element of fatalistic acceptance in pity, and to feel sorry for characters may weaken a simulation of active coping with the situation.

Although sympathetic emotions are important to our experience of film, they cannot be our only means of relating to the characters on screen because this would often impoverish our experience. Thus the rule of thumb for predicting whether a given salient film situation will induce simulation or sympathy is whether that situation offers the potential for relief through action. Clearly, pity and compassion are the appropriate reactions when a tragic hero is dying, but they would be inappropriate in the middle of an action film when the hero is temporarily at the mercy of villains, for in this case pity might diminish the simulation of the urge to escape or take revenge. Furthermore, as we saw in the case of *Free Willie*, the sympathetic emotions experienced by the viewer are often based directly on a first-person simulation of the characters' own sympathetic emotions and actions. This is obviously the case in Spielberg's *E.T.* as well. The film evokes strong sympathetic emotions that mimic those felt by the boy in the film as he cares for the helpless alien E.T. The viewer's empathetic feelings are therefore cued by intradiegetic actions and emotions. Sympathetic emotions arise principally at the end of a film when the diegetic action is coming to an end.

The Importance of Salience and Relevance for Character Simulation

My argument so far has focused on the ways that films prompt us to simulate emotions or elicit our sympathy, but I have also mentioned that our immersion and empathy are not always total; thus we may experience large parts of the film from a more distanced position, and different films have different ratios between immersion and distance. Murray Smith (1995) has shown how our relation to film characters may be described by terms such as *recognition, alignment*, and *allegiance*. In addition to this, I will examine some of the elements that influence our degree of immersion.

Let us start with salience. The depth of our simulation of the characters in a film is deeply influenced by the degree of salience in their representation. A close-up revealing strong interest or emotion in the face of a character is much more salient than a long shot, since the resolution with which, for instance, facial expressions and eye movements are shown is so much higher. All other factors being equal, then, the higher the resolution, the stronger the salience. Big screens create greater salience than small screens. There is a quantitative element in our motivation that is also indicated by Smith's term *alignment*: as Reeves and Nass (1996) have shown, strong salience is more motivating than weak salience, irrespective of the viewer's beliefs. Audiovisual salience is important for mental agenda setting.

An important part of the meaning of what we see when seeing a film or seeing in real life lies in the possible future consequences of the present situations. Seeing and hearing cover the here-and-now dimension of the experience, whereas imagination gives us emotionally informed cognitions concerning the future: what phenomenologists call protensions (Merleau-Ponty 1962; Gallagher and Zahavi 2008). The depth of our immersion is also strongly influenced by the importance of the issues at stake, especially if there is a chance that a negative situation will be transformed into a positive one. Action potentials are central to the experience of personal identity, and when these are blocked we may, instead, experience subjective and impersonal feelings that prevent us from simulating the diegetic world and the characters in it and lead us to feel that our experience, as viewers, is a purely mental phenomenon. In this case, we may speak of a mental "invasion" of our experience that inhibits the simulation of distinct characters with action potentials.

Immersion is further influenced by the relationship between the viewer's concerns and value structure and that of the protagonists. Viewers who have a strong aversion to violence may have trouble simulating the main character in Kubrick's *A Clockwork Orange*. Many men have difficulty in fully empathizing with some of the concerns in women's soap operas.

However, as we saw in chapter 4, most viewers do not have a consistent value system: they may hate burglars but share their desire to get rich; they may be in favor of faithfulness in relationships but also excited by clandestine affairs. Thus films that offer very salient portrayals of burglars or adulterous lovers may strike a chord with some of the viewers' concerns while leading them to suppress others, and they will often lure viewers into simulating characters that they would dislike in real life. We do not always act according to our dominant value system; sometimes we commit actions that we would consider reprehensible in the light of our stated values, and we may even hate what we do. Similarly, we may get fully immersed in simulating saliently presented characters, even though their behavior conflicts with our dominant value structure.

Salient presentations may even change viewers' concerns and value structures temporarily or permanently. Unlike Carroll (1998), I would thus agree with a number of theorists from Plato onward that salient character emotions can simply transmigrate into us. The film experience does not consist merely in a distant viewer's projecting his or her values onto the film; rather, there is a constant interaction between viewer and film.

The degree of our immersion in a film's characters and their concerns is also influenced by the overall value structure of the film and by various emotional filters, of which laughter is the most important. Laughter diminishes or blocks the simulation of characters from the inside (Grodal 1997) and constitutes perhaps the most popular form of distancing. Laughter can express sympathy or disgust. Most film comedies oscillate between offering cues for character simulation and creating distance through laughter. For decades, comedy has been the most popular film genre, and one of the main reasons for this is that it allows us to simulate even the most painful experiences by giving us a permanent option to bail out of emotional states through laughter, which transforms the reality of the eliciting emotions so that they are not taken as real (Grodal 1997), thereby renewing our mental energy for further character simulations. From an evolutionary perspective, laughter is an emotional reaction rooted in playing, grooming, and bonding (Provine 2000), and the importance of laughter for humans reflects the increasingly important role of social interaction, with laughter acting as an antidote to a series of empathy-induced emotions such as shame and embarrassment.

In table 8.1 I have described four different prototypes for the way in which viewers relate to film. The distant observer watches the characters from outside the diegetic world with a graded range of distances, from Olympic distance to closeness, and with a range of emotional temperatures, from coldness to warmth in pity, admiration, warm comic distance, or sympathy. Extreme distance may be enhanced by taking a metafictional stance so that the artificiality of the fiction is highlighted, thereby impeding emotional resonance.

I shall not comment further on immersed simulators, which have been a focus of this chapter. Rather, I will make some brief remarks on invaded simulators and interactors. I define an objective world as one that can be the scene of actions or action tendencies. The radical blocking of action therefore leads to

TABLE 8.1. Prototypes by Which Viewers Relate to Film

Distant observer	Immersed simulator	Invaded simulator	Interactors
Viewer takes protagonist as object (pity, laughter, admiration, disgust, cool observational distance), and the distance may be highlighted by taking a metafictional stance	Viewer simulates protagonist from within the diegetic world; the simulation is focused by actions	Viewer simulates nonnarrative experiences; the unfocused experience dissolves the concept of a diegetic world	Viewer interacts with protagonist by elimination of diegetic boundaries, indirectly, as in films like musicals where protagonists address the audience, or by being addressed directly, or by interacting with the diegesis in video games

what I have called invaded experiences: ones that, unlike distant and immersed experiences, are perceived as mental and impersonal, as described in chapter 10. The distinction between viewer and diegetic world disappears. Invaded experiences such as lyrical and subjective experiences are, paradoxically enough, often impersonal; in extreme cases of schizophrenia, the body-world distinction disappears permanently.

Other types of film, by contrast, destroy the diegetic fourth wall by addressing the viewer directly, thereby returning him or her to the reality of the cinema and his or her role as spectator placed in a nonfiction real world. Films such as musicals often have scenes in which the characters perform for the audience; other films have sequences in which characters address the audience. Given finite mental capacity, the attention required to simulate diegetic characters and their diegetic worlds competes with the attention required to focus on one's role as a viewer in the real world. When a protagonist communicates directly with the viewer, he or she therefore diminishes or destroys the latter's ability to simulate the characters. Interactive media such as video games have given rise to new types of experience that allow for the fusion between the roles of spectator and participant (see Grodal 2000; chapter 7, this volume). These interactive media games offer the possibility of an entirely new type of immersion, involving even the element of concrete motor action in the PECMA flow.

A special type of interaction fictions may be called ritualistic interaction. Some scenes in sad melodramas, like those described in chapter 6, are made in such a way that the audience members feel they are participating in a ritual of mourning (as discussed in chapter 6). Similarly, many comedies and sitcoms are made in such a way that the audience members feel they are participating in a ritual of social bonding by defusing through laughter a series of negative emotions such as shame, pity, and embarrassment, indicated in sitcoms by the laugh track, which of course is made to cue contagious mirth but also to position the viewer as a participant in a mutual "grooming ritual" to defuse negative social emotions.

Some of my arguments in this chapter can be summed up in the following theory of film viewing: To begin with, film viewing is based on online perceptions of worlds that are simulated by technical means on screens. Through their higher order mental functions, viewers are aware of the fact that films are representations, and even get pleasure from evaluating the artistic qualities of the show. But these evaluations do not as a rule interfere with the experience of online perceptual realism. Viewers will often simulate the diegetic world from an immersed point of view through character simulation, which resembles what in ordinary language is called identification (though this should not be confused with the psychoanalytic definition of the word). The simulation is usually carried out from points of view within diegetic worlds cued by diegetic concerns and action potentials, rather than starting from the viewer's optical point of view. The simulation is both mental and physical, involving both brain and body.

9

Art Film, the Transient Body, and the Permanent Soul

In this chapter, I analyze some of the concepts and modes of representation that characterize films as art and discuss some of the reasons for the limited appeal of high art to a mass audience. The main argument is that a key difference between art films and mainstream films rests on the difference between portraying permanent as opposed to transient meanings. Our basic experiences of the world are transient in the sense that they stem from concrete, present-tense interactions with the world, involving a constant PECMA flow. However, not all our experiences are of this kind. Our ability to recall the past and to construct schemas creates fields of more permanent meanings, and our ability to produce abstract concepts likewise gives rise to experiences that are beyond the transient level of concrete interaction. High art typically avoids the middle level of concrete (narrative) interaction in order either to evoke abstract or subjective permanent meanings, or to activate a "lower" level of perceptual meaning, style. Permanent meanings are often felt to exist only in our minds, not in the objective exterior world. Works of high art will therefore appear to us both as subjective and as expressing certain permanent, eternal, or spiritual meanings.

Film Art and High Art

The concept of art (and derivatives such as art film) is difficult to define, perhaps because art is a series of different things, related by a Wittgensteinian family resemblance (Lakoff's [1987] description of categorization by prototypes). Aristotle saw art as a craft, based on skills (*techne*) of representation, while for Plato the core of art was mimesis, representations of nature and other aspects of the external world. David Bordwell and Kristin Thompson's (2001) neoformalist concept of film art, in which art is defined through style, has neo-Aristotelian features in its emphasis on stylistic craft. However, their concept is also informed by classical ideas concerning unity (parametric style) and complexity, dear to the aestheticians of New Criticism such as Monroe C. Beardsley (1958). Underlying the romantic notion of art, on the other hand, were two linked ideas: art should present an individualized, original, and subjective vision of the world, and it should express emotions. The creative artistic genius was the source of new (as well as eternal) insights into man and world. Aspects of the romantic attitude underpin many derivatives of auteur theory. It might be suggested that the romantic attitude also involves an aspect of cult, insofar as art is seen as a vehicle for expressing profound and eternal truths about man and world. This is partly due to the fact that, from the early 19th century onward, high art to some extent supplanted religion as the means for worshipping transcendental values. Linked to notions of transcendence is the preromantic idea of the sublime and the Kantian idea of art as a playful freedom from the constraints of necessity in ordinary life and from the drive to fulfill mundane human interests. In the 20th century, Edward Bullock transformed the idea of disinterestedness into a theory of psychological distance, one that is not very friendly to those (often popular) works of art that are based on the strong emotional involvement of the viewer, though it is compatible with Brecht's idea of distancing, *Verfremdung*, as a precondition for the intellectual function of art.

The notion of the artwork as a dense, inexhaustible source of meaning (see Cooper 1995), demanding never-ending interpretation, can be seen as a development of the romantic idea of the rich, original vision, while the idea of art as an institution belongs primarily to the modern day. Clearly the concept of film as high art is influenced by institutions such as festivals, art film houses, film archives, film journals, university departments, and the special audiences created by such institutions. Describing art in terms of institutions avoids having to come up with an essentialist definition. Art is defined historically through the shifting norms and practices of the relevant institutions: thus art is whatever certain art institutions accept as such. A recent theory of art offers, instead, an evolutionary and functionalist explanation: in *Homo Aestheticus*, Ellen Dissanayake (1995; see also Dissanayake 2000) argues that art functions as a means of emphasis, rendering its objects special. It therefore leads us to allocate additional focused and shared attention to a given field and its objects and events if they by style and other features of art are marked as important.

In what follows I do not choose between these definitions of art, on the pragmatic assumption that all the various notions of (film) art in circulation make their contribution to the evaluative processes by which certain films are judged more worthy tokens of art than others. Moreover, it is reasonable to assume that the various criteria can often work together. Manifesting a high level of craftsmanship (*techne*) or emphasis ("making special") are certainly important criteria for high art, but may not by themselves be sufficient. Lars von Trier's *The Element of Crime* or Wenders's *Wings of Desire* are both films that required distinctive professional skills in their making. But it is not easy to determine whether such films demand more professional skill than mainstream films that few would define as high art—say, McTiernan's *Die Hard*—although the skills involved are certainly different. It is fair to suppose that the reason *The Element of Crime* and *Wings of Desire* are conceived as high art, whereas *Die Hard* is not, has something to do with the romantic idea that an original and individual vision of the world, and perhaps some distancing from strong embodied emotions, are prerequisites of art. Such evaluations may also be based on the idea (backed up by art film institutions) that a work of art must be inexhaustible. Moreover, personalized visions may often be thought of as possessing some higher or deeper meaning (I use the phrase *higher meaning* as subsuming these two metaphors). An art film is supposed to express not only formal (stylistic) skills, but also skills relating to content: deeper "visions," for example, into certain central and permanent aspects of the world, society, or the human psyche. This makes the art film well suited for the purposes of a cult, a social institution involving rites that relate to the idea of some permanent and possibly transcendental meanings. On the one hand, therefore, the concept of high art highlights the concrete perceptual level of style, but on the other it focuses on an abstract level of permanent (transcendental) meaning. By contrast, the typical narrative mainstream film concentrates on the middle level of meaning, which is experienced as concrete and transient.

The distinctions drawn between high art, art, and nonartistic mainstream films are of course not absolute. These categories are prototypes from which central and peripheral examples can be chosen. Art film is a subcategory within film art in general. Films that qualify as film art may possess one of several features typical of art films, and art films are sometimes badly crafted. To be an art film is therefore a descriptive, not an evaluative, label. So, although in this chapter I predominantly focus on art films, I also use examples from other films that in one or several dimensions may qualify as film art. *Wings of Desire* and Lynch's *Lost Highway* would certainly count as central examples of high art, whereas some viewers might categorize Almodóvar's *Women on the Verge of a Nervous Breakdown* as a slightly more peripheral example, since the film has a relatively simple narrative. Many "made for an Academy Award" Hollywood films have pretensions to higher meaning, and therefore by some are evaluated as a kind of art, although their lack of a distinctive, salient style means that they too will be regarded as more peripheral examples. Because of its visual originality, some might consider a mainstream film like Fincher's *Se7en* as an example of film art that has more affinity to art films than *Die Hard* or *The Bridges of Madison County*, although others might be more fascinated by the lofty morality of *The Bridges of Madison County* than by the sordid morality portrayed in *Se7en*. Many Academy Award–winning American films express higher meanings by focusing on strong prosocial and altruistic themes and portraying lofty moral ideals, but these films often lack audiovisual originality.

I will argue that the prototypical art film combines stylistic innovation with a claim to higher meaning. The ultimate art film classic, *Last Year in Marienbad* (1961), exemplifies this beautifully, but so do more recent works such as Trier's Europe trilogy (*The Element of Crime, Epidemic, Europa*), the films of Peter Greenaway, and David Lynch's *Lost Highway* and *Mulholland Drive*. All of these are notable both for their stylistic innovation and their suggestion of higher meaning. However, I will also consider films like *Blade Runner* as possible examples of film art because they share several features such as prominent style and higher meaning with art films, although their narrative drive is stronger than that of art films.

Abstraction, Higher Meaning, and Disembodiedness

Films with higher meaning are often characterized by a certain "disembodiedness," in striking contrast to the typical mainstream action film, which is based on embodied interaction with an online reality. David Bordwell (1986) has pointed out that in the classical Hollywood cinema, deviant style needs to be motivated by plot, whereas style in the art film (and the parametric film) may enjoy a certain autonomy vis-à-vis the narrative. I would suggest a psychological explanation for this: narrative films are based on concrete embodiment; they concern actions carried out by human agents for whom mental processes are intimately linked with physical actions aimed at concrete goals. Style in such films thus serves to flesh out these concrete actions and the emotions that go with them. In art films, by contrast, style is often associated with the portrayal of a deviant reality, one that is not accessible through standard online interaction.

These deviant realities typically fall into three categories: levels of meaning that are abstract, symbolic, and above basic embodiment; representations of states of reality that are not embodied online (memories, fantasies, visions); and representations of (possibly online) perceptions that are experienced as subjective because they are not motivated by (or are isolated from) the narrative.

In ordinary experience, we draw a distinction between concrete phenomena with which we can interact physically and abstract phenomena that are beyond embodied interaction. In *Philosophy in the Flesh*, Lakoff and Johnson (1999) describe the way in which the human mind is programmed to deal with basic-level phenomena. They define the basic level as the highest level at which a single mental image can represent an entire category (we can visualize *chair* but not *furniture*) and the highest level at which a person uses similar motor actions for interacting with members of a category. In language, categories that are placed above the basic-level categories, which are called superordinate categories, may acquire a certain concreteness by virtue of their signifiers; the concrete signifier *furniture* leads us to perceive it as a thing that we can interact with. But despite Eisenstein's and others' efforts to produce a visual language, such abstract categories cannot, in audiovisual representations, acquire flesh and blood. An example: at the beginning of *Wings of Desire* we are shown a series of people engaged in various activities (biking, watching TV, reading, and so on) who together clearly represent concrete tokens of a more abstract (superordinate) category, humans (or "suffering humanity"), but our inference here is abstract; none of these people, taken alone, can provide a mental image that represents the whole category, nor prompt some motor schema that would enable us concretely to interact with that category. Thus the superordinate category remains disembodied. Similarly, the film carries a series of meanings that presuppose our understanding of such abstract categories as German history. The abstract, disembodied nature of this type of representation has emotional consequences, for here the viewer cannot have the tense emotional involvement that he or she experiences with concrete phenomena that allow for embodied interaction.

Such disembodied categories may nevertheless exert a powerful fascination. In *Wings of Desire*, Wenders throughout the film uses motions of a feathered "bird-angel" wing that are marked as symbolic, and often in the context of eyes and opening of eyes; the visual closeness of wings and eyes creates explicit or implicit graphic matches between eyelashes opening and closing and wing movements. The spectacular wing movement and the possible graphic link to eyes evokes a feeling of deep significance arising from the synthesis of the two images, for, as Eisenstein argued in his theory of montage (e.g., Eisenstein 1949), the juxtaposition of two heterogeneous shots creates a new, third meaning. The angel wings are further associated with many other scenes and images. The very fact that the viewer has difficulty in visualizing and comprehending the precise mean-ing of the wing symbolism and creates a concrete mental image of the meaning paradoxically enhances the salience of the metaphoric symbolism. Therefore the symbolism provides the sense that it signifies some higher meaning. This feeling of a hidden meaning thus gives rise to disembodied feelings that act in combina-tion with the steady accumulation of salient embodied images that are linked to the symbolic field (e.g., links between flying and hanging from a trapeze). Embodied narratives are based on a full PECMA flow in which perceptions and emotions result in actions; the emotions are thus full of tension and the scene of the film narrative is the intersubjective world. Disembodied narratives, by contrast, block the PECMA flow to some degree; here the emotions are chan-neled into saturated webs of associations, and the film narrative as a rule takes place in an inner, subjective world. Watching films with extended scenes that cue saturated (mental, disembodied) emotions is a minority taste; most people prefer films that cue tense (embodied) emotions based on action tendencies.

Lakoff and Johnson (1999) provide some clues as to why many people have problems with abstract representations. They show that key elements of human thought are based on the basic level of sensory-motor experience associated with such activities as seeing, walking along a path, manipulating objects, and so on. The more concrete the phenomena we deal with—the more easily they can be comprehended through schemas derived from our basic interaction with external reality—the easier the thought processes involved, because they are both concep-tually and emotionally backed up by our basic embodiedness. Our capacity for abstract thought is a higher extension of these basic-level schemas that involves the use of metaphor. One can project the schema "walk along a trajectory with a few obstacles" to create a metaphoric representation of one's life: "My life has been an easy journey with a few obstacles." Allegorical films are based on this mapping of basic-level schemas onto abstract levels of meaning, and the experi-ence of higher meaning is linked to a metaconsciousness of the "metaphoricity" of the representation. If we experience Travis's journey in Wenders's *Paris, Texas* (1984) as a nonmetaphorical, concrete journey, the experience of higher meaning will disappear. In order to experience the metaphorical version with its higher meaning, we have to switch mental modes, from the embodied and concrete to the disembodied and abstract. Such abstract models may be difficult, as when *Wings of Desire* poses the difficult task of recognizing the angel in the film as a metaphor for the disembodied intellectual observer (figure 9.1). Even if the viewer solves such intellectual tasks, the categories involved are still far from the basic concrete level. The viewer may feel that the filmmaker has imposed these tasks, just as he or she may feel forced, in Angelopoulos's *Ulysses' Gaze*, to con-struct some abstract metaphorical projections from the dialogue.

FIGURE 9.1. Art films often convey abstract and symbolic messages that challenge and strain viewers' interpretational capacities. The visible middle-level world of art films demands interpretive support from abstract categories. In Wenders's *Wings of Desire*, for instance, we observe how a symbol for an intellectual, the angel Damiel, played by Bruno Ganz, tries to come down to earth and the warm, trivial life of street food, ordinary people, and mass culture, represented by Peter Falk. Damiel is still an invisible angel and cannot get in contact with Falk and ordinary life. *Wings of Desire* © Road Movie Filmproduktion 1987.

Higher Meaning and the Question of Permanence

In the paragraph above I looked at the superordinate nature of higher meaning: at the fact that it rests on something other than our basic, concrete interactions with the world. But disembodied representations may also arise where the dominant experiences are offline (memories, hallucinations, expectations about future states) or where they are based on online perceptions from which an action perspective is bleached out, as occurs, for instance, with *temps mort*, periods in a film when nothing happens. Such experiences are felt to be more permanent than the emotions and feelings cued by an ever-changing online narrative. This sense of permanence is central to the experience of higher meaning; since the meanings cannot be straightforwardly visualized, it is the saturated sense of some transcendent and abstract meaning that anchors the experience. These saturated feelings may be active even when the film has ended because there are no final solutions to the quest for hidden meaning. Mainstream films are often considered transient, in the sense that they provide instant but passing gratification, whereas a work of art is considered to be something of lasting value. The very fact that higher meaning is often based on categories at a level superior to those of the visible and audible diegetic world cues the feeling of being confronted with certain permanent essentials.

The term *feeling* is important in this connection, because the experience of higher meaning is based not only on cognitive phenomena, such as the thought that Terence Davies's *Distant Voices, Still Lives* provides deep insight into the life of the English working class. It arises also from a strong feeling of permanent salience in the images. In *Distant Voices, Still Lives*, for instance, the characters are shown confronting the camera as if posing to be photographed. This tableau style activates a double experience: the nostalgia of family photos and the promise of finding a lost life in the stills. Davies constructs a network of atemporal associations. Those hoping for a live, forward-moving narrative will be frustrated by the antinarrative devices in the film, which include splitting up voices and images (using diegetic voice-overs) in order to underpin the eternal, museumlike still-life quality of the shots. There is no prescribed way to release the saturated emotions associated with nonnarrative experiences, and these feelings therefore remain permanent. The process here is different from that in which emotions are elicited, but also released, in mainstream narrative films. In such films, emotions are mainly elicited by narrative problems and released when these problems are solved: the bomb is defused, the criminals arrested, the couple married.

For this reason, it has often been claimed that art films should have an open narrative as opposed to the closed form of the mainstream film (see, e.g., Bordwell 1986). Critics have often proposed realist arguments for creating open texts, as exemplified, for instance, in Italian neorealist films. However, the ordinary viewer will often perceive an open neorealist film as being an art film portraying a higher meaning. *Die Hard* is a closed text because at the end of the film the major narrative problems are solved (the evildoers are contained and the family reunited). *Last Year in Marienbad*, by contrast, is an open text; no solution to the narrative problems is offered, and the emotions and meanings attached to the text will therefore persist in the viewer's mind once the film experience is over. However, narrative openness is not necessarily a precondition for higher meaning. Formally speaking, *Wings of Desire* is a closed text: the film starts with a problem, the experience of emotional isolation felt by Damiel (Bruno Ganz) because of his position as a spiritual creature (an angel) and his cultural removal from the warm mainstream experiences associated with American mass culture (Peter Falk), circus life, and other aspects of embodied existence. Eventually he is transformed into a human being and integrated by marriage into the warm earthly life of the circus. But the film aspires to higher meaning by presenting Damiel's life as symbolic: he is not an individualized human being like Bruce Willis in *Die Hard*, but a symbolic construct intended to subsume certain key human experiences, and the narrative closure represents a mediation between abstract opposites: German high culture versus French and American low culture, or the soul versus the body. Thus closure is not in itself an indication of lower meaning. It is only because closure generally goes hand in hand with the nonsymbolic, embodied representation of the world that it tends to be associated with profane meanings, particularly the achievement of mundane goals through concrete actions.

Neurologist Antonio Damasio (1999) has put forward a theory of consciousness that might be of help in defining higher meaning. His basic idea is that the phenomenon of consciousness reflects and is rooted in our embodiedness. The interests of our bodies are represented in the brain by means of emotions. Using neurological evidence, he shows that if the brain is cut off from information about our bodily state that evokes feelings and emotions, we lose consciousness. Damasio's theory is also based on evolutionary considerations. He identifies three stages in the development of consciousness, respectively represented in three distinct neurological systems. The first system is unconscious and linked to the unity of the body and its organic processes; people in deep sleep or coma (like Jan at a certain point in *Breaking the Waves*) are in this state. The body regulates breathing, body temperature, and so on, but does not engage in actions directed at the outside world.

The next level is that of core consciousness and the core self. This system takes care of the basic interaction between the embodied mind and the world. Here, perceptions of the external world are evaluated in relation to the body's preferences and feelings. The mental system that constitutes core consciousness and the core self is based on limited conscious memories of a person's global identity—the form of identity that consists of his or her experiences over time, his or her autobiography, and future-directed aspirations. The core self is consequently transient: it confronts the world directly on the basis of a relatively limited memory of personal identity, as the typical action hero does in response to a given situation. The core self is therefore transient and opportunistic: it responds immediately to incoming impulses from the external world. Because of this transience, its perceptions are salient. Damasio gives examples of mental patients who have only a core self with a memory span of up to three minutes. The heroes in mainstream films of course act on the basis of a much more flexible time frame than this; they may even have goals that take a very long time to fulfill. But they still live in the PECMA flow and their goals are mostly material, not psychological. Damasio's description of people living in the present because they are unable to form long-term memories inspired Nolan's *Memento*, although for narrative reasons the film has to circumvent the lack of memory by having the hero use the device of bodily tattoos.

The third level consists in the autobiographical self: online experiences are evaluated in relation to memories of past experiences and the plans for the future that these memories give rise to. The autobiographical self may conflict in certain ways with the core self, because the core self wants to solve problems in the light of the salient events of the present, whereas the autobiographical self seeks to solve problems on the basis of experiences and norms laid down over a lifetime—as happens in *Memento*, where the protagonist searches for his lost autobiography. Take, for example, a simple scenario in which the autobiographical self functions to some extent as Freud's superego: in a confrontation with a troublesome person the core self may have the urge to kill his opponent, whereas the autobiographical self may point to the consequences of such acts, and thus restrain the core self from acting rashly. But the concept of the autobiographical self is much more comprehensive than this, covering all aspects of a given person's life that constitute his or her identity. Thus Travis in *Paris, Texas* seeks to reconstruct his identity by reconstructing his life story, and Tarkovsky's *The Mirror* likewise centers on the reconstruction of an autobiography. However, Tarkovsky presents this autobiography not only as a narrative in time, but also as a nonnarrative associative context for the present. Had he chosen to present his life story in the form of a canonical narrative, of the kind found in August's *Pelle the Conqueror*, it would have consisted in a series of transient core self experiences, rather than a portrayal of the way that the past exists in the mind of the present-day person, providing a "context of pastness." Numerous art films and novels have sought by different means to convey the experience of a permanent context for transient present experiences.

Thus the shorthand version of Damasio's (1999) model is that there are three prototypical ways in which humans may experience the self: (1) as an unconscious protoself that undergoes basic biological processes, but—as in the case of coma—does not interact with the world; (2) as a core self with a transient consciousness, living in the online present; and (3) as a permanent self with an extended consciousness that interprets the online present in the context of past memories and future goals and aspirations. These ways are prototypes with intermediate forms. The representation of higher meaning in film is often associated with the different problems involved in establishing a permanent self based on an extended consciousness. Narrative embodied mainstream films are of course not totally transient, so total transience and complete permanence are the extreme poles and a given film may choose a level in between or alternate between different positions in relation to transience and permanence.

Permanence, Postmodern Decenteredness, Identity, and Soul

As Lakoff and Johnson (1999, 267–289, passim) have pointed out, however, the sense of a permanent identity that should in principle result from having full access to the memorized autobiographical records of one's life is only a mental construct, a kind of wishful thinking created for the purpose of establishing a unified agent as the source of one's actions and relationships. The life experiences of a given person do not, as a rule, add up to a unified whole from which the subject, the agency of the person's actions, can be derived. Most people have contradictory experiences that give rise to different selves. The heroine Bess in Lars von Trier's *Breaking the Waves* is torn between her religious upbringing and her sexual desire for Jan, which springs from a more mature self. Many dramas and films center on people who are torn between incompatible motives arising from life experiences that have produced different and sometimes conflicting preferences (as in the case of Romeo and Juliet, who are torn between their mutual love and their feelings for their families, or as in Trier's *Pictures of Liberation*, in which tender childhood experiences conflict with those of being a Nazi soldier). Because humans have only one body and are therefore constrained to act as if they were unified selves, there is a strong functional motive for constructing a unified agency (subject) that can carry out actions and solve conflicts. As mentioned earlier, Panksepp (1999) has pointed out that the basic self is located in subcortical systems that generate primitive self-centered emotions and motivations such as pain, fear, anger, separation anxiety, and sexual and maternal urges. The self is linked to motor-related processes and acts as a motivator for voluntary actions. Clearly, higher order functions may easily find difficulties in unifying the different transient version of the self-agency.

For this reason, the autobiographical consciousness not only provides the potential basis for the experience of identity but may give rise to a feeling of fragmentation, as exemplified in numerous art films, in which there are no functional solutions to the protagonist's conflicting emotions and motivations. By contrast, the subject in the typical mainstream film tends to be a unified self (although it sometimes changes and there may be mental conflicts during the transition from one unified self to another). The problem for Bruce Willis in *Die Hard* is not to integrate his motives and preferences—these are unambiguous—but to implement them in the physical world; for example, by killing the evil German terrorists. The problem for Travis in *Paris, Texas*, on the other hand, is the mental task of reestablishing his autobiographical self and integrating different and for the most part conflicting motives into a unified self-conception. Similarly, it is vital for Clementine and Joel in Gondry's *Eternal Sunshine of the Spotless Mind* to recover the erased memories that constitute their autobiographical selves.

The fact that a given individual is motivated by a series of often contradictory experiences, many of which may even be unconscious, has led many film scholars to claim that the Cartesian notion of a unified conscious self is a Western, male, ideological construction, and that the human subject is essentially decentered (see Stam 2000 for an overview). Lakoff and Johnson (1999) agree with the postmodern view that in certain respects human lives are based on conflicting and often unconscious experiences. However, they strongly disagree with the postmodern claim that the concept of self is only an ideological construct. They argue, on the contrary, that the concept of unified, conscious subjecthood is universal. The reason for this is functional: the conscious will needs to carry out unambiguous actions and therefore constructs a unified identity that can carry out those actions and, where necessary, suppress all experiences (identities) that conflict with the chosen course of action. Thus the motivation for constructing a centered subject is not ideological but practical (cf. the introduction to part II). Because a central function of the conscious subject is to control the body, moreover, there is a universal tendency to experience this subject as disembodied and spiritual, separate from, and possibly opposed to, the physical self. The will seeks to exert control over the body, issuing commands such as "Pull yourself together" or pronouncing judgment: "I do not like what I [the body as other] did." The erroneous notion that there exists a disembodied, spiritual self, a soul, is therefore based on an experience that arises for functional reasons, not as a result of ideology. Popular psychology reasons that the body must be controlled by some disembodied force.

Over and above the practical functions outlined above, there are several cognitive and emotional reasons for creating a centered subject—an agency with intentions, beliefs, and moral responsibilities that is required to perform centered, embodied actions. Even the poststructuralists and postmodernists cannot do without some concept of agency, although they have tried to veil this fact (perhaps even from themselves) by using obscure terminology, as Mette Hjort (1993) has shown in her analysis of concepts of agency in postmodernist writings. The fact that conscious agency is influenced by a series of unconscious and possibly conflicting forces, and by social factors that the subject, the agency, cannot fully comprehend, does not exclude the obvious commonsense truth that conscious agency matters.

Memory and the Problems of a Unified Self-Experience

Let me offer some examples of the way that memory and ideas of the future function in the constitution of the autobiographical self in films. The basic problem in *Last Year in Marienbad* consists in the relationship between the memories of an autobiographical self on the one hand, and the present experiences of a core self on the other. A man meets a woman in Marienbad, and, in principle, they might have a sexual relationship based on this online meeting. But in the film it is extremely important that the present accords with their memories of the past. The two cannot engage in a relationship before they have straightened out the past and evaluated the present in the light of it (i.e., in the light of inner records of previous perceptions, as opposed to online perceptions). Their arguments dwell on whether they had a relationship last year in Marienbad and under what circumstances. The experience of the present, moreover, is stylistically more difficult to apprehend because the present is for the most part shown in one modality only: either the present-day images are accompanied by dialogue from the past, or, vice versa, present-day dialogues are accompanied by images from the past. The viewer therefore has a sense of higher meaning, because the discourse offers no input for the online construction of a canonical story line, and hence no experience of direct interaction. Rather, the sounds and images give rise to associations and salient stylistic experiences aimed at reconstructing an elusive autobiographical self. Thus when the film is over, the viewer is left with a series of mental associations labeled as "past" (and "subjective," because of the dispute between the man and the woman about the true nature of their previous experiences). We feel that these are higher meanings because they involve riddles of the soul, the inner life, and because they are permanent: they cannot be dissolved by action. We do not have any direct access to the workings of our minds; we can only conceptualize the terra incognita of our inner lives by projecting onto it metaphors drawn from our basic-level experience of the external world: "I battled with myself," "I trawled through my recollections," "I sealed off those memories."

The hero in Trier's *The Element of Crime* is also faced with a problem of autobiography. The narrative is set in the past and presented by the hero (Fisher) in a state of hypnosis. Thus there is no online action in the film; all the events have already taken place and are filtered through Fisher's imagination. Moreover, the story turns on several possible identities: Fisher starts out by seeking to solve a series of crimes involving child molestation and for this purpose tries imaginatively to relive the experiences of a possible suspect, Grey, by seeking out situations that Grey may have lived through, in order to understand the crime. Fisher accordingly undergoes hypnosis in his efforts to recall what has happened in the past and to come up with material that is even more elusive: to simulate Grey's possible experiences. In the process, any authentic core self experience is totally blocked by memory and imagination. The film does not arrive at any real closure, because the important experiences (reliving memory and imagination) are not set in a context of online action. This visually stunning film thus offers an experience in which the salience of the images suggests higher meanings that transcend their obvious, basic-level significance: meanings that are permanent because they find no outlet in action.

It might be objected that, because *The Element of Crime* portrays a world utterly devoid of permanence—Fisher is unable to establish a stable autobiographical self—it must surely advocate a postmodern vision of a decentered subject with only a transient core self. A similar statement might be read into *Last Year in Marienbad*, where the protagonists, unable to establish fixed autobiographical selves, are condemned forever to inhabit the physical and mental mazes of Marienbad. As we saw above, their immediate core self bodily experiences are continuously supplanted by recalled or fantasized experiences. The possible lovers in *Last Year in Marienbad* have no strong sense of their bodies or their online desires. And, as Damasio (1999) argues, it is our indivisible bodies that provide the basis for a unified self and unified consciousness. Similarly, Lakoff and Johnson (1999) have shown how our (false but necessary) experience of a centered subject arises from our embodiedness, and described the way in which this experience of unity can break down if a person is confronted with conflicting demands and experiences, whether the confrontation is online or resides in the person's conscious or nonconscious autobiography.

Resnais's and Trier's films are full of higher permanent meanings because they establish a mental universe in which the embodied mind in the form of memory (and the seat of possible spiritual permanence) takes precedence over the online experience of an embodied mind in online (and transient) contact with the world. However, the characters in *Last Year in Marienbad* are not decentered agents in a postmodern narrative, because the main male character experiences pain at the loss of autobiographical coherence and seeks to solve the riddles of the past, while the main female character perhaps seeks to create coherence in her present autobiographical self-understanding by blocking access to certain memories. Through a series of clinical examples, Damasio (1999, 202–219) has shown that only those whose access to the autobiographical self is blocked by brain damage can live as truly transient (decentered) agents. For although the mind of an ordinary person may be unable to synthesize different and perhaps contradictory experiences and action impulses, as in the case of the German soldier in Trier's *Pictures of Liberation*, there are very good (and universally manifested) reasons for trying to construct a unified (essentialist) subject as the control mechanism for actions.

The most radical conclusion drawn from the paradox that the mind is at once embodied, the seat of all our experience of the external world, yet (in its capacity for memory and future anticipation) appears to be autonomous vis-à-vis the body that supports it, is of course the folk psychological and Cartesian idea of the soul as a symbol of permanence that can exist quite independently of the embodied mind. I discussed the traumatic versions of that dualism in chapter 5 in relation to the undead that were severed from their live bodies.

The question of the soul and the idea of posing a radical division between the embodied core self and the disembodied autobiographical self might seem remote from the world of modern art film. But one need look no further than Trier's *Breaking the Waves* to find a film that advocates this conception of the soul as a disembodied version of the autobiographical self. The heroine, Bess, starts out by trying to combine physical, embodied love with some kind of disembodied, spiritual love. But she soon finds herself in a situation where she has to sacrifice her body. Her physical love for Jan can no longer be fulfilled, and she can only fulfill his demand for salvation by allowing her body to be sexually abused and physically tortured to death. In line with traditional Christian thinking—the body is sacrificed so that the permanent spiritual powers can be released from their bodily container—Bess heals Jan's illness and acquires saintly status through the heavenly bells that ring at her second funeral at sea. It is, of course, an extreme position to advocate the destruction of the body in the belief that the spirit thereby fulfills a higher destiny. But even in more profane narratives, higher meaning is often associated with the transcendence of basic bodily needs in the performance of altruistic deeds.

An extreme rupture of the links between core self and autobiographical self is not a typical experience. A more modest rupture can be found in Kieslowski's *Blue*. The main character, Julie, loses her husband and child in a car accident. Many of her memories are intimately linked to a series of future-oriented projects, including the project of bringing up her child: thus she dwells in her memory on an autobiographical self as the mother who would follow her child's future development. Similarly, her relationship to her husband and to his projects as a composer reflects a project-oriented aspect of her identity, her autobiographical self. Thus the death of her beloved deprives her existence of meaning, because her memories no longer generate online core experiences or a sense of the future. Julie is therefore traumatized. She tries to get rid of all the possessions associated with her life before the accident and seeks out primitive core self experiences, such as swimming, in which her body is in uncomplicated interaction with the world. Her desire for contact with water, her need to run her knuckles over the wall of a house, her interest in reflections of light, and so on require no psychoanalytic explanation (e.g., the suggestion that water symbolizes a regression to the womb) but can be seen as an effort to generate new core self experiences. Little by little, she builds up a small stock of experiences that not only serve to provide new memories but contribute to core self experiences such as undertaking to complete her dead husband's project, the composition of the *Europe* symphony.

However, the project of composing the *Europe* symphony indicates that Julie's recovery does not only lie in establishing new core experiences—had this been the case, the film would not have been an art film but just a melodrama with a happy ending. It is the combination of visual style and serious music (the drafts for the *Europe* symphony) that indicates that this is not just a film about a woman traumatized by a car accident, but concerns permanent cultural values associated with the concept of Europe.

My final example of the importance of memory and the blocking of action in art films comes from Tarkovsky's *The Mirror*. The project of the film is to describe aspects of the main character's life. This could have been done using classical narrative form, starting with the early life of the hero and ending with his maturity. By offering a steady flow of present-tense moments, shaped by a series of online actions, such a representation would strongly activate core consciousness experiences. But Tarkovsky seeks to portray the different situations in the form of memories: as scenes from the mind that are sealed off from online interaction. He has therefore chosen an associative presentation with significant perforations in ongoing linear time. As he asserts in his book *Sculpting in Time*, the purpose of the cinematic image is to gain permanence, to speak the eternal "truth of human existence" (Tarkovsky 1987, 102 passim). This idea is in harmony with his religious belief that the body is only a transient bearer of permanent spiritual ideas and perceptions.

Perceptual Presence as Higher Permanence

Although the narrative in art films often aims to explore the individual past of the characters, as we see in films such as Bergman's *Wild Strawberries*, Fellini's *8½*, Tarkovsky's *The Mirror*, Wenders's *Im Lauf der Zeit* (*Kings of the Road*) and *Paris, Texas*, or Trier's *The Element of Crime*, it also offers a deeper representation of present experience. Bordwell (1986) notices the marked tendency in art film narration toward *temps mort*, that is, sequences in which nothing takes place (see the description of subjectivity by default in chapter 10). Because of the pragmatic, action-oriented bias of classical narration, the present will often be experienced as important only in relation to the future, that is, future actions. The classic narrative moves toward some future action deadline, reaching a series of climactic points along the way. By contrast, art film narration tends to focus on the experiential stream of perception, without the peak moments of classical dramatic presentation. Tarkovsky's and Wenders's films, for example, often include long pauses in conversation or long periods in which there is no present movement toward the future. This "dead time" thus presents highly charged online sensations in isolation from any motive, that is, without suggesting their relevance to some future-directed, action-driven, or problem-solving narrative. These streams of perceptions appear both objective and subjective: objective in the sense that they offer an experience of time as a process cued by the objective external world (rather than by subjective actions), and subjective in the sense that they highlight the experiencing subject rather than the pragmatic, action-oriented agent. Whereas canonical narration is largely pragmatic and behavioristic, art film narration is often phenomenological. The main characters are more often observers than participants, as we see in the case of Travis in *Paris, Texas*, who contemplates life as he gazes at the traffic on the freeways of Los Angeles.

Periods of *temps mort* evoke a sense of higher meaning for two intertwined reasons. The first is that streams of perceptions are disembodied, insofar as they are isolated from any pragmatic concerns that might link them to action. *Temps mort* thus serves expressive and lyrical functions that give a feeling of permanence. The second reason is a special case of the first: since the viewer is unable to detect any narrative motivation for a given *temps mort*—a given salient and expressive perceptual experience—he or she may look for such motivation in his or her concept of the addresser, the filmmaker. As Bordwell (1986) has pointed out, art films are often seen as authored, whereas mainstream narratives are often perceived as anonymous. It might therefore be suggested that *temps mort* derives its higher, subjective toning from the fact that we see it as an indication of a particular auteur's permanent and distinctive vision of the world. Our experience of these salient sequences does not therefore seem to us fully online and embodied, since we are not invited to see for ourselves, but to see what the auteur saw. The perceptual present is ultimately transformed into the permanent perceptual past of the auteur's experience.

Higher Meaning and Epistemological Uncertainty

On the surface, many films are preoccupied with questions of truth and reality, and thus with questions of objectivity. *Distant Voices, Still Lives* is a quest for the truths of working-class life, while *Wings of Desire* represents a search for the true identity of Berlin, Germany, and humanity. At first sight it therefore seems paradoxical that art films often transform objective, online experiences into subjective ones. Bordwell (1986) sees a strong surface conflict between the quest for truth and objectivity on the one hand, and the strongly subjective form of art film narration on the other, and argues that the standard solution to this conflict is to create ambiguity and epistemological uncertainty. Art films appear to offer representations of the world that are much truer than those of mainstream film, yet at the same time suggest that there are no objective representations of the world, just ambiguous and transient ones. Thus subjective, ambiguous, and transient representations—anchored in the visions of an auteur—are presented as being more true and realistic than unambiguous and supposedly objective representations.

As mentioned earlier, Bordwell (1986, 212) has pointed out that one of the differences between canonical and art film narration lies in epistemological differences between the two types of narration. The canonical narrative assumes unproblematic access to reality. There are no problems of representation as such; the problems we encounter in a canonical narrative are those that the characters confront and seek to deal with in their lives, whereas the main characters in art films often experience the world as opaque and difficult to understand. *Last Year in Marienbad* offers a prime example of this. Wim Wenders's *Lisbon Story* (1994) likewise focuses on questions of knowing and representing reality, while Greenaway's films provide an ongoing commentary on the problems and uncertainties of representation. Similarly, Lars von Trier's *The Element of Crime* presents an extremely opaque world that raises a series of epistemological questions.

The obvious explanation for this emphasis on epistemological uncertainty is that art film directors are more skeptical as to the possibility of understanding the true nature and outline of the world than directors of mainstream narrative films. But there may be aesthetic reasons for this tendency as well. One of the main consequences of epistemological uncertainty is that online, embodied actions are impeded or blocked. In the canonical mainstream film, epistemological certainty allows the characters to interact continuously with their environment. The environment throws up certain problems or opportunities for the characters, who respond accordingly. We thus witness the following sequence: external causes → physical and mental processing of these causes → action in response to these causes. No epistemological problems arise in a film like *Die Hard*, only the practical problems that the characters face in seeking to control the world according to their preferences. Classical Hollywood films have often been accused of presenting a Western, idealist type of narration, although their narratives accord with materialist philosophy. Marx claimed that earlier idealist philosophers were occupied with how to interpret the world, whereas his materialist philosophy was aimed at changing the world. This is also the main purpose of the characters in classical narration.

The term *idealist* could be applied, on the other hand, to many art film narratives. In art films, the problem of interpreting and understanding the world precedes concrete action and often renders it impossible. To a great extent, art film narration thus inherits the romantic worldview and its critique of rationalism. Some versions of modernism and postmodernism are indeed closely related to neoromantic epistemology (Grodal 1992). Mental interiors are seen as alienated, cut off from authentic contact with the external world, and suffer from lack of authentic communication.

Trier's *The Element of Crime* offers a good example of an art film that favors epistemological uncertainty. The entire film is based on modes of representation that block online interaction and create doubt as to the reality status of the phenomena represented. As we saw above, *The Element of Crime* is narrated in retrospect and through several filters (such as hypnosis), rendering uncertain Fisher's efforts to reestablish aspects of his autobiography. Visually, the film appears disembodied through being shot in dark spaces lit by yellowish sodium light, which lends an eerie, unreal glow to the images. Moreover, the main characters have no stable identities or preferences that might provide them with clear-cut motives and support their actions. Determined to track down an alleged child molester, Grey, Fisher tries to imagine himself into the mind and body of the criminal, whom we never see and whose very existence we come to doubt. Fisher's old mentor, Osborne, has also previously tried to emulate Grey. Both Fisher and Osborne succeed so well in their quest that they both turn into child molesters themselves. It is their bodies that perpetrate the acts they perform, but these bodies are controlled by Grey's mind (and life story)—although Fisher, at least, has relived certain aspects of that life story. Thus mind and body are split and the relations between the characters and world are opaque, partly because of the lack of a focused relationship between the characters and the world they inhabit. The result is an intriguing, lyrical film. Because of the epistemological problems involved, the viewer gives up trying to create a coherent and unambiguous diegetic world, and instead enjoys the film lyrically by absorbing its various themes and associations.

From an aesthetic point of view, it might therefore be argued that epistemological uncertainty serves the purpose of transforming narrative modes into lyrical modes of experience. These lyrical modes are characterized by a certain degree of disembodiedness: the associations take place in inward-looking minds, not in embodied minds that interact with the world. In *The Element of Crime*, Trier borrows certain narrative patterns from mainstream genres: film noir, spy thrillers, and science fiction films, all of which use epistemological uncertainty as a means of creating suspense that is ultimately dissolved through action. But Trier uses the means—uncertainty—as an end in itself: even at the close of the film, the world and the identities of the characters remain opaque and uncertain, full of higher meaning about the mysteries of the human mind. The question that such films raise is therefore: do the directors choose epistemological uncertainty for cognitive or for affective-aesthetic reasons? It might be argued that it is precisely the preference for the romantic, saturated aesthetic feelings typical of art films that leads their directors to choose epistemological uncertainty.

Alternatively, one might argue that there is a strong link between the preference for a certain kind of romantic, saturated aesthetic and the choice of a particular epistemology. Many art film directors dissent to some degree from the rationalist worldview. There are various reasons for this. Adherents of a religious, metaphysical worldview, like Tarkovsky, may object to science and rationalism because they block our access to spiritual experiences. Those who profess an antimetaphysical world view—as expressed in the various strands of grand theory and critical thinking—may object to rationalism on the basis that it is an ideological, Western, and patriarchal mode of representation. Sometimes the nostalgic and the radical critique of rationalism are combined. One example can be found in Lars von Trier's TV series *The Kingdom*, inspired in turn by David Lynch's series *Twin Peaks*. Trier's TV series is based on a classic romantic dualism portrayed through postmodern filters. Evil in the film is associated with reason and enlightenment, embodied in the (male) doctors and their belief in science. These men do not suffer from any epistemological doubt, but all their projects have monstrous or problematic consequences: from the abuse of children through malpractice, to reckless experimentation, to the monstrous scientific project initiated by one of the doctors, who aims to preserve a certain type of cancer by operating the cancer cells into his healthy liver. Irony notwithstanding, the good forces in the film are those who rely on superstition, on magic and witchcraft, as exemplified by the main character, Mrs. Drusse. By presenting this strong undercurrent of anti-enlightenment sentiment (including central aspects of critical theory, for which enlightenment is equated with the kind of instrumental reason that arguably led ultimately to the "rational" mass destruction practiced at Auschwitz), Lars von Trier has created an extremely ambiguous world—partly bracketed by irony—in which epistemological doubt dissolves the unambiguous world of science and rationalism.

But historical factors, as well as aesthetic preferences, may also account for the tendency in art films toward epistemological uncertainty. Directors like Bergman, Antonioni, Godard, Resnais, and Tarkovsky offered new ways of representing subjective experiences. However, the search for stylistic innovation was also linked to feelings of unease in relation to modernity. Although the Italian and French new waves can be seen in part as a revolt against traditional aspects of European life and often express an ambivalent fascination with the American mainstream film, they also emanate a pronounced feeling of angst and identity crisis vis-à-vis Americanization. Stylistic innovations were often used to represent worldviews with a metaphysical or religious undertone. The pathos and sense of higher meaning that we find in many auteurist films (one thinks of Bergman's oeuvre, Kubrick's *2001: A Space Odyssey*, Ridley Scott's *Blade Runner*, Kar Wai Wong's *2046*) link the theme of a crisis in personal identity with that of the collective crisis of modernity.

Style and Higher Meaning in Art Films

The importance of style in film art is partly due to the fact that it tends to focus on subjective experiences. In mainstream cinema, the objective experiences that constitute its central concerns are presented transparently. The diegetic world is unmarked and uncolored by the characters' subjective emotions, states of mind, or special perceptual conditions. By contrast, representations of subjective experiences are often stylistically marked: since the viewer's basic assumption is that the screen represents a view of an objective, external time-space, the stylistic marking of a subjective experience may serve to indicate its deviant status.

Just as important, however, perceptual salience—style—serves to create a sense of permanence. Bordwell (1986) has shown that in mainstream films, style figures as a raw material that is transformed by its use in the construction of the *fabula*, the story line. Because of this transformation, which destroys the conscious memory of stylistic features, it is difficult to remember the stylistic surface in mainstream films. In cinematic art, however, style is not so strongly tied to a salient story line, and cannot therefore be transformed into mere information to support the plot. Trier's *Pictures of Liberation*, *The Element of Crime*, and *Europa* all have salient styles that can only partly—if at all—be transformed into narrative meaning. This perceptual meaning is often referred to as excess (Thompson 1999) that makes the artwork special and attention demanding (Dissanayake 1995).

The reason that this excess still represents part of the film's meaning, even though it defies conceptual analysis, is that it offers the same kind of emotional experience as do meaningful signifiers and cues: an experience that emotionally triggers the viewer's quest for meaning. Our minds continuously scan the world for salient phenomena and events, and the sense that a given phenomenon is meaningful motivates us to allocate mental resources to it and, in some cases, respond to it through action. But whereas certain stylistic features can be fully transformed into story information, excess perceptual salience cannot. These excess features therefore activate particularly marked attention, switching on feelings and emotions which suggest that these features contain a meaning that the viewer cannot fully conceptualize. The viewer is therefore left with the sense that there must be some deep meaning embedded in these stylistic features, because the emotional motivation for making meaning out of salient features cannot be switched off. Style thus serves as an additional guarantee for some higher or deeper meaning, while at the same time giving rise to a feeling of permanence, since the perceptual, stylistic cues continue to trigger meaning-producing processes without reaching any final result. Some of the phenomena associated with *temps mort* serve to activate similar processes. Thus the best art films employ two intertwined procedures for creating higher and permanent meanings: a symbolic representation of certain fields of meaning above the basic level (for instance, permanent subjective meanings, based on individual or collective memory, that may conflict with experiences in the present), and a series of salient stylistic features that are rendered permanent by their relative independence from any transparent narrative function. Kubrick's *2001: A Space Odyssey* superbly uses all three procedures: the film evokes certain abstract ideas about man's true identity and destiny, offers a "metabiography" of man, and at the same time has an extremely salient perceptual style that supports the sense of some higher cosmic meaning.

Higher Meaning, Existential Needs, and Modes of Experience

Art film representations of subjective and symbolic experiences clearly serve certain existential needs. But even the more metaphysical quests for the transcendental origins of subjecthood (the search for a soul or an identity, the anchoring of altruism in certain transcendental values, the establishment of a hierarchy of art forms as a basis for a vernacular cult) may partly be seen as a consequence of our innate quest for causality.

The impressive appeal of art films to their core audience of intellectuals is not matched by an equal appeal to the mainstream film audience, although this audience may like exemplars of film art (Hitchcock's films or *Blade Runner*, just to mention a few examples). Some of the reasons for this are fleshed out in Noël Carroll's (1998) *A Philosophy of Mass Art*: high art presupposes special skills and for this reason is not addressed to the masses that logically enough tend (at least partially) to reject it. Another reason for the relatively narrow appeal of high art has to do with the question of embodiment and style. Terence Davies's *Distant Voices, Still Lives* deals with ordinary working-class life, and most of the content does not demand special interpretive skills. Moreover, some of the stylistic features—for instance, the use of family photos—are not in themselves difficult to grasp. But the fact that the film deprives the viewer of any concrete, embodied, canonical narrative and instead cues a mental, disembodied experience of implied profilmic events suggests that it is addressed to viewers for whom symbolic and abstract meanings have more appeal than a more concrete narrative. The question of high art styles and the types of feelings and emotions linked to such styles are therefore important.

In order to create a sense of permanence and transcendence, high art styles need to block the PECMA flow—the embodied acting out of emotions in response to the narrative. Melancholia, nostalgia, and empathetic distance are among the emotions that art films tend to cue, because by blocking enactment, such emotions promote in the viewer a mental experience instead. Even in a film such as Besson's *Subway*, which to some extent emulates American mainstream film, the main character is a melancholic romantic wanderer who dies for love, and the film thus aspires to be disembodied art. All Trier's early works evoke such negatively colored, saturated emotions, whereas his TV series *The Kingdom* is a comedy that evokes pleasurable laughter. Although Trier himself has labeled *The Kingdom* a "left-hand" film rather than a work of high art, the series has a stylistic salience and thematic richness comparable to that of many of his "right-hand" films. Thus the main reason for regarding the series as not entirely a work of high art is an emotional one: as a comedy, it does not evoke the negative or melancholic feelings typical of high art. Ingmar Bergman's most acclaimed high art films almost all evoke negative feelings. In his *New German Cinema*, Elsaesser (1989) explains the negative and pessimistic tone of German art film by the fact that its audience typically consisted of lonely and frustrated intellectuals. This may be true, but it does not explain why tragedies are often felt to be a higher form of art than comedies. A commonsense explanation would be that—except for metaphysical "hymns" such as the *Europe* symphony in *Blue*, the bells at the end of *Breaking the Waves*, or the resurrection in Dreyer's *Ordet*—negative experiences tend to be more disembodied than joy. The obvious reason for this is that negative emotional experiences are normally opposed to the preferences of the body, just as death is one of the greatest motivators for (metaphysical) thoughts concerning a spiritual essence that exists independently of the body.

Negative experiences and emotions are not exclusive to art film. Many mainstream films, like many melodramas, have tragic endings: take, for instance, *Gone with the Wind* (1939). But such films are intended not so much to create negative saturated feelings such as melancholia as to evoke strong, body-based, autonomic reactions like sorrow, which can be released through tears. The lower value that some accord to sentimental sorrow is expressed in the terms *weepy* or *tear-jerker* to denote mainstream films that are intended to make us cry. In general, sad films with mainstream appeal rely on emphasizing bonding (pair, male, tribal, kin, or offspring bonding) as I discussed in chapter 6. Even if this is also sometimes the case in art films that evoke sad melancholia, the typical art film melancholia more fully expresses despair. I shall not speculate about the reasons that fans of art films prefer melancholia and despair, for instance, to embodied sorrow and to the emphasis on bonding by means of loss, except to point out that melancholia may be experienced as a more permanent feeling than sorrow. It is significant that many people feel that the director's-cut version of *Blade Runner* is closer to film art than the commercial version, in which the protagonist's hope of escape is embodied and visualized. By refraining from visualizing this possible escape, Scott makes the melancholia of the film the permanent experience.

Conclusion

Art films express a key tendency in the evolution of the human mind: the increasing importance of the inner mental landscape brought about through a massive expansion in mental resources. Art films tend to focus on how experiences are processed in the inner world, as opposed to focusing on experiences in an exterior world. They use visual means to indicate abstract meanings, including stylistic devices aimed at making visual phenomena special and suggestive of higher meaning. Moreover, art films tend to focus on the search for common denominators among the various inner layers of feelings, memories, action tendencies, and so on in order to create autobiographical unity and permanence. They use various techniques to impede the PECMA flow and refocus our attention on inner dimensions. One consequence of this is that art films often produce saturated emotions with a negative hedonic valence such as sadness, despair, and nostalgia. The different features of art films are also used in film art in general.

10

Subjective Aesthetics
in Film

We experience some audiovisual phenomena as subjective, while others appear to us as objective. Subjective representations appear to be toned by certain inner emotions or show signs of being filtered and molded by particular personal experiences, whereas objective representations seem to provide direct access to a given scene, untoned by embodied mental processes. The experience of visual phenomena that formally belong to some exterior world but appear to stem from or be filtered through certain inner mechanisms plays a key role in film aesthetics. The PECMA flow model offers a general explanation for this: aspects of a film that are easily linked to the actions of one of the main characters are experienced as objective, but if there are no protagonists, or the characters' or viewers' action tendencies are blocked or impeded, this will lend a subjective toning to our experience of the film. This subjective toning expresses intuitive feelings of the action affordances of what we see: subjective experiences may be more intense and saturated but at the same time felt as being less real, because the feeling as to whether a given phenomenon is real depends on whether it offers the potential for action. This feeling of a special reality status is not congruent with our cognitive evaluations of reality status but represents what Panksepp (1999) calls equalia, basic emotional feelings that inform organisms where they stand with respect to environments and actions.

Such equalia have only later in the evolutionary process been supplemented with higher, explicit cognitive evaluations. Art films make prominent use of subjective sequences, whereas mainstream films use them more sparingly and by way of support for objective narrative sequences (Bordwell 1986). In this chapter, I give a functionalist account of how to cue subjective and objective phenomena in film and offer a way to categorize the kinds of phenomena that create subjective experiences.

Our intuitive sense of objectivity or subjectivity depends on the issue of control rather than on whether something is evaluated as real or not in an absolute sense. The reason for this is that our perceptual experiences of the world are constructed in such a way as to provide quick support for our actions. Experiences that allow little scope for action are flagged in our minds as less real, whereas perceptions on which we can act appear to us more real. This way of looking at our perceptions is at first blush counterintuitive, because we think of our perceptions as being separate from our actions and action tendencies. But it makes perfect functional sense: we can feel directly that we must act with caution when it is dark and that we cannot interact with distant mountains, which we experience as something sublime and beyond our reach. Film viewing is based on our standard experience of the world, and this experience is not objective but is affected by the extent to which the world favors (affords) or impedes our projects.

Our conscious visual attention is linked to what Gibson (1986) would call affordances. It is our concerns and interests that determine which aspects of the visual input we receive gain vividness and prominence in our conscious experience. And, as Nico Frijda, among others, has agued, emotions and feelings are "modes of relational action readiness, either in the form of tendencies to establish, maintain, or disrupt a relationship with the environment or in the form of modes of relational readiness as such" (1986, 71). It follows from this view that emotions and feelings play a central role in our visual consciousness, because they are important determinants of our visual attention and our action readiness in relation to what we see. As Georges Mandler has argued, "Consciousness is limited in capacity and it is constructed so as to respond to the current situational and intentional imperatives" (1997, 482).

If we combine the points made by Gibson, Frijda, Panksepp, and Mandler, we arrive at the following: our conscious experience expresses our current situational and intentional imperatives, including the emotions that represent our action tendencies. These emotions also represent the situational affordances, equalia that is, whether or not a given situation affords or offers scope for action. A subjective feeling would therefore indicate that a given situation does not (fully) support action. Action may be blocked because there is insufficient visual information to support it: scenes that take place in foggy weather are often experienced as subjective. Fog impedes visual access to space and therefore impedes actions, thereby eliciting subjective feelings because, as we have seen, feelings of subjectivity represent innate warning signals: be careful when acting on this information.

Ray Jackendoff (1987) has shown that feelings are an important element in our consciousness. He argues that what we are conscious of are perceptual surfaces, such as images or words, whereas we have no direct access to our cognitive processes, which take place at a nonconscious level. Feelings are ways in which we can consciously communicate with these unconscious processes. Tip-of-the-tongue feelings—the sensation that there is something just below the surface—both direct our attention to unconscious processes and provide some assurance that we can get in contact with these processes. Feelings of subjectivity and reality are conscious representations of nonconscious or semiconscious mental processes, and act as motivators for stop or go tendencies. The subjective feelings evoked by film sequences are mostly intersubjective—that is, shared: there is seldom any debate about whether a given film sequence is subjective or not.

Objective Propositional Acts and Subjective Mental Associations

In earlier chapters we have discussed action and the blocking of action in relation to agencies acting in an external world. When Indiana Jones runs from a boulder in *Raiders of the Lost Ark*, we simulate his actions as taking place in an objective, distal world (the surfaces from which the light information has originated). However, we may also perform actions that take place in our sensory organs and in our minds (in our proximal space). When we state a proposition such as "elephants are gray and have trunks," we perform a mental act that probably relies on some of the premotor circuits that played an important role in the development of language. I argue that propositional mental acts use some of the mental structures that were developed to control actions. Thus some of the procedures that enable us physically to manipulate and act within the external world are reused at a symbolic or mental level to make thought-actions, and this constitutes an important part of our mental processing. Cognitive linguists such as George Lakoff (e.g., Lakoff 1987) and Mark Johnson (e.g., Johnson 1987) have shown how many key linguistic structures are based on image schemata, either referring to simple perceptual activities ("We see a solution to our problem") or using aspects of motion in space as metaphors for mental processes ("We are trying to find a way to solve the problem, but most paths seem to be blocked"). One of the key language centers in the brain, Broca's center, is part of the premotor cortex, and it has been argued (Gallese and Stamenov 2002) that language originally developed from hand gesticulation, another indication of the close link between propositional language and action. Thus language and propositions may simulate the action aspects of the PECMA flow.

Making a proposition therefore gives rise to the same feeling of dealing with real, objective phenomena as one gets from undertaking physical actions in an external space. Propositions such as "The blue ghost ate all the tomatoes," or "The ghost had two ears" feel objective on the surface because it requires active agency to assert or process such propositions. If we assume that propositional sentences represent a new use of mental mechanisms originally developed for controlling actions and the perceptual processes linked to actions and affordances, it follows that the mental actions involved when watching a film will evoke a feeling of reality similar to that evoked by physical action. A documentary that makes a number of propositions thus gives us a sense of reality; similarly, even a fiction film that uses establishing shots or cutaways to support certain propositions will give us a feeling of objectivity. If, for example, a film presents a short establishing shot showing the skyline of New York City, it will cue a brief sequence of thoughts and propositions in the head of the viewer: this is New York City; there's the Empire State Building; and so on. Documentaries, online reporting, and so on are usually designed precisely to cue such a sequence of propositional acts in the viewer.

However, if there is no opportunity to perform propositional acts in response to media products (or online perceptions), what we experience, instead, is a series of associations that seem partly to belong to an interior mental space. This interior space consists of more unfocused (associative) perceptual elements to which we relate only through largely involuntary mechanisms that are isolated from action tendencies. Feelings of objectivity or subjectivity allow us to form a conscious representation of whether the situational and intentional imperatives elicit mental processes mapped on an external (distal) space or perceived as belonging to an internal (proximal) mental space. The switch between the two spaces, world and mind, occurs through activating or deactivating action tendencies and is represented in our consciousness by a switch in feelings, from objectivity to subjectivity. If we froze a film sequence to a still, for example, it would no longer give rise to action tendencies and the frozen image would therefore elicit subjective feelings: we would experience our perceptions as proximal, that is, as belonging to the interior mental realm.

Films use many different procedures to evoke subjective feelings by impeding or blocking our ability to project what we see onto an objective, exterior space. The simplest way to evoke a feeling of subjectivity is to present images that elicit only a very limited number of propositions and which have no obvious links with the concerns of the protagonists. If the sequence persists beyond the brief time required for the viewer to make all the propositions cued by the images, the mind will shift to subjective mode. Our first procedure in watching a film sequence is to deal with it as a stream of information that cues the construction of objective spaces and processes. But if we fail to find anything that can focus our attention—such as the protagonists and their concerns, or some proposition-eliciting phenomena—we will shift into an unfocused default mode. In this default mode, the mind tries out all the various associations that may pop up. This method of creating subjectivity can therefore be called subjectivity by default.

Many of Marguerite Duras's films have long-drawn-out, perceptually realistic scenes depicting spaces in which little or nothing happens. Despite the fact that these spaces are very real, such scenes elicit a subjective feeling. Perceptual realism is not sufficient for eliciting objective feelings. A film scene depicting an ordinary three-dimensional space is perceptually real and objective, but subjective feelings are elicited by spaces in which little occurs and which do not cue propositions. In other words, feelings of subjectivity and objectivity relate to the kinds of physical and mental processes that a given sequence cues. If the time-spaces presented cue a form of mental activity that is linked to the implementation of the protagonists' concerns in the film, or which give rise to propositions, they will elicit feelings of objectivity. But if the protagonists in the film are prevented from acting on their concerns, or if the sequence provides audiovisual information that does not cue propositions, we experience the given film sequence as subjective.

Good examples of subjectivity by default can be found in Marguerite Duras's films, for example, *Aurélia Steiner*. A randomly picked shot from this film shows a railway station, but the scene lasts so long, and the narrative motivation for showing it is so slender, that we quickly exhaust the possibilities for making propositions from it ("This is a railway station"). Thus we are forced to switch into a more unfocused mode; diffuse semiconscious or unconscious associations and subjective feelings indicate that no actions or focused propositions are possible. The film thus acquires a lyrical associative toning. In this context, the blocking of the mental flow prompts us to enter the default mode. If what we experience cannot be transformed through physical or mental action (the construction of propositions), the brain returns to an earlier, more unfocused stage of the PECMA flow in which the various components of our perceptions are linked in a diffuse, lyrical-associative way.

A less obvious example of subjectivity by default can be seen in Jean-Luc Godard's *Two or Three Things I Know about Her*. The film makes extensive use of shots that resemble documentary footage, first because they lack any close connection to the concerns of the fictitious protagonists (often, indeed, the protagonists are not physically present at any of the locations shown in this documentary mode), and second because certain aspects of the film suggest that it is intended to be propositional, that is, to offer a portrait of the "new" Paris of the early 1960s. Thus the footage might give rise to propositions such as "These images show how Paris has been transformed into an alienated modern city." Let us look at three shots from the beginning of the film. We first see a shot of a flyover, then a shot under a flyover, and finally a street with pedestrians. All three shots could be part of a documentary on Paris, but other aspects of the film make it difficult to construe it as such. There is an obvious change from real sound being turned off in the first shot, to sound on in the second, to sound off in the third. The whispering voice-over also prevents us from experiencing what we see in full documentary mode. But most important, the shots are not sufficiently anchored by cognitive procedures that would make it possible to transform what we see into propositions. The film therefore acquires a lyrical associative toning, and (as in the example from Duras's film above) the blocking of the mental flow leads us to experience it in default mode.

Subjectivity by default is much more obvious when it is cued in films than in real life. In real life, our attention is controlled mainly by our current interests. If we have exhausted our interest in one aspect of our surroundings, we turn our attention to something else. But when we watch a film, we are no longer able to focus our attention on the basis of our own interests because the camera prefocuses our attention. Provided that the film catches our attention by presenting us with a focused narrative or salient audiovisual information, this lack of control of our attention does not disturb us. Potential conflict over control of the viewer's attention surfaces only when the filmmaker confronts the viewer with images that do not cue focused propositions or that have no links to the protagonists' concerns. Most ordinary filmgoers shun such films, labeling them dull because they do not have the motivation or the skills necessary to enjoy what they see. More sophisticated viewers switch into a subjective-lyrical mode, seeking at the same time to unravel parts of the associative network to which the film gives rise. A lyrical director such as Tarkovsky often uses long takes and extended scenes in which very little happens and in which it is difficult to pinpoint clear-cut protagonist concerns. Just after the credit sequence in *The Mirror*, for instance, there is a long sequence in which very little occurs: a man walks through a meadow, talks to a girl, and then slowly walks away. Viewers attuned to such scenes will shift from a propositional to a lyrical mode, in which percepts are associated in an unfocused search for subjective meaning.

Subjectivity by default offers the most obvious illustration of the fact that subjectivity in film depends on the circumstances of the film experience, not on the reality status of the phenomena viewed. The most common way of generating a sense of subjectivity in film, however, is to block or impede the viewer's ability to simulate an enactional (i.e., action-based) relationship to the world depicted on the screen. It is a precondition for simulating such a relationship to a given film space that the viewer has full, unimpeded perceptual access to that space. Thus distortions in (audio)visual access contribute to blocking enaction and creating subjectivity. But it is not essential to objectivity that the scenes viewed should be plausible or realistic. A scene from Spielberg's *E.T.* illustrates this point. In a famous sequence, Elliott bicycles up into the air, and although this act is fantastic, we do not initially feel it to be strongly unreal because Elliott is performing a meaningful action in a three-dimensional space. But when, for a brief moment, Elliott and E.T. are silhouetted against the moon (and later in the film against the setting sun), and thus brought into an abstract, visual proximity to enormous cosmic forces with which they and the viewer can interact only in a passive, perceptual manner, the experience is strongly symbolic and subjective. The external three-dimensional world has suddenly been transformed into a mental, two-dimensional, mythical world. In the viewer's nonconscious reasoning, whatever cannot be acted on must belong to the mental realm. The imagery in these scenes also suggests a sublime, action-blocking mismatch between the protagonist and the setting. When the boy rides past the rising moon, and later on past the enormous, glowing sun, the experience belongs to the interior world, for it highlights the ways in which these cosmic elements function as mental, mythic percepts. These film sequences focus on prime cosmic forces, the sun and the moon, to which we have only a passive perceptual relation. A documentary film might show the sun and the moon in another context that emphasized objectivity and control: images of the sun and moon might be accompanied, for instance, by a voice-over telling us that these are some of the closest celestial objects to the earth and are notable for their round luminous surfaces. *E.T.* and our hypothetical documentary both take place in a symbolically exterior space, but in the case of *E.T.* no action follows from our perception of the images, whereas the documentary scene inspires us to construct propositions concerning the sun and moon, thus transforming the percept to mental activity that generates a sense of reality.

The *E.T.* example highlights the way in which our sense of subjectivity often arises from stop effects or time-out effects. When Elliot starts riding up into the air we recognize that the scene is unreal, but because of the strong action cues—Elliot is riding vigorously along a trajectory, albeit an unusual one—we are lured into attributing a kind of realism to the images. However, the shift from three dimensions to two dimensions that occurs when the figures turn into silhouettes, and the mismatch between the middle ground and the background, together put a stop to any enactive, objective simulation of the scene. For a short while the viewer introjects the images, feeling that they express some unfocused, atemporal, symbolic meaning belonging to the mental rather than the external world. The blocking of enactive simulation by the symbolic sequence also evokes strong, saturated feelings, fueling an unfocused search into unconscious associative processes. The stop effect represents a reaction to ambiguous input, and there are good evolutionary reasons—in terms of survival value—to explain why we immediately respond to such input by attempting to sort out and clarify the ambiguity.

A Typology of Factors That Give Rise to Subjectivity in Film

Film subjectivity can be elicited by six main factors:

1. Subjectivity by default, as discussed above: this effect stems from sequences in which there are few or no actions and little or no scope for focused propositions.
2. A represented space that impedes perceptual access
3. Deviant or distorted enactional or perceptual access to a represented space
4. Actions and processes that deviate in certain ways from normal objective actions and processes
5. Situations with a problematic reality status that block interaction
6. Deviant emotional phenomena and reactions

I now proceed to a more detailed account of the key ways in which subjectivity is represented in film and show how these various ways fit into the overall pattern, in which subjectivity arises from the blocking or absence of action tendencies. I will examine these different approaches by describing prototypical phenomena that cue subjectivity. These prototypes do not represent an exhaustive list: films can deviate from our reality schemata and our knowledge of reality in more or less infinite ways. Furthermore, I have isolated the various prototypes for analytical purposes, but they often work together or are intertwined.

A Given Film Sequence Includes Scenes in Which Nothing Occurs

The simplest way to create subjectivity, as we have seen, is to present scenes in which little or nothing happens and which do not offer any focused cues as to their propositional meaning. The mind of the viewer will embark on an intense search for meaning by activating unfocused associations. The strong subjective feelings that arise in this case express this unfocused search for associational meaning. Although it is a simple matter in principle to create subjectivity by default, many viewers may refuse to respond by activating strong emotions and searching for hidden meanings. Filmmakers such as Tarkovsky, who make extensive use of the pathos of minimal action, attract a relatively small audience. Subjectivity by default must therefore rely either on strong motivations built up in previous scenes (as when Truffaut's *The 400 Blows* ends with a freeze frame), or on a more select audience that is strongly motivated to engage in a subjective, lyrical search for unfocused, associative meaning and to be open to the feelings involved.

The Represented Space Blocks or Impedes Perceptual Access

The optimal scene for objective actions is a well-lit three-dimensional world, in which we see clearly delineated objects (Grodal 2005). Light and air are optimally invisible media through which to view the world. They allow us to get maximum information about our environment, affording us a clear view of trees, cars, houses, people, and so on by which to orient our actions. In certain situations, however, our access to information is impeded—for example, by fog, rain, darkness, complex shadows, heat haze, or confusing assemblies of objects with blurred and indistinct boundaries. Such scenes hamper our ability to orient ourselves and thus impede our actions. Normally, the mental processes that mediate our perception of the world are masked; like the air around us, these unconscious media are transparent. But when our vision or hearing is impeded, we become conscious of these mediating processes.

Thus scenes designed to elicit subjective feelings make frequent use of deviant types of weather and light. Such motifs gained particular popularity in the romantic period. Painters and poets sought to block access to the spaces they depicted in order to highlight subjective experiences, and later on the impressionists, among others, developed new techniques for blocking our perceptions of spaces and blurring the boundaries of objects. Filmmakers have reused many of these devices; most famous, perhaps, among the romantic film effects are the wet, foggy streets that recur in film noir, while Jean Renoir, Kurosawa, and Bergman are notable for their impressionistic effects: blurred figures and shapes, for example, in mysterious forests where sunshine is filtered through foliage (figure 10.1). But mood-inspiring uses of fluctuations in light and weather are so widespread that they almost escape our conscious attention, except insofar as we think of them as clichés.

FIGURE 10.1. Subjective representations diminish or block an experience of a space of unimpeded action, resulting in a mentalist toning of the experience. In this dream scene in Bergman's *Wild Strawberries*, the subjective toning is done by backlighting so that the objects and space tend to be flat, two-dimensional, and the gaze of Victor Sjöström as Dr. Borg is averted toward the sky; this emphasizes the subjective, mental experience because its objects are invisible memories. *Wild Strawberries* © Svensk Filmindustri 1957.

The feeling of cliché attached to deviant light and weather arises partly from our innate mental architecture (Grodal 2005). Normally, our perception of space is linked to the mental functions that control our actions. When our view is unimpeded, spaces and objects appear as objective, distal phenomena that invite specific, focused attention. When our vision is impeded, however, our experience becomes proximal and subjective, as we know from sunset moods. To take an example from the first part of Fincher's *Se7en*: police detectives are investigating a murder during a downpour (and in an environment with numerous obstacles). The rain creates a claustrophobic feeling of lack of control and activates strong simulations of tactile qualities such as wetness, dirt, and so on. Our distal experience of space is impeded and our proximal awareness activated, as if the intentional-affective beam had been blocked, causing diffuse emotional arousal. Another way of describing this is that our experiential space has been narrowed to the confines of our bodies as we simulate the scene. This experience may be intensified by activating imaginary tactile sensations—for instance, by showing the protagonists getting soaked in the rain. Whether this narrowing of space and activation of tactile sensations is a positive or a negative experience depends, of course, on the context. In *Se7en* the constant rain cues claustrophobia, whereas in other films rain and water cue positive feelings. Such positive feelings are linked to an acceptance of the fact that voluntary action is blocked, whereas negative feelings stem from frustration. In a lyrical film, fog might be experienced as providing a positive, subjective freedom for the mind to wander, unconstrained by the external world (here, the mind is engaged in free "top-down" processes), and in a mainstream film the sunset may be associated with feelings of lyricism and a relaxation of control. In a mystery or thriller, however, a foggy scene might be associated with painful disorientation and loss of control.

It is obvious that foggy, rainy, or dark landscapes are just as real as sunny landscapes or cityscapes. Thus, as we have seen, the sense of subjectivity or objectivity depends not on the reality or otherwise of a given scene but on its affordances, on the extent to which it supports or impedes the protagonist's or the viewer's current situational and intentional imperatives.

Action-Based or Perceptual Access to a Space Is Deviant or Distorted

In the previous section I dealt with the ways in which our perceptual access to visual space can be impeded by deviant features of that world. I now turn to the ways in which special or deviant relationships between the viewer-protagonist and a given space can likewise create feelings of subjectivity.

In order to interact with the world, we need it to be middle-sized, that is, to be able to see it in medium shots or close-ups. In these formats, people can reach out for coffee cups, kiss, fight with their opponents, and so on. However, subjective representations often use extreme formats that make human action difficult or impossible: long shots showing sublime mountain views, for instance, or cosmic perspectives such as we find in Kubrick's *2001: A Space Odyssey* or in Lucas's *Star Wars*. In the typical romantic mountain scene, the viewer-protagonist can interact perceptually with the places seen in far-off vistas, but there is no chance of physical interaction with them. Space films often depict spaces and objects that are beyond normal interaction. In traditional aesthetics, experiences in which perception is dissociated from interaction are called sublime.

On the surface it is paradoxical that a confrontation with something manifestly real, such as a mountain, can elicit subjective feelings, yet it is logical enough that we experience as subjective processes that can be dealt with only in the mind. These experiences and many of those described below illustrate the paradoxical rule of thumb, that the more the protagonists are turned into objects or passive subjects, perhaps through their absorption into larger social, biological, or cosmic totalities, the more the viewer will experience a feeling of subjectivity induced by stalled interaction.

Subjective representations may also go to the other extreme, using ultra-close-ups—for example, of microscopic objects—that render normal interaction impossible. In other cases the framing, scale, or angle may be unusual, making it difficult to recognize the objects and creating a feeling of unfamiliarity. Our experience of objective reality is based on a series of prototypical views of objects: if a given object is represented in a way that markedly deviates from the prototype, it will take time to perform the mental rotation necessary to recognize it and thus highlight the mental, top-down aspect of vision.

In order to interact with the world, we seek optimal clarity by focusing our eyes and filtering the sounds that come to our ears. This gives us the sense of objective, unmediated access to the world and enables us to interact with it. Distorted or unfocused images block this access and draw attention to the subjective and mediated aspects of our experience. Strong emotions—sometimes accompanied by tears—are among the factors that distort our perceptual control, and expressionist and horror films emulate this distortion. At the other extreme, complete relaxation can also soften our focus. Thus classic Hollywood films create an emotional, romantic atmosphere by using soft-focus photography, thereby blocking action tendencies and replacing them with relaxed, unfocused contemplation. A mismatch between visual and acoustic cues can also prompt a feeling of subjectivity. The cues may be incongruent in their temporal source (as in many film noirs, when a voice-over comments in the past tense on images from the past) or in their geographic location (for example, a medium shot of a person may be accompanied by an apparently distant voice). Such sequences cannot be synthesized into a unified experience of reality and will therefore create a feeling of subjectivity.

A rich means of eliciting subjective feelings (one that is functionally related to perceptual distortion, comprehensively analyzed in Branigan 1984, 1992) consists in highlighting the fact that the viewer does not have access to an objectively given space; rather, his view of the scene is limited to that of a given character. Although all film spaces in principle are seen from a specific point of view—that of the camera—viewers process moving images by understanding them as cues to perceive objective spaces and objects that exist independently, regardless of the camera's position, just as we in the real world move eyes and head to soak in information to construct objective, object-centered representations of the world. There is normally enough information in film images to enable the viewer to work out the position from which it was filmed, but it is uneconomical to base our comprehension of the scene on this subjective point of view (Marr 1982). However, the filmmaker may want to highlight the fact that a given image is subjective, thereby activating the feeling that our view is restricted. Here, as elsewhere, subjectivity often entails restriction: the subjective feeling results from the constraints imposed on potentially unimpeded access. A famous example of subjective point of view can be found in Montgomery's *Lady in the Lake*; here, the entire film is shot from the main character's point of view. The resulting information deficit makes the viewer feel that he or she has no control over the fictitious world, and this elicits strong subjective feelings which also reflect that the experience is disembodied, not only because there is no (visual) body to anchor the experience but also because of the way in which those primitive self-feelings that I discussed in chapter 8 and that constitute emotion-charged agency functions are blocked because of the felt lack of control of vision.

The Actions and Processes Deviate in Certain Ways

To interact with the world, we need to be in a position to act as individualized agents who are able to perform voluntary goal-directed actions. Subjective film sequences use various means to block this sense of voluntary individualized agency.

One means of doing so is to create actions that can be acted out only by superhuman agencies or by collective identities, which reduce the individual to being a token of a type. In some of the key scenes of Spielberg's *Close Encounters of the Third Kind*, humankind as a species interacts with aliens as a species. Individual agencies are obliged to forswear individual action and enter into a shared identity as humans. Viewers shed tears when they vicariously give up their individual identities in order to assume a sublime identity as members of a species. Similarly powerful subjective feelings and autonomic reactions are often elicited by melodramas in which individuals incarnate social roles, such as *mother, man, woman, American*, thus giving up their own free will to act as social symbols.

Another way to block individual subjectivity is to introduce scenes in which the protagonists participate only passively. Melodramas often involve situations in which natural phenomena or human-caused disasters—wind, waves, fire, war, or biological growth and decay—are the main forces. The protagonists are therefore forced to switch off their voluntary reactions and participate passively in the experience. *Gone with the Wind* offers a classical example of this, *Titanic* a modern one.

In the previous paragraphs, I have dealt with different types of mismatch between representations and actions that are nevertheless linked in time and space. But many films create a temporal mismatch by expanding or compressing normal time. Montage sequences, like the one depicting the concert tour in Welles's *Citizen Kane*, offer a simple way to do this. A more complex method can be seen in Laughton's *The Night of the Hunter*, where two children are shown traveling down a river in a boat. The scene that we witness in normal time is clearly supposed to take place in an extended, mythical time with no clear temporal boundaries. The odyssey in *2001: A Space Odyssey* likewise represents an eternal journey from birth to old age, from Earth to some strange cosmic place. Such undefined time obviously blocks interaction and creates sublime subjective feelings: unable to simulate the situation through active coping mechanisms, the viewer is reduced to a passive onlooker. As we can see, then, one way of blocking voluntary action is to rise above the level of the autonomous individual. Another way is to descend below that level. The autonomic aspect of our embodied lives is normally masked by our voluntary endeavors. But filmmakers can focus attention on these autonomic processes by including heartbeats or heavy breathing in the soundtrack or by showing muscular spasms or eye movements. Alternatively, they can isolate parts of the body, removing them from a motivated totality and perhaps showing subjective reactions such as hands in convulsion. They may also use rhythm, either in physical movement or in music, to suggest a more primitive, subjective form of motion than voluntary, goal-directed action. Many musicals or music videos use rhythm to show people losing free will and succumbing to orgiastic forces. In Parker's *Pink Floyd: The Wall*, for instance, rhythm creates a subjective feeling arising from loss of voluntary control. In many cases, superindividual and subindividual processes are linked (as in the case of marching soldiers or orgiastic dances that express generic rather than individual identity).

Film as a medium has powerful means at its disposal to depict the loss of voluntary individual control. Slow motion, accelerated motion, and repetitive mechanical action are some of the devices used to create a feeling of subjectivity by blocking voluntary action. Music videos, in particular, use and abuse such effects in order to create this sense of subjectivity.

All the subjective processes outlined above are formally anchored in an external space, although the images of that space activated interior and subjective forms of experience. But many scenes that elicit subjectivity are designed instead to simulate mental processes such as dreams, hallucinations, daydreams, memories, or associative streams of consciousness. Normally, we order our experience of the external world through using schemata that slot spaces, objects, and events into linear time linked to discrete time-spaces because those processes that define time in stories as well as in real life develop linearly from beginning to end. However, our memory and imagination are not limited by such time-space-object schemata. Quite disparate spaces, objects, and events can be linked or even fused in our imagination, because our minds consist of enormous networks of associations with no constraints of time and space. Films can simulate aspects of these associative networks by various means: through flashbacks, double exposures, or montage sequences, different times, spaces, objects, or events can all be fused into a unified experience.

Such rearrangements of time and place create a feeling of subjectivity for three intertwined reasons. First, when the temporal order is scrambled, we can no longer simulate what we see as a series of forward-directed actions and processes, and this disrupts the normal irreversible linear interaction between emotion, cognition, and action in the PECMA flow. Second, many memories refer to events that have already been enacted and have led to consequences that cannot be undone, so the experience of these events is sealed off from online enaction. Third, our minds work precisely through the associative ordering of phenomena. The subjective, lyrical scrambling of narrative order thus dams up our emotions and creates saturated experiences.

Resnais's *Last Year in Marienbad* offers a prototypical case of the scrambled, associative narrative. The film has no clear temporal structure and the situations and spaces we encounter in it are confusing and disorienting. In music videos, too, the linear narrative is often scrambled or completely absent. Instead of clear actions and goals, we are bombarded with scenes and images that can only be assembled in the form of associative fields. There is no scope for action that would release the tension from painful or seductive images.

We often use the term *dreamlike* to describe associative, scrambled narratives, precisely because in dreams our associations work without any higher mental control and our ability to act is completely blocked.

A common source of subjectivity is images that the viewer interprets as mental figures or metaphors (Whittock 1990). When a machine in Lang's *Metropolis* is transformed by a series of superimpositions into a man-eating Moloch, the viewer interprets what he or she sees as a mental figure or metaphor. Similarly, in Cronenberg's *Videodrome* we see a man's stomach equipped with a videocassette slot—a metaphor for the way that we have been transformed by audiovisual media.

A borderline case of experiences that are perceived partly as subjective, partly as objective consists of spaces that are real, but which in one way or another violate innate conceptions of reality. Our minds are preset to certain expectations about the way the world looks: we expect the natural environment to conform to certain rules. Here are three assumptions that we tend to make about the natural world:

1. It is a fractal world, that is, one that has certain regularities but a great many variations within these regularities. Thus all trees share the same basic features but each individual tree has many singular features and cannot be described by simple geometric figures alone.
2. The world is made up of concrete-composite objects: the eyes are placed in a certain position in relation to the nose and eyebrows; the door is positioned between or alongside the windows, and so on.
3. The world is made up of objects that have both a structural outline and an irregular, fractal texture.

However, our present culture produces many artifacts that violate these assumptions. Modern designs, for example, often consist of simple geometric figures that could be identically reproduced and which may be noncomposite and completely lacking in texture. Such artifacts are of course just as real as many natural phenomena, and familiarity makes us accept them as such. Nevertheless, they can easily be used to cue a feeling of unreality and subjectivity. The reason for this is perhaps that phenomena such as geometric figures, pure surfaces, and paradigms of similar objects echo the way that our minds typically work: extracting types from tokens that are analyzed by means of innate geometric filters and dispensing with textures in order to compress our mental data files. An example of this can be seen in Burton's *Edward Scissorhands*. The suburban houses in the film consist of neat geometric elements painted in pastel colors. This creates an eerie subjective effect that is also cued by the narrative, and although this effect certainly has a cultural component (based on cultural norms as to what constitutes reality), it is tempting to suggest that we also embark from innate assumptions about what is real.

Situations with a Special or Problematic Reality Status

So far we have looked at ways in which deviant exterior worlds, perceptions, or mental experiences create subjectivity. Although the above-mentioned mental experiences relate to real phenomena (fog is real, dreams are real, and so on), we experience them as unreal, because they allow no scope for action. Another group of subjectivity-eliciting stimuli are phenomena that are unreal in the sense that they violate basic assumptions about the world. In Coppola's *Bram Stoker's Dracula*, Jonathan Harker is confronted with three female vampires. The interaction between vampires or ghosts and humans cannot, of course, be construed as real since humans cannot react to supernatural phenomena, and this blocking thus gives rise to subjective feelings. This resembles the way in which mental experiences are elicited (for instance, through lack of modality synthesis: the ghosts may be seen but not felt, and cannot be harmed by physical acts), but the difference is that supernatural scenes indicate that our naturalistic perception of the exterior world may be wrong. Many horror films use all kinds of supernatural gimmicks to block interaction and thereby create strong saturated effects.

Often such supernatural experiences closely resemble the experience of dreams. In Bergman's *Wild Strawberries*, an old professor has a dream in which he sees his own face as a dead man. The strong subjective feeling that this scene elicits arises not only because we sense that it must be a dream, but because we get the feeling that the exterior world may be ruled by supernatural laws that make normal interactions and representations impossible. But if a filmmaker creates a film in which all the agents act at this supernatural level, and are therefore completely able to interact, the subjective effect disappears.

Sometimes it is unclear whether a given phenomenon in a film is to be understood as supernatural or as the projection of an interior, deviant consciousness. Take, for example, Wiene's *The Cabinet of Dr. Caligari*, in which there are numerous unreal deviations from the normal world. Such borderline scenes allow for two competing hypotheses: either this is an artificial expression of mental phenomena or it is an unreal, supernatural space.

Deviant Emotional Phenomena and Reactions

I have previously mentioned (Grodal 1997) how comic reactions may function as a defense against the impact of emotions such as empathy with suffering people. Hitchcock's *The Trouble with Harry* offers an example of the way in which a subjectivizing effect can be created by blocking normal empathetic feelings. When subjectivity functions as an emotional defense, there is a complex relationship between cause and effect, because the subjective feeling is not only a reaction to certain action-blocking phenomena but also contributes to the pragmatic verdict that what we are looking at is unreal and subjective, thereby diminishing the impact that such situations would otherwise have on the viewer. When we watch a scene with a strong emotional content, such as the shower scene in *Psycho*, we feel it to be unreal, even though it may be very realistic, because such scenes activate defense mechanisms that allow us to place their reality status in subjective brackets in order to make the strong emotions bearable. Scenes that depict violent and irreparable mutilations to the body block coping actions and provide emotional muffling by using the only coping strategy available and redefining the reality status of what we are seeing. People in a state of shock often find the experience dreamlike or nightmarish, indicating this kind of defense through subjectivization.

The subjectivity that we experience in watching films like *Se7en*, which deal with all sorts of sordid aspects of the human body and human desires, is in part a response to the fact that enaction is blocked, but also represents a defense mechanism against the full impact of what is seen. Representations of repellent scenes, from gory mutilations to garbage, are often filtered and muffled by a subjective setting. But subjective framings can also be used with scenes that elicit strong positive affects (for instance, explicit sexual representations), thereby acting as control mechanisms that muffle these scenes' affective impact.

A sense of subjective unreality can also be activated by sudden powerful emotional shifts, whether from negative to positive or vice versa. Take, for example, the ending of Gary Marshall's *Pretty Woman*, where (strongly cued) feelings of subjectivity bracket the positive emotions we feel. Similarly, the marked reversal to positive experiences in *Blade Runner* leads us to experience the happy ending as unreal.

The feeling of subjectivity can further be aroused by depictions of characters with deviant, psychopathic emotions. Deviant emotions relating to sex and death are the hallmark of many psycho-thrillers: take, for example, *Psycho* or Kershner's *Eyes of Laura Mars*. These subjective feelings serve to block our identification with the actions depicted. The subjectivizing effect of deviant emotional responses is even more striking where they appear incongruously in otherwise normal settings, as in Godard's *Pierrot le Fou*, when a dead body is found in the apartment, but the actors continue to behave as if they were part of a happy musical.

Conclusion

In this chapter, I have shown how feelings of subjectivity are linked to different phenomena that have one thing in common, namely that they impede or block the PECMA flow by impeding or blocking action or propositional cognition. There are many ways to cue subjective experiences: opaque spaces, perceptual distortions, deviant processes, emotions or supernatural phenomena, or sudden emotional shifts in which subjective feelings are part of a process of reorientation.

The reorientation that accompanies subjectivity may take the form of a reflection on the blocking of action, or of a simple time-out—what is it we are witnessing here? Or it may involve a shift from interpreting what we see as part of an exterior world, to understanding it as the projection of an interior world. The subjective feelings associated with our mental processes therefore serve a cognitive function, telling us not to confuse these mental events with exterior phenomena. Subjective feelings of unreality are probably the shorthand version of semiconscious or unconscious cognitive judgments, equalias that tell us to postpone or block action because of insufficient information. Feelings of unreality in relation to very strong (mainly negative) emotions may serve to prevent emotional overload that would make action impossible; here, the emotion-eliciting situation is evaluated as unreal, thus enabling us to filter the emotional impact.

The shift from objective to subjective mode usually seems to be followed by a shift from a more focused to a more unfocused state of consciousness. The strong voluntary attitude associated with being an active agency is replaced by a more autonomic mental attitude, such as we feel in a romantic twilight scene. Subjective states are mostly passive associative states, in which our unfocused experience of the nonmuscular parts of our bodies and the unfocused parts of our minds come to the fore. But this shift to a more unfocused state of consciousness may also be part of a reorienting process, as when ambiguous images fail to provide any obvious clues to their meaning and cue a diffuse mental search, or distorted images block action and cue us to try to clarify what is happening. Subjectivity by default also acts as part of a reorienting process: thus lyrical scenes elicit a reorientation from focused, linear processes to unfocused, associative processes.

The mental overload resulting from ambiguous images or from the activation of large networks of semiconscious or unconscious associations and processes may lead to subjective feelings. Powerful subjective feelings that seem to point to profound meanings do not guarantee that a given film actually possesses such meanings. Filmmakers can easily use blind spots in our mental machinery as input in creating ambiguous film sequences that lure the spectator into endless puzzles, prompting feelings that fuel the hermeneutic process in which the brain automatically searches for some hidden meaning. A filmmaker can activate so many associations that our short-term memory becomes overloaded, giving us the sense of some ungraspable fundamental significance (see chapter 9). Directors like Tarkovsky activate many different associations that are impossible to compress by categorization. Complex subjective images may be gratifying. Tarkovsky's activation of uncompressible associations linked to memories and fundamentals such as fire, water, or wind cues strong feelings of experiential plenitude. The passage across the sun and moon in *E.T.* is universally gratifying, because it draws on the fundamental experience of enormous cosmic forces,

placing the two characters in sudden close proximity to these forces by silhouett-
ing them against the sun and moon. Such scenes derive their strength from the
way in which they activate our senses and our past experiences.

Some philosophers and filmmakers define the difference between the action-
related linear mode, based on the focused use of short-term memory, and the
association-based alinear mode (which activates associations in a more unfocused
way) as an opposition between a Western mode of thinking versus a deconstruc-
tive, poststructural, Eastern mode. Deleuze's (1989) distinction between images
of movement and images of time represents a variation on this. But the shift from
objective to subjective film experiences is mainly a shift between two innate foci
and modes, two complementary experiential fields, and whether the viewer pre-
fers one or the other is more a question of individual taste than an epistemological choice. Because of constraints on the capacity of our consciousness, we cannot
at one and the same time have very focused and detailed experiences and very
comprehensive experiences. Nor can we simultaneously be in a state of heightened self-awareness (including an awareness of the huge number of associations
that stem from our experience of the world) and yet focus on our action-oriented
relationship to that world.

Film scholars often link subjectivity with perversions such as voyeurism or
fetishism, because the types of films that elicit such experiences are felt to be
strongly subjective. There is a good reason for this: voyeurism and fetishism activate sex-related phenomena but block the acting out of the desires elicited, so
that the viewer experiences a saturated activation of sexual associations without the tension associated with acting out those desires. Freud's description of
"fore-pleasure" and final pleasure provides a good framework for understanding
the subjective effect in terms of blocked action tendencies. However, there is no
need to resort to explanations like castration anxiety to account for the subjective toning of voyeuristic or fetishistic film scenes. By blocking enaction in such
films, the director cues powerful subjective experiences, just as he or she would
in creating a horror scene in which there was no enactive outlet. Subjective feelings contribute to the stop process that occurs whenever an action tendency is
impeded or blocked. This blocking is experienced as a sense of unreality, which
in turn represents an emotional representation of the blockage (whether the latter is caused by external constraints on perceptual access or by the reality status
of the input—i.e., by the fact that it consists of memories, dreams, supernatural
phenomena, or lyrical associations). Subjective feelings may take the form either
of a positive relaxation or of a negatively felt blocked urge. Often, the subjective
feeling is also motivationally linked to the process of reorientation, when the
mind shifts toward unfocused inner processes in order to clarify and objectiv-
ize the blocked input or, more generally, to search for mental associations. But

these inner processes can also be objective and focused when they are linked to propositional thinking.

The film viewing situation possesses elements that can serve to enhance subjective experiences. In real life, our perception of the exterior world is often a bottom-up process: the world just pops up in our mind. At the same time, the focus of our attention is mainly determined by our own current concerns and interests, and thus our perception and attention usually appear to us to be an expression of our free, voluntary control. Salient changes in weather and light are a notable exception. But when we watch a film, the focus of our attention is determined by the film sequence. Mainstream films generally mask this by presenting salient events that are linked to the characters' actions. But if the film sequence blocks our experience of control, by using some of the above-mentioned subjectivity-eliciting devices, we cannot—as we often can in real life—regain control by shifting our attention elsewhere or by self-generated coping strategies. Cinema is therefore a powerful medium for eliciting subjective feelings that are often larger than life.

11

The Experience of
Audiovisual Realism

In this chapter, I analyze some of the ways in which viewers experience realism. I seek to describe and characterize some of the processes and elements that cause viewers of audiovisual representations to have the sensation of realism. I assume that this sensation can be described in terms of the explicit or tacit feelings through which we evaluate the reality status of our perceptions, cognitions, and actions. Such feelings are shorthand tags for experiences that express the way in which frontal brain circuits evaluate the reality status of given perceptual phenomena. The core element in the sense of something being real is that it is a pragmatic feeling that involves a go signal to the embodied brain, just as the sense of unreality involves a stop signal. These feelings have evolved to support actions in a physical world by evaluating their feasibility and to distinguish information coming from inside body and brain from information coming from the exterior world. The development of sophisticated mental activities and the evolution of external media of representation have added further complexity to the cognitive-emotional responses that underlie our evaluations of reality status (Grodal 1997).

I start with a discussion of how the experience of realism is linked both to perceptual specificity and to certain mental schemas that give rise to a sense of typicality and familiarity, or recognizability. I then discuss how certain types of realism are based on the idea of the audiovisual screen as a transparent window on the real world, while others emphasize the role of filmmakers, reporters, or protagonists; for instance, by making subjective deconstructions of transparency to indicate the presence of the communicator. I discuss how some types of realism focus on a specific external reference, whereas other forms, constituting what I call categorical realism, seek to portray the general essence of things, and yet others, which I group under the term lyrical realism, activate subjective-associative references. Reality can also be constituted by assertions, as when certain human agencies assert that something is real, or through interaction with the agencies represented in the given medium. I go on to discuss how and why realism is often associated with seriousness and even with negative and painful experiences. Finally, I suggest that the postmodern reflexive skepticism toward realism in audiovisual media represents an emotional stance.

Reality and realism are among the central terms used to describe media representations. Because they are central, it is no wonder that they are used in many different ways, giving rise to ambiguity and inconsistency. Moreover, the concept of reality (and derivatives like *real*) plays a key role not only in describing media representations but in understanding real life, and here too the concept is used in many different ways. Our notions of what is real are based on many different elements, and in a given representation these various elements may each have their own reality status (Grodal 1997). A fiction film shot on location in New York may offer realistic acting and a realistic visual picture of the city but involve a wildly improbable story. Animators of fantasy films often devote considerable energy to making the movements of fantasy creatures look realistic—making them accord, that is, with the movement schemas that viewers have developed on the basis of experience. A nonfiction film may tell a true story but with pictures that offer only a weak sense of reality. That our concepts of reality and realism are based on many different parameters (schemas) in a given audiovisual representation means that the viewer performs a series of mental operations to assess the reality status of each parameter. The viewer may also evaluate the reality status of the film or program as a whole.

The concept of realism may be applied to fiction as well as nonfiction, because it does not require that what is represented be true and real in all its aspects, only that we experience it as a concrete representation that is or might be true. Our evaluation of realism in a given representation is based on a characterization of the representation, some concept of what the real world looks like, and a judgment as to the relationship between the given representation and that concept of the real world. The degree to which there is a positive match between representation and concepts of reality determines the degree to which the representation will be judged realistic. Thus, the question of realism involves not only characterizing representations, but giving an account of what different individuals, groups, cultures, or epochs understand as real, and that is a rather difficult and complex task. Some of the parameters on which we base our evaluations of what is real are relatively universal. Thus, for instance, our basic perception of the physical world is based largely on innate dispositions and on certain anthropocentric presuppositions (such as "earth is down," "heaven is up"; Lakoff 1987; Johnson 1987).

Universal norms exist by which we judge the degree of realism in the perceptual dimensions of a given representation. Such judgments, however, do not necessarily express the way in which a given culture evaluates the representation, since perceived realism may be relative to other representations. Thus, although the way in which people in the Middle Ages perceived the basic features of the world closely resembled our own, they were not able to represent their perceptions of exterior reality to the same degree that we can. They may therefore have perceived their medieval paintings as more realistic representations than we do, because our context for experiencing representations is different. Parameters other than basic perception—for instance, the norms of human behavior on which our evaluations of realism are based—may vary over time and from group to group. Although nonverbal communication is based on innate and universal dispositions, different groups emphasize or suppress certain features of their body language when engaging in such communication (Ekman and Friesen 1975). Moral norms that are unrealistic or deviant in one society may be considered normal in another culture. Knowledge of what exists in the world differs from person to person and from epoch to epoch. Thus, in evaluating whether a given representation may be labeled realistic, we need to perform a historical or cultural analysis that takes into account the knowledge of modes of representation and of the world that the representation maker, and the intended or actual viewers or audience, had at their disposal.

A further complication in evaluating realism derives from the fact that the term is often used to imply not only that a given representation must provide a good match to reality, but that it should also match those aspects of reality that are considered typical. Thus our concepts of realism and reality are not merely descriptive but often involve normative judgments as to what is typical in real life. Representations of the private lives of film stars or millionaires may be just as realistic as "kitchen sink" representations of the lives of ordinary people, but the latter will often be considered more typical and therefore more realistic than the former.

The concept of realism is defined not only by reference to reality but also by contrast to two other concepts, the abstract and the fantastic. This complicates things, because the abstract is not necessarily unreal: abstract scientific models, such as those showing the structure of atoms, have a very concrete correspondence to reality, and you might argue similarly that many (although certainly not all) abstract representations within the arts and media relate to certain general schematic features of objects and can thus be considered realistic representations of phenomena. Indeed, abstraction is to be found not only in the models and external representations we make, but in all the simplified schemas that we use in our basic mental representations of the world. It is therefore evident that realism has a different meaning when contrasted with abstraction than when contrasted with the fantastic (or the subjective). Thus the contrast between what is abstractly realistic and what is concretely realistic points to an experiential bias in the dominant use of the term realism. What is essential is not so much that a given representation be real as that viewers experience it as real. To understand the experience of the real in media representation, we must examine the basic mechanisms that constitute our experience of reality in general.

Perceptual Specificity

A basic component in our experience of physical and social reality is that what we perceive, what we see and hear, is perceptually determinate, that is, particular, complex, and unique. Few objects are exactly identical (except when factory-made), and no situations will repeat themselves in exactly the same way in real life. But even if we perceive a given situation or object as something unique, our minds will process these particular and unique phenomena into something simpler and more general. We perceive the particular uniqueness of a given tree, but at the same time our minds recognize that it possesses certain nonspecific structural features such as a trunk, branches, and leaves. When we store what we have perceived in our memories, we will tend to store it under a rather compressed, general description, and over time we will form mental schemas that reflect the invariant and typical features, although we may recall the specificities when we see the same phenomenon again. Our ability to slot what we perceive into existing schemas enables us to develop the superior categorization that provides the background for our comprehension of reality.

This general schematic description of the world's phenomena is close to what Lakoff (1987) has called basic-level categorization, the level of specificity that we normally use to interact with the world. Normally, in order to know how to act, all we need to know is that, for example, the creature in front of us is a dog, although sometimes it is important to be more specific—for instance, to register whether this particular dog is a pit bull or a dalmatian. Usually the general category *cup* is sufficient to describe the vessel we want to drink from, although sometimes we may require a particular shape or color. Likewise, to be able to open a given door and go through it, it is usually sufficient simply to identify the exit in question as a door. So, at one level—the level associated with our basic ability to act and maneuver in the world—the PECMA flow involves a powerful reduction of complexity. Bordwell (1986) has pointed out that in our comprehension of narratives we tend to throw away the stylistic complexity in order to uncover the *fabula*, the general story line. However, the perceptual complexity remains as a background that we can inspect when needed: is this an edible or a poisonous mushroom; does this door have a scratch; is there mildew on the corn; and so on. Thus, specificity is important as a background, represented in consciousness as a feeling of realism, to which we can return to get new or more specific information when we need to. Several types of aesthetics are based on going against the grain of our standard perceptions, focusing on specificity and blocking the transformation of the perception into something general. By contrast, animated films for children often save the children some of the work of transforming complex, texture-rich images into more general schematic representations by leaving out a lot of detail and focusing children's attention on the basic level.

If we take a developmental and historical perspective, we see that both children and early humans start out with abstract, schematic representation, drawing other human beings, for example, by making circles for heads and eyes, lines for limbs, and so on (Gardner 1982; Arnheim 1974). Verbal descriptions likewise start at a very general categorical level—man, woman, river, and so on—and, as Erich Auerbach (1974) has shown in his book *Mimesis*, the ability to create very specific and detailed realistic verbal descriptions developed only through a long historical process. Thus, from a historical perspective, the particular and unique have become the hallmark of direct perception, because only they can provide the necessarily complex-specific salience typical of the experience of the real, whereas mental or physical representations may be more abstract and schematic.

This complex-specific salience gives the viewer the sense of being confronted with real physical events and phenomena. Other things being equal, perceptual uniqueness and complexity enhance the feeling of realism, because the representation is directly simulated in our brains as if we were confronted with reality. Stick men or computer graphics with poor texture are less realistic than good photographs. Perceptual realism is often described in relation to indexicality, that is, realistic representations index, point to, or are an imprint of phenomena that exist in real worlds. Bazin (1967) pointed out that a photograph or film is supposed to be a true imprint of reality, generated via the photographic process. However, from an experiential point of view it is not only our knowledge of the photographic process that gives us the feeling of realism but the very salience of the experience of seeing it, and this salience may be created independently of any indexical relation: in other words, the picture may have been staged or the image may have been produced by a computer and if this is well done, the effect of realism by visual salience is driven by innate specifications, not by any true indexicality.

From a developmental perspective, knowledge of indexicality is acquired, not innate; small children take film and television for granted; they are fascinated by audiovisual representations and they may draw crude distinctions between more or less realistic programs without possessing the faintest knowledge of how films or photographs are produced. The impression of reality caused by a complex-particular film sequence represents an immediate reaction, based on innate dispositions combined with the fundamental and universal experience of reality. Furthermore, a Bazinian indexicality demands cultural knowledge: small children may not know whether green or blue people as portrayed in many fantasy films or science fiction films exist or not, and even previously only cost or public control prevented distorted film representations of reality.

Our basic attitude is that what we see exists. So if we see an angel in a film, we intuitively and at first blush feel that it exists in the same way as all those real creatures that we see, because, as mentioned earlier, seeing is believing and disconfirmation needs a special effort (Gilbert et al. 1990). The frontal brain needs to perform reality status evaluations, cognitive evaluations to qualify that what we see has no reference in real worlds; angels are fantasy creatures. Except where memories, dreams, and thoughts are concerned, the innate functioning of our brains presupposes that anything seen must exist, because our brains were not constructed in a media environment. Thus, small children may not perceive realistic films as representations of certain profilmic events, but rather as a display of certain people and events that enjoy a special reality status (they cannot be touched or interacted with). Even in the case of adults, a special effort is required to imagine the profilmic event as distinct from the immediate experience. We constantly add to our knowledge and thereby enrich our phenomenal experience; thus, for example, we may learn about the earth's rotation, and this may enrich our basic experience of the sun rising in the morning, crossing the sky, and setting in the evening without, however, replacing the basic phenomenological experience. I know when I watch the evening news that what I am seeing is a profilmic event in some remote TV studio, but my immediate experience does not reflect this fact. The images are somehow present on my TV screen and in my consciousness as an "adjacent room," and only by making a special effort can I concretely imagine the studio as located far away.

Our knowledge modifies our experience of realism. We know that a science fiction film is staged or animated, just as we know that, even though it is of poor quality, the famous Rodney King videotape shows us real events. There is thus a potential conflict between the kind of realism established by perception and that established by knowledge. Wolterstorff has argued (see Plantinga 1997) that fiction films do not assert anything about the truth of a given story, but merely invite us to consider a given state of affairs, whereas nonfiction films assert that the scenes they present actually occurred in the real world as portrayed. However, perceptual salience acts as an assertion of existence even where imaginary creatures are concerned. These assertions may be contradicted to a greater or lesser degree by our cognitive assessment of the realism or otherwise of the scenes in question—that is, our judgment as to whether the scene, as portrayed, could have occurred in reality. Thus all audiovisual representations are assertions of existence. The judgment as to what type of existence they represent is determined by what Branigan (1992) calls "decisions about assigning reference," based on our knowledge of the world, including our trust or otherwise in the agencies addressing us (filmmakers, TV stations, etc.) and their assertion of the reality status of a given film or program (true, invented, and so on).

Schematic Typicality and Familiarity

The experience of realism in terms of perceptual salience, including the uniqueness and complexity of a given scene, (mostly) occurs on the basis of a certain familiarity and typicality, since our understanding of what reality looks like is founded on previous, stored experiences that constitute our sense of familiarity and serve as schematic descriptions of movements, objects, persons, or situations. We all generate certain mental schemas as to how people walk, for instance, or how working-class people behave, which we use in order to evaluate whether a given representation is realistic or not. If the representation differs greatly from our existing schemas, we may judge it unrealistic. At the same time, if it precisely resembles our schemas yet lacks any specificity, we may likewise deem it not very realistic. Overschematic representation may seem to us stereotypical, in that it lacks the flavor of the particular and unique time, place, and object. As the Russian formalists observed, salience, and hence the sense of realism, decays with overfamiliarity and habituation.

Realism could therefore be seen as a balancing act between the unique, which provides the salience of the real, and the typical, which provides the cognitive credibility and familiarity of the real. Since our imagination and ability to create mental representations often rely on schemas and typicality, filmmakers often need to confront nonfiction reality to get inspiration to create scenes with a flavor of being a specific, unique slice of reality.

The bias toward typicality introduces a certain normative dimension to the concept of realism, since there are many real phenomena and representations of real phenomena that are neither typical nor familiar. As mentioned above, for instance, there is an anthropocentric bias to our understanding of realism. A high-angle shot seems to us less realistic than a shot from human eye level, unless we are given to understand that what we are seeing is a bird's-eye view or that of a person flying. But even if there is a reason for the unusual angle, we still have a sense of its deviation from the typical. Moreover, our norms for what constitutes realism are influenced by considerations of the canonical view (Grodal 1997; Humphreys and Bruce 1989). The recognition of an object is not equally easy from all angles. A horse seen from behind is more difficult to recognize than a horse seen sideways on. Most people will draw or record objects from a canonical angle in order to make them more easily recognizable. Canonical angles may also be considered more realistic and less expressive, even if the object is also in principle familiar from noncanonical angles and in an abstract sense just as realistic.

Historically, realism has been associated with the representation of scenes from everyday life, especially the life of the middle and lower classes. Thus many critics regard De Sica's *Bicycle Thieves* as the prototypical realist film because it portrays everyday problems encountered by ordinary working-class people. Clearly, brushing your teeth is a more ordinary and therefore a more typical event than having a heart attack, winning a million dollars, or being raped. However, confining realism to the depiction only of the most statistically common actions would go counter to the general understanding of the concept among both viewers and critics. Thus, scenes of intense activity in critical situations, such as an emergency room or a workers' strike—as, for example, in Biberman's *Salt of the Earth*—may be perceived as realistic. The preference among some critics for films depicting uneventful daily life may be seen as a polemic against fiction films that stage improbable actions that are irrelevant to ordinary life, rather than against those that portray exceptional situations (such as sudden illness or social conflict) that may nevertheless be highly relevant to ordinary people. Indeed, the emotional impact made by such films is seen by many as a valid measure of their realism. Scenes that portray all the gory details of a mutilation, for instance, may be considered very realistic because of the emotional impact they make on the audience, and the same goes in some respects for pornography. Kracauer (1960) observed that the depiction in films of garbage, dirt, or sewers plays an important role in establishing physical existence, precisely because these phenomena normally go unnoticed. I would add that the emotional impact of what Kracauer called "the refuse" is also an important component in the experience of realism. Thus our sense of what is real is linked not only to the factual existence of certain phenomena but also to their (negative or positive) emotional relevance. Perceptual realism may not be salient unless it serves to activate emotional concerns.

Transparent Access or Mediated Realism

In several respects, the typical fiction film is better able to provide a transparent experience of realism than the typical nonfiction film. A realistic fiction film gives us the sense of being confronted with a unique and concrete world despite the fact that its realism is general and hypothetical: we believe, in other words, that such a world might exist. Ford's *The Grapes of Wrath* and August's *Pelle the Conqueror* portray many scenes that appear to be true to life on a general level, even though the specific circumstances depicted have been staged. As they watch such films, viewers will often experience the images as if they referred to real people or events, even though they know that their reference to reality is only general and hypothetical. The narrative form of the typical fiction film allows the actions and events to develop in time in a way that resembles everyday experience. Fiction films often focus our attention on one particular person, and our identification with that person gives us the sense of online, concrete interaction with what is shown. Our experience of the film thus matches our experience of the real world, which we view through the filter of our own specific emotions and concerns. Moreover, the classic, seamless mode of presentation that developed especially in Hollywood seeks to follow the basic perceptual and cognitive rules governing our experience of events in real life (Bordwell 1986; Bordwell et al. 1988).

Fiction films can stage events that are inaccessible or accessible only with difficulty to the nonfiction filmmaker. Thus nonfiction films cannot usually provide a firsthand view of a murder or of secret negotiations in government or business. Even where the events in question are in principle accessible (as in the case of a plane crash, street riots, etc.), it is rare that a professional camera is present at the proper moment to record them. And even if a professional camera is present, the circumstances will not usually allow for optimal angles, lighting, and so on of the kind that could be arranged if a similar scene were shot in a fiction film. The widespread private use of video cameras may provide some footage, but this will generally be of a low quality and shot only from certain angles. Moreover, the sheer presence of a camera may alter the behavior of the people filmed, whereas a good actor should be able to perform as if there were no camera present.

Documentary films or programs can compensate for these shortcomings by several means. The simplest is to emulate the narrative form, with some kind of narrative agency playing the role of "focalizer," whether in the form of a voice-over, intertitles or subtitles, or a reporter or documentarist who is visually present in the film. So-called docudramas take the more radical step of restaging a real event. Here we get a firsthand impression as to how the murder happened, what took place at the secret negotiations, or what went on in the small everyday dramas arising from accidents or illnesses. Thus the docudrama can lend a perceptual realism to the events portrayed. It may even use the real-life protagonists as actors in the docudrama and thus acquire a personal specificity that affords the viewer a sense of full involvement, since both the drama and the protagonists are concretely and uniquely real. Even the fact that the acting may look amateurish compared with that of professional actors can lend a special salience and specificity to such films.

However, there are certain problems with the docudrama procedure. The docudrama has to be created after the fact, whereas most fiction films, including those that are realistic, relate the events in a hypothetical present. Docudramas may therefore offer an experience similar to that of the passive melodrama, which is often told from a temporal position later than that of the events depicted. Because the viewers are aware of the fact that they are watching a reenactment, they may speculate as to its correctness, whereas in the case of the typical realist fiction film the filmmakers are credited with knowledge of the hypothetical phenomena portrayed. Thus docudramas may succeed in making certain events visually salient but may fail to activate the strong emotions that arise when we feel we are witnessing real, unique happenings that take place right now.

A more radical or paradoxical way of compensating for the lack of perceptual realism in nonfiction consists in emphasizing the very shortcomings of the genre, making imperfect perceptual realism into a sign of reality. Such a method undermines the status of perceptual realism as a measure of authenticity by implying that the perfect realism of many fiction films is unrealistic and artificially staged. Thus many documentarists and nonfiction filmmakers, far from seeking to achieve perceptual realism, prefer to stick with grainy pictures, imperfect focus and framing, erratic camera movements, and bad lighting. Although the images produced do not emulate the way in which the human eye would perceive the situations in question, they serve to indicate that the film was shot under nonstaged, nonfiction conditions. Thus a film that follows real policemen or firemen at work may give us only an obscure sense of what is happening in the murky alleys of Los Angeles, but at the same time—so it is argued—offer us the sensation of unstaged reality. Certain fiction filmmakers—for instance, the Dogma group—have used similar techniques in making realist fiction films. The method is exemplified in the genre of the fake documentary (or fake home movie), such as Myrick and Sánchez's *The Blair Witch Project*. Here we see one of the typical effects of imperfect perceptual realism, namely subjectivization. The erratic, handheld camera and often poor resolution enhance the feeling of stress and isolation and the weirdness of the goings-on, and the amateurish quality of the representation corresponds to the helplessness of the supposed filmmakers, the young people in the woods.

The fact that subjectivization is an important aspect of imperfect perceptual realism ("antiseamless" presentation) offers an interesting insight into the relation between the innate and the acquired aspects of realism. Viewers obviously learn to connect certain features of audiovisual representation with the circumstances of their recording; thus, for example, we may in certain contexts associate imperfect pictures with live reports transmitted by satellite over vast distances. So, just as we learn what zebras look like, we can also learn about media recording and media transmission, applying rules such as that short distances allow for good transmission, while long distances mean poorer quality images. At the same time, the fact that imperfect transmissions often evoke the feeling of subjective experience points to certain innate characteristics of human perception. The imperfections block easy recognition of the objects portrayed. Our innate way of categorizing deviant perceptions is to assume and feel that certain subjective factors are blocking the basic interaction between our minds and the external world. Deviations from perfect vision and hearing in film representation disturb our normal obliviousness to the subjective (proximal) aspects of perception. Moreover, they create stress and arousal in the viewer. Given the proper context (for instance, the horrible experiences in Myrick and Sánchez's *The Blair Witch Project* or the stressful work of a policeman in the Los Angeles streets), you might argue that the lack of perceptual realism is transformed into an emotional realism by inducing nervous, stressful feelings in the viewer that are appropriate to the scenes depicted. In the more trivial uses of imperfect perceptual realism, the aesthetics may either serve as a rhetorical device (the lack of salience in the object is compensated for by unusual camera movements and odd framings and angles that provide a rhetorical salience) or as a self-conscious means of emphasizing the role of the filmmaker ("We were here; we did the recording"). Thus the central question is whether or not the imperfections are motivated by the recording situation.

The distinction between perceptual realism and emotional realism reminds us that the term realism is usually applied only partially. Many different kinds of filmmakers claim to be realists, but portray only certain aspects of reality. Terms such as magic realism, extreme realism, poetic realism, psychological realism, or social realism show how variously realism can be understood. Even mainstream films may use elements derived, for instance, from expressionism in order realistically to portray deviant mental states.

The different applications of the word *realism* are a logical consequence of the fact that reality is multifaceted and open ended: our developing knowledge constantly adds new elements to what we understand and experience as real. And this sense of the real represents a practical tool in our relationship to the world and to the mind, so that when we augment our tools for dealing with the world and the mind, our feelings of reality and realism will also become more complex. We may, however, have a graded, pragmatic understanding of realism: we tend to consider certain aspects of reality more normal and intersubjective than others. Thus films such as De Sica's *Bicycle Thieves* or Wiseman's *High School* can be defined as realistic without any further specification, whereas others require a more specific designation: for example, we apply the term psychological realism to Polanski's *Repulsion*. Not only are there different types of realism corresponding to the representation of different aspects of reality, but such types are evaluated and graded, with some deemed more central than others.

The aesthetics of imperfect perceptual realism represent the very opposite of Bazinian aesthetics. According to Bazin (1967), the essence of film art lies in its ability to create an objective mechanical recording of the world that leaves no trace of an intervening human subject. Films and photographs should be the perfect replication of the external world. We thus have two different ideas of realism: one centered on the subjective vision of the "experiencer," the person addressing us, the other centered on the objective external world—assuming that it is possible to create a neutral representation of that world. Certain scholars and filmmakers have disputed this. In his book about documentaries, *Representing Reality*, Bill Nichols (1991), for example, argues that supposedly neutral presentations of reality are in fact ideological representations posing as neutral and natural, and that nonfiction films or programs must therefore be self-reflexive and admit that they are specific representations. Imperfect perceptual realism is one way of marking the presence of an addresser or experiencer. But it might also be argued—in line with Bazin—that we are sometimes able to minimize our awareness of our subjective situation as observers and therefore have the sense of witnessing an objective, disinterested observation of the world. That this sense of disinterestedness may be characterized as a feeling does not necessarily make it subjective, because certain feelings and emotions are key tools for assessing the reality status of a given experience. Thus both kinds of realism—that which focuses on the objective, external world and that which focuses on the subjective world of the filmmaker addressing us—are equally valid forms of representation.

Abstract Categorical Realism and Lyrical Representations

However, perceptual realism is not the only means by which we experience reality, just as the narrative form is not the only form that we use to assemble data (Branigan 1992). Many audiovisual representations use a categorical form (Bordwell and Thompson 2001) that aims not so much to provide a vivid portrayal of certain concrete situations and experiences as to extract a more abstract understanding from concrete examples. Although the famous documentary *Night Mail* uses certain narrative elements (a train ride from London to Glasgow) and some illustrative visual examples of some of the activities that take place en route, the purpose is not only to convey the concrete experience of a night on the mail train, but to offer more general, abstract information about certain aspects of the British postal system. Although a significant proportion of nonfiction programs seek to portray certain highly specified, concrete situations, many others aim to give a generalized view and therefore deal with the abstract and typical rather than the concrete and unique. Categorizations and mental models often serve as the tacit background to our understanding of concrete situations. In the categorical film, the focus of the representation is on the abstract schematic level. A photograph of a tiger in an encyclopedia is not intended to denote the specific tiger depicted, but the category *tigers* at a schematic level (Branigan 1992). The comic troupe Monty Python derives much fun from conflating the concrete and schematic use of images of trees and larks. The experience of reality conveyed by such abstract portrayals of external phenomena could be called cognitive realism or categorical realism, as opposed to perceptual realism. In chapter 9 I discussed how superordinate categories are linked to an experience of (disembodied) permanence, whereas the experience of transience is associated with perceptual, embodied, basic-level categories.

The difference between perceptual-narrative representations and categorical representations may be illustrated in the nonfiction montage sequence at the beginning of *Beverly Hills Cop*. Here we are presented with various shots that apparently have no narrative connection with one another. Yet they appear to have a common theme: all the shots show some aspect of the life of poor people in a black ghetto in Detroit. The different people and locations depicted have a very concrete, unique, realistic specificity. Had the scenes been linked by a narrative, they might have been perceived merely as elements of concrete perceptual realism. But since the viewer cannot find a narrative link, he or she will search by default for a thematic, categorical connection, such as poverty or black ghetto life. This process does not completely deprive the individual pictures of their concrete reference, but they nevertheless acquire a double status both as concrete references and as illustrations of a more abstract theme, poverty. The narrative part of the film takes place mainly in the rich Beverly Hills area, and although it is possible to see the scenes and events portrayed here as presenting a contrasting theme—wealth or white upper-class life—this kind of categorical understanding now serves only as a background to the events in the story, since the narrative form leads us to focus on the concrete and specific.

Where does our sense of categorical realism come from? Plato and other thinkers within the idealist tradition believed that ideas were more real than appearances (or more real than perceptual realism, in the language of this book); they were in fact the essence of reality. But this fails of course to provide a psychologically satisfying explanation, especially since perceptual realism plays such an important role in eliciting feelings of reality. As mentioned earlier, however, small children often draw only the formal essences of objects or people, using lines to represent legs and circles to stand for stomach and head.

Such abstract representations constitute the mentally pertinent features in our experience of the ever-changing phenomenal world. I therefore suggest that a certain kind of schematic salience provides a feeling of reality that is abstract and atemporal and derives its power from being the mental essence or schema of many different experiences, whereas the feeling of perceptual salience is connected to the temporal, specific, and unique. In fiction films, mental schemas or abstract representations often become redundant themes in the concrete narrative progression. In order to make them salient, the film needs to offer us concrete illustrations or exemplifications of the abstract theme, thereby supporting schematic salience with perceptual salience. But schematic realism presupposes that the final reference is not only to the concrete and unique but also to the general and pertinent. *Night Mail* is not a documentary about a specific night and a particular train; rather, the concrete illustrations refer to the general, atemporal, and repeatable.

An illustrated, focused categorical presentation elicits a double feeling of realism and reality. Its illustrations create a unique perceptual salience, while its categorical presentation offers an essentialist salience. The reason I emphasize that the presentation must be focused is that, if it is not, it will give rise to yet another type of experience, a lyrical mental-associative mood that is far more detached from exterior, intersubjective reality. Many critics have pointed out that certain documentaries evoke a lyrical mood, and Plantinga (1997) has distinguished three typical voices in nonfiction films: the formal, the open, and the poetic. However, no explanation has been offered for the seemingly paradoxical phenomenon that certain apparently factual films may often intentionally or unintentionally elicit lyrical feelings in the viewer. Let us take a look at one of the best-known lyrical documentaries, Ruttmann's *Berlin, Symphony of a Great City.* The film consists of an extended series of shots of Berlin life, apparently taken on a single day since the film begins in the early morning and ends late in the evening. Sometimes we are shown a sequence of similar happenings; at other times different kinds of events are contrasted. But apart from the fact that all the shots are taken in Berlin and present a diurnal cycle, there is no clear focus, no arguments are put forward, and no clear categorical analysis provided. Viewers therefore build up by default a web of associations between the different objects and events depicted: one that has only a diffuse center in the idea that what we are witnessing is life in a modern city, Berlin.

In real life, everything is concrete and fixed in contiguous space and continuous forward-directed time. Associations between widely different times, spaces, and objects, as well as those based on similarity and other formal features, usually exist only in representations or in our minds (thus we may associate New York with Tokyo, both being important cities, or find links between different historical periods, or a similarity between eyes and sun). Such associations are typical of lyrical films, which, unlike most narrative fictions or more concrete forms of documentary, do not refer primarily to an external concrete reality, but rather to the internal reality of experiences in the mind. In focused categorical audiovisual representation, categorical assertion provides the link between the external world and mental representations, but in unfocused presentations this assertion of external existence is absent. This gives rise to curious effects: many lyrical films—some of Marguerite Duras's films, for example (chapter 10)—are in principle straightforward or even extreme documentaries, but nevertheless evoke an intensely lyrical mood. The reason for this is that viewers cannot find in such films any focused categorical assertion, and therefore by default search their minds for possible associations, thereby establishing in response to the film a subjective associative web. Even a typical documentary such as *Night Mail* hovers between concrete, focused reference and lyrical mental reference, the latter assisted by the words of the poet W. H. Auden on the sound track. The film's apotheosis of speed and efficiency sometimes evokes a purely idealistic-internal reference.

Assertions of Existence and Realism

Many scholars have been interested in assertions from an epistemological point of view. Thus Plantinga (1997) points to the fact that nonfiction films perform pragmatic acts by which they assert that what is shown and told is a true fact in the world. Some theoreticians, such as Nichols (1991), are very skeptical about the overt assertive aspect of certain nonfiction films—those made in what Nichols calls the expository mode, involving for instance a "voice of God" in the form of an omniscient voice-over.

The problem of assertion in establishing reality and fiction could also, however, be approached from a psychological point of view. As discussed earlier, our basic experience of reality is linked not only to perceptual processes but to enactive ones: our motor-based relations to the world. The objects and perceptions that can guide our (re)actions are real, as are the feelings behind our reality-status judgments as to whether a given phenomenon allows for action or not. Certain computer applications, and especially computer games, produce a strong sense of reality, despite the fact that their perceptual definition is often quite poor, because users can physically interact with the represented world. This suggests that (inter)action constitutes an important element in our experience of reality.

Thus, the question of reality and realism poses the problem of agency. In the typical narrative fiction film, the question of agency is solved through the existence of a protagonist whose actions are oriented by his perceptions. The diegetic world derives its relevance and reality through being the object of the protagonist's concerns. In certain types of observational film, the nonfictional protagonists have a salience that enables the viewer to experience a kind of vicarious agency and hence to find the necessary relevance. But this is by no means true of all types of film: the categorical documentary, for instance, has no such onscreen agency. However, the filmmaker—the person who implicitly or explicitly addresses us in such films—may serve as an agency for the viewer, performing nonconcrete actions by asserting that this or that is the case. As Austin and Searle have shown, the performatives or symbolic actions which assert that something exists are a central feature of human communication. Assertive-performative activity is one of the main ways that we transmit the feeling that something is real and factual. Assertions need not be verbal: any framing or presentation is in principle an assertion, although it may not be experienced as such if the viewer cannot reconstruct the principles on which the assertion is made.

The assertions made during a film play a vital role in creating a concrete focus or reference for a representation that might otherwise be perceived in a subjective-lyrical mode. Nichols's distrust of overt assertions as a form of ideological imposition leads him to exclude a key means of communicating about reality. Of course it is possible that the addresser may abuse his or her position, but we cannot abolish the role of addresser in general just because it may be abused. Indeed, it could be argued that there is a kind of honesty in making overt assertions that allows us to form a clear impression of the asserting agency. We can see this if we compare an expository film involving a voice-over or intertitles with a so-called fly-on-the-wall observational film that appears to present an objective recording without any asserting agency. Most viewers of Wiseman's observational documentary *High School* will assume that the film makes certain general assertions about the American high school system, albeit on the basis of concrete observation. But the film conceals the addresser-agency—the person or persons responsible for actually shooting and editing the film—so that what we see is seemingly asserted by reality itself. This problem with the observational mode has been noticed (for an overview, see Carroll 1996b, 224–252), and scholars such as Nichols therefore prefer the reflexive film that openly reveals the fact that it is a specific representation. It might be argued, however, that the average, nonnaive viewer of an overtly assertive expository film is very well aware that what he or she is watching is a film made by some human agency; it is not essential to this understanding that the addressing agency be reflexively represented.

Reality and Realism as Genuineness, Seriousness, and Pain

Our experience of realism in film is often linked to judgments about the seriousness of the intentions and consequences involved and about the genuineness of what is represented. Fiction films are not fully real, since, for example, the actors do not intend to kill each other; they only pretend to have that intention, and the consequences of their actions are likewise only pretended. Our experience of reality and realism demands that some vital human (or animal) concerns are at stake. When playing or pretending, we are supposed to be free to discontinue that behavior, which is not the case with acts that arise from our genuine self and our vital concerns. A transmission of a football match is less likely to be described as being realistic than the transmission of a fight between police and demonstrators, in which vital concerns appear to be at stake, although they are evaluated as equally real. But if a documentary peeps into the locker room, revealing the true backstage identity of the players and showing that real concerns are at stake for them as well, we may well judge the product realistic. In a television genre often called reality TV (*Survivor, Big Brother*, etc.), based on performances by ordinary people—amateur actors—the program makers often emphasize that the participants are acting in accordance with serious and therefore real motives.

It is difficult to draw a clear line between what is just pretense, a role, and what is genuine. People's acts and pretense in real life, their "front-stage" appearance as Goffmann (1986) calls it (see also Meyrowitz 1985), may be determined by stronger motives than their relaxed, private, and intimate (backstage) behavior, although a behind-the-scenes documentary about actors, politicians, or football players will be judged more realistic than a presentation of their front-stage performance. To sing a song, act in a play, or perform a comic sketch is just as real as to work on an assembly line, but often we do not see it that way. It seems that an attitude of seriousness and genuineness and a certain lack of playful freedom play an important role in our judgment as to what is real or realistic. The fact that realist films often feature situations in which agents are supposed to have limited capacity to act may be an implicit reflection on this problem. Although in one sense the life of the hero of *Bicycle Thieves* is trivial and uneventful, the loss of his bicycle and therefore possibly his job represents for him an existential crisis that guarantees that his behavior is serious and genuine. The reality TV series *Big Brother* emphasizes its ability to evoke genuine behavior by involving elements of possible deprivation (confinement for a long period of time in a limited space that is under surveillance, the exclusion of nine out of ten participants by painful processes, the fact that they often have to live in basic conditions without the normal comforts of modern life, and so on).

FIGURE II.I. John Ford's *The Grapes of Wrath* exemplifies several of the cues that typically evoke feelings of realism. The scene shown has perceptual salience and a concrete physical space in which people may exert intentional agency (indicated by the gaze structure and body posture). Further, the scene fits into prototypical concepts of how poor farmers and working-class people look and behave and, in the overall context of the film, it shows slices of life in which serious concerns are at stake, involving possible pain. *The Grapes of Wrath* © Twentieth Century-Fox Film Corporation 1940.

One consequence of the principle that a strong feeling of reality demands that vital human or animal concerns are at stake is that realism is more often attributed to those representations that portray negative emotions than those that portray positive emotions. This is perhaps based on the assumption that pain is more real than pleasure and thus evokes more genuine behavior. A documentary about deprived and suffering people is probably more likely to be labeled realistic than a documentary about happy jet-setters, even though the first group may not necessarily be more typical than the second. Some of the classic realist films, such as Ford's *The Grapes of Wrath* or Biberman's *Salt of the Earth*, focus on deprivation and pain (figure II.I). Certain philosophers and artists consider death the ultimate reality. Freud even gave the term reality principle, as opposed to pleasure principle, to the mechanisms associated with our reflections on pain. Although Freud's terminology does not make sense from an evolutionary perspective, it may reflect a fundamental aspect of the way that humans experience reality. The psychologist Nico Frijda (1988, 353) has claimed that there is a "hedonic asymmetry" in our experience: "Pleasure is always contingent upon change and disappears with continuous satisfaction. Pain may persist under persisting adverse conditions." Thus, the bias in realist representations toward portrayals of suffering or deprivation may reflect not only a political intention to advocate empathy, but also a feeling that pain and deprivation are more real than pleasure.

Realism in an Age of Pervasive Representations

Several scholars, among them Jean Baudrillard, have argued that the fact that nowadays natural experiences play a decreasing role in comparison with experiences associated with audiovisual representations has led to the dissolution of our sense of reality, and this in turn means that the concept of realism has become increasingly problematic (Grodal 1992). The salience of images does not guarantee any real, concrete, and unique reference, and as even the perceptual world becomes increasingly artificial, there are no absolute and natural norms to anchor an authentic experience of reality.

The present pervasiveness of representations even in everyday life certainly raises questions as to what is true or probable (realistic), and what is only invented and improbable (fantastic or just false and misrepresented). However, the problem of illusion and the miscalculation of reality status is a quite general effect of the overall increase in human intelligence and culture that has enhanced our ability to fantasize and make hypotheses. The cultural explosion that followed the invention of language (Mithen 1996) increased the scope for both realistic and fantastic representation. Ever since language, sculpture, and painting were invented, strange tales have been told about gods, magical causation, or Cyclops with only one eye, and humans have offered visual representations of gods and fantastic creatures, asserting and believing them to be true representations of genuinely existing beings. Although premodern humans had visual and acoustic access only to a relatively narrow concrete environment, many of their beliefs about the world were molded by what they had been told existed elsewhere. It is not obvious that modern viewers of fantasy and science fiction films have more belief in the realism of such representations than premodern humans had in fairies and gods—on the contrary. Although perceptual realism activates innate dispositions, the massive exposure to audiovisual representations probably does not create more credulous viewers than verbal communication created credulous listeners in the past. Indeed, certain questionable representations are more easily created in verbal than in audiovisual media. Thus generalizations such as

"New Yorkers are happy and active" are easy to make verbally, but if they are illustrated visually even naive viewers may have some doubts about the validity of the claim.

It is not obvious therefore that the world is moving in the direction of a crisis in the representation of reality (except in the sense that greater knowledge increases awareness of the potentially problematic relationship between the world and the way we represent it). Even those who use the media a great deal have extensive experience of the nonmedia world, including experience of media platforms as physical objects, and their firsthand experience of other cultures will tend to be greater than in earlier times. There is no reason to believe that our basic perceptual experience of the everyday intersubjective world has changed radically; it still provides the norm by which the representation of specific phenomena is evaluated and characterized. Moreover, public debate about the validity of representations is more complex than ever before, so the proliferation of (audiovisual) representations has been matched by an expansion of the critical discourse. This does not mean that people cannot be seduced into believing that biased and stereotypical representations are real or realistic. All types of human communication constitute possible opportunities for learning as well as for propagating misleading or biased representations.

High modernist and postmodernist discourses concerning the crisis of representation and reality may therefore best be understood in the light of the emotional dimensions of our cognitive appraisal of what is real and realistic. As briefly mentioned earlier, a vital component of our experience of reality is emotional: the feeling that something exists and can thus serve as a possible object of or arena for action. A key aspect of this feeling of reality is the sense of a certain basic familiarity. Periods of rapid change, involving the expansion of representation, may cause alienation, an emotional dissociation that makes it, for many people, more difficult to gain a feeling of familiarity and thus a sense of reality. To some extent, therefore, certain aspects of high modernism and postmodernism do not so much reflect the essence of the present period seen from a perspective of familiarity; rather, they are emotionally and experientially rooted in the conflict between past and present. Thus modern and postmodern critics and artists who express skepticism about the quest for realism and focus their interest instead on metafiction, reflexivity, and intertextuality may be seen as the product of a period of cognitive transition that for emotional reasons needs to foreground the "representedness" of representations. Although postmodernists are in principle against grand narratives and grand generalizations, their negative epistemological claim concerning the inherent uncertainty of our knowledge is in itself a grand historical narrative that implicitly expresses a longing for the lost Cartesian world in which certain divine principles guaranteed the link between world and mind.

The feeling of reality and realism is based on and serves our pragmatic interaction with the world. Whether we communicate with grunts, with words, or by means of audiovisual media, we need to trust certain communicators or representations as better guides for our actions and concerns than others. Some of the critics who have made the point that representations are constructions and that reality is socially constructed tend to use *construction* as synonymous with *illusion*. From an evolutionary point of view, however, not only the media but all our mental processes represent constructions, and realist representations establish and negotiate an intersubjective world that facilitates or makes possible our experiences and actions as human beings. For this reason, I believe that concepts such as reality, realism, and truth are even more pertinent today, in a postindustrial society with pervasive audiovisual representations, than they were in the past.

12

Conclusion

*The Gene-Culture Stream
and Bioculturalism*

The purpose of this book has been to demonstrate how films are sophisticated products of culture and at the same time are supported by a human nature that has evolved through a process that has taken millions of years. The shorter cultural development has had centrifugal elements of cultural differentiation as well as centripetal developments based first on Eurasian–North African communication and later on a global communication (Diamond 1997). Our universally shared embodiment and its multitude of dispositions are the foundation on which we create new cultural adaptations, new salient forms. The purpose has further been to show how inspiration from the natural sciences is able to fertilize the study of culture and film studies. It is important for studies within the humanities to take advantage of research within a natural science paradigm when explaining what aspects of the film experience are determined by local causal factors such as a given cultural environment and what are determined by universal elements in the biological makeup of humans.

As I have shown, the history of the evolution of our embodiment is ingrained in the way in which the constants and variables of our abilities to create cultural products are molded. Central aspects of our emotional dispositions exert a constant influence on how films are crafted and experienced. In the chapters on children's film, on romantic films and pornography, on morality, on our relation to counterintuitive agents, and on bonding through sadness, I have discussed how our fascinations are motivated by basic emotional dispositions. The fascinations that glue us to screens when we are exposed to hide-and-seek scenarios and to emotion-evoking hazard precaution scenes in horror stories are products of our biological nature. Similarly, those hermeneutic mechanisms that are hyperstimulated in different fashions in, for example, art films and crime fictions rely on our emotional nature and cognitive wiring. That modern societies have monopolized the exertion of justice by means of special institutions does not make vigilante films, which activate deep-seated emotions supporting personal revenge, less activating even if such films raise ethical problems. Stories about counterintuitive agents are, as discussed in chapter 5, still fascinating for modern viewers despite the advances of science.

The architecture of our brain is fundamental for molding the film experience. The general layout of our brain, which supports the PECMA flow, provides the general framework of film aesthetics. The perceptual system grounds basic aesthetic effects linked to figure ground, light and shadow, color, contrast, and so on, which generate feelings of intensity linked to salient images (see also Grodal 2005, in press). The association cortices in the parietal and temporal lobes support lyrical associations and are activated by hermeneutic riddles and provide saturated emotions to the experience. The general framework of the frontal lobe determines how narratives focus on actions and goal achievement for agencies, and mechanisms in the frontal lobe parse stories into a temporal framework that supports action schemes and theory of mind mechanisms. Such narrative mechanisms create tense emotions by the subliminal activation of action tendencies and expectations, and such tense processes are supported by dopamine gratifications. The basic canonical narrative is a solution made by evolution to make schematic models of agencies and actions. Late adaptations support the quest for autobiographical and abstract categorical unity in combination with perceptual salience, as manifested in art films.

The universal features in films are explained by psychological and evolutionary theories and models that in several respects are similar to some of those models favored by structuralists in the 1960s, based on a distinction between surface structure and deep structure. The constants are the deep structures that express fundamental aspects of our embodied minds and embodied visions. In contrast, the surface structures are determined by the profound historicity of culture within the framework of these biologically determined deep structures. The thousands of different embodied mental mechanisms in their interaction with the world may be combined in infinitely many ways, although mental hierarchies provide specifications of how different elements have different degrees of compatibility, as discussed in chapter 2. There is therefore no limit on surface variations, although function optimization in relation to deep-seated dispositions such as watching stories fueled by biological fundamentals (e.g., bonding, fear, love, or death) tends to provide a relatively limited number of story formats.

What from a systemic point of view are surface variations can, however, express vital differences for individuals or cultures. Familiarity is a powerful reason for liking, and therefore viewers will often prefer films that contain elements with which they are familiar. Films express ideological views on political institutions, gender roles, ethnicity, and so on, and although, for example, the ethnic background of villains or heroes is a surface variation from a systemic point of view, it is extremely important from the point of view of cultural politics. Whether the action hero is a man or a woman is a surface variation in relation to fundamental narrative norms; however, the gender of a hero may be highly significant in relation to a given cultural discussion of gender roles. Cultural development is a continuous negotiation of and struggle over such values and norms. Bioculturalism is therefore not an alternative to the ongoing critical negotiation of representations; evolution has not stopped, and a fast-paced cultural evolution takes place on top of a slow-paced biological evolution. The basic emotional dispositions are, as discussed in the text, not internally well-ordered but are calibrated differently in different contexts, in different individuals, and in different cultures. The urge to survive may be in conflict with offspring bonding, mate bonding, bonding to brothers in arms, kin bonding, or tribal bonding. Economic considerations may conflict with love; love and desire may conflict; and different films and different cultural backgrounds provide different calibrations and evaluations of the emotional dispositions. The aim of a biocultural study of films is therefore not to ground ethics or political convictions in some fixed and inflexible human nature, because there is no such thing as natural ethics, natural morality, or a natural political order.

In chapter 6 I have focused on the way in which the motivation for film viewing cannot be explained solely within a narrow hedonic framework of viewers pursuing pleasure and avoiding pain in the same way as very low-order organisms, although to pursue pleasure is certainly an important motivation for watching movies. The human motivation system seems to be activated by many different adaptations. Playing and coping pose challenges, but the process of coping with and overcoming those challenges may be rewarding in itself (for instance, by pleasure-evoking dopamine release). Playing and coping are pleasurable not only because of a final positive goal achievement but also because motivational systems support coping by providing pleasure to offset the negative aspects of the challenges. Elsewhere (Grodal 1997) I have discussed the distinction between paratelic gratifications (i.e., means-oriented pleasures) and telic gratifications (i.e., goal-oriented gratifications). Furthermore, humans are curious not only about positive events but also very much in relation to negative events, prob-ably because in general it is fitness enhancing to tune and exercise one's hazard precaution systems to be prepared for dangers before they arrive—although not all mental preoccupations with negative events are fitness enhancing in a modern environment.

It is important in film viewing as well as when consuming other types of fiction to train one's emotional skills, social intelligence, and cognition (Fiske and Taylor 1991). Consuming fiction is a vital source of training one's abilities to simulate other minds and to expand one's theories of mind. Comedies are, for in-stance, often a pleasurable way of working through a series of negative emotions, from fear of falling and losing motor control in physical comedy to the intense occupation with central social emotions such as shame, embarrassment, and other emotional reactions linked to transgression of social norms. Innate mecha-nisms make it possible to transform the negative emotions induced by simula-tion and empathic resonance to pleasure (Grodal 1997). The origin of comic joy is probably play mechanisms (Panksepp 1998; Provine 2000), and comic fiction supports bonding. The laugh track in situation comedies simulates how viewers in ideal theater conditions bond. Social conflicts and individual embarrassments are transformed to common pleasure because the audience, by laughing, allevi-ates social tensions and transforms such arousals to pleasure.

Similarly, tragic films are often rituals of bonding in which viewers are in-duced into group mourning, which in the negative expresses the value of human bonding, whether it is kin bonding, pair-bonding, or tribal bonding. Such rituals of mourning seem to be an adaptation to group living. From a purely hedonic point of view, it is difficult to explain why viewers watch sad melodramas because to watch such films induces sadness and pain in the viewer. However, the interest in sad melodramas makes sense from the point of view of evolution as a way to affirm bonding in the negative, in the willingness to participate in the separation sadness of others as a ritual of bonding.

There are therefore several ways in which viewers relate to films: a first-person simulation, a distanced observation, a subjective assimilation, and (especially in comedies and tragedies) a ritualized participation in the working through of cen-tral negative emotional situations from shame to loss, as well as positive emotional situations of bonding and achievement. This points to the double nature of how viewers may experience films. Viewers may participate in a first-person simulation of possible worlds and possible actions. Additionally, viewers have a tacit or ex-plicit feeling of participating in a public communication and of being constituted as an audience. In these capacities, viewers participate in an experience of shared attention and shared emotions due to the fact that films and other audiovisual ar-tifacts are public events and that by watching films viewers are sharing experiences with other people (the filmmakers as well as the actual or virtual community of onlookers). Ellen Dissanayake (1995, 2000) has proposed the simple but intriguing theory of art that art making consists of making something special, and that this making special is intimately linked to the way in which humans have developed their cultural excellence by being able to share attention and emotions, and thereby to be ultrasocial, as Boyd and Richerson (1998) have argued.

Culture powerfully influences the embodied mind even if the flexibility is not as great as presupposed by extreme social constructivism, because often cultural calibrations only work under conditions of biological resistance. A good example of this is body language. As shown in Ekman and Friesen's (1975) classic study, the basic aspects of facial expressions for emotions are innate, and differences between the public use of facial expressions due to cultural display rules demand continuous control; thus Japanese and Americans displayed the same expressions of disgust when unobserved, although they differed when observed. However, that does not produce any absolute norms about how to act, how to communicate through facial expression. Social groups, acting communities, and so on have throughout history worked on inhibiting or increasing the innate facial expressions. Similarly, the canonical narrative is the mental default mode, but that does not mean that it is not possible to make noncanonical narratives, say, to tell the sad ending first to transform tense expectations into saturated experiences (Grodal 1997) or to tell a story with a chronology that is difficult to ascertain, a story with numerous flashbacks or flash-forwards, and so on. There are, for instance, good reasons for some makers of film art to deviate strongly from the canonical mode at a cost of demanding additional brainpower, training, and motivation for story comprehension. Film art and especially art films may try to provide metaperspectives on different phenomena. Prominently, art films provide what Damasio has called understanding of the autobiographical self, that is, to take a metaperspective on the course of a story of someone's life in order to be able to recalibrate values and goals in view of such a metaperspective. Film art can also take metaperspectives on human perception (aesthetic salience), on the process of mediation, on the meaning of life, or whatever. Thus, culture, including film art, has enhanced not only the ability to simulate canonical actions and a canonical PECMA flow, but also, although at a greater emotional and cognitive cost, to reflect on such actions and such a flow from metaperspectives.

The cultural (r)evolution has changed the ecological niche of humans as humans have made a deep imprint on their environment, an environment that is increasingly not only physical but representational and mediated. One of the central features of culture has been the invention of external storage media for information. The invention of picture making, writing, photographic recording, and digital simulations has enhanced the way in which cultural evolution is able to refine storytelling by creating new solutions and new techniques. For instance, the romantic period in the 19th century integrated stories that had circulated widely in oral tradition into a written form and experimented with new variations. This romantic literature became the input for film stories in the 20th century. Story formats such as attachment stories for children, fantastic stories, horror stories, and romantic love stories were developed from their literary predecessors and provided with audiovisual dimensions, partly by integrating inspiration from drawings, paintings, theater, and architecture.

However, it is important to emphasize that sophistication in achieving certain objectives is not identical to absolute progress or absolute value. As discussed in chapter 2, often film art and the other arts return to abandoned techniques for different reasons, as part of a novelty-habituation cycle, for instance, or because of a shift in preferred function, as when Bazin (1967) advocated abandoning the heavily edited film to present the phenomenology of basic experience, or when artists for various reasons return to black and white. Cave paintings that date back to the Stone Age cultural explosion still fascinate.

The way in which media professionalized the production of fiction created a new subgroup of professionals and thereby enabled the creation of sophisticated products for these professional elites (Carroll 1998). Such high art or avant-garde art products often play with narrative, hermeneutical, or perceptual fundamentals and often appeal to a minority of viewers. This indicates the amount of mental resources and learning needed to appreciate films that play with fundamentals and take a metaperspective on a series of phenomena. The existence of such sophisticated products does not disprove the universality thesis. It highlights the way in which cultural development is not uniformly directed at common-denominator products but also supports niche products.

The biological underpinnings for audiovisual storytelling might encourage the idea that there are simple and unambiguous ways of optimizing such storytelling, say, to exaggerate all likely triggers of innate emotional reactions. For example, people may use the cartoon fashion of making unnatural big eyes and big heads for sweet transitional objects, portray big-shouldered heroes with deep voices and heroines with high-pitched voices and big breasts and hips, or monsters with big, poisonous teeth, and make mutually reinforcing clusters of such features, say darkness and dangerous biting agencies. Ramachandran and Hirstein (1999b) have described a so-called peak-shift theory: extreme inputs will provide extreme mental reactions. They have therefore argued that due to brain reinforcement mechanisms, art equals caricature in the sense that art tends to exaggerate features to evoke limbic reactions. Clearly, films sometimes and in some dimensions might be described as strongly caricatured or idealized versions of life with bravery, love, or despair bigger than life. But there are mechanisms that pull in other directions, like realism and the novelty-habituation mechanisms. Idealized or caricatured representations may wipe out salient surface specificity. Whereas small children like to hear or see the same story over and over again, older children and adults like stories that have similar canonical deep structure but variations on the surface structures. Repetitions lead to a loss of salience over time. The novelty-habituation mechanisms are linked to the "salience by specificity" mechanism. As discussed in chapter 11, specificity is the hallmark of the exterior world, whereas the inner world consists of more general schemas, images, and ideas. Thus, specificity provides the rhetoric and the feel of the real to narratives, and the surface of specificity enables our minds to provide some distinct perceptual signatures to the experience and to the memories of the experience.

For some film scholars, all that matters is specificity and surface uniqueness, whether the uniqueness is based on realism, on expressive trait optimization, or some other aesthetic principles. Admittedly, it is gratifying to analyze how a given film is the unique product of a certain time, a certain cultural background, and even a specific group of people working on a given film, each with his or her own background. To this specificity I may add the specific reception in an individual mind configuration among the billions of viewers who each have an individual background and whose tastes and cultural preferences are products of their life stories, including the stories of the thousands of hours that many of them have spent in theaters or in front of television sets. The interest in specificity is based on intellectual curiosity to explain those complicated historical causal chains that have produced the uniqueness of a given film or unique receptions. Moreover, the interest in specificity is also rooted in emotional layers, in the film lover's deep emotional fascination with specific films.

However, the specificity cannot fully be understood except as we appreciate those general mechanisms that support the specific film, the specific cultural manifestation. Miyazaki's *My Neighbor Totoro* fascinates children and adults all over the world. The film is clearly influenced by its Japanese origin, from the use of Shinto gods to the rice fields and sliding doors. But the fact that children all over the world are fascinated by the film is only loosely related to those cultural specificities that may provide a specific visual salience. The main reason for the fascination is the superb way that Miyazaki uses a series of devices that tap into innate and universal mental mechanisms and emotions. Central, of course, is the fascination with the soft, organic counterintuitive agent, Totoro, who provides attachment security and empowerment for the little girl, Mei, in the absence of the parents (especially the sick mother). Similarly, the film uses distortions of universal body language movements and facial expressions in its mimetic as well as its expressive dimensions in the portrayal of Mei in order to fascinate by letting us resonate with her body language. A bus that is also a cat fascinates because of the counterintuitive violation of innate distinctions between the ontological categories animate and inanimate. Although comprehension demands a bit of cultural knowledge about buses that has only become quasi universal within the past century, the fascination is rooted in activation of images of powerful counterintuitive agencies as tools for personal empowerment.

Bioculturalism allocates equal importance to analyzing universal mechanisms and specific configurations and does not shy away from combining a reductionism stemming from the natural sciences with the historical analysis of specific configurations. *Embodied Visions* has focused on theoretical issues in relation to universalism. However, I hope that future research can show in detail how cultural history constitutes an open-ended diverse evolutionary process based on our common biological heritage.

Appendix

Frozen PECMA Flows in Trier's Oeuvre

In chapters 9 and 10 I looked at aspects of art film narration and the various ways in which subjective experiences are elicited. In what follows here, I illustrate some of the points made in the previous chapters through an analysis of Lars von Trier's films. Trier is a distinctive auteur who has maintained tight control over his productions, so that he has continuously been able to develop his personal and aesthetic ideas. He has explored the aesthetic and emotional possibilities of some of the central mainstream genres by synthesizing them with features of European art film narration. His earliest films had a strong lyrical toning that can also be sensed in the undertone of his later, more narrative films. His first "professional" film, *The Element of Crime*, a dark, obsessive work, inaugurated a series of films that systematically explored the genre system. The TV movie *Medea* is a tragedy, *Epidemic* a metafilm about filmmaking that includes elements of fantasy, *Europa* (*Zentropa* in the United States) a tragi-melodramatic film noir, *Breaking the Waves* a love melodrama, and *The Kingdom* a comedy that mixes elements of the gothic horror story with *General Hospital*–style soap opera. *The Idiots* is a naturalist film, *Dancer in the Dark* a tragic, operatic musical, and *Dogville* a mixture of avant-garde theater and a parody of social realism. All these films experiment with the emotions traditionally linked with the genres in question, and the key devices in these experiments serve to block and freeze the PECMA flow.

In chapter 9 I argued that art films often are inspired by and focus on the interpretation and creation of continuity in a person's life and values, that is, the creation of unity in what Damasio has called the autobiographical self. By contrast, most mainstream films are concerned with more concrete subgoals, such as marriage, death, or money. Trier's films are also part of his ongoing interpretation of central problems in his own life—especially those relating to establishing unambiguous relationships with other people and achieving some kind of personal control. Trier's films reveal an ongoing exploration of lyrical and distancing effects designed to achieve representations of subjective images, the hallmark of art film. Most of his films deal with people who are able to act only partially, or act under the influence of fate, as shown in his frozen flows, that is, lyrical sequences of blocked or impeded action. A cognitive analysis might describe how value uncertainty is related to this impeded ability to act freely.

Lyrical-Associational Forms and Saturated Emotions

In the mental flow model of the film experience, PECMA (perception, emotion, cognition, and motor action), I describe how the main film forms are based on innate features of the mind and body. Basic narrative forms presuppose specific mental mechanisms that are the biologically necessary conditions for the development of these forms, although they are not sufficient without other, culture-dependent factors. Significant and salient film genres are constructed to evoke certain characteristic emotions: aggressive tension (action, adventure), fear (horror films), laughter (comedy), desire (pornography), sorrow (tragedy), and romantic love (romantic fiction) (Grodal 1997). The evocation of these feelings is intimately connected with the narrative structure and themes of the films concerned. Emotions are always defined through a cognitive interpretation of their cause, and through a cognitive evaluation of the kinds of actions possible within the given narrative context.

The flow model (PECMA) provides tools with which to characterize the relationship between feelings, emotions, and cognitions and to identify two basic forms of aesthetic experience: narrative experience and lyrical-associative experience. Standard canonical narratives based on action must be linear and causal or teleological, because processes take place in linear time, and because strong emotions are linked to causes and effects or goal and means. The linear, narrative mode of experience is not the only basic mental format. Another is the lyrical-associative mode. Consciousness may be focused on complex mental associations that do not directly lead to action tendencies, and whose web of associations is multidimensional and, in principle, atemporal, because it does not involve the causal or goal-oriented processes and actions that could constitute a temporal dimension. Action and irreversible processes are what constitute temporal experience, whereas experiences linked to associations are atemporal. Whereas the emotions that are linked to potential or actual activations of the muscles give rise to feelings of tension, the associational web gives rise to saturated feelings, because the affective activation builds up in the absence of any potential outlet or release in action.

An example of this kind of lyrical-associative web can be found in an extremely salient sequence from *The Element of Crime*. A horse-drawn cart loaded with apples falls into the water, and as the horse goes through its death throes, the apples are seen floating

in the dirty water of the harbor. Various torchlike sources of light are reflected in the
water and cast dynamic, flickering lights on walls and other surfaces. We are also shown
close-ups of the dead horse gently rolling with the motion of the water as small air
bubbles ascend. The sequence has no narrative function; it neither motivates nor initiates
any action. The viewer is invited to experience the situation as a fabric of associations
linked to features of the visual space. These associations consist of elements of decay and
death: the run-down harbor, the yellow sodium lighting, the dead horse, and the apples
that get spoiled through contact with the dirty water. Death is obviously a supercategory
in blocking actions, since by definition it puts an end to further goals.

Moreover, the scene is charged with contrasts between fire, water, stone (earth), and
air (bubbles) and invokes a strong sense of passive, diffuse agency. The apples float, the
horse gently rolls, the light flickers. Thus, the sequence does not evoke emotions and
actions, but moods that relate to floating, drifting, flickering, and bubbling. Because
of its powerful visual salience and the affective charge produced by thoughts of death,
the sequence evokes strongly saturated feelings, blending the melancholia attached to
death and decay with euphoria generated by the complex, yet somehow thematically
ordered perceptual elements. Ramachandran and Hirstein (1999b) have described the
way in which we derive pleasure from isolating patterns in a complex array of perceptual
stimuli.

Action versus Melodrama

There are cognitive and emotional reasons for the popularity of the narrative film. Our
mental equipment has developed through evolution to solve problems and guide our
actions. A scene such as that of the drowning horse in *The Element of Crime* does not
pose well-defined problems or suggest solutions. The viewer is forced to try to deduce
certain thematic structures, inner connections, and so on, and the relationship between
this scene and the rest of the film is not immediately evident to the viewer. There are
emotional as well as intellectual barriers to appreciate such lyrical sequences. Wilhelm Wundt, writing in the late 19th century, argued that the experience of pleasure
is based on change. Increasing activation and arousal creates pleasure up to a certain
point, beyond which it will start to create displeasure, whereas continuous activation does not create pleasure. Wundt also showed that a decrease in stimulation and
arousal also created pleasure (Berlyne 1971). Most narrative films offer precisely this
kind of roller-coaster ride, increasing and decreasing arousal to maximize pleasure. In
the lyrical-associative film, there are no such phasic changes between increasing and
decreasing stimulation and tension, because no tension-releasing actions and goals are
presented or defined. Many viewers will feel that such a constant level of excitement is
not pleasurable, and they will reject those sequences that do not offer a phasic modulation of arousal. For the sophisticated viewer, on the other hand, the lyrical-associative
elements will provide an extraordinarily strong cognitive challenge because of the need
for sophisticated perception and analysis. The viewer may experience his or her analytic
work as a mental action involving certain phasic elements and hence arousal-relaxation

through perceptual and associative problem solving. The saturated images offer experiential complexity.

Perverse film sequences may easily evoke a lyrical-associative mode of experience, because there are no obvious, clear-cut actions that would bring the perverse impulse to a halt. There are several masochistic scenes in Trier's work, including *The Element of Crime*. In one such scene from this film, a young man is lying on a pallet of very sharp objects. This worship of suffering may create arousal as well as pain, and the arousal has no clear conditions of satisfaction. Even the pseudopleasure involved in the buildup of arousal through pain is ambiguous. By contrast, erotic excitement may be released in orgasm. In perverse scenes, the blocking of the narrative drive may also result from the viewer's difficulties in feeling empathy for the characters involved. When small girls are molested in *The Element of Crime* and there is no one to come to their rescue, the viewer may become a distant observer and experience the scene only in lyrical-associative mode. The timelessness of lyrical-associative sequences, and the fact that any forward-directed actions in such scenes are weak or blocked, help explain a central aspect of Trier's films. The focus on the past plays a key role in blocking voluntary action and hence in cueing lyrical-associative experiences. Even where the past situation is seemingly able to motivate or produce actions, these are narrated in retrospect so that the viewer is focally aware of the fact that the events have already found their solution before they are represented. They are not free acts, carried out in an indeterminate now with a masked future, but events that have already been finalized and transformed into fate.

Trier has not made a single film that can unambiguously be described as a canonical active narrative. Most of his films are variations on passive melodrama, that is, stories in which the characters are passive victims of fate. The contrast between active and passive narration is linked to a contrast between emotions that support goal-oriented coping, such as love, hate, or the desire for fame and money, and autonomic reactions such as sorrow or laughter that serve to release inner tension rather than alter the external world. Certain kinds of love stories also involve an element of fatalistic abandonment, as in *Breaking the Waves*. The title is inspired by *The French Lieutenant's Woman*, where we see the heroine waiting by the sea, but whereas the theme of passive passion and waves in *The French Lieutenant's Woman* strongly enhances the heroine's erotic abandonment, Trier uses passive melodrama to portray abuse or self-sacrifice. Passive narrations often have a lyrical toning, because even active sequences—such as the song-and-dance scene in the train in *Dancer in the Dark*—may serve to generate an empathetic, atemporal web of associations.

Melodramatic effects have often been described as excess, that is, as a transgression and deconstruction of the classical Hollywood narrative. It is true that the retarding, empathetic, and lyrical narrative elements in melodramas such as those of Douglas Sirk deviate from the canonical goal-oriented narrative. However, if the word *excess* is interpreted to mean a kind of guerrilla warfare activity that breaks down the classical narrative film, it is misleading. Melodramatic-excessive modes of representation activate innate feelings of pleasurable abandonment and of yielding to sublime and saturated experiences, and are thus expressive elements that have no essential transgressive purpose.

The lyrical elements in melodrama indicate its orientation toward inner experience rather than action. Tense emotions ignite motor activation, whereas melodrama releases tears. As the default mode of humans is active and goal oriented, melodramatic modes require the action to be retarded, blocked, or filtered. In film after film, Trier has experimented with different ways of creating excessive strategies and evoking passive, saturated emotions, although his later films include more elements of active narrative.

Static Tableaux and Obsessive Narrative

Trier's preference for passive narration is evident already in *Pictures of Liberation*. The film centers around three static tableaux. The historical-nostalgic opening highlights the blocking of action. The story takes place in a strongly marked past, the days preceding and following Denmark's liberation from the German occupation, which is partly represented through authentic, tinted black-and-white documentary footage. The film deals with events that have already taken place, and the characters are seen not as individuals exercising their free will but as passive objects of destiny. They are pawns in a grand historical drama that transcends the individual. Moreover, action is blocked for psychological and ethical reasons. First and foremost, the viewer's attempts to simulate events are stymied because each of the main characters displays highly contradictory emotions and action tendencies. A German soldier is seen as both perpetrator and victim; he is drawn toward his childhood fascination with nature but at the same time acts as an accomplice in the molestation of a child (putting out her eye). A Danish woman is attracted to the German soldier, but she is also an avenger who punishes him by putting out his eyes, then weeps painfully over his fate; meanwhile, she is also attracted to a black American soldier. The viewer's participation in a goal-oriented narrative presupposes a certain degree of unambiguousness in the characterization of the main characters' motives. Thus, when a film presents characters with ambivalent or contradictory action tendencies, narrative drive is lost. The viewer may therefore experience the film only in a lyrical-associative mode, as the orchestration of a series of thematic oppositions. The emotional impulses appear to be isolated, passive, and molded by destiny. At the same time, Trier uses a whole arsenal of elements of passive experience, many of them borrowed from Tarkovsky (rain, flickering torches, mechanical sounds produced by wheels and metal chains), to evoke saturated passive experiences.

The ambivalence in the depiction of the main characters is linked to a theme that is prominent in most of Trier's films, namely the ambiguous coupling of sexuality (pleasure) and pain (suffering). This paradoxical association is not Trier's invention but a common theme in art. It stems from the fact that both intense sexual pleasure and intense pain cause a very high level of arousal, which in turn sets off a series of autonomic reactions, such as involuntary muscular contractions in the face and body. It might be that only through analyzing a given situation could anyone observing the body language of pain or pleasure determine which of the two experiences a person was undergoing. Drawing a relatively unambiguous distinction between pleasure and pain presupposes the ability to empathize, to be able mentally and affectively to understand another person and to share his or her emotions. In a perverse relationship, empathy is not dominant: a person is pleasurably aroused by another person's arousal irrespective of its hedonic tone, that is, whether the arousal expresses pain or pleasure. From an evolutionary point of view, the life of hunters and warriors may suggest certain functional reasons for being excited by the arousal of enemies or animals of prey. However, a generalized annihilation of the difference between pain and pleasure, which would make sadomasochism the norm in interpersonal relations and exclude the possibility of empathy, would clearly fail to enhance survival because it would annihilate all types of bonding.

Trier's first feature film, *The Element of Crime*, offers a much more complex version of the passive narrative than we find in *Pictures of Liberation*. It could be labeled an obsessive narration (Grodal 1997), because it combines certain narrative elements that seem to be forward directed and goal oriented with others that are based on passive and non-goal-oriented elements, that is, obsessive, paratelic features such as one finds in other noir-inspired crime movies. Trier himself has called the film a modern film noir (Schepelern 2000). The framing story is passive: the main protagonist, Fisher, is in Cairo and relates his story to a doctor while under hypnosis. On the surface, the story appears to be highly active. Fisher is investigating a series of sexual crimes against little girls that may have been committed by a mysterious figure called Harry Grey. Earlier, Fisher's old teacher, Osborne, trailed Grey by using his special investigative technique: seeking to simulate completely the mind of the criminal. Now Fisher is trying out this method himself and ends up abusing and murdering a little girl. The narrative deals with obsessive individuals and obsessive acts in multiple dimensions. It deals with obsession in its study of the central criminal motive, a sexual impulse directed toward little girls, and the criminal acts themselves involve a series of compulsive ritual elements (for instance, a graphic structure that controls the choice of crime scene). The obsessive element is likewise evident in the fact that Fisher, like Osborne, is pursuing a phantom criminal, Harry Grey, and that the simulation of Grey's supposed behavior eliminates Fisher's and Osborne's free will. It is also apparent in the way the story is told, under hypnosis, and in the story's portrayal through images that suggest a passive and unreal world.

Many music videos make extensive use of images depicting unfree, obsessive behavior (e.g., by running the same sequence backward and forward to the rhythm of the music) with the aim of generating a strong lyrical toning in these audiovisual poems. This expressive representation of obsessions rests on the idea that obsessive behavior cannot be experienced as flexible, voluntary, and goal oriented as is the case when frontal lobe control is in place, but rather as compulsive and expressive, controlled by brain stem mechanisms. Unlike goal-oriented behavior, it is driven by causes that are unknown to the viewer. The absence of external goals also makes it difficult to imagine conditions for emotional release or satisfaction. As we saw in chapter 9, art films often portray characters with very salient, non-goal-oriented behavior to evoke impressions of strong, inner, subjective experiences.

The blocking of voluntary, goal-oriented behavior in *The Element of Crime* is enhanced by a series of stylistic features, especially the film's mise-en-scène and its use of lyrical sequences that serve to retard the narrative drive. The story takes place in a dilapidated, worn-out Europe of the future, in conditions of such social decay as to make active coping meaningless. A series of episodes portrays the transformation of active coping into passive abandonment or obsession. There are also a number of minor lyrical retardations in the film, from scenes showing characters passively drifting at night on a raft to lyrical-emphatic scenes that dwell on objects longer than would be needed purely for the purposes of descriptive representation. In addition, there is the extensive use of optical lyrical effects, from the dissolution of time-space through superimpositions and dissolves to the use of lyrical, action-retarding slow motion. All these effects dissolve the objective and unambiguous representation of time and space. Deep focus and long takes are also extensively used. For example, a deep-focus shot shows a naked woman in the middle ground who, impassioned and afraid, tries to jump out of a window while Fisher in the background prevents her leaping by holding onto her foot. The camera tracks backward and reveals in the foreground the power receptors of a train that generate electric sparks as they touch the power cable. The pornographic picture is made lyrical by an Eisensteinian attraction montage that joins sex, electricity, and the train, but without any cutting. Montage through camera movements creates the sense of accidental association and chance spatial contiguity, whereas edited montage is more obviously deliberate: a visible act of juxtaposition by the director. At the same time, this form of internal montage evokes a sense of significance and destiny.

The main format of the film is the obsession narrative, but Trier also boosts the lyrical aspect through his postmodern integration of a series of genre elements. The art film is brutally integrated with the B film and there is also a strong pornographic undertone. Lyrical scenes reminiscent of Tarkovsky are welded together with elements from American war films, detective flicks, science fiction, and pornography. The B film genre elements also create internal connections: for example, the link between German themes and the Vietnam War. The result of these genre amalgamations is that they are cleansed of their inner narrative dynamics, so that their function becomes purely lyrical-associative and expressive. Moreover, *The Element of Crime*, like *Blade Runner*, evokes sublime imperial grandeur by splicing together elements from the first and third worlds and presenting the story in terms of the decline of a grand (European) civilization, thus emphasizing still further the experience of larger-than-life destinies. The film's purpose, however, is not political; rather, it is a purely aesthetic experiment with sublime and saturated lyrical forms.

Europa and the Classical Melodrama

Europa transformed the obsessive narrative and the themes found in *Pictures of Liberation* and *The Element of Crime* into a more classical melodramatic story. Like *Pictures of Liberation*, *Europa* is set just after World War II, but like *The Element of Crime* it takes place in Germany. It is a classic melodrama in the sense that the main character, Leo Kessler, is not driven by inner obsessions; formally speaking, his actions are voluntary. However, his life is controlled by powerful external forces, especially in the form of a femme fatale. The film takes place in a railway environment, thus reusing a cliché from the classical tradition of melodrama. Kessler, a young American with German parents, arrives in Germany after the Nazi collapse in 1945 and becomes an assistant ticket collector on the railway. Leo is weak and is therefore easy prey for a mature woman, Katharina, who is the daughter of the railway owner and a secret member of the Werewolves, who want to continue the Nazi struggle. She takes advantage of Leo and forces him to place a bomb on a train by pretending that she has been kidnapped by the Werewolves. Although she and her accomplices are exposed, the bomb nevertheless explodes on a bridge; Leo's compartment falls into the water and he drowns.

The narrative structure is thus based on the classic conflict between virtue and temptation, with the weak Leo wanting to act morally but being led astray, to crime and eventual death, by his erotic and emotional fascination with Katharina. The melodramatic impact of the film derives, however, from the fact that Leo's choices, though formally free, are fundamentally the consequence of an overwhelming fate. This fatalism is enhanced by a number of highly salient stylistic and thematic features. Let me make a few comments on the concept of fate to identify its functional core and thus rid the term of its metaphysical connotations (in German and Danish there is only one word, *schicksal* and *skæbne*, respectively, for fate and destiny). Fate is the opposite of free will. Any account of a life story that highlights the individual's voluntary actions must necessarily be relative, emphasizing those elements that are under his or her control. But seen in a larger perspective, the fate of an individual is strongly influenced by numerous other factors: innate characteristics, socialization, war, accidents, macroeconomic elements, random events, and so on—factors that can be neither controlled nor fully comprehended due to the millions of intersecting causal chains involved. The typical action or adventure film evokes active emotions by focusing on the microlevel at which the individual is in control of his life. But other kinds of film may represent the events in a person's life from a bird's-eye macroperspective; seen from that vantage point, the individual is a tiny creature who has little or no control. Such melodramatic or tragic representations evoke passive-autonomic responses such as crying and sorrow (but may also take a positive melodramatic form, in which a sudden change of fortune cues strong positive emotions that are likewise released in tears of joy).

It is the experience of being under the sway of gigantic forces that is central in *Europa*. By setting the narrative in Germany in 1945, that is, at a time when one epoch is over and another has not quite started, the film removes the active dynamic from the course of history. The causes of the German tragedy are not analyzed, and both executioners and victims suffer the same fate: death and destruction. Trier cues saturated, passive, melodramatic emotions by including both a sequence showing concentration camp prisoners bound for their destruction on a train and sequences involving Nazis.

Europa strengthens these passive, subjective experiences by using a series of visual effects: the use of front projections, contrasting black-and-white and colored elements, and long, complicated camera movements. These three devices may appear to be self-conscious, metafictional elements, serving to emphasize that the film is a construction rather than an imitation of reality. Because the visual representations in the film deviate greatly from normal representation, the viewer may interpret them as the filmmaker's self-conscious efforts to exhibit his film craft. But he or she is more likely to experience them as cues to enter the inner life of the characters, reasoning that since such phenomena do not exist in external reality they must be drawn from some inner, subjective, mental reality. Let me first illustrate this with Trier's use of front projections. These often serve to highlight an incongruity in size between two objects, for instance, between Kessler's natural face and his supernaturally enlarged one, or between Kessler and Katharina projected in oversize, or between the face of a boy and the oversize face of a major that the boy has killed. The incongruity in scale and texture between projected images and images that are directly photographed may be interpreted as a (metaphorical) expression of the mental impact of the projected images on the minds of the main character or the viewer. At the same time, the exaggerated size poses a further obstacle to concrete interaction (these enlarged figures seem to belong to another type of reality). This use of projections is well known from other films; take, for instance, the very large picture of the mother in Bergman's *Persona*, which symbolizes the psychic size of the mother in the mind of the son, and his difficulty in establishing contact with her. Trier's recycling of Bergman makes explicit that the aim of the front projections is to portray a blocking of (inter)action. Like the front projections, the use of colored characters and objects on a black-and-white background could be seen as self-conscious and antinaturalistic. In combination with slow-motion action, these effects can also create the sense of witnessing an inner life. Trier further uses long and complex camera movements that dissolve spatial orientation to create an antinaturalistic effect. In addition to these devices, Trier uses a great many theatrical effects, above all tableaux: scenes that have a figurative meaning and no narrative function.

Tragedy and the Melodrama of Love

Whereas *Europa* is a fully fleshed melodrama in which the main characters are all driven by destiny, the TV movie *Medea* portrays a much more violent conflict between active and passive elements. The main character, Medea, is a classic, tragic heroine. Jason, with whom she has two children, has expelled her from her home because he wants to marry Kreon's daughter Glauce. But Medea kills Glauce by poisoning her and afterward hangs her own two sons. Jason is driven to insanity, whereas Medea, in a serene mood, sails away to another land. From one point of view, *Medea* is a classical tragedy, and this is not surprising since the story is borrowed from Euripides' play. Several of the characters die a violent death, and the two main characters survive only with severe mental damage. From another point of view, however, Medea can be seen as a rather active protagonist, who kills her rival and hurts Jason severely by murdering her own children. Nor are these actions a consequence of some general destiny (such as the cursedness of Europe); they result from Jason's and Medea's own will. Unlike the actions of the weak Leo Kessler, who passively submits to death and becomes united with the water, Medea's actions lead to a kind of liberation, and the tide and the wind carry her ship away from the scene of the tragedy. The aesthetic challenge that Trier faced in *Medea* was to imbue even the active elements and Medea's perverse murder of her own children with passive, fatalistic emotions so that the audience feels sorrow rather than moral revulsion at the story. Trier uses style to evoke passive, fatalistic emotions. His romantic use of nature evokes the feeling that it is an anonymous and overwhelming agency. The leaves and the canvas of the love tent tremble and the grasses wave in the wind. In scenes on the moor, the fog and the water dissolve contours, and the film freely uses romantic clichés such as rolling waves or the passive power of the tide. Trier unabashedly uses a horse as a symbol of primitive organic forces: a poisoned horse is shown making a desperate escape to freedom from a primitive castle, suffering its final death throes at sea, while Jason is depicted riding in romantic despair through the wild landscape. These lyrical devices successfully put a brake on forward-directed emotions. Even the brutal execution of the children appears to be a consequence of Medea's destiny.

The development, from characters who are completely under the control of obsessive impulses to those who take active coresponsibility for their fate, is reflected in the viewer's emotional experience. Whereas Trier's first film evokes only static, saturated feelings in which melancholia predominates, the films that follow evoke not only saturated, lyrical feelings, but also passive emotions cued by empathy with the characters' tragic fate. In *Europa* we feel sorrow when Kessler fails to save the train and dies. Medea's fate evokes a more dynamic sorrow, as the film ends with Medea being slowly moved away from the scene of death. In *Moving Pictures* I used the term *paratelic* to describe a kind of non-goal-oriented action controlled by autonomic forces (Grodal 1997).

In *Breaking the Waves*, some of the basic narrative and visual strategies of Trier's early films are modified. Here, the story is more goal oriented and active. Although the film displays a number of melodramatic and lyrical retardations, the main character, Bess, is in some respects an active, goal-oriented heroine. Bess is a religious, neurotic, and slightly retarded girl who has grown up in a backward community on a Scottish island. She falls in love with and marries an oil rig worker, Jan, and her fascination with him is powerfully erotic. Soon Jan has to return to work, and Bess prays to God to let him come back. Her wish is tragically fulfilled when he falls victim to an accident that leaves him paralyzed. He now demands that she have sexual relations with other men and relate her encounters in all their exciting details. He claims that this is the only way he can stay alive. Feeling that she caused his accident by her prayer to God, she submits to increasingly brutal sexual humiliations, finally dying as a result of sexual violence. But she saves Jan, who is miraculously cured, and during her burial at sea a great mythic bell chimes in the sky.

Although Bess is a victim of destiny, she wins Jan back, both in having him return from the oil rig and in curing him of his paralysis. Despite various antinaturalistic devices, the narrative is much closer to normal film realism than Trier's previous films. The active elements are "paid for" by the creation of a highly metaphysical dimension in the diegetic world, where prayers are real actions, and Christlike suffering results in miraculous healing, in accordance with social exchange principles (Boyer 2001). The extreme passive act of suffering and death is interpreted as active coping. The male hero, by contrast, is paralyzed throughout most of the film, so in this respect, too, *Breaking the Waves* is romantic in its emphasis on healing femininity. The film is set in a prototypically romantic landscape, Ossian's Scotland, and the title indicates that Bess's life is subject to a wavelike destiny that is miraculously broken only at the end of the film. Trier uses a romantic-metafictional frame by dividing the film's episodes into chapters with captions that indicate the nature of the next episode, set against a background of highly romantic scenes. By evoking historic associations, the chapter division blocks the present-tense qualities of the film; the story is set in the past, and the film merely recounts what has already been decided by fate. Thus the epic aspects of the film are lyrically colored by a fatalistic melancholia. The use of handheld camera and grainy pictures is yet another distance-creating and antinaturalistic device (handheld camera often goes against natural vision, in the sense that our eyes have a sort of biological steady-cam function).

Metafiction and Affective Filters

In the preceding paragraphs I have used the difference between narrative and lyrical elements on the one hand, and between active and passive narrative elements on the other, as important parameters. In the following, I will look at a third key parameter: the framing and filtering of the viewer's empathetic relationship to the diegetic characters. The normal action-oriented film is designed in such a way that the viewer establishes an empathetic relationship to the characters and simulates their experiences. In *Breaking the Waves*, for instance, the viewer sees what is happening through the eyes of Bess or from a point of view close to her horizon, so that we are cued to simulate her emotional and cognitive processes (on the problems of identification and simulation, see chapter 8; Gaut 1999).

Two filters, two aesthetic procedures, can be used to modify or alter empathetic identification with the main character. The first procedure is based on laughter, humor, and irony. Laughter and similar reactions lead to radical changes in the emotional relationship between the viewer and the characters. Consider, for example, the way we react to clowns and other comic figures. If viewers empathized fully with the clown, as small children often do, they might begin to weep at the clown's degradation and suffering, whereas the more mature viewer will use the comic relabeling function and see that the situation is not quite real, thus enabling him or her to transform painful arousal into pleasure that is expressed in laughter. The ability to transform unpleasant emotions into pleasant ones, for example, by blocking empathy, is innate but does not appear until a certain age. It serves as an emotional safety valve in relation to excessive, painful arousal. The comic episodes in Trier's *The Kingdom* consist in a long series of embarrassing and absurd scenes that would be extremely painful without the comic filter.

The other main filter is created when the conditions of observation cause the viewer to become a more or less interested, but distant, observer of the events and characters in the film, rather than identifying with the characters and simulating their emotional experiences. The most extreme version of this device consists in the metafiction, a narrative that combines a diegetic world with extradiegetic elements, ensuring that the audience maintains a distanced view by making them conscious of their own position vis-à-vis the film. This awareness makes certain cognitive and emotional demands on viewers that leave them with less capacity for an emotional and cognitive simulation of the intradiegetic narrative. As I mentioned above, for example, the intertitles in *Breaking the Waves* act as a metafictional frame that facilitates the transformation of the film's active emotional elements into a more passive, fatalistic, and saturated form.

Epidemic is a full-blown metafiction. Large parts of the film consist in portraying a real-life frame story: Trier and his scriptwriter Vørsel are seen working on a manuscript. In the five days in which the frame narrative takes place, they try to write a manuscript titled *Epidemic*. As the writing takes place, fictional elements—pieces of the future film—are introduced. The film is about a plague epidemic in the past. The viewer's affective and cognitive simulation of the plague story is diminished by several factors. First, the scenes are too brief to allow for deep simulation. Second, the viewer is continuously reminded that the story is not quite real, but a product of the filmmaker's and the scriptwriter's imagination. At the same time, the film suggests that it is difficult to separate reality and imagination, because the imaginary epidemic world threatens to infect the supposedly real world of the frame, so that the reality status of both frame and fiction becomes problematic.

Self-conscious metafictional distance is often used as a means to circumvent cognitive or affective censorship. As we discussed in chapter 4, it is clear that viewers do not have a fixed value system. In *The Kingdom*, Trier uses metafictional features to deny the reality of the fiction and to emphasize that the film is like a game. After each episode, Trier steps forward as the empirical author and comments on the fictional world. He exposes the gimmicks of the TV series and describes what he thinks are the viewers' expectations. But in doing so he also permits the audience to abandon themselves to tales of the supernatural—just as Hitchcock, in presenting his TV films, allowed viewers to enjoy murder as a game. Metafictional distance may therefore serve to satisfy moral, cognitive, or affective objections. Trier's experiments with distance are functionally linked to the undertone of perverse sexuality in his films, from the early experimental films such as *The Orchid Gardener* and *Menthe la Bienheureuse* to *Breaking the Waves* and *Dogville*. Perverse scenes block the narrative and the viewer's empathetic identification, thus preventing any buildup of emotions; the viewer is placed as a distant observer who eventually activates feelings. Perversion is therefore one of several ways of creating lyrical-saturated experiences (see a similar lyrical use of perversion in Cronenberg's *Crash*).

We may divide these emotional filters into three types, according to function: one concerns affective valorization (e.g., the way laughter transforms pain into pleasure); another concerns the intensity or "temperature" of the experience (as when distance is used to reduce emotional activation); and a third concerns the modal form of the affect (tense emotions vs. saturated emotions). Trier's art makes extensive use of all three types of emotional filters.

Comic Filters

The TV series *The Kingdom* uses all types of emotional filters continuously, but focuses especially, of course, on the comic transformations of pain and embarrassment into pleasure. On a thematic level, there is a large degree of continuity between Trier's earlier films and *The Kingdom*. The Danish title, *Riget*, is the popular version of the name of the national hospital in Copenhagen, and it corresponds to the German word *Reich*; there is thus a link between this story of the possible demise of the hospital and Trier's previous concern with the fall of the Third Reich. The labyrinthine corridors of the hospital bear a resemblance to the postwar interiors of his previous films, and much of what goes on at the hospital is tragic, embarrassing, or absurd. The introductory images are lyrical depictions of the swampy foundations on which the hospital is built, on the site of what was once a bleaching pond. But the bleaching evokes a crime that still haunts the hospital: the Nazi-type experiments with chloride carried out by a doctor on his illegitimate child, Mona. She cannot rest and haunts the hospital buildings. As in the previous films, the maltreatment of children is a prominent theme in *The Kingdom*. Mona's fate is mirrored in a more recent case of "patriarchal" abuse: a doctor's negligence during an operation on a little girl leaves her mentally retarded. The conflicts between present-day characters, which center on the abuse of power, are doubled and mirrored in the spirits of the past, with the ghosts of the evil father and the abused girl intervening in hospital life to gain power or redemption.

The central function of a hospital is to treat suffering people who have been transformed from agents into patients, and the series uses devices from hospital soaps and science fiction to show the frail, mortal human body and the emotions that mental and physical frailty evoke. In the series, Trier continues his experiments with the lyrical transformation of actions to portray action as destiny, and to transform active, tense emotions into passive, saturated emotions. Although the prime filter used in the series is comedy, *The Kingdom* has strong melodramatic elements, especially in the gothic description of the hospital's prehistory, so that it at once evokes emotions melodramatically and transforms them via comic effects.

The format of the TV series offers scope for new aesthetic devices, allowing for (lyrical) repetition as well as the portrayal of unique events. The repetitive daily routines of the hospital (e.g., the morning conference) exemplify this. The transformation of dramatic dynamics into lyrical repetition is emphasized by the use of repetitive style features borrowed from music videos and other television products. There is the mood-creating, lyrical recurrent establishing high-angle shot of the hospital, a recurring shot of the elevator shaft, and a recurring image of a mysterious ambulance. To this is added the use of a Greek chorus: two hospital employees with Down syndrome who make metacommentaries that correspond with Trier's own metacommentaries at the end of each episode. All these effects enhance the impression of the film as a mixture of lyrical repetition and of unique, forward-directed action.

There are two new types of elements in the TV series compared with the earlier films. First, there is a series of explicitly goal-oriented story elements. The main character, Mrs. Drusse, is strictly speaking a patient, and as such the incarnation of the passive object—the passive sufferer of illness and treatment. But in reality she is a very goal-oriented person, responsible for a series of actions aimed at lifting the curse that haunts the hospital. Many of her actions are, by normal standards, absurd, induced by her superstition and credulity. But they have their own twisted logic and prove to be effective. Several other individuals are also very active, although their actions are often absurd, embarrassing, or shameful. The change from passive to active behavior is most clearly manifested in the two child abuse cases. In the earlier films, the abuse was not punished or redeemed (except through the investigation in *The Element of Crime*, which facilitates the criminal actions of the investigator), but in *The Kingdom*, child molestation is the central motivating force behind two of the main story lines: the dissolution of the curse on the Kingdom that arose from the abuse and murder of Mary, and the effort to fight the doctor whose malpractice caused Mona's mental handicap.

The other new element in the film is linked to the way in which the emotions are labeled and filtered. In Trier's earlier films, the painful or embarrassing emotional tone of a given situation is maintained, engendering empathy with the sufferers. In *The Kingdom* there is a comic rejection of any empathy with suffering, absurdity, shame, or embarrassment. Any such emotions are transformed into comic pleasure. At first blush it may seem paradoxical that this transformation of empathy to an often brutal laughter represents a breakthrough to a far more humane universe. From a cynical point of view, the audience is spared the most painful forms of empathy and they are able to protect themselves through laughter. Yet it could be argued that the filmmaker is being humane in sparing the viewer the most painful aspects of empathy by relabeling the characters' pain and providing comic relief. One of the ways in which this relabeling takes place is that the reality status of the story elements is constantly manipulated: first because the series explicitly indicates that it is a farce, a caricature of reality; and second, because the horror elements make us uncertain about the reality status of the supernatural phenomena. The horror elements are visually and acoustically realistic, but will, of course, be seen as unreal by most people. The fear evoked by the sensuous representation of an unreal situation may more easily be dissolved in a comic reaction afterward because the viewer's cognitive evaluation ("this scene cannot be real") chimes with the sense of unreality or absurdity produced by the comic filter. Laughter overrules the motivation for action that a scene might otherwise produce. We may observe that in film aesthetics, one step forward plus one step backward does not return us to square one. Horrifying and melodramatic representations evoke unpleasant experiences that are larger than life; laughter reverses the whole thing and makes these experiences smaller than life, or unreal. The pain-laughter sequence gives us a roller-coaster ride on the Wundt curve, that is, the curve that describes how changes in levels of arousal create pleasure, regardless of whether the level is increased or decreased.

Several of the characters in the series display obsessive features: Mrs. Drusse does so, and so do the head doctors, whose projects of enlightenment always end in absurd or tragic acts. Thus the stronger element of goal-oriented behavior in *The Kingdom* has not stopped Trier from portraying the kinds of obsessive characters that we saw in *The Element of Crime*; he has simply replaced the dynamic lyricism of the obsessive narrative with laughter as an affective discharger.

The move toward real, goal-oriented action in *The Kingdom* ties up with a modification in the way that the characters are portrayed, a modification that was already evident in *Breaking the Waves*. Whereas the main characters in the previous films were fragmented and torn between conflicting emotions that were often perverse, especially in relation to children, the main character in *The Kingdom*, Mrs. Drusse, is motivated by an (almost) unambiguously altruistic maternal love for the abused children and a virtually obsessive need to care for the weak. Mrs. Drusse's altruistic motherly bonding is mirrored in one of *The Kingdom*'s more grotesque elements. A young woman has been made pregnant by the evil demon of the series, Krüger, and gives birth to a grotesque monster. However, her motherly love for the monster is absolute. Although Bess's love for Jan in *Breaking the Waves* has egoistic elements in the beginning, it is soon transformed into a total, altruistic love for the handicapped and perverted man, despite the fact that this leads her into degradation and destruction. Absolute motherly love is even more prominent in the story of *The Idiots*. The simpleminded Karen has lost her baby, and when she meets an "idiot," her instincts to tend him unconditionally are activated. The focus in the later films (except for the last part of *Dogville*) on women who save men or children through motherly love shows the interrelationship between theme and generic filtering. In its most simple form, the theme is sentimental, violating good taste and ideas of feminine emancipation. Trier therefore filters the theme through various distance-creating generic devices. The story of Bess's love is filtered partly because it takes the form of a religious melodrama, partly because it is spiced with pornographic elements. Similarly, Mrs. Drusse's all-embracing altruism is filtered through absurd elements of spiritualism. The pinnacle of motherly love is of course achieved by Björk as Selma in *Dancer in the Dark*. Here, the sentimental love theme is filtered by the style of the film and its adherence to formal, operatic rules. Whereas Medea hangs her children, Björk is hanged to save her son's eyes. But both mothers are (traumatically) linked to death and suffocation.

Dogma Realism

It is somewhat paradoxical that Trier has become famous for launching the Dogma movement, a supposedly realist film concept, since in his oeuvre it represents only a short, ascetic interlude, negating all those features that made him an auteur of lyrical art films. The language he used to formulate the Dogma is borrowed from the monastic world. The 10 Dogma rules are negations of everything he did before *The Idiots* and everything he has done since. The use of artificial lighting is banned; nondiegetic music is banned; sophisticated postproduction methods or superficial effect-evoking story elements are banned; genre films do not qualify; and the film must be set in the present day. However, *The Idiots* is not a straightforwardly realistic film, because although it eschews certain traditional antirealistic effects, such as guns, it includes pornographic scenes, including group sex and voyeurism, that might be judged superficial teasers. The main story is about a commune of young people who play at being idiots in order to discover their "inner idiot," an authentic core, and because they want to provoke their bourgeois neighbors and members of their own families to expose their prejudices against the mentally handicapped. The film cues powerful feelings of shame and embarrassment in the viewer, because the realist setting makes some of the sex scenes, and the scenes in which the characters act as if they were mentally retarded, more painful than the embarrassing elements in earlier films.

One of the filters used in *The Idiots* is self-conscious metafiction. The characters only act as if they were idiots, so the film concerns a happening, or series of happenings; it is not a piece of social realism about the life of handicapped people. Moreover, it contains certain metafictional scenes in which the actors reflect on their acting. In *The Idiots*, Trier renounces some of the lyrical visual effects used in the earlier films, but the handheld camera, natural lighting, and so on that he uses in place of these likewise serve to produce an antinaturalistic visual style. The human eye is constructed to act as a steady-cam, with highly sophisticated functions that enable us to focus on objects and adapt to changes in lighting, making our ordinary vision much closer to the experience of continuity editing. It is almost impossible with natural vision to sever objects or figures through framing, or to produce shaky images and brutal shifts in lighting. Thus Trier's version of the Dogma style is not a complete break from his earlier films but a sophisticated experiment in new types of visual distancing (the use of a handheld camera, for example, could be seen as a form of addresser realism that serves to remind us of the filmmaker's presence; cf. chapter 11).

Melodramatic Americana

Whereas *Breaking the Waves* for the most part fulfills the generic expectations of melodrama, *Dancer in the Dark* has a more complicated relationship to genre norms. Some critics went so far as to allege that the film was a cold, ugly parody or caricature of the classical American musical, whereas others found it very moving. Compared even with *Breaking the Waves*, the story line and the setup have an operatic, libretto-like simplicity which in some respects is intended as a parody of (social realist) melodrama. The characters' motives appear willfully improbable or clichéd, and the characters and the scenes have been drawn with a simple, cartoonlike salience. Selma, for instance, is the tragic blind girl of all time, outperforming the heroines of all the most tearjerking "blind girl" films, and she is also the most unselfish mother ever to breathe. The contrast between the black-and-white inserts on the one hand, with their quotations from happy old American musicals, and, on the other, the tragic social melodrama in color, showing Selma's drab life in the factory and the cruel judicial system, is spelled out in letters larger than those of Trier's name in the credit sequence. How does this apparent simplicity fit with Trier's art film image (and with the sophisticated images from the world of painting that we see in the precredit sequence)? One explanation may be that the simplicity is an indicator of allegory, of deeper symbolic meaning, of art.

The story is as follows: a Czech immigrant in the United States, Selma (Björk) is about to go blind due to a genetic illness. She is working in a kitchen sink factory to earn money for an eye operation for her son, so that he can avoid the same fate. A friend steals her money and she kills him to get the money back. She is convicted of the murder, but because she does not tell the background story—explaining her desire to retrieve the money so that it could be used for her son's operation—she is executed. Stylistically, the film is made up of two contrasting systems. One system consists of the nonmusical sequences, in which Selma's tragic everyday life is filmed with hand-held cameras, so that the camera movements are often hectic and noisy, there is a lack of in-depth sharpness, and the framing is often unfocused, cutting even through key objects. Some scenes were shot with as many as 100 cameras and edited for single-shot salience, not for classical continuity. The color saturation is often deficient. The other system consists of the song numbers, which express a utopian or dreamlike dimension in which all the conflicts of normal life are transformed into an idyllic world of rosy, upbeat feelings, warm community, and shared values. The color in these sequences is highly saturated and they are shot entirely in classical continuity style with steady, focused, meticulously composed images. The order of the compositions is underlined by the fact that they are often cut to the beat of the music, especially in the railroad song, where the railroad, as an established metaphor of passive melodramatic immersion in fatal processes, is integrated into the music. However, Björk's voice and the music itself do not belong to the style of the classic musical. Her markedly individual and expressive voice produces the diametrically opposite effect of the classic musical, which suggests the integration of the individual in a harmonious social system. The musical interludes serve the same function as the chapter images in *Breaking the Waves*, transforming and transfiguring the ordinary flow of life into sublime atemporal vistas.

Most of the musical scenes are rather peculiar and can be seen to refer to the moral collapse that marked earlier films. The execution of Selma begins with grim portrayals of her suffering, fear of death, and so on. But then the musical version shows a happy Selma who sings, enchanted, with the rope around her neck, apparently in a joyful embrace with death, her attitude quite similar to that of Medea's eldest son, who willingly asks for the robe. In another musical episode, Selma and the man she has murdered dance happily together, expressing a joyful submission to fate: nobody is to blame; you had to steal my money; I happened to kill you; but let's be friends. In a third musical interlude, the court sings and dances happily despite the fact that it is dealing with a murder trial. The musical elements achieve their sublime effects by annihilating central motivators for actions. If lambs and wolves or murderers and victims dance happily with each other, then any motivational machine is short-circuited.

Some critics of *Dancer in the Dark* argued that the film was a caricature of American society, inspired by Soviet cold war kitsch and influenced by Trier's communist parents. Others, as mentioned, felt that it was a cold, ugly deconstruction of the Hollywood musical tradition. In some respects, Selma represents the Artist as opposed to American mainstream culture. Björk, as a singer, may not have been directly influenced by 20th-century experimental opera, but if we compare her performance with that of, say, the actors in the musical *Chicago*, it appears to be avant-garde and experimental rather than parody, fueled by an archetypal melodramatic story that gives an emotional charge to the audiovisual experiments. There might be some truth to the criticism that the film contains an implicit critique of Hollywood, although the utopian sequences are those that have classical continuity, and it is also true that *Dancer in the Dark* focuses on some of the more sordid aspects of the United States. However, the United States has the same structural function in the later films as the Third Reich or Europe had in the earlier work, namely to be the bearer of a fate that integrates the life of the individual into a quasi-metaphysical tragedy. It is difficult to see the political element as the inspirational core of these films, since *Medea* contains many of the same ingredients. Rather, at the center of the films is the question of basic affective relations between people; for example, the story of Björk, the ugly duckling with a weird voice, who expresses a love that transcends the evil world, sacrifices her life out of motherly love, and becomes a kind of blind seer.

Whereas *Dancer in the Dark* represented a further experiment in combining the art film tradition with mainstream fiction, in *Dogville* a cast-iron art film frame surrounds the mainstream inspiration with self-conscious props, in an effort to ensure that no tears are spilled in true compassion (in vain, since many viewers are moved to tears by the film). The dominant affective mode is that of irony, the cold eye of the camera recording sordid human life; but some viewers may read it as farce, comedy, or even pornographic fantasy. The film leans on the Brechtian tradition of metafictional framing and the prominent use of allegory. The film is played out on a theater stage, with only a very few props, and this allows for an abstract, symbolic presentation of what appears, on the surface, to be a social realist drama. With mocking playfulness, even the symbolic dog in Dogville is merely indicated by a chalk outline, as is most of the layout of the small village. The voice-over narrator is omniscient and ironic and provides a fatalistic commentary on events as they unfold. This "God's-eye" view is even symbolized visually, because Trier went to great lengths to provide a completely vertical view of the scene, making the three-dimensional world shrink almost down to a two-dimensional diagram. This bird's-eye pictorialism offers a classic aesthetic contrast to the scenes in which the play's microcosmic world is shown through restless, handheld cameras, and the beauty of the scene in which we get a sudden glimpse of Grace surrounded by apples in a van is partly due to this reduction to two dimensions.

The story deals, as usual, with the question of whether warm personal relations are possible. The inhabitants of the miserable village are more or less reluctantly involved in a moral rearmament drive to raise morality, and when a girl who appears to be running away from gangsters arrives at the village, their moral values are tested. Initially they pass the test, but soon they begin to exploit her, first economically and then sexually. Unlike Bess, whose sole purpose in submitting to sexual abuse is to save Jan, Grace gradually assumes the role of a female Jesus who will perhaps succeed through her sufferings in finally redeeming the rotten village and giving it grace. But toward the end, the story turns from the New Testament to the Old and the God who destroyed Sodom, Gomorrah, and Babylon. To our surprise, we find out that the heroine is not a damsel for whom the (divine) boss has evil intentions; on the contrary, she is his daughter, and has run away in order to become good and meek. She ends up acting as an avenging angel who performs an Endlösung, a final solution, not of "the Jewish question" but of the problems in Dogville. In this respect, *Dogville* clearly represents a somewhat nihilistic mockery of Marxist as well as American values. The working class cherished by

Marxists are not nice people; they will readily exploit and enslave anyone available for the purpose.

Whereas the emotional frame of the film is ironic, the content is imbued with an aggression that leads to humiliation and sexual perversion. The scene in which Grace is put in chains and forced to have sex with all the men in the village—in full public view in a sense, given the lack of walls—could be seen as slightly veiled pornography. However, the context in which these scenes are presented transforms arousal into shame, embarrassment, and empathy. The art film context, including the allegorical elements, could have served as a classical Freudian secondary elaboration, except for the fact that even the primary material is shown in broad daylight or floodlight.

Trier's Development from a Biographical Perspective

In understanding the ways in which Trier has been inspired both by European art film and by American genre films, we also need to take into account certain aspects of his personality. Trier's works stage universal types of experience, but the recurring themes of his films and their development also have their background in very personal problems. This is not the place for a detailed account of his life (see Schepelern 2000, 2004), but I would like to focus here on a few important elements that are central to his themes and narratives. Trier had a neurotic childhood and suffered from an intense inferiority complex, feeling himself an unloved ugly duckling. But he also grew up in an environment that encouraged ambition. His mother was a strong-willed communist and purveyor of abstract altruistic feelings, which she nevertheless felt bound to defend aggressively because the immediate environment did not live up to her ideals (the Communist Party was an insignificant minority party in Denmark and was despised after the Hungarian uprising). Problematic mother-son relations are central to most of Trier's films.

Trier also thought he was Jewish because his mother was married to a Jew whom Trier assumed to be his father. His early films show a fearful fascination with the world of the Third Reich and the Holocaust. The aggressive ambivalence in Trier's outlook is expressed by the fact that he added *von* to his surname and for a short while flirted with a Nazilike identity, dressing like a Prussian Junker, while at the same time making films that focus on victimization. It is easy to see that for a physically small Jewish boy, raised in a communist family and growing up in the radical '60s and '70s, it is a gesture of extreme ambivalence to identify formally with the aggressor as well as the victim. It is therefore not surprising that many of his films take a passive melodramatic form. There is no obvious narrative solution for these personal and historical ambivalences, and therefore a lyrical-thematic network of associations linked to ambiguous emotions was the logical aesthetic choice.

On her deathbed in 1989, Trier's mother told him that he was the fruit of a liaison with her non-Jewish boss. This appears to have lessened Trier's interest in the fateful world and the victims of World War II: although the relationship between hangman and victim has remained central to his universe, his later stories are set in the Anglo-Saxon world or in Denmark. His ambivalence toward America seems to have two main roots: his communist upbringing and his love-hate relationship with American mass culture, whose basic emotional salience evidently appeals to Trier, yet conflicts with his high-art ambitions, his aesthetic sensibility, and his fascination with subjective images arising from his own personal traumas. The knowledge that he was not a Jew came at a time when he was beginning to gain social success through his filmmaking. In the 1990s and early 2000s, with films and TV serials such as *The Kingdom*, *Breaking the Waves*, *The Idiots*, *Dancer in the Dark*, and *Dogville*, Trier's work shifted in a more narrative direction. On the surface, it has become a bit more upbeat, although it continues fundamentally to express a tragic vision of the world.

Trier's Work, Agency, Biology, and Culture

The basic aesthetic framework for Trier's films is provided by biology: the genres and emotions that he draws on and the aesthetic possibilities he uses are determined by fundamental features of the brain's architecture—for instance, by the set of features that evokes a freezing of the PECMA flow and the feature that determines how such manipulations are linked to certain emotions. He inherits and elaborates on knowledge from more than 100 years of film culture experiments with the way certain audiovisual effects influence brains.

On another level, however, his films express the confluence of a series of different historical and cultural factors. Just to mention a few: World War II and the Holocaust were still very present when Trier grew up, and they produced a field of fearful fascination for a boy who believed he was Jewish, providing a framework for stories of individuals who are the passive victims of destiny. The Vietnam War led to associations between America and the Third Reich. Trier belonged to the first generation who grew up with television, and his films reflect the conflict between the European art film and American mainstream film and TV fiction. Through a series of experiments in passive and distanced narrative, his films also express his personal development. The biographical facts of Trier's life contribute to an understanding of the motivational force behind his fascination with strong and ambivalent emotions, with lyrical-associative and expressive modes of representation, and with metafictional forms. In his work Trier portrays powerful and often deviant subjective feelings, whether these consist in dystopian visions of a decaying future, depictions of a community threatened by supernatural agents, stories of people in the grip of perverted minds, or characters who are strongly moved by love. Because the constituent devices in most mainstream genres are geared to evoking strong emotions, generic formulas have proved good vehicles for Trier's fascination with strong, deviant emotions. His synthesis of elements from high and mass culture involves filtering the action and emotions that typify mass culture through a high cultural lyrical toning.

Although Trier's films are the products of a specific cultural situation and certain personal psychological elements, his films also activate cognitive and emotional dispositions that are universal and innate. The general narrative forms used in mainstream films define, or label, the emotions portrayed in a given film through its choice of narrative formula, be it tragedy, melodrama, or comedy. Over the centuries, the specific forms of fiction have changed, from the epics, tragedies, comedies, and farces of ancient times to modern film genres, but the continuities in general narrative forms and their relationship to particular emotional types are much greater than the discontinuities. Trier's *Medea* is not identical to Euripides' version, but the two versions share certain key narrative and affective elements. Classical and modern comedies have many common features that distinguish them systematically from tragedies. A cognitive-emotional account of film takes as its point of departure the functioning of the adult individual. Some of the situations that adults face demand active coping, as reflected in stories about willed, heroic efforts to find solutions to crises. Other situations demand passive adaptation to fate and unchangeable conditions, as reflected in films that show reactions of sorrow or lyrical contemplation. Thus it is important to distinguish the biographical reasons for problematic interpersonal relations in Trier's work from the way in which such relationships are presented in his films, which appeal to people who do not share his life story.

References

Alcorta, Candace S., and Richard Sosis. 2005. "Ritual, Emotion, and Sacred Symbols: The Evolution of Religion as an Adaptive Complex." *Human Nature* 16, no. 4: 323–359.

Altman, Rick. 1999. *Film/Genre*. London: BFI.

Anderson, Joseph D. 1996. *The Reality of Illusion: An Ecological Approach to Cognitive Film Theory*. Carbondale: Southern Illinois University Press.

Anderson, Joseph, and Barbara Anderson, eds. 2005. *Motion Picture Theory: Ecological Considerations*. Carbondale: Southern Illinois University Press.

Arnheim, Rudolf. 1957. *Film as Art*. Berkeley: University of California Press.

———. 1974. *Art and Visual Perception: A Psychology of the Creative Eye*. Berkeley: University of California Press.

Atran, Scott. 1994. "Core Domains versus Scientific Theories: Evidence from Systematics and Itza-Maya Folkbiology." In *Mapping the Mind: Domain Specificity in Cognition and Culture*, ed. Lawrence Hirschfeld and Susan Gelman, 316–340. Cambridge: Cambridge University Press.

———. 2002. *In Gods We Trust: The Evolutionary Landscape of Religion*. Oxford: Oxford University Press.

Auerbach, Eric. 1974. *Mimesis: The Representation of Reality in Western Literature*. New York: Doubleday Anchor Books.

Aunger, Robert, ed. 2000. *Darwinizing Culture: The Status of Memetics as a Science*. New York: Oxford University Press.

Averill, James B. 1968. "Grief: Its Nature and Significance." *Psychological Bulletin* 70, no. 6: 721–748.

Baars, Bernard J. 1988. *A Cognitive Theory of Consciousness.* Cambridge: Cambridge University Press.

Balazs, Bela. 1970. *Theory of the Film.* New York: Dover.

Bandura, Albert. 1994. "Social Cognitive Theory of Mass Communication." In *Media Effects: Advances in Theory and Research,* ed. Jennings Bryant and Dolf Zillmann, 61–90. Hillsdale, N.J.: Erlbaum.

Barkow, Jerome H., Leda Cosmides, and John Tooby, eds. 1992. *The Adapted Mind: Evolutionary Psychology and the Generation of Culture.* New York: Oxford University Press, 1992.

Baron-Cohen, Simon. 1995. *Mindblindness.* Cambridge, Mass.: MIT Press.

———. 2003. *The Essential Difference: Men, Women and the Extreme Male Brain.* London: Allan Lane/Penguin.

Baron-Cohen, Simon, and John E. Harrison, eds. 1997. *Synaesthesia.* Cambridge, Mass.: Blackwell.

Barrett, Justin. 2004. *Why Would Anyone Believe in God?* Walnut Creek: Altamira.

Barrett, Louise, Robert Dunbar, and John Lycett. 2002. *Human Evolutionary Pscyhology.* Houndmills, U.K.: Palgrave.

Barsalou, Lawrence, W. 1999. "Perceptual Symbol Systems." *Behavioral and Brain Sciences* 22: 577–660.

Bartels, Andreas, and Semur Zeki. 2004. "The Neural Correlates of Maternal and Romantic Love." *Neuroimage* 21, no. 3: 1156–1166.

Barthes, Roland. 1974. *S/Z.* Translated by Richard Miller. New York: Hill and Wang.

———. 1977. "Introduction to the Structural Analysis of Narratives." In *Image Music Text.* London: Fontana.

Bazin, André. 1967. *What Is Cinema?* Berkeley: University of California Press.

Beardsley, Monroe C. 1958. *Aesthetics: Problems in the Philosophy of Criticism.* New York: Harcourt, Brace.

Benjamin, Walter. 1977. "The Work of Art in the Age of Mechanical Reproduction." In *Mass Communication and Society,* ed. James Curran, Michael Gurevitch, and Janet Wollacott, 384–408. London: Edward Arnold.

Berlyne, Daniel E. 1971. *Aesthetics and Psychobiology.* New York: Appleton-Century-Crofts.

Björklund, David, and Anthony Pellegrini. 2002. *The Origins of Human Nature: Evolutionary Developmental Psychology.* Washington, D.C.: American Psychological Association.

Blackmore, Susan. 1999. *The Meme Machine.* Oxford: Oxford University Press.

Bloch, Maurice. 1992. *Prey into Hunter: The Politics of Religious Experience.* Cambridge: Cambridge University Press.

Bordewijk, Jan L., and Ben van Kaam. 1986. "Towards a New Classification of TeleInformation Services." *Inter-Media* 14, no. 1: 16–21.

Bordwell, David. 1986. *Narration in the Fiction Film.* London: Methuen.

———. 1989a. "A Case for Cognitivism." *Iris* 9: 11–40.

———. 1989b. *Making Meaning.* Cambridge, Mass.: Harvard University Press.

———. 1996a. "Contemporary Film Studies and the Vicissitudes of Grand Theory." In *Post-Theory*, ed. David Bordwell and Noël Carroll, 3–36. Madison: University of Wisconsin Press.

———. 1996b. "Convention, Construction and Cinematic Vision." In *Post-Theory*, ed. David Bordwell and Noël Carroll, 87–107. Madison: University of Wisconsin Press.

———. 1998. *On the History of Film Style*. Cambridge, Mass.: Harvard University Press.

———. 2002. "Film Futures." *Substance* 31, no. 1: 88–104.

Bordwell, David, and Noël Carroll, eds. 1996. *Post-Theory*. Madison: University of Wisconsin Press.

Bordwell, David, Janet Staiger, and Kristin Thompson. 1988. *The Classical Hollywood Cinema: Film Style and Mode of Production to 1960*. London: Routledge.

Bordwell, David, and Kristin Thompson. 2001. *Film Art: An Introduction*. New York: McGraw-Hill.

Bourdieu, Pierre. 1984. *Distinction: A Social Critique of the Judgement of Taste*. London: Routledge Kegan Paul.

Bowlby, John. 1980. *Loss: Sadness and Depression* (Vol. 3 of *Attachment and Loss*). London: Hogarth Press.

———. 1982. *Attachment*. New York: Basic Books.

Boyd, Robert, and Peter Richerson. 1998. "The Evolution of Human Ultrasociality." In *Indoctrinability, Ideology and Warfare*, ed. Irenäus Eibl-Eibesfeldt and Frank Kemp Salter, 71–93. New York: Berghahn Books.

Boyer, Pascal. 1999. "Cognitive Tracks of Cultural Inheritance: How Evolved Intuitive Ontology Governs Cultural Transmission." *American Anthropologist* 100, no. 4: 876–899.

———. 2001. *Religion Explained: The Human Instincts That Fashion Gods, Spirits and Ancestors*. London: William Heinemann.

———. 2007. "Specialized Inference Engines as Precursors of Creative Imagination?" *Proceedings of the British Academy* 147: 239–258.

Boyer, Pascal, and Pierre Liénard. 2006. "Why Ritualized Behavior? Precaution Systems and Action Parsing in Developmental, Pathological and Cultural Rituals." *Behavioral and Brain Sciences* 29, no. 6: 1–56.

Branigan, Edward. 1984. *Point of View in the Cinema*. Berlin: Mouton.

———. 1992. *Narrative Comprehension and Film*. London: Routledge.

Bråten, Stein. 2002. "Altercentric Perception by Infants and Adults in Dialogue." In *Mirror Neurons and the Evolution of Brain and Language*, ed. Maxim Stamenov and Vittorio Gallese, 273–294. Amsterdam: John Benjamins.

Bremond, Claude. 1964. "Le Message Narrative." *Communications* 4: 4–32.

Brockman, John. 1995. *The Third Culture*. New York: Touchstone.

Brown, Donald E. 1991. *Human Universals*. New York: McGraw-Hill.

Brown, Steven. 2000. "Evolutionary Models of Music: From Sexual Selection to Group Selection." In *Perspectives in Ethology. 13: Behavior, Evolution and Culture*, ed. François Tonneau and Nicolas S. Thompson, 231–281. New York: Plenum.

Browne, Nicholas. 1982. *The Rhetoric of Filmic Narration.* Ann Arbor, Mich.: UMI Research Press.

Bruce, Vicky. 1988. *Recognizing Faces.* Hillsdale, N.J.: Erlbaum.

Bundesen, Klaus, Thomas Habekost, and Søren Kyllingsbæk. 2005. "A Neural Theory of Visual Attention: Bridging Cognition and Neurophysiology." *Psychological Review* 112, no. 2: 291–328.

Burgoon, Judee, David B. Buller, and Gill W. Woodall. 1989. *Nonverbal Communication: The Unspoken Dialogue.* New York: Harper and Row.

Buss, David M. 1994. *The Evolution of Desire: Strategies of Human Mating.* New York: Basic Books.

———, ed. 2005. *The Handbook of Evolutionary Psychology.* Hoboken, N.J.: Wiley.

Caillois, Roger. 1958. *Les Jeux et les Hommes.* Paris: Gallimard.

Campbell, Anne. 2002. *A Mind of Her Own.* Oxford: Oxford University Press.

Carey, Susan, and Elisabeth Spelke. 1994. "Domain-Specific Knowledge and Conceptual Change." In *Mapping the Mind: Domain Specificity in Cognition and Culture,* ed. Lawrence Hirschfeld and Susan Gelman, 168–200. Cambridge: Cambridge University Press.

Carroll, Joseph. 2008. "An Evolutionary Paradigm for Literary Study." *Style* 42 (2–3): in press.

Carroll, Noël. 1988. *Mystifying Movies: Fads and Fallacies in Contemporary Film Theory.* New York: Columbia University Press.

———. 1990. *The Philosophy of Horror or Paradoxes of the Heart.* New York: Routledge.

———. 1996a. "The Paradox of Suspense." In *Suspense: Conceptualizations, Theoretical Analyses, and Empirical Explorations,* ed. Peter Vorderer, Hans J. Wulff, and Mike Friedrichsen, 71–91. Mahwah, N.J.: Erlbaum.

———. 1996b. *Theorizing the Moving Image.* Cambridge: Cambridge University Press.

———. 1998. *A Philosophy of Mass Art.* Oxford: Clarendon/Oxford University Press.

Cawelti, John D. 1976. *Adventure, Mystery and Romance.* Chicago: University of Chicago Press.

Chatman, Seymour. 1978. *Story and Discourse: Narrative Structure in Fiction and Film.* Ithaca, N.Y.: Cornell University Press.

Churchland, Patricia. 2002. *Brain-Wise: Studies in Neurophilosophy.* Cambridge, Mass.: MIT Press.

Clover, Carol. 1992. *Men, Women, and Chain Saws.* London: BFI.

Cooper, David, ed. 1995. *A Companion to Aesthetics.* Oxford: Blackwell.

Corballis, Michael C. 1991. *The Lopsided Ape: Evolution of the Generative Mind.* New York: Oxford University Press.

Cosmides, Leda, and John Tooby. 1997. "Evolutionary Psychology: A Primer." Available at: http://www.psych.ucsb.edu/research/cep/primer.html, January.

———. 2000. "Consider the Source. The Evolution of Adaptations for Decoupling and Metarepresentation." In *Metarepresentations: A Multidisciplinary Perspective,* ed. Dan Sperber, 53–115. New York: Oxford University Press.

Crick, Francis, and Christof Koch. 1993. "The Problem of Consciousness." In *Mind and Brain: Readings from Scientific American*, 125–136. New York: W. H. Freeman.

Csikszentmihalyi, Mihaly. 1990. *Flow: The Psychology of Optimal Experience.* New York: Harper and Row.

Currie, Gregory. 1995. *Image and Mind: Film, Philosophy and Cognitive Science.* Cambridge: Cambridge University Press.

Damasio, Antonio. 1994. *Descartes' Error: Emotions, Reason, and the Human Brain.* New York: Grosset.

———. 1999. *The Feeling of What Happens: Body and Emotion in the Making of Consciousness.* New York: Harcourt, Brace.

———. 2003. *Looking for Spinoza: Joy, Sorrow, and the Feeling Brain.* Orlando, Fla.: Harcourt.

Damasio, Antonio, and Hannah Damasio. 1993. "Brain and Language." In *Mind and Brain: Readings from Scientific American*, 54–65. New York: W. H. Freeman.

Darley, John M., and Daniel C. Batson. 1973. "From Jerusalem to Jericho: A Study of Situational and Dispositional Variables in Helping Behavior." *Journal of Personality and Social Psychology* 27: 100–108.

Dawkins, Richard. 1976. *The Selfish Gene.* Oxford: Oxford University Press.

Deleuze, Gilles. 1989. *Cinema 2: The Time Image.* Minneapolis: University of Minnesota Press.

Dennett, Daniel. 1991. *Consciousness Explained.* London: Penguin.

———. 1995. *Darwin's Dangerous Ideas.* London: Penguin.

Derrida, Jacques. 1994. *Spectres of Marx.* London: Routledge.

Diamond, Jared. 1997. *Guns, Germs, and Steel: The Fates of Human Societies.* New York: W. W. Norton.

DiMaggio, Paul. 1997. "Culture and Cognition." *Annual Revue of Sociology* 23: 263–267.

Dissanayake, Ellen. 1995. *Homo Aestheticus: Where Art Comes From and Why.* Seattle: University of Washington Press.

———. 2000. *Art and Intimacy: How the Arts Began.* Seattle: University of Washington Press.

Doane, Mary Ann. 2002. *The Emergence of Cinematic Time: Modernity, Contingency, the Archive.* Cambridge, Mass.: Harvard University Press.

Dunbar, Robin. 1996. *Grooming, Gossip, and the Evolution of Language.* London: Faber.

Ebert, Roger. 1991. "The Silence of the Lambs." *Chicago Sun-Times*, February 14.

Eco, Umberto. 1970. "Sémiologie des messages visuel." *Communications* 15: 11–51.

Edelman, Gerald, and Giulio Tononi. 2000. *Consciousness: How Matter Becomes Imagination.* London: Penguin.

Eibl-Eibesfeldt, Irenäus. 1979. *The Biology of Peace and War.* (No place): Thames and Hudson.

———. 1989. *Human Ethology.* New York: Aldine de Gruyter.

Eisenstein, Sergei. 1949. *Film Form: Essays in Film Theory.* New York: Harcourt, Brace, Jovanovich.

Ekman, Paul, and Wallace V. Friesen. 1975. *Unmasking the Face: A Guide to Recognizing Emotions from Facial Clues.* Englewood Cliffs, N.J.: Prentice Hall.

Elsaesser, Thomas. 1989. *New German Cinema: A History.* New Brunswick, N.J.: Rutgers University Press.

Ewen, Robert B. 1993. *An Introduction to Theories of Personality.* Hove, U.K.: Psychology Press.

Fauconnier, Gilles, and Mark Turner. 2002. *The Way We Think: Conceptual Blending and the Mind.* New York: Basic Books.

Field, Syd. 1984. *Screenplay.* New York: Dell.

Fisher, Helen. 1992. *The Anatomy of Love: The Natural History of Monogamy, Adultery, and Divorce.* London: Simon and Schuster.

———. 2004. *Why We Love: The Nature and Chemistry of Romantic Love.* New York: Henry Holt.

Fiske, Susan T., and Shelley E. Taylor. 1991. *Social Cognition*, 2nd ed. New York: McGraw-Hill.

Fonagy, Peter. 2001. *Attachment Theory and Psychoanalysis.* New York: Other Press.

Foucault, Michel. 1971. *The Order of Things.* New York: Pantheon Books.

Fox, Robin. 2005. "Male Bonding in Epics and Romances." In *The Literary Animal: Evolution and the Nature of Narrative*, ed. Jonathan Gottschall and David S. Wilson, 126–144. Evanston, Ill.: Northwestern University Press.

Freeman, Derek. 1983. *Margaret Mead and Samoa: The Making and Unmaking of a Myth.* Cambridge, Mass.: Harvard University Press.

Frijda, Nico. 1986. *The Emotions.* Cambridge: Cambridge University Press.

———. 1988. "The Laws of Emotion." *American Psychologist* 43, no. 5: 349–358.

Gallagher, Helen L., and Christopher D. Frith. 2003. "Functional Imaging of 'Theory of Mind.'" *Trends in Cognitive Sciences* 7, no. 2: 77–83.

Gallagher, Shaun, and Dan Zahavi. 2008. *The Phenomenological Mind: An Introduction to Philosophy of Mind and Cognitive Science.* Routledge: London.

Gallese, Vittorio. 1998. "Mirror Neurons: From Grasping to Language." Paper presented at the conference Toward a Science of Consciousness 1998, Tucson III, April 27–May 2.

Gallese, Vittorio, and Maxim Stamenov, eds. 2002. *Mirror Neurons and the Evolution of Brain and Language.* Amsterdam: John Benjamins.

Gardner, Howard. 1982. *Art, Mind and Brain: A Cognitive Approach to Creativity.* New York: Basic Books.

Gaut, Berys. 1999. "Identification and Emotion in Narrative Film." In *Passionate Views: Film, Cognition, and Emotion*, ed. Carl Plantinga and Greg Smith, 200–216. Baltimore: Johns Hopkins University Press.

Geary, David C. 2005. *The Origin of Mind: Evolution of Brain, Cognition, and General Intelligence.* Washington, D.C.: American Psychological Association.

Genette, Gerard. 1983. *Narrative Discourse: An Essay in Method.* Ithaca, N.Y.: Cornell University Press.

German, Tim, Jeffrey L. Niehaus, Meghan P. Roarty, Barry Giesbrecht, and Michael B. Miller. 2004. "Neural Correlates of Detecting Pretense: Automatic Engagement of the

Intentional Stance under Covert Conditions." *Journal of Cognitive Neuroscience* 16, no. 10: 1805–1817.

Gerth, Hans H., and Charles Wright Mills, eds. 1958. *From Max Weber*. New York: Galaxy.

Gibson, James J. 1986. *The Ecological Approach to Visual Perception*. Hillsdale, N.J.: Erlbaum.

Giddens, Anthony. 1984. *The Constitution of Society: Outline of the Theory of Structuration*. Oxford: Polity Press.

Gilbert, Daniel T., Douglas S. Krull, and Patrick S. Malone. 1990. "Unbelieving the Unbelievable: Some Problems in the Rejection of False Information." *Journal of Personality and Social Psychology* 59: 601–613.

Gilbert, Paul. 2005. "Evolution and Depression: Issues and Implications." *Psychological Medicine* 36: 287–297.

Goffmann, Erving. 1986. *Frame Analysis: An Essay on the Organization of Experience*. Boston: Northeastern University Press.

Goldberg, Elkhonon. 2001. *The Executive Brain. Frontal Lobes and the Civilized Mind*. New York: Oxford University Press.

Goldman, Alvin L. 2006. *Simulating Minds: The Philosophy, Psychology, and Neuroscience of Mindreading*. New York: Oxford University Press.

Gombrich, Ernst. 1968. "Style." In *The International Encyclopedia of the Social Science*, ed. David Sills, Vol. 15, 352–361. New York: Free Press.

Gregersen, Andreas, and Torben Grodal. 2008. "Embodiment and Interface." In *Video Game Theory Reader 2*, ed. Bernard Perron and Mark J. P. Wolf. London: Routledge.

Greimas, Julien A. 1983. *Structural Semantics: An Attempt at a Method*. Lincoln: University of Nebraska Press.

Grodal, Torben. 1992. "Romanticism, Postmodernism and Irrationalism." In *Postmodernism and the Visual Media (Sekvens 1992)*, ed. Eva Jørholt and Peter Schepelern, 9–29. Copenhagen: Institut for Film og Medievidenskab.

———. 1997. *Moving Pictures: A New Theory of Film Genres, Feelings, and Cognition*. Oxford: Clarendon/Oxford University Press.

———. 1999. "Intertextuality in a Cognitive Perspective." In *Sekvens 99: Intertextuality and Visual Media*, ed. Ib Bondebjerg and Helle K. Haastrup, 47–63. Copenhagen: Department of Film and Media Studies, University of Copenhagen.

———. 2000. "Video Games and the Pleasures of Control." In *Media Entertainment: The Psychology of Its Appeal*, ed. Dolf Zillmann and Peter Vorderer, 197–213. Mahwah, N.J.: Erlbaum.

———. 2003a. "Stories for Eyes, Ears, and Muscles." In *Video Game Theory Reader*, ed. Mark J. P. Wolf and Bernard Perron, 129–156. London: Routledge.

———. 2003b. "Tales from the Crypt." Available at: http://www.filmint.nu/netonly/eng/debgrodal.htm.

———. 2004. "Agency in Films, Filmmaking, and Reception." In *Visual Authorship: Creativity and Intentionality in Media*, ed. Torben Grodal, Bente Larsen, and Iben T. Laursen, 15–36. Copenhagen: Tusculanum.

———. 2005. "Film Lighting and Mood." In *Motion Picture Theory: Ecological Considerations*, ed. Joseph Anderson and Barbara Anderson, 152–163. Carbondale: Southern Illinois University Press.

———. 2006. "The PECMA Flow: A General Model of Visual Aesthetics." *Film Studies* no. 8: 1–11.

———. 2007. *Filmoplevelse: En indføring i audiovisuel teori og analyse*. Copenhagen: Samfundslitteratur.

———. In press. "Film Aesthetics and the Embodied Brain." In *Neuroaesthetics*, ed. Martin Skov and Oshin Vartanian. New York: Baywood.

Gunning, Tom. 1994. "An Aesthetic of Astonishment." In *Viewing Positions*, ed. Linda Williams, 114–133. New Brunswick, N.J.: Rutgers University Press.

Gunter, Barrie. 1994. "The Question of Media Violence." In *Media Effects: Advances in Theory and Research*, ed. Jennings Bryant and Dolf Zillmann, 163–212. Hillsdale, N.J.: Erlbaum.

Haidt, Jonathan. 2001. "The Emotional Dog and Its Rational Tail: A Social Intuitionist Approach to Moral Judgment." *Psychological Review* 108: 814–834.

Harrison, Neil A., Tania Singer, Pia Rotstein, Ray J. Dolan, and Hugo D. Critchley. 2006. "Pupillary Contagion: Central Mechanisms Engaged in Sadness Processing." *Social Cognitive and Affective Neuroscience* 1: 5–17.

Hasson, Uri, Orit Furman, Dav Clark, Yadin Dudai, and Lila Davachi. 2008. "Enhanced Intersubjective Correlations during Movie Watching Correlate with Successful Episodic Encoding." *Neuron* 57, February 7: 452–462.

Hirschfeld, Lawrence, and Susan A. Gelman, eds. 1994. *Mapping the Mind: Domain Specificity in Cognition and Culture*. Cambridge: Cambridge University Press.

Hjort, Mette. 1993. *The Strategy of Letters*. Cambridge, Mass.: Harvard University Press.

Humphreys, Glyn W., and Vicki Bruce. 1989. *Visual Cognition: Computational, Experimental and Neuropsychological Perspectives*. Hove, U.K.: Erlbaum.

Izard, Carroll E. 1991. *The Psychology of Emotions*. New York: Springer.

Jackendoff, Ray. 1987. *Consciousness and the Computational Mind*. Cambridge, Mass.: MIT Press.

Jakobson, Roman. 1960. "Closing Statement: Linguistics and Poetics." In *Style in Language*, ed. Thomas Sebeok, 350–377. Cambridge, Mass.: MIT Press.

Jameson, Fredric. 1984. *Postmodernism*. Durham, N.C.: Duke University Press.

Johnson, Mark. 1987. *The Body in the Mind: The Bodily Basis of Meaning, Imagination and Reason*. Chicago: University of Chicago Press.

Johnston, Claire. 1988. "Double Indemnity." In *Women in Film Noir*, ed. E. Ann Kaplan, 89–98. London: BFI.

Jones, Steve, Robert Martin, and David Philbeam. 1992. *The Cambridge Encyclopedia of Human Evolution*. Cambridge: Cambridge University Press.

Jullier, Laurent. 2002. *Cinéma et Cognition*. Paris: L'Harmattan.

Katz, Leonard D., ed. 2000. *Evolutionary Origin of Morality*. Thorverton: Imprint Academic.

Keil, Frank C. 1994. "The Birth and Nurturance of Concepts by Domains: The Origins of Concepts of Living Things." In *Mapping the Mind: Domain Specificity in Cognition and Culture*, ed. Lawrence Hirschfeld and Susan A. Gelman, 234–254. Cambridge: Cambridge University Press.

Koepp, Matthias J., Roger N. Gunn, Andrew D. Lawrence, Vin J. Cunningham, Alain Dagher, Therese Jones, David J. Brooks, Christopher J. Bench, and Paul M. Gralsby. 1998. "Evidence for Striatal Dopamine Release during a Video Game." *Nature* 393: 266–268.

Kohlberg, Lawrence. 1984. *Essays in Moral Development: Vol. 2. The Psychology of Moral Development*. New York: Harper and Row.

Kracauer, Siegfried. 1960. *The Nature of Film. The Redemption of Physical Reality*. Oxford: Oxford University Press.

Kramer, Mette. 2004. "The Mating Game in Hollywood Cinema—A Darwinian Approach." *New Review of Film and Television Studies* 2, no. 2: 137–159.

———. 2008. *Romancing the Mind: Women, Emotion, Cognition, and Film*. Unpublished PhD dissertation.

Krebs, Dennis L. 2005. "The Evolution of Morality." In *The Handbook of Evolutionary Psychology*, ed. Donald Buss, 747–771. Hoboken, N.J.: John Wiley.

Krebs, Dennis L., and Kathy Denton. 2005. "Toward a More Pragmatic Approach to Morality: A Critical Evaluation of Kohlberg's Model." *Psychological Review* 112, no. 3: 629–649.

Kringelbach, Morten L., and Edmund T. Rolls. 2004. "The Functional Neuroanatomy of the Human Orbitofrontal Cortex: Evidence from Neuroimaging and Neuropsychology." *Progress in Neurobiology* 72, no. 5: 341–372.

Kuper, Adam. 1999. *Culture: The Anthropologist's Account*. Cambridge, Mass.: Harvard University Press.

Lakoff, Georges. 1987. *Women, Fire and Dangerous Things: What Categories Reveal about the Mind*. Chicago: University of Chicago Press.

Lakoff, Georges, and Mark Johnson. 1999. *Philosophy in the Flesh*. New York: Basic Books.

Laland, Kevin N., and Gillian R. Brown. 2002. *Sense and Nonsense: Evolutionary Perspectives on Human Behaviour*. Oxford: Oxford University Press.

Lamm, Claus C., Daniel Batson, and Jean Decety. 2007. "The Neural Substrate of Human Empathy: Effects of Perspective-Taking and Cognitive Appraisal." *Journal of Cognitive Neuroscience* 19: 42–58.

Larkin, Kevin T., Ronald R. Martin, and Susan E. McClain. 2002. "Cynical Hostility and the Accuracy of Decoding Facial Expressions of Emotions." *Journal of Behavioral Medicine* 25, no. 3: 285–292.

Laurel, Brenda. 1993. *Computers as Theatre*. Reading, Mass.: Addison-Wesley.

Ledoux, Joseph. 1998. *The Emotional Brain*. London: Weidenfeld and Nicholson.

———. 2002. *Synaptic Self*. London: Macmillan.

Leslie, Alan M. 1987. "Pretense and Representation: The Origin of 'Theory of Mind.'" *Psychological Review* 94, no 4: 412–426.

Lévi-Strauss, Claude. 1961. *La Pensée Sauvage*. Paris: Plon.

———. 1963. *Structural Anthropology*. New York: Basic Books.

———. 1964–1971. *Mythologiques*. 4 vols. Paris: Plon.

Liebes, Tamar, and Elihu Katz. 1993. *The Export of Meaning: Crosscultural Readings of Dallas*. Cambridge: Polity Press.

Livingstone, Margaret. 2002. *The Biology of Seeing*. New York: Harry N. Abrams.

Lorenz, Konrad. 1966. *On Aggression*. Orlando, Fla.: Harcourt Brace.

MacLean, Paul D. 1986. "Ictal Symptoms Relating to the Nature of Affects and Their Cerebral Substrate." In *Emotion: Theory, Research and Experience, III*, ed. Robert Plutchik and Henry Kellerman, 61–90. New York: Academic Press.

Mandler, George. 1997. "Consciousness Redux." In *Scientific Approaches to Consciousness*, ed. Jonathan Cohen and Jonathan Schooler, 479–498. Mahwah, N.J.: Erlbaum.

Mandler, Jean M. 1984. *Stories, Scripts and Scenes: Aspects of Schema Theory*. Hillsdale, N.J.: Erlbaum.

Mar, Raymond A. 2004. "The Neuropsychology of Narrative: Story Comprehension, Story Production and Their Interrelation." *Neuropsychologia* 42: 1414–1434.

Marayanski, Alexandra, and Jonathan Turner. 1992. *The Social Cage: Human Nature and the Evolution of Society*. Palo Alto: Stanford University Press.

Marr, David. 1982. *Vision: A Computational Investigation into the Human Representation and Processing of Visual Information*. San Francisco: W. H. Freeman.

Martindale, Colin. 1990. *The Clockwork Muse*. New York: Basic Books.

McCauley, Robert N., and Thomas Lawson. 2002. *Bringing Ritual to Mind: Psychological Foundations of Cultural Forms*. Cambridge: Cambridge University Press.

McKee, Robert. 1997. *Story: Substance, Structure, Style, and the Principles of Screenwriting*. New York: HarperCollins.

Merleau-Ponty, Maurice. 1962. *Phenomenology of Perception*. Trans. Colin Smith. London: Routledge and Kegan Paul.

Messaris, Paul. 1994. *Visual Literacy*. Bolder, Colo.: Westview.

Meyrowitz, Joshua. 1985. *No Sense of Place: The Impact of Electronic Media on Social Behavior*. Oxford: Oxford University Press.

Milner, David, and Melwyn Goodale. 1996. *The Visual Brain in Action*. Oxford: Oxford University Press.

Mithen, Steven. 1996. *The Prehistory of the Mind: A Search for the Origins of Art, Religion and Science*. London: Thames and Hudson.

Mook, Douglas G. 1987. *Motivation: The Organization of Action*. New York: W. W. Norton.

Mulvey, Laura. 1975. "Visual Pleasure and Narrative Cinema." *Screen* 16, no. 3: 6–18.

Münsterberg, Hugo. 1970. *The Film: A Psychological Study*. New York: Dover. Originally published 1916.

Murray, Janet. 1997. *Hamlet on the Holodeck*. Cambridge, Mass.: MIT Press.

Naremore, James. 1998. *More Than Night: Film Noir and Its Contexts*. Berkeley: University of California Press.

Nichols, Bill. 1991. *Representing Reality*. Bloomington: Indiana University Press.

Noë, Alva, and Kevin O'Regan. 2001. "A Sensori-Motor Account of Vision and Visual Consciousness." *Behavioral and Brain Sciences* 24, no. 5: 939–1011.

Norenzayan, Ara, Scott Atran, Jason Faulkner, and Mark Schaller. 2006. "Memory and Mystery: The Cultural Selection of Minimally Counterintuitive Narratives." *Cognitive Science* 30: 531–553.

Oliver, Mary Beth. 1993. "Exploring the Paradox of Sad Films." *Human Communication Research* 19: 315–342.

Panksepp, Jaak. 1998. *Affective Neuroscience: The Foundations of Human and Animal Emotions*. New York: Oxford University Press.

———. 1999. "The Periconscious Substrates of Consciousness—Affective States and the Evolutionary Origins of the Self." In *Models of the Self*, ed. Shaun Gallagher and Jonathan Shear, 113–130. Exeter: Imprint Academic.

Panksepp, Jaak, and Günther Bernatzky. 2002. "Emotional Sounds and the Brain: The Neuro-affective Foundations of Musical Appreciation." *Behavioural Processes* 60: 133–155.

Pellegrini, Anthony D., Danielle Dupuis, and Peter K. Smith. 2007. "Play in Evolution and Development." *Developmental Review* 27, no. 2: 261–276.

Pervin, Lawrence A., and Oliver P. John, eds. 1999. *Handbook of Personality: Theory and Research*. New York: Guilford.

Plantinga, Carl. 1997. *Rhetoric and Representation in Nonfiction Film*. Cambridge: Cambridge University Press.

Plantinga, Carl, and Greg Smith. 1999. *Passionate Views: Film, Cognition, and Emotion*. Baltimore: Johns Hopkins University Press.

Propp, Vladimir. 1968. *Morphology of the Folktale*. Austin: University of Texas Press.

Provine, Robert R. 2000. *Laughter: A Scientific Investigation*. New York: Penguin.

Pylyshyn, Zenon. 1991. "The Role of Cognitive Architectures in the Theory of Cognition." In *Architectures for Intelligence*, ed. Kurt VanLehn, 189–223. Hillsdale, N.J.: Erlbaum.

Ramachandran, Vilaymur S., Sandra Blakeslee, and Oliver Sachs. 1999. *Phantoms in the Brain*. London: Fourth Estate.

Ramachandran, Vilaymur S., and William Hirstein. 1999a. "Biological Functions of Consciousness, Qualia and the Self." In *Models of the Self*, ed. Shaun Gallagher and Jonathan Shear, 83–111. Exeter: Imprint Academic.

———. 1999b. "The Science of Art." *Journal of Consciousness Studies* 6 (June/July): 15–51.

Ravaja, Niklas, Timo Saari, Mikko Salminen, Jari Laarni, and Kari Kallinen. 2006. "Phasic Emotional Reactions to Video Game Events: A Psychophysiological Investigation." *Media Psychology* 8, no. 4: 343–367.

Reeves, Byron, and Clifford Nass. 1996. *The Media Equation: How People Treat Computers, Television, and New Media Like Real People and Places*. Cambridge: Cambridge University Press.

Richerson, Peter, and Robert Boyd. 2001. "The Evolution of Subjective Commitment to Groups: A Tribal Instincts Hypothesis." In *Evolution and the Capacity for Commitment*, ed. Randolph M. Nesse, 186–220. New York: Russel Sage.

———. 2005. *Not by Genes Alone: How Culture Transformed Human Evolution.* Chicago: University of Chicago Press.

Riis, Johannes. 2003. "Film Acting and the Communication of Emotions." In *Film Style and Story: A Tribute to Torben Grodal,* ed. Lennard Højbjerg and Peter Schepelern, 139–152. Copenhagen: Museum Tusculanum.

———. 2004a. "Naturalist and Classical Styles in Early Sound Film Acting." *Cinema Journal* 43, no. 3: 3–17.

———. 2004b. *The Nature of Film Acting: A Realist Approach.* Unpublished PhD dissertation, University of Copenhagen.

Rizzolatti, Giacomo, Laila Craighero, and Luciano Fadiga. 2002. "The Mirror System in Humans." In *Mirror Neurons and the Evolution of Brain and Language,* ed. Maxim Stamenov and Vittorio Gallese, 37–59. Amsterdam: John Benjamin.

Rock, Irvin. 1995. *Perception.* New York: W. H. Freeman.

Rubin, Alan M. 1994. "Uses, Gratifications, and Media Effects Research." In *Media Effects: Advances in Theory and Research,* ed. Jennings Bryant and Dolf Zillman, 417–436. Hillsdale, N.J.: Erlbaum.

Ryan, Marie-Laure. 1991. *Possible Worlds: Artificial Intelligence and Narrative Theory.* Bloomington: Indiana University Press.

———. 2001. "Beyond Myth and Metaphor—the Case of Narrative in Digital Media." *Game Studies* no. 1 (July). Available at: http://www.gamestudies.org/0101/ryan/.

Salt, Barry. 2003. *Film Style and Technology: History and Analysis,* 2nd ed. London: Starword.

Schatz, Thomas. 1981. *Hollywood Genre: Formulas, Filmmaking, and the Studio System.* New York: Random House.

Schepelern, Peter. 2000. *Lars von Triers Film: Tvang og Befrielse.* Copenhagen: Rosinante.

———. 2004. "The Making of an Auteur." In *Visual Authorship,* ed. Torben Grodal, Bente Laursen, and Iben Larsen, 103–127. Copenhagen: Tusculanum Press.

Schulte-Rüther, Martin, Hans J. Markowitsch, Gereon R. Fink, and Martina Piefke. 2007. "Mirror Neuron and Theory of Mind Mechanisms Involved in Face-to-Face Interactions: A Functional Magnetic Resonance Imaging Approach to Empathy." *Journal of Cognitive Neuroscience* 19, no. 8: 1354–1372.

Singer, Ben. 2001. *Melodrama and Modernity.* New York: Columbia University Press.

Slingerland, Edward. 2008. *What Science Offers the Humanities.* New York: Cambridge University Press.

Sloboda, John. 2005. *Exploring the Musical Mind: Cognition, Emotion, Ability, Function.* Oxford: Oxford University Press.

Smelser, Neil J. 1992. "Culture: Coherent or Incoherent." In *Theory of Culture,* ed. Neil J. Smelser and Ricard Münch, 3–28. Berkeley: University of California Press.

Smith, Murray. 1995. *Engaging Characters: Fiction, Emotion, and the Cinema.* Oxford: Clarendon/Oxford University Press.

———. 1999. "Gangsters, Cannibals, Aesthetes, or Apparently Perverse Allegiances." In *Passionate Views,* ed. Carl Plantinga and Greg Smith, 217–238. Baltimore: Johns Hopkins University Press.

Snow, Charles P. 1993 (first pub. 1959). *The Two Cultures.* Cambridge: Cambridge University Press.

Sober, Elliott, and David Sloan Wilson. 1998. *Unto Others: The Evolution and Psychology of Unselfish Behavior.* Cambridge, Mass.: Harvard University Press.

Solso, Robert L. 1994. *Cognition and the Visual Arts.* Cambridge, Mass.: MIT Press.

Sørensen, Lars-Martin. 2008. "The Bestseller Recipe: A Natural Explanation of the Global Success of Anime." *Post Script* 27, no. 1.

Sosis, Richard, and Eric R. Bressler. 2003. "Cooperation and Commune Longevity: A Test of the Costly Signaling Theory of Religion." *Cross-Cultural Research* 37, no. 2: 211–239.

Sperber, Dan. 1996. *Explaining Culture: A Naturalistic Approach.* Oxford: Blackwell.

Sperber, Dan, and Deidre Wilson. 1986. *Relevance: Communication and Cognition.* Oxford: Blackwell.

Stam, Robert. 2000. *Film Theory: An Introduction.* Malden, Mass.: Blackwell.

Steen, Francis F., and Stephanie A. Owens. 2001. "Evolution's Pedagogy: An Adaptationist Model of Pretense and Entertainment." *Journal of Cognition and Culture* 1, no. 4: 289–321.

Stern, Daniel. 2000. *The Interpersonal World of the Infant: A View from Psychoanalysis and Developmental Psychology.* New York: Basic Books.

Strauss, Claudia, and Naomi Quinn. 1997. *A Cognitive Theory of Cultural Meaning.* Cambridge: Cambridge University Press.

Tan, Ed. 1996. *Emotion and the Structure of Narrative Film: Film as an Emotion Machine.* Mahwah, N.J.: Erlbaum.

Tan, Ed, and Nico Frijda. 1999. "Sentiment in Film Viewing." In *Passionate Views*, ed. Carl Plantinga and Greg Smith, 48–64. Baltimore: Johns Hopkins University Press.

Tarkovsky, Andrey. 1987. *Sculpting in Time.* Austin: University of Texas Press.

Tattersall, Ian. 2001. *The Monkey in the Mirror.* New York: Harcourt Brace.

Thompson, Kristin. 1988. *Breaking the Glass Armor.* Princeton, N.J.: Princeton University Press.

———. 1999. *Storytelling in the New Hollywood.* Cambridge, Mass.: Harvard University Press.

Todorov, Tzvetan. 1975. *The Fantastic: A Structural Approach to Literary Genre.* Ithaca, N.Y.: Cornell University Press.

Tomasello, Michael. 1999. *The Cultural Origins of Human Cognition.* Cambridge, Mass.: Harvard University Press.

Trivers, Robert S. 1971. "Parental Investment and Sexual Selection." In *Sexual Selection and the Descent of Man 1871–1971*, ed. Bernard G. Campbell, 136–179. Chicago: Aldine.

Tynianov, Jurij. 1967. *Die literarischen Kunstmittel und die Evolution in der Literatur.* Frankfurt am Main: Suhrkamp.

van der Gaag, Christiaan, Ruud B. Minderaa, and Christian Keysers. 2007. "Facial Expressions: What the Mirror Neuron System Can and Cannot Tell Us." *Social Neuroscience* 2, no. 3: 179–222.

Vogeley, Kai, and Albert Newen. 2002. "Mirror Neurons and the Self Construct." In *Mirror Neurons and the Evolution of Brain and Language*, ed. Maxim Stamenov and Vittorio Gallese. Amsterdam: John Benjamins.

Vorderer, Peter, Hans J. Wulff, and Mike Friedrichsen, eds. 1996. *Suspense: Conceptualizations, Theoretical Analyses, and Empirical Explorations.* Mahwah, N.J.: Erlbaum.

Whittock, Trevor. 1990. *Metaphor and Film.* Cambridge: Cambridge University Press.

Williams, David L. 2002. *The Mind in the Cave.* London: Thames and Hudson.

Williams, Linda. 1989. *Hard Core: Power, Pleasure, and the "Frenzy of the Visible."* Berkeley: University of California Press.

———, ed. 1994. *Viewing Positions: Ways of Seeing Films.* New Brunswick, N.J.: Rutgers University Press.

———. 2000. "Film Bodies: Gender, Genre, and Excess." In *Film and Theory: An Anthology*, ed. Robert Stam and Toby Miller, 207–221. Malden, Mass.: Blackwell.

Wilson, David Sloan. 2002. *Darwin's Cathedral: Evolution, Religion, and the Nature of Society.* Chicago: University of Chicago Press.

Winnicott, Donald W. 1971. *Playing and Reality.* London: Tavistock.

Young, Kay, and Jeffrey L. Saver. 2001. "The Neurology of Narrative." *SubStance* 30, nos. 1 and 2: 72–84.

Young, Larry J., and Wang Zuoxin. 2004. "The Neurology of Pair Bonding." *Nature Neurology* 7, no. 10: 1048–1054.

Zajonc, Robert B. 2000. "Feeling and Thinking." In *Feeling and Thinking: The Role of Affect in Social Cognition*, ed. Joseph Forgas. Cambridge: Cambridge University Press.

Zeki, Semir. 1993. *A Vision of the Brain.* London: Blackwell.

———. 1999. *Inner Vision: An Exploration of Art and the Brain.* Oxford: Oxford University Press.

Zillmann, Dolf. 1991. "Empathy: Affect from Bearing Witness to the Emotions of Others." In *Responding to the Screen: Reception and Reaction Processes*, ed. Jennings Bryant and Dolf Zillmann, 135–167. Hillsdale, N.J.: Erlbaum.

———. 2000. "Basic Morality in Drama Appreciation." In *Moving Images, Culture and the Mind*, ed. Ib Bondebjerg, 53–63. Luton: University of Luton Press.

Zillmann, Dolf, and Jennings Bryant. 1994. "Entertainment as Media Effects." In *Media Effects*, ed. Jennnings Bryant and Dolf Zillmann, 437–461. Hillsdale, N.J.: Erlbaum.

Zwaan, Rolf A. 2004. "The Immersed Experiencer: Towards an Embodied Theory of Language." *Psychology of Learning and Motivation: Advances in Research and Theory* 44: 35–62.

Index